Memoir Writing

FOR

DUMMIES®

by Ryan G. Van Cleave, PhD

Memoir writing instructor

John Wiley & Sons Canada, Ltd.

Memoir Writing For Dummies®

Published by
John Wiley & Sons Canada, Ltd.
6045 Freemont Blvd.
Mississauga, ON L5R 4J3
www.wiley.com

For general information on John Wiley & Sons Canada, Ltd., including all books published by Wiley Publishing Inc., please call our distribution centre at 1-800-567-4797. For reseller information, including discounts and premium sales, please call our sales department at 416-646-7992. For press review copies, author interviews, or other publicity information, please contact our publicity department, Tel. 416-646-4582, Fax 416-236-4448.

Wiley also publishes its books in a variety of electronic formats. Some content that appears in print may not be available in electronic books.

Library and Archives Canada Cataloguing in Publication

Van Cleave, Ryan G.
 Memoir writing for dummies / Ryan Van Cleave.

(–For dummies)
Includes index.
Issued also in electronic formats.
ISBN 978-1-118-41464-4

1. Autobiography–Authorship. I. Title. II. Series:
For dummies

CT25.V37 2013   808.06'692   C2012-908419-0

ISBN 978-1-118-41464-4 (pbk); 978-1-118-41466-8 (ebk); 978-1-118-41467-5 (ebk); 978-1-118-41465-1 (ebk)

Printed in the United States

WILEY

About the Author

Ryan G. Van Cleave is the award-winning author of 20 books, including two creative writing textbooks, an illustrated humor book, and a memoir. Ryan graduated from Florida State University with an MA and PhD in English. He then taught at such places as Clemson University, Eckerd College, the University of Wisconsin-Green Bay, the University of Wisconsin-Madison, as well as at prisons, community centers, and urban at-risk youth facilities. His literary honors include a Gold Medal in the Florida Book Awards, a Edward H. and Marie C. Kingsbury Fellowship at Florida State University, the Anastasia C. Hoffman Fellowship at the University of Wisconsin-Madison's Institute for Creative Writing, and the Jenny McKean Moore Writer-in-Washington Fellowship at George Washington University, among others.

Ryan currently works as a freelance writer, a writing coach, an international speaker on video games and digital media, a professor of liberal arts and coordinator of creative writing at the Ringling College of Art and Design, and the executive director of a nonprofit publishing house, C&R Press (www.crpress.org) that he co-founded in 2006. Check out Ryan's website at www.ryangvancleave.com.

Dedication

To the many writing students of all ages who have ever entered my classroom, let *Writing Memoir For Dummies* serve as my answer to your two most common questions: Is my life worth writing about? Do I have what it takes to write a memoir? (The answers are yes and yes!)

Author Acknowledgments

I want to thank the many individuals whose efforts, commitment, and expertise helped make this book better at every stage of its development. Specifically, I thank the fine people at Wiley who immediately recognized the value of a book on memoir writing, including Anam Ahmed, Chad Sievers, Therese Garnett, and Erika Zupko. Heartfelt thanks also to my talented technical editor Dinty Moore, a gifted teacher and writer whose memoir *Between Panic & Desire* is a lesson itself in how to write memoirs.

I also thank my wife Victoria and our kids — Valerie and Veronica — for holding down the fort during the months it took to research and write the book you now hold in your hands.

Publisher's Acknowledgments

We're proud of this book; please send us your comments through our online registration form located at http://dummies.custhelp.com. For other comments, please contact our Customer Care Department within the U.S. at 877-762-2974, outside the U.S. at 317-572-3993, or fax 317-572-4002.

Some of the people who helped bring this book to market include the following:

Acquisitions and Editorial

Associate Acquisitions Editor: Anam Ahmed

Production Editor: Pamela Vokey

Project Editor: Chad R. Sievers

Copy Editor: Chad R. Sievers

Editorial Assistant: Kathy Deady

Cartoons: Rich Tennant
(www.the5thwave.com)

Cover photo: © Barbara Ferra Fotografia /
   Getty Images (main image);
   © Dave White / iStockphoto (SD card);
   © Agnieszka Kirinicjanow / iStockphoto
   (photo of children)

Composition Services

Senior Project Coordinator: Kristie Rees

Layout and Graphics: Carl Byers

Proofreaders: John Greenough,
   Shannon Ramsey

Indexer: Palmer Publishing Services

John Wiley & Sons Canada, Ltd.

   Deborah Barton, Vice President and Director of Operations

   Jennifer Smith, Vice-President and Publisher, Professional & Trade Division

   Alison Maclean, Managing Editor

Publishing and Editorial for Consumer Dummies

   Kathleen Nebenhaus, Vice President and Executive Publisher

   David Palmer, Associate Publisher

   Kristin Ferguson-Wagstaffe, Product Development Director

Publishing for Technology Dummies

   Andy Cummings, Vice President and Publisher

Composition Services

   Debbie Stailey, Director of Composition Services

Contents at a Glance

Table of Contents

Introduction

A few years back, I worked with a twenty-something elementary school teacher who wanted to work on a memoir. We chatted a bit about the different themes in her life she was interested in exploring through writing. A coworker walked past and must've overheard us because he asked one of the big questions about memoir: "Why on earth would you write a memoir? You're so young!"

Her answer: "Last year, at my grandmother's funeral, I heard so many stories from my aunts and uncles that I realized I didn't know my grandmother at all. Each of us had a story or two about her, but it was always a different story. Together, we had more than a few tales about her childhood in Romania, her job waitressing on cruise ships, her violent first marriage, and her life as a nanny for a count's daughter, but we all realized that there were pieces of her life missing. Huge pieces. I can't stand the idea that my family and my future kids might not know me either."

What a great reason to write a memoir! It's true that she didn't cure cancer, survive a terrorist attack, nor did she inherit billions, but she found value and relevance in her own experiences. She thought that, properly told, her story could impact the lives of others, whether they're her immediate family or not. She's absolutely right.

Whatever the reason that you want to write your memoir, I welcome you. *Memoir Writing For Dummies* is ultimately an invitation to make sense of your life through writing. If you've ever felt the need for clarity or truth in this confusing, difficult world, writing a memoir may be the answer. To struggle with truth, honesty, and history brings revelation and understanding. It can also bring closure and healing. Who doesn't need more of those things in his or her life?

About this Book

If you've picked up *Memoir Writing For Dummies,* you've probably either tried to write a memoir before or you've been thinking about it for some time and want a little guidance to get started. Either situation is fine. There's no wrong way to enter the world of memoir — doing so is a worthy task to undertake, no matter how you come to it.

In my 20 years of teaching, I've encountered a lot of people just like you who at some point try their hand at writing a memoir. My goal with this book is to reveal all that you need to succeed with that task. In the pages to come, I identify the reasons why you should write a memoir, share the writing tips you need, and discuss what to do after you have a complete, well-edited, well-written manuscript. I also reveal the main pitfalls and how to steer clear of them. For those who want some extra inspiration and suggestions, I have you covered as well.

The ability to write sometimes doesn't get enough respect. This bias about writing is simply one of life's little injustices, I'm afraid. It comes from the realization people have: "Everyone can scribble something on paper, right? Big deal!" Well, you wouldn't expect to pick up a guitar or a paintbrush and create masterpieces in a week or two. The same is true for writing. Anyone *can* scribble something on paper, but to do it well is another thing entirely. But here's the reality: Writing is a craft. That means you can discover practical skills to improve your writing ability. This book gives you what you need to know to succeed in writing your own memoir, no matter the reason or goals you have for writing one.

I wrote this book with the idea in mind that everything that's included would've helped me a great deal during my first few years of being a writer. If anything doesn't make sense to you or runs counter to the way you choose to do things, that's fine. Break any rule I give. Avoid any tip or technique I share that feels unhelpful. Just remember, though — this book represents the insight of two dozen years of my professional writing life and career as a writing teacher and writing coach. It also brings in the wisdom of my colleagues and friends in the writing, editing, and literary agenting business. It's time-tested, solid stuff. All I request is this: Give all of it a good faith, earnest effort. You may be surprised at how often you'll strike gold.

The one golden rule of writing is that you can do anything you want . . . as long as the end result is good writing.

Conventions Used in this Book

I use the following conventions and guiding principles throughout the text to make everything clear and accessible to readers:

- ✔ I use *italics* when I define a term. I also use italics for all book, movie, and TV show titles.
- ✔ I use **bold** to emphasize keywords or statements in bulleted lists. I also use bold for specific steps you take in numbered lists.
- ✔ I format all Internet addresses in monofont.

✔ All song names, short story titles, and poem titles appear in quotation marks.

✔ Although I wish it were otherwise, I'm a realist. I know that most budding memoir writers haven't read enough memoirs for me to exclusively use memoir examples throughout the book. Referring to texts you've never encountered isn't helpful, so I bring in lots of popular movie, novel, and TV examples to illustrate key points.

What Not to Read

More than anyone, I understand how crazy busy life can be. You're juggling half dozen things at once and trying to keep your head above the fray. You want to write a memoir, but you don't have tons of time. Although I would love for you to (at least at some time or other) read every word, I do offer some things you can skip if you just need the essential, need-to-know information:

✔ **Sidebars:** These gray-shaded boxes are supplemental tidbits of information, but you don't have to read them.

✔ **Paragraphs marked with Technical Stuff icon:** These paragraphs have more technical bits of information that you may find interesting, but you don't need to write your memoir.

Foolish Assumptions

All writers know that you stand the best chance of hitting the mark with your audience if at some point in the writing process you stop and really think about who your audience is. I spent a good while thinking about you. Here is what I assume about you, the reader:

✔ You want to write or have started writing a full-length (book-length) memoir.

✔ You want to publish that memoir in one manner or another.

✔ You realize that you can use many different blueprints for telling a great story.

✔ You want this book to focus more on effective story-telling than grammar concerns.

✔ You want expert, tried-and-true guidance on writing memoirs.

✔ You want to only have to buy a single book that gives you all the need to know on writing and publishing memoirs.

If you've already put time into developing your ability to write on your own or in formal classes, no problem. Some of this book will serve as a useful refresher. Regardless of your current level of writing ability, I hope to reveal a few new insights along the way. The tips and techniques here can help you with writing memoir, but they also can help you if you decide to one day move on to writing screenplays, poems, short stories, or self-help books. Good writing is good writing.

How This Book Is Organized

This section describes what's in each of the five main parts of the book so you can more quickly locate what you need. Leap right in at whatever spot you like or start at the beginning. It's all up to you!

Part I: The First Steps to Writing a Memoir

Although you may think this part is mostly about what to do after you have pen in hand (or a Word file open), here I focus on what to do *before* that step. Chapter 1 gives a basic overview on writing memoirs. Chapter 2 furthers that by exploring what a memoir is, who writes them, and why. In Chapter 3, I show how stories work, and how to use that information to help create audience-pleasing stories in your own memoir. Chapter 4 deals directly with two key elements of any memoir — researching and remembering. Chapter 5 puts all that together and helps you develop your ideas just like experienced authors do. In short, this part gives you all the preparatory work to do before you start the actual writing.

Part II: Telling Your Story with Pizzazz

Now you're knee-deep (or for some, neck-deep) into the writing portion of your memoir. To write a memoir that's going to be well-received — no matter the size or scope of your publishing plan — you need to control several main aspects of effective story-telling. Chapter 6 covers all you need to know about structuring your story, including showcasing how other memoirists have structured their books. Chapter 7 focuses on how to create vivid settings and scenes. In Chapter 8, I go over the ins and outs of creating compelling characters. Because you can't have characters without dialogue, I give you Chapter 9 to reveal how best to handle all that talking. Chapter 10 has a different look at talking — it's all about the writing voice you have or wish to create. Chapter 11 discusses your point of view options as well as the pros of and cons of each choice. Finally, Chapter 12 tackles how to start your memoir strong and finish it even stronger. Taken together, these chapters give you step-by-step advice on how to utilize these core skills to great effect. After you finish this part, you have what you need to write that complete first draft.

Part III: Revising, Editing, and Pushing Your Story to the Next Level

After you have a first draft, it's time to go back and smooth out the bumps, correct the gaffes, and polish up all the shiny parts. These chapters help isolate many of the issues that memoir writers don't get right the first time. Chapter 13 covers the main ways you can fine-tune your memoir's structure and story for maximum effect. Chapter 14 examines how writers create theme and meaning, and shows you ways to make the most of those in your memoir. Chapter 15 is all about revision — the large-scale choices you make when working with an already-written section, chapter, or manuscript. If you want help at the sentence level, Chapter 16 is for you. This chapter also explains how to bring in and work with a professional editor, if you need that extra help. Chapter 17 explains how to know what and what not to write in your memoir. This covers how to handle painful memories, how to deal with family (living or dead), and how to circumvent any ethical or legal issues that may cause you grief once your book is published.

Part IV: Sharing Your Story: A Publishing Primer

This part covers all the basics of finding the best mode of publication for your manuscript. From finding and working with a literary agent (Chapter 18) to sending out a manuscript on your own (Chapter 19) to self-publishing to e-publishing (Chapter 20), these chapters give clear, up-to-date advice on all your main options. With a little planning and a lot of legwork, you can discover exactly how to proceed toward the best publication method for your memoir. And if you want useful, actionable ideas on how to promote your finished product to prospective readers, Chapter 21 is for you. You can also check out my website (www.ryangvancleave.com/bonuschapter. pdf) for a bonus chapter on joining a writers' group to improve your writing before you submit your manuscript.

Part V: The Part of Tens

This section follows the *Dummies*-wide practice with quick resources, checklists, and reminders (all in sets of 10, of course!). This part does that, detailing the most common myths about memoirs (Chapter 22), the main reasons memoirs are rejected by literary agents and publishers (Chapter 23), and the most useful advice on writing your first book (Chapter 24). Don't be fooled by the size of this part — these chapters may be short, but they're chock-full of good information every memoir writer can put to good use. You can also find a bonus Part of Tens chapter online at www.dummies.com/extras/writersconference about ten perks of attending a writers' conference.

Icons Used in this Book

To make this book easier for readers to read and understand, I include icons in the margins to help you find and make sense of key ideas and information.

These are the hints, guides, and suggestions that pro writers know. They represent some of the best available advice. They're worth reading twice when you encounter them.

If you've ever clipped something from a book or magazine and taped it on your wall to revisit regularly, then you know what type of stuff you'll find after this icon. It's the bumper-sticker good material memoir writers need.

If you want to immerse yourself in all the historical and technical things about writing memoir, look for these icons. They can offer up some of the pretty cerebral things that can impress your writer friends at parties.

This icon gives you a heads-up on specific memoir-writing problems that you may encounter. Pay attention to avoid these hazards that other writers may succumb to.

Where to Go from Here

A great thing about any _For Dummies_ book is that they're modular, meaning each chapter works well on its own. You can read any chapter at any time and not worry that you'll be lost because you skipped earlier chapters. If you're at all like me, then you may be inclined to skip to the parts that speak to what you're most interested in.

If you want information on story structure, focus on Chapters 3 and 6. If you're completely new to the business of writing — memoir, poems, essays, or otherwise — you may want to begin with Chapter 1 and work your way straight through at your own pace. You can also flip to the table of contents or index and find a topic that interests you.

Whatever the situation, you're here and there's a wealth of information on the pages to follow. Onward!

Part I

The First Steps to Writing a Memoir

The 5th Wave — By Rich Tennant

"I want to become a memoirist. I'm just not sure I have that much prose in me."

In this part . . .

Although you're excited to plunge into the actual writing of your memoir, you need to do some preparatory reading, thinking, and writing before going any further. In this part, I explain the basic characteristics of a memoir, consider the reasons for writing a memoir, discuss the best ways to gather and shape material, and outline the basic structures available to create an effective story. I also delve deeply into a host of inspiration-building writing prompts and techniques to help you think of yourself as a writer as well as get you prepared to succeed with creating your own memoir.

Chapter 1

The Lowdown on Memoir Writing: Just the Basics

*F*or a long time, writing a memoir was the province of celebrities and people living in retirement homes. Thanks to an explosion of exciting memoirs written by people of all ages, the memoir as a form is now a viable way for anyone to meaningfully share their story. There's something incredibly rewarding to finding the leisure time to think, remember, reflect, and then write about your past. In doing so, you can discover the emotional truths that create the undercurrent of your life.

The Bowker Industry Report shows that memoirs generated $170 million in sales in 1999, and nearly $300 million a decade later. That's a lot more than just chump change! There's a growing audience for memoirs and that's good news for you.

This chapter serves as your stepping stone to everything you need to know about writing your memoir. Find the information you need here, depending on where you are in the writing process, to get your story down.

Although I've been a teacher of writing for nearly 20 years, I'm not coming to you as a teacher now. I'm simply someone who's been down this path before and who's willing to share the wisdom I've gained and gathered throughout the years. There are no grades, no deadlines, and no penalties for mistakes. What matters is that you commit to reaching across the chasm of memory and start retrieving the deep past, then recording it faithfully and vibrantly on the page. Memory by memory, moment by moment, you'll see a story take shape and grow into something that is a lesson in compassion, understanding, and humanity. That's memoir.

Understanding What Makes a Memoir a Memoir

The short answer for what makes a memoir a memoir is that like a novel, it tells a story, but unlike a novel, a memoir is 100 percent truthful. But that's an insufficient definition. A memoir also has other obligations that make it unique and distinct from other literary utterances. Understanding those differences is to understand the memoir's strengths. To know those is to know what areas you should play up when writing your own.

In order to be considered a memoir, your book needs to be in-line with the following:

- ✔ **Be book length.** Generally, a memoir is between 60,000 and 120,000 words.

- ✔ **Limit what's included:** A memoir is focused on parts or elements of a life, whereas an autobiography strives to include everything about a life, from birth to death.

- ✔ **Be truthful.** You can't play loose and free with the truth and still be called a memoir.

- ✔ **Use the elements of narrative.** Fiction writers know how to tell a story and make it interesting. See the next section for more on this.

- ✔ **Show desire.** A story gets interesting when the main character wants something — desperately so. Be specific and clear about what your main character wants, and readers will care.

- ✔ **Have conflict.** If a character can just get what he or she wants, who cares? That's not drama, that's grocery shopping. It's when a character *can't* get what he or she desires that things get interesting. Tell that story and you have the makings of a strong memoir.

Check out Chapter 2 for more information about the concepts of a memoir in far greater details.

Naming the Essential Parts of a Memoir

Like any good work of art, numerous parts comprise a memoir. Getting the best end product comes from knowing and having control over all of those smaller elements. Most of what a memoirist needs are skills borrowed from the world of fiction writing, though those skills are used somewhat differently in the world of nonfiction in general, and memoir in specific. For instance, you can't generate more conflict to heighten reader interest in a chapter if the scene you're writing simply didn't have that level of conflict. You can't reinvent the past to make a better story. With fiction, you can (and should).

Some of the main elements that make up a memoir include

- **Structure:** This is the shape of your story on the page. You may assume that the *structure* of your story has to be chronological, from beginning to end, but you have many more options than that. See Chapter 6 for the skinny.

- **Setting:** *Setting* is the where and when that a story takes place. A memoir may have two, three, or even as many as 23 different settings if you traveled or moved around a lot. Setting matters because it has a direct influence on character. See Chapter 7 for details on how to create and utilize setting to best effect.

- **Characters:** *Characters* are the people who populate the scenes and settings of your story. Yes, they're real-life people, but memoirists still call them characters, as novelists do. For more on why as well as how to make them come alive on the page, visit Chapter 8.

- **Dialogue:** The conversations that your characters have are called *dialogue*. This is a particularly tricky thing to use in memoir because memory is imperfect. Who walks around recording all conversations so you can accurately quote people later? You can discover more about the challenges and strengths of dialogue use in memoirs in Chapter 9.

- **Voice:** *Voice* is the unique manner in which a writer writes. It comprises distinctive decisions, such as word choice, rhythm, and the way a writer says things — taken together, voice creates a powerful effect on the reader. Interested in knowing more? Chapter 10 covers voice in depth.

- **Point of view:** The perspective through which the story is seen is called *point of view*. This in an important choice because it can drastically change how your story is conveyed. Read more about point of view in Chapter 11.

- **Theme:** *Theme* is what your memoir is about. It speaks to universal truths, core ideas, and emotional truths through the development of key scenes, moments, and tensions in your story. See more about theme in Chapter 14.

Making the Necessary Revisions and Edits to Help Your Memoir Shine

A great memoir doesn't appear by magic, but rather it's the result of good revision (to get the big stuff under control) and careful editing (to get the little stuff under control). How often in life do you wish you had a Do Over button? With writing, you do. You get a second, a third, or tenth chance if you require it, which is good news because you can improve the mistakes and poor decisions that you made earlier in the writing process.

After you have a rough draft of either your entire manuscript or even just a chapter, you can begin the revision process. Revision is important because it asks you to focus on large story elements without worrying much about specific word choices or sentence-level issues. While revising, you certainly look over all of the essential parts of a memoir (which I discuss in the previous section) to make sure each is functioning well on its own as well as connecting meaningfully to the entire book. You have another obligation, though. You need to think like a reader, not the writer. You handle revision first because you may revise and remove an entire chapter or scene from a book. You don't need to spend the extra time polishing those sentences that won't appear in the first edition. Stay efficient revising first and then editing after. Refer to Chapter 15 for more on making revisions.

Meanwhile there is also a time to edit, which is before you finish and start thinking of publication. Editing asks you to re-examine every word choice, reevaluate sentence structure, and think about how you're using paragraphs. Editing is a sentence-by-sentence level of attention that can feel tedious, but it's often the difference between a promising book that gets published or not. Some of the things that occur at this level of editing are adding or improving imagery, cutting clichés, removing most adverbs and adjectives, and tightening language across the board. Refer to Chapter 16 for more on line-by-line editing.

Focusing on the End Goal: Publishing

When I was in high school, an English teacher who recognized that I devoured F. Scott Fitzgerald's *The Great Gatsby* (Scribner), William Faulkner's *As I Lay Dying* (Modern Library), and John Steinbeck's *The Grapes of Wrath* (Penguin Classics), gave me a copy of Ernest Hemingway's *A Moveable Feast* (Scribner). I was blown away by it as fully as I'd ever been by any work of fiction. This book had grace, excitement, lovely language, melancholy, and a nearly-perfect sense of the extraordinary place Paris was in the 1920s. And most impressive to me? It was all true.

From that point on, I recognized that part of my goal of being a writer wasn't just to write a great memoir one day, but to have people read it and hopefully be swept up by that same kind of reaction I had to Hemingway. (A tall order, I realize, but it's okay to dream big!) I wanted others to experience the same visceral sense of wonder and awe that I did about the past with Hemingway's book. And the way to do that is through publishing your book. It's your avenue to finding readers and inviting them into the magic of a story only you can share. These prospective readers won't be sneaking into your house at night, rummaging in your file drawers or peeking into your computer files in pursuit of great literature. You have to send it to them, and the best way to do so is publishing.

Attending a writers' conference

If you want some community with people who will understand your impulse to tell stories, consider attending a writers' conference. There are hundreds of these throughout the country to choose from. Some specialize in the type of books they talk about, and others are more general. Here are just ten of the many writers' conferences that might suit the needs of a memoir writer. Research each online for more information.

✔ Writers in Paradise (St. Petersburg, Florida)

✔ Antioch Writers' Workshop (Yellow Springs, Ohio)

✔ San Miguel de Allende Writers' Conference & Literary Festival (San Miguel de Allende, Mexico)

✔ Orange County Christian Writers Conference (Fullerton, California)

✔ Wesleyan Writers Conference (Middletown, Connecticut)

✔ Stonecoast Writers' Conference (Portland, Maine)

✔ Taos Summer Writers' Conference (Taos, New Mexico)

✔ Green Mountain Writers Conference (Tinmouth, Vermont)

✔ ArtsQuest Memoir Writing Conference (Bethlehem, Pennsylvania)

✔ Story Circle Network's Annual Women's Memoir Conference (Austin, Texas)

Check out the website for the National Association of Memoir Writers (www.namw.org). Their "Writing Resources" link shows many online and real-world workshops and events all around the country.

Even if you decide your target audience is small — your family, or the people of your hometown — the idea of making something publishable quality is important. It means that it's the best that you can make it. It means you're understandably and honestly proud of it. It means that the writing you've labored over is likely to be engaging, memorable, and lasting for those special readers. And if you want to reach millions like Stephen King did with his memoir *On Writing: A Memoir of the Craft* (Scribner), publishing a well-written, publishable-quality book is your only way to approaching that size of an audience.

Before you seek a publisher, you may want to seek advice and feedback from your peers or even a literary agent to ensure what you have is the best that it can be. A writing critique group can be a great help in terms of getting advice on the quality of writing or receiving revision ideas (see www.ryangvancleave.com/bonuschapter.pdf for a bonus chapter on writing groups). One step further, a literary agent can take this manuscript and showcase it to publishing houses that have the infrastructure in place to print your book and distribute it to online and real-world bookstores throughout the world. Chapter 18 provides more insight about what an agent can do for you.

You have a few publishing options when you're ready to publish your book:

- ✔ **Traditional publishing:** For the last century or so, this is the main route that authors had to seek print book publication. You write the book, send a letter of inquiry (a query letter) to a publisher, and then hope for a positive response. If the publisher likes your letter, it asks for the manuscript. If the publisher likes the manuscript, it sends you a contract, and two years later (give or take), the memoir appears in bookstores. For more information on this time-honored option, Chapter 19 awaits.

- ✔ **Self-publishing:** If you're interested in writing, printing, and selling your own memoir, then *self-publishing* is a fine choice. With 211,000 self-published books appearing in 2011 alone, other authors have clearly liked this choice a great deal. If self-publishing interests you as well, see Chapter 20.

- ✔ **E-publishing:** This is a subcategory of self-publishing that's emerged as a viable outlet for books in the past few years. An e-book isn't a print book, but with so many people having e-readers or e-reader capabilities on their computers, getting published in an e-book format is no longer a disincentive for an author. Chapter 20 has what you need to know about this new publishing option.

No matter what publishing method you decide on, you want to promote your finished work. If you don't promote your memoir (for example, with a website for your book, or with social media to alert people that your book is available to purchase), then people won't know about it and won't buy it. In today's publishing world, publishers do very little marketing and publicity for a book unless you're getting a huge amount of money from them upfront; this reality shifts the responsibility for book marketing and publicity duties to your shoulder. Chapter 21 offers some great suggestions for promoting your book, whether you do it on your own or hire a professional to help out with some or all of it. With more than 4,000,000 new books (or new editions of existing books) published in 2011, you need to find ways to get the attention of readers.

Answering the Question: Why Do You Want to Write a Memoir?

People ask me all the time about why I ever chose to write a memoir. "Why put yourself through that? Why put your family through that?" They ask — sometimes by dancing around the topic, and sometimes saying it outright — why I'm interested in sharing pain and experiencing the potential shame of revealing secrets, mistakes, and transgressions?

If you're serious about being a memoirist, be prepared to answer these questions. You need to be able to answer them yourself, in your own words, in a way that makes sense to you. Don't duck the hard questions. Think them through and come to a sense of peace with your reasons, no matter what they are.

Here's something else you'll encounter beyond those questions — even if you obscure the names of real-world people who appear in your book, your friends and family will make great effort to figure out who is who. Whether people guess at which character is them or if you use their names and exact likenesses, they will (a) feel proud to have been immortalized in print, (b) nitpick all the things about themselves that you got "wrong," (c) feel a little exploited/ violated, or (d) have some other reaction that's impossible to predict.

Here are some of the most popular and self-justifying reasons to write a memoir. See if you identify with any of them. You want to

- ✔ Find some kind of meaning and order to the often-chaotic swirl of existence
- ✔ Discover who you really are by confronting the truth(s) of your life
- ✔ Be the star of the show versus remain someone who stands behind a curtain offstage, or worse, stays in the audience (or even worse, never arrives to the show at all)
- ✔ (Re)witness the most important stages of your life
- ✔ Overcome fear, guilt, shame, and regret
- ✔ Preserve your family's history
- ✔ Improve your ability to communicate with others
- ✔ Build self-esteem through valuing yourself and listening to your own voice
- ✔ Figure out who you are
- ✔ Become a better thinker because good writing isn't from the seat-of-your-pants; it's from reflecting, making connections, and creatively engaging with your material
- ✔ Learn how to forgive yourself
- ✔ Create a deep empathetic connection with readers who will learn and be inspired from your life
- ✔ Confess something — confession is, as they say, good for the soul
- ✔ Defy the aphorism "it's all been said before," because you haven't said it

To deny the validity of memoir is to deny that the past powerfully affects the present. Whether your past is full of darkness, bright with joy, or a chiaroscuro containing both, examining that and bringing the chaos of disarray (which memories generally are) into order can change lives for the better. I've seen it happen many, many times. Through the writing of a memoir, you can take full possession of your life — possibly for the first time. You don't have to be famous. You don't even have to be a professional writer. You just have to be honest, faithful to the past, and generous in the telling. That's memoir.

Celebrity doesn't sell memoirs

You don't have to be a famous person to write a memoir. Still, your memoir will probably sell more copies if you won *Dancing with the Stars* or if your face has graced a box of Wheaties. But simply having celebrity is no guarantee that your memoir will sell and be successful. See this for yourself from this list of celebrity memoir stinkers:

✔ *Jersey Shore* star Snooki's memoir only sold 4,000 copies during its first week. (She had more than a million Twitter followers at the time, and the premiere episode of season three of *Jersey Shore* drew almost 8.5 million viewers.)

✔ Wikileaks founder Julian Assange's unauthorized biography barely sold 600 copies in its first week. He received a $1.5 million advance in 2011 for this title.

✔ Actor Alec Baldwin's *A Promise to Ourselves: A Journey through Fatherhood* (St. Martin's Griffin) is reported to have sold only 13,000 hardcover copies in four years.

Although having a famous person's name attached to a book can guarantee a few sales, a bad book is a bad book, period. After people figure that out, the sales will scream to a stop.

A well-written, honest, interesting memoir, however, can actually make you a celebrity. Amy Chua, the author of *Battle Hymn of the Tiger Mother* (Penguin Press), received a ton of media attention over how she humorously portrayed the "superiority" of super-strict Chinese mothers. That attention turned into huge sales for the book and made Chua a prominent media figure.

Chapter 2

Getting Started: What You Need to Know about Writing Your Memoir

In This Chapter

▶ Recognizing why people write memoirs

▶ Allowing yourself to write

▶ Ignoring fame and fortune

▶ Exploring the vaults of memory

▶ Considering the role of reading

*W*riting a memoir is a noble endeavor that involves the author in ways that poetry, fiction, and other types of nonfiction simply don't. With a memoir, you, the author, are front and center with the spotlight burning down from above, and the world is watching — waiting and expectant.

Question: What type of person volunteers to put him or herself under that kind of scrutiny?

Answer: Writers who want to create, discover, witness, preserve, and uncover something real and honest about themselves and their past.

What makes memoirs even more alluring is that people like to read real-life stories. Memoir isn't just based on true events; it *is* true events. And thus, readers feel more is at stake.

This chapter identifies the main reasons why people yearn to write memoirs. It also covers some of the main challenges as well as the rewards memoir writers may encounter. The final part of this chapter examines the role that reading plays in any writer's development.

Figuring Out Why Anyone Would Want to Write a Memoir

Before you set pen to paper (or fingers to keyboard), though, I want to explain why people write memoirs. They obviously write memoirs for various reasons. Knowing why you're writing one can help determine your intended outcome. If you don't have a clear target, you can't expect to hit the bull's-eye. Read on to see which one(s) resonate with you most clearly.

You're an authority in your field (or you aspire to be one)

Say that you've been involved with helping senior citizens re-enter the work-force so they can have a higher standard of living, keep active and healthy, and be financially able to get better insurance than the government offers. To help the most people, you need to reach a lot of people, right? Writing a memoir that details your life and how you came to commit yourself to help-ing this particular demographic of citizens can do exactly that. In this hypo-thetical memoir, you'd probably detail a few of the most compelling stories you had about helping someone find a life-changing job at age 60 (or 70, or 80). Anyone reading the book may well take away a few how-to tips from those case studies alone, which is a good thing.

A possible outcome for a memoir like this is media coverage. A well-written memoir on any topic can net the author radio and TV interviews, magazine stories, blog write-ups, and word-of-mouth. A good memoir can help raise awareness of what you do in a very big way.

You could then follow up your memoir with a good self-help or how-to nonfic-tion book, and you're even closer to cornering the market on your topic.

Here are a few other success stories where a published memoir helped estab-lish someone as an authority on his or her topic:

✔ **Elie Wiesel's *Night* (Hill and Wang):** It's considered one of the bedrocks of Holocaust literature.

✔ **David Pelzer's *A Child Called "It": One Child's Courage to Survive* (HCI):** This 1995 memoir of childhood abuse led him to write other books and become a highly-paid motivational speaker.

✔ **David Mura's *Turning Japanese: Memoirs of a Sansei* (Atlantic Monthly Press) and *Where the Body Meets Memory: An Odyssey of Race, Sexuality & Identity* (Anchor):** Mura, a third-generation

Japanese-American, gives educational presentations at schools, businesses, and organizations. His events combine poetry, presentation, and personal testament that tackle some of the most powerful cultural issues faced today.

You have a powerful, unique story to share

Another reason authors seek to write a memoir is to share their incredible story. Say for instance, you cured whooping cough. You took a snowboard journey across the Arctic. You won 35 blueberry pie eating contests in the past two years, and you still fit into a size zero miniskirt. You developed a blackjack strategy that helped you take Las Vegas casinos for $35 million. You swam from Hawaii to Australia . . . and you're blind!

If you did any of these things — or something equally amazing — you *should* write a memoir so other people learn about it. Your barber knows, as does the fellow in the cubicle next to you at work, and maybe the kid who delivers your newspaper does too, but the rest of the world doesn't. The rest of the world salivates for amazing real-life stories like yours. It makes everyone feel warm and squishy inside when they see the heights the human spirit can achieve.

Here are a few examples of this type of memoir:

- ✔ **Isobella Jade's *Almost 5'4* (Gamine Press):** This book details her struggles with being one of the smallest models in the business. Even more amazing was that she wrote it at the Apple Store on Prince Street in Soho, because she was homeless and living on McDonald's dollar menu items.

- ✔ **Ernesto Che Guevara's *The Motorcycle Diaries: Notes on a Latin American Journey* (Ocean Press):** This book, which has been a *New York Times* bestseller multiple times, details Che's travels across South America with his biochemist friend. Together, they witnessed so much social injustice that Guevara became an iconic revolutionary for the rest of his life.

- ✔ **Julie Metz's *Perfection: A Memoir of Betrayal and Renewal* (Voice):** Seven months after her husband dropped dead, she found out that he'd been cheating. So this brutally honest memoir recounts how Metz does what every cheated-on person dreams of — she hunted down and confronted every single woman. (Although the situation of being cheated on isn't that unique, how she handled it indeed was.)

Legitimized my story: My own authority-figure experience

A few weeks after my own memoir (*Unplugged*) came out, I was invited out of the blue to do a three-hour interview with George Noory on *Coast to Coast,* a radio program that averages three million listeners. After the interview, the Amazon sales ranking for my book jumped from more than one million to well under 1,000 and stayed there for quite some time. And from that single interview, I got three invitations to do other radio interviews and dozens of requests for advice on my topic from regular people. Because of that single book, I have more speaking event opportunities than I can possibly do, and I've been on shows like *Dr. Drew, Issues* with Jane Velez-Mitchell, and *ABC News.* I've even had an Associated Press story on me that ran in more than 100 newspapers and appeared in 15+ countries. In essence, writing this one book made me an authority on my topic — video games and video game addiction — overnight.

If I didn't have a book published on this subject, I wouldn't have been featured in all those media outlets. I didn't get any more knowledgeable on my subject by virtue of writing or publishing a book — I knew the same stuff before. But the book validated it in a public way that people understand and respect. A memoir can make you seem more legitimate in their eyes.

You want to understand/know yourself better

Self-knowledge is a great goal, and more people seek this goal as they mature. Writing a memoir is the careful observation of your inner world. Stick it out through the entire process, and you'll have a much stronger handle on who you are, what you're about, what you believe in, and why you're the person you are today.

A real benefit of this reason for writing a memoir is that publication for the masses isn't a huge motivation. You may even choose to keep the final book-length product in the family, or amongst a select group of friends, which is no problem. Make sure you do read the chapters on publication, just in case. Told well, any memoir has value to others.

You want to document your life

If you're like most people, around age 50 you start to realize how much you didn't know about your parents, and their parents, and *their* parents, all of whom are likely no longer with you. You've lost access to a rich, meaningful past that is part of your family's legacy. You don't have to be a genius to realize that your own kids or other family members might one day feel the same way.

You can use the writing of a memoir as an opportunity to document yourself and your experiences. Keep your story — your family's story — immune to the ravages of time. Plus you just might build family unity, create memories, and establish traditions for generations to come along the way.

Families with rich oral histories can benefit from this type of reason for writing a memoir. For that type of book, a lot of Q&A may be effective because it'll capture the tempo and tenor of people's speech. It'll place the stories in a strong social context that you won't have to develop as much in exposition.

You want to set the record straight

People write this type of memoir to clarify the truth of an event or series of events. For most people, this reason isn't the main one for writing a memoir unless they were thrown out of office, accused of a sordid sex scandal, or falsely imprisoned for 11 years for a hate crime.

Although you can try to get your record-setting story out via newspapers, radio, TV, and the Internet, none of those options has the respect and lasting power of a well-published, well-written book. In fact, publishing a book that details the true account of how you *didn't* do something will likely earn you plenty of media coverage, but the reverse isn't always true. Plenty of people get a radio interview or two-minutes on a TV show to tell their side of a story, and that doesn't lead to a book deal. So just write the book in the first place and utilize the publicity techniques in Chapter 21 to know with confidence that you're taking the best option to revise the incorrect "truth" most people believe.

Some memoirists aren't trying to show that the events are untrue, but rather set the record straight by offering the full context that created the events. Some readers and critics may see this as the author trying to absolve himself or herself of guilt or culpability, which is okay. Giving people a fuller appreciation for something that happened is a fine motive for writing a memoir.

A few examples of this type of book include

- ✔ **Jose Baez and Peter Golenbock's** *Presumed Guilty: Casey Anthony, The Inside Story* **(BenBella Books):** Here, Anthony's lawyer says Florida detectives should've realized Casey Anthony "wasn't playing with a full deck."

- ✔ **Courtney Love's untitled forthcoming memoir:** In this tell-all, Love gives the real scoop on her life with Kurt Cobain, his suicide in 1994, her own drug problems, and her Hollywood career. Her goal is to get past all the tabloid falsehoods and literally "set the record straight," as she explained to the Associated Press.

✔ Michael Vick's *Michael Vick: Finally Free* (Worthy Publishing): With this memoir, Vick tries to explain how his exposure to dog fighting at age eight plus his poverty-stricken youth led him to make poor later choices, including most famously being arrested in 2007 for running an illegal dog-fighting ring.

You enjoy a challenge

Writing a memoir *is* a sizable challenge. Some people simply aren't equipped to write it, at least at this specific point in their life.

But this doesn't apply to you because you're reading this book right now. The ones who aren't equipped to write a memoir never get past the "Oh, I'll write it one day . . . " mindset. Or they may not even formulate that thought, which they'll never act on.

You're proactive and seeking expert advice and tips. You're on the right path. Now to go from the impulse to write a memoir to producing 100, 200, or 300 manuscript pages is still challenging, but it's a different type of challenge. It's the sort of challenge a tough deadline is at work. You can meet it, but you may have to skip watching TV all week, and you may need to put in a couple of late nights. Make those sacrifices, however, and you're golden. You can do it.

The same is true of a memoir. Come at it with the right determination, and you're equipped to overcome any challenges you encounter in the writing process.

You enjoy playing with language

If you enjoy solving word problems and playing word games, you may find great delight in puzzling together the words of a memoir. Just as those games have restrictions that force you to be creative and expand beyond your initial thoughts, writing a memoir insists on the same type of play to uncover/ discover the actual solution. In this case, the solution is a quality, readable, enjoyable memoir.

Although you can write anything and still tickle your word puzzle-bone, a memoir may be a better choice because you have all the clues inside you.

Any type of writing is like playing a word puzzle game. Going with one answer changes what comes before and after it; it's all deeply interrelated. Puzzle enthusiasts thrive on the give and take, the guesswork, the rethinking required to succeed. The execution of a memoir has plenty of those things.

You find writing therapeutic

I teach writing to lots of teens and college-age kids, but the most rewarding populations of writers and would-be writers? Rape victims. At-risk youth groups. Prisoners. Trauma victims. Soldiers. Divorcees. Widows. Orphans. Groups who have had a rough shake of things for one reason or another. People whose lives are in a serious state of disrepair.

You don't even have to have some huge reason to feel damaged, sad, or broken — sometimes life itself is reason enough to feel that way. Languishing away with those tumultuous feelings inside you is a mistake. Writing is a wonderful option to take ownership of whatever you feel, explore it, and ideally purge yourself of those feelings so you can move forward into the future without being trapped in the past. Writing a memoir can be a self-generated, private catharsis. It's transformative. It frees you from shame and guilt. It can quite literally change your world for the better.

Even the most well-adjusted, fully-realized, happy and content people can find healing in writing, so don't think you need rock star–rehab type of problems to write a memoir. Everyday problems can be assuaged via writing, too. The only thing I need to remind you of is this: Be aware of what writing serves the overall purpose of the memoir and what writing is purely for therapy. Just keep the entirely therapeutic stuff in a separate drawer. Don't include that in your memoir. Always decide what goes in by thinking of your readers. They want to see your pain and share in what you learned, but they're not likely to choose to sit through years of therapy with you.

You can't help but write

If you simply love writing, you already know it. You probably have drawers full of love notes and letters and poems and other stuff you've scribbled over the years. You may even be writing notes or thoughts in the margins of this book as you go (not recommended, though, if you're still in a bookstore or reading a library copy!).

Judge to criminal: "Write your memoir!"

I'm not the only one who seems to realize that writing a memoir is a good, healthy thing to do. When former Bristol-Myers Squibb exec Andrew Bodnar pled guilty to a white-collar crime in 2009 (providing false information to pharmaceutical regulators), Judge Ricardo M. Urbina sentenced him to writing a memoir. Yes, you read that correctly. The punishment for this criminal was a $5,000 fine, two years of probation, and the *mandatory* writing of his cautionary tale and mistakes in a book of at least 75,000 words.

If you're a writer, go ahead and write. I can't think of a better subject material than your own life, so go for it. Unleash the literary hounds!

Granting Yourself Permission to Write a Memoir

For some people, writing a memoir feels inappropriate, like they don't deserve it. I refuse to do the "we're all as unique as snowflakes" thing, but I will say this with certainty — having worked with at-risk youth groups, prisoners, seniors, and stay-at-home-moms (not to mention oodles of college and high school students) — your life does matter. You can easily forget that when you may get signals from the world that says so from time to time. The world is wrong. Your life does matter.

Somehow, far too many people feel they don't have permission to articulate their own experiences and feelings. In the delicate framework of their own lives, their families, and their friends, they believe it's off-limits to be so revealing. They have this vague sense of the taboo to writing their memoir.

I give you that permission.

This book gives you that permission.

Your own crucial story gives you that permission.

Through the act of writing a memoir, you can uncover a braver, stronger, more forgiving version of yourself. I've witnessed too many success stories to believe anything but this to be true.

The next sections offer ideas on how to make your own success story through memoir by making smart choices about what to share and what to leave out. It also acknowledges that nonfiction writers in general, and memoirists in specific, all have a lot to learn from novelists, who really know how to tell a story. With a little guidance, you can take the facts of your life and turn them into riveting, powerful, truthful prose that stands up well against any work of fiction.

Creating the reading experience of fiction with facts

Aspiring memoirists are often concerned with being stuck with the truth. You're not stuck with the truth — you're freed by it. You have the raw data of every single chapter already in your head. All you need to do is figure out the best way to translate that onto the page for your future readers.

Fiction writers spend a lot of time on this very issue because they want to create a seamless, compelling, convincing reading experience. They do this by managing things like time, atmosphere, tone, pace, and characterization. Memoir writers need to be cognizant of those same elements and utilize them to their best effect, too. The chapters in Part II examine many of those narrative elements and techniques, and reveal how you can make every moment that's important to your life journey feel important to a reader, too.

You have permission to use the techniques and tactics of fiction writers to tell your story better. Readers don't want a laundry list of names and dates and blow-by-blow data from every moment of your life. What they want is a well-written, reflective, emotionally charged literary representation of the most crucial moments of a life.

You absolutely have my permission to aspire to that.

You may have encountered the term *creative nonfiction,* which is what memoir really is. Memoir is *nonfiction* (true) that's told using the creative techniques of storytelling (fiction, screenwriters, and so on). In many ways, memoir is a lot like literary journalism; however, it's more expansive in that it covers such a wide variety of potential topics: memoir, history, documentary, biography, social criticism, personal essays, *belles lettres,* cultural criticism, travel writing, nature writing, and science writing.

Using elements of your life versus your entire life

People commonly feel obligated to write their entire life story if they're going to write about themselves at all. That kind of memoir is actually an *autobiography,* a book that runs the entire span of a life, from birth until death. You can save that type of personal story for presidents, Bill Gates, and other people who are so famous or important that even the minutiae of their lives makes people listen.

You have permission to exclude from your memoir the parts of your life that you don't want to write about or that don't fit the theme or themes you've chosen to focus on. Plenty of memoirs gloss over childhood, school years, or even careers in order to more quickly get to the juiciest, most relevant stuff.

Don't exclude events or experiences from your memoir because they're difficult to write about, or because you'll be embarrassed about what readers (or Grandma Jackson from Oklahoma, or your beloved Bible school teacher) might think. If you're potentially embarrassed, that's a sign you *should* include them because they're deeply important, hard-to-put-into-words happenings. Readers will be getting a peek into the most powerful moments of your life — good, awful, silly, foolish, amazing, horrifying, whatever. They're all good.

Memoirs: Writing in truth and subjectivity while reporting the facts

You may hear people refer to "new journalism" when the topic of memoir comes up. The journalism part is easy enough to understand — writing that favors the who, what, when, where, why, and how like you see in newspaper articles. Some time ago, readers who saw the facts of a life written that way in memoirs and biographies realized that it was a bit boring. That's where the "new" comes in. The new twist on the long-standing journalistic tradition is to use the techniques of fiction to tell a better story, that's still based in good reporting (truth) and subjectivity.

A few books worth reading that can give you a good sense of this literary movement that emerged in the 1960s and 1970s include the following:

- ✔ Hunter S. Thompson's *Hell's Angels: The Strange and Terrible Saga of the Outlaw Motorcycle Gangs* (Penguin)

- ✔ Tom Wolfe's *The Electric Kool-Aid Acid Test* (Picador)

- ✔ Truman Capote's *In Cold Blood* (Random House)

- ✔ Joan Didion's *Slouching Toward Bethlehem: Essays* (Farrar, Straus and Giroux) (a study in the New Journalism of the 1960s)

Just make sure you give your readers that type of access. Give yourself permission to give us that kind of access, and you'll create readers who will love you.

Focusing on More Than Just Fame and Fortune

If you're writing your memoir because you want to become famous and rich, think again. Fame and fortune are fleeting, if you even manage to attain them. What lasts is a well-written, honest book. Do that, and your words will last far beyond the span of your own life.

Face it. The average memoir receives an *advance* against royalties — that is the money you receive upfront that a publisher fully expects to recoup via later sales — that comes to well under $5,000. Consider that you may spend a year or two writing the book, and you can suddenly see that you're better off financially by working part-time at the local convenience store, buying lottery tickets than trying to become the next big name memoirist.

And fame is even more elusive. Perhaps 1 out of every 100 memoirs grabs the public's attention and makes the author a household name. And even then, it's usually for only 15 minutes, until it moves on to the next hot writer.

Have you ever heard of Nicole Lea Helget? She was the next hot writer in 2007 after writing the debut memoir *The Summer of Ordinary Ways: A Memoir* (Borealis Books), which is terrific. I read about her in the *Chicago Tribune*, which raved about this book. She received coverage from *People* to *The Washington Post*, which is the type of attention any writer dreams of. Since then she's done great for herself, having published a half-dozen titles. But the same level of attention doesn't stay, even though her later books were just as good. In fact, *The Turtle Catcher* (Mariner Books), a 2010 novel about a small Minnesota town struggling with change in post-WWI times, is pretty darn good. Does it mean that *The Summer of Ordinary Ways* is no longer worth reading? Nope. It just means that the media world and the general public hurry on to the next new thing quickly.

Want to know how much creating a great piece of art really means to people? Just look at how many A-list celebrities who command many millions per picture are turning down anything except Oscar-worthy roles. They're passing on huge dollars to chase that lasting, meaningful artistic opportunity because as long as they can afford to pay the bills and take a vacation now and then, money doesn't mean all that much. Someone who's struggling to make ends meet can't relate, but one day, the truth of this may smack you existentially. Creating something beautiful that speaks to the world for generations to come is priceless and worth committing a lifetime to.

Tapping into the Vaults of Memory

As a memoir writer, your main goal is to capture memories and record them accurately on the page. Unfortunately doing so isn't always easy. Your memory vaults aren't as secure as you may hope, and you need actual information to give your story depth and texture.

Memory is a fickle thing, my mother — or was it my father — once told me. See how that happens? A quote I heard 30 years ago is stuck word for word in my mind, but I have zero clarity on the context of who said it to me. That's how fickle memory can be. Worse, I have incidents from my past where I'm certain I know what happened. My brother disagrees. My mother tells us we're both wrong. And my father reminds us that we were living in a different state at the time (which is wrong, too — I can prove that one!).

Many teachers of writing harp on the two Rs of writing: Reading and (w) Riting. Memoir has two more crucial Rs: Remembering and Reflecting.

These sections delve deeper into your vaults and help you understand the importance of memory and what you do to help you more easily remember.

Doing your best to remember

You know your limitations, and therefore you should be skeptical of what you (and others) recall. Maybe you don't remember it all wrong, but it's certainly been warped out of its initial shape by your re-remembering.

All you can do is your best. That's the promise every memoir needs to make. You essentially say this to the reader: "This is what happened. To the best of my ability and knowledge, this is what I did and saw and thought and felt." (For more insight into how to handle memory, visit Chapters 4 and 17.)

Probably no one will know if you embroider your story with memories that didn't happen. But I strongly urge you to stick with the truth as you know it. Whatever it was, it was yours. Own it. It's already good enough to share so don't rev it up to the point that you're fictionalizing your own life. If you really feel compelled to do that, write a novel that's loosely based on your life, which plenty of novelists do.

Discovering your past

You know your story because after all you lived it. Think about all the things you've forgotten. What your Aunt Betty looked like before she turned blue from cancer. What the crickets' song from the back porch of your neighbor's vacation home sounded like. How old you were when you first masturbated, or told a lie, or realized everyone dies and that means one day *you'll* die. Wow, that's heavy stuff.

Be open to remembering anew the world of your past. Discover what you didn't bother to remember before, or never noticed until now. Keep that kind of childlike wonder close as you delve into the deep past. Writing about something is to have a conversation with it — listen for what it says back to you, and that's sometimes the more important thing to discover.

Revisiting the places of your past are a fantastic way to suddenly recall things, such as the glowing reflection of light on the stainless steel stovetop your mother spent most of her life at or the smell of fresh herbs and flowers in your parents' backyard. Grabbing those kinds of details from your past and including them in your memoir can create a captivating world that pulls the reader in. Do your research. Go back to your past. Revisit the people and the places you need to. Read. w(R)ite. Remember. Reflect. (Refer to Chapter 4 for more ideas when researching your past.)

Memoirs are for young and old alike

In the past only people at a certain age, such as 35, 40, 50, or some specific age, could write memoirs. These days, people recognize that life experiences can be powerful, meaningful, and worth sharing at any age. A memoirist doesn't need to be a certain age. She only needs to be faithful to the truth and generous in the telling.

A couple good examples of memoirs written by young authors that I suggest reading are

✔ Blake Taylor's *ADHD & Me: What I Learned from Lighting Fires at the Dinner Table*

(New Harbringer Publications): This book was published when he was 18.

✔ Hannah Friedman's *Everything Sucks: Losing My Mind and Finding Myself in a High School Quest for Cool* (HCI Teens): This was published when she was 23.

✔ Samantha Abeel's *My Thirteenth Winter: A Memoir* (Scholastic): This was published when she was 25.

Engaging your history

Memoir is an act of preservation, of loving recovery. Just as you may travel to Greece to witness firsthand the ruins of ancient civilizations and be swept up in the past, so too should your memoir find ways to invite future readers to choke down your father's beef pies, smell the lavender hairspray your third grade teacher hosed you down with when you misbehaved, and run the three miles home, sobbing, because the playground jerk yanked out a handful of your hair.

You've surely heard variations on American philosopher George Santayana's famous quote: "Those who cannot remember the past are condemned to repeat it." That's terribly true, but it also speaks to an opportunity every memoir has. It can save others from making the same mistakes you did, too. What a noble role memoirs can play!

So engage with history. Learn what you did. Learn why you did it. Learn from it in such a way that you'll make better choices in the future. Write a memoir where those things happen, and readers will be able to follow along, taking lessons and ideas and inspiration from the pages, genuinely thankful for your efforts.

Contemplating Reading's Role

Other books can provide inspiration, possibilities, and good models for your memoir. You don't have to just read memoirs to figure out how to tell stories. Novels, plays, essays, and even poetry have a lot to offer in terms of how to craft powerful, moving language.

You do want to read some memoirs before you start just to see how other people tackled the exact challenge before you — how to locate and reveal the emotional truths and realities just beneath the surface that create, drive, and transform a life.

Reading does a lot of good things for writers, including:

- Helps you develop and strengthen language skills
- Allows you to see what's been done before so you don't repeat it (you can find a way to creatively add to the tradition of literature)
- Serves as models for good (or bad) writing
- Gives you information
- Offers pleasure and enjoyment
- Reminds you why you love to write
- Affirms that you're not alone

Because writing your memoir is all about reading, I heartily suggest Anna Quindlen's very thin (84 pages), very readable *How Reading Changed My Life* (Ballantine Books), which is a kind of memoir of her relationship with books and reading.

These sections show how you can read and elevate your writing as a result.

Examining bestseller lists

Many bestsellers are widely read because they're well-written, timely, and touch on certain universal truths that speak to the heat of living. Don't get caught up in the pushback against bestsellers — it's generated from jealousy, ignorance, or the wrong-minded idea that all things popular must be bad (or crass commercialism). It's simply untrue.

A quick search for bestselling memoirs of 2012 turns up the following terrific memoirs:

- *Let's Pretend This Never Happened: (A Mostly True Memoir)* by Jenny Lawson (Amy Einhorn Books/Putnam)

- *I Suck at Girls* by Justin Halpern (It Books)
- *Wild: From Lost to Found on the Pacific Crest Trail* by Cheryl Strayed (Knopf)
- *Most Talkative: Stories from the Front Lines of Pop Culture* by Adam Cohen (Henry Holt and Co.)
- *Lots of Candles, Plenty of Cake: A Memoir* (Random House) by Anna Quindlen (Yep, Quindlen again)
- *Bossypants* (Reagan Arthur Books) by Tina Fey
- *Prague Winter: A Personal Story of Remembrance and War, 1937-1948* by Madeleine Albright (Harper)

You can do much worse than reading Strayed's amazing story (an Oprah pick, no less!) or Lawson's weird/funny/wild book or anything by Quindlen. You may want to take a long look at Halpern's effort, a Kindle-only book (yes, you read that right; it doesn't have any print option available; you can read more about this phenomenon in Chapter 21) that's a follow-up to his smash hit *Sh*t My Dad Says*.

You can also search online for a list of bestselling memoirs for any year you choose. (God love the Internet, which apparently *is* good for something other than video games and porn!) There's no wrong way to come at successful memoirs. Read them. See how they work. Take note of what you like, what you don't like.

Then put them away and go after your own story.

Imitating how to write

You wouldn't expect to pick up a guitar for the first time and jump on stage to play lead for a big time rock band, would you? Instead, you get a guitar, noodle some on it, and then start to learn how to play by watching others do it (either from a teacher, a better player, or perhaps videos of a professional playing). Although you may complement your lessons with a how-to book, nothing helps you master as fast as the "monkey see, monkey [try to] do" approach.

Old world painters learned in this same manner, too; as soon as they showed a little skill, they began a long apprenticeship period. For awhile, they simply observed. Before long, they'd be asked to imitate, and finally, after years of copying the attitudes and techniques and commitments of others, they finally became a master and painted entirely on their own.

Writing works just like those models. You imitate not to steal but to discover how — it's a form of flattery. You imitate the writers you respect because you want to be as good as they are. You want the same level of artistry that they have.

My experience with imitating

During the early part of my writing career, I kept hitting plateaus where it seemed like I'd be stuck at that level of achievement forever. I got past it each time by imitation. I would take a poem, or a story, or in a few cases, an entire book, and copy it word by word. Now I can type 80+ words per minute, though that's not how I copied them. I went slowly, methodically, and carefully. I stopped periodically and looked at what I'd just typed, and then asked, "If this were my piece, what would I say next?" And then I compared my guesses to what the original writer did. It was incredibly informative and helped me absorb some of the techniques of great writers.

Hunter S. Thompson supposedly retyped *The Great Gatsby* and *A Farewell to Arms* to fundamentally understand the styles of F. Scott Fitzgerald and Ernest Hemingway, so maybe my own typing assignments weren't a poor idea!

If you see a memoir that you adore, try this same thing on a page or two. See if by making some of the author's story your own, you figure out a better way to tell *your* own story. (And if you feel so moved, copy a chapter, or even the whole thing. Doing so won't hurt you and it just may help a ton!)

Finding your audience

Despite being able to say, "Hey, if you love Anna Quindlen's memoir, you'll *love* mine too!", the reality is that you won't steal her entire audience. You may have some crossover, though that's not a guarantee either.

Figuring out your audience is always a challenge. Part of this is a publicity issue (see Chapter 21 for more on this topic). Part of this is the story you're telling and the manner in which you tell it. Some books will never be bestsellers, and some will. Don't stress over this point. Whatever size audience is out there for your book is the right audience for your book. Simple as that.

Pro writers know that you can't take a square and bang its corners down to make it look like a circle just because you suspect a circle will play better to readers. In short, pro writers write the stories they like in the best ways they can. They don't get too caught up in audience concerns and issues until *after* the first draft is done and it's time to revise (see Chapter 15) and edit (refer to Chapter 16). Try to please everyone too soon in a writing project, and you'll end up pleasing no one, most especially, not yourself.

Writing Exercises to Just Get You Started in the Right Direction

No writing book is complete without some hands-on activities and exercises to help get you moving in the right direction. Although other chapters are targeted to address specific aspects of memoir writing, these are most useful at the start of the entire process. Try one, try three, or try them all if you choose. There's no wrong way to get started writing.

❑ **Start building up your writing muscles.** For a week straight, write at least 100 words a day. It doesn't matter what you write about. Just get in the habit of putting pen to paper (or fingers to keyboard) at a 100-word-a-day pace. The stories will come.

❑ **In a single sentence, write down what you think — at this very moment — your memoir will be about.** Then compare that to the various reasons listed about why people write memoirs (that I discuss in this chapter). Are they a match? Does your intended memoir satisfy the reason you want to write one? (You'd be surprised at how often this happens.) Adjust accordingly.

❑ **Make a list of at least a dozen firsts you remember from your life.** The first day of school. The first car accident. The first time you fell in love. Select one and write the full scene of that event, taking care to relate what you were thinking, feeling, and doing (and why!). This scene may turn into one of the foundation scenes of your book.

❑ **Write your own nano-memoir in only six words.** The online literary magazine *Smith Magazine* has a focus on personal narrative. One of its most interesting projects in that vein is the Six-Word Memoir Project. After you take a crack at it, visit `www.smithmag.net` to see an archive of other six-word memoirs. (If you like this kind of thing, check out its book version entitled *Not Quite What I Was Planning: Six-Word Memoirs* [Harper Perennial] by Writers Famous and Obscure.)

❑ **Get visual!** Researchers know that for a host of reasons (TV, video games, films, and so on) people are becoming more visually oriented. They also know that thinking visually can help people remember more effectively. Go through old photographs. Make year-by-year charts of your life. Draw scenes from your past using stick figures. Get out highlighters and mark up your notebooks with whatever you find interesting. Get visual and get ready to write that memoir!

❑ **The next time you dine at a Chinese restaurant, save the fortune cookie.** Break out the fortune at the next writing session and write for five minutes about what would happen to you if you followed the advice verbatim. (Another option: Write five fortune cookie fortunes that would have been a great help had you encountered them — and followed them — years ago.)

❑ **Try writing immediately after you wake up for three days straight.** The moment you get up, before you do *anything* else, get writing. Don't talk to anyone, don't eat, and don't even brush your teeth. Give yourself at least five minutes of writing. Does your fresh-out-of-bed morning voice sound different from your normal one? (Change up your routine as needed to creatively try out the various possibilities for your voice.)

❑ **Focus on writing about little moments.** Some writers get bogged down trying to write about big moments in their past so they can get at the big themes. Start small. Start by capturing as faithfully as possible two of the little, self-contained moments from your past that you deeply recall. What you'll soon realize is that it's these little moments that often contain the largest truths. Write enough of these little moments and you'll have all the big themes, the large truths that your book ever needs.

Chapter 3

Understanding What Readers Expect: The Story Behind a Good Story

*E*very reader comes to a book with a small mountain of biases and expectations. They can't help it — it's just the natural outcome of their experiences, upbringing, education, family, and so forth. As a writer, you can't do anything about a reader's personal biases, such as someone who believes:

✓ I hate books about baseball. Or all sports for that matter.

✓ Books should be no longer than 175 pages.

✓ The only books worth reading have two car chases, one shootout, and an X-rated love scene.

You (or any writer for that fact) can't do anything about a reader's biases, but you certainly can do a lot to meet their story expectations. Readers may not have the specific terms and language to talk about stories as specifically as academics and writers do, but readers immediately recognize certain things as right and others as confusing (which typically leads to readers moving on to other stories).

This chapter identifies those reader expectations and shows you how to work with them to maximize your chances of success. If you want your memoir to be something readers can't put down, consider reading this chapter more than once because understanding basic story structure empowers you to tell the most effective story possible. Even if you intend to share your story with only a select few, knowing what's in this chapter can still serve you well in creating a lasting effect in your readers. They may even start bugging you to get it published with a big New York publisher or have the movie made, it's so good.

Following the Traditional Story

Stories have been around since cavemen have been painting on walls. They're the tales around a campfire about what happened out in the darkness. They're the stories about the type of love that literally causes mountains to be moved. They're the chronicles of battles and triumphs and sorrows. They're the things that help people see and understand and make better sense of the swirling world of experiences.

The traditional story — or rather, the elements of the traditional story — emerged after generations upon generations used the same techniques to make their stories more effective. In the most basic definition possible, the *traditional story* is a series of events that brings a character from the normal happenings of his or her life to a moment of importance. From those moments, inner change often happens.

Some examples that show the setup for how a character can move to a moment of great importance in his or her life are as follows:

- ✔ **Testament of Youth by Vera Brittain (Weidenfeld & Nicolson):** In this memoir, a sleepy English village is devastated by WWI. All the young boys enlist and don't come back. Talk about a change from the norm in the world of this little village!

- ✔ **Angela's Ashes: A Memoir by Frank McCourt (Scribner):** In this memoir, Brooklyn-born McCourt goes with his family to Limerick, Ireland, the poverty-stricken land of their ancestors.

The following sections identify the four main parts of the traditional story. In the rest of this chapter (and in Chapter 6), I look at many different ways of thinking about and understanding stories. If this one doesn't quite jive with you, no worries! I start here for a reason. The traditional story is clear and easy to examine. In fact, nearly 99 percent of stories you encounter will fit into the traditional story structure. As for the other 1 percent? They're oddball pieces, experimental stuff, and hybrid things that more than likely aren't successful, unless the author is incredibly talented and fully understands story structure first. (This is that whole "you have to know the rules before you can break them" thing you probably heard from a sports coach or English teacher.)

Building your character's history: Pattern

For your readers to understand and care about a character, they have to know some of the events and experiences that helped shape your character. A character's *pattern* provides the context for the story. His patterns are his histories; histories inform who and what a character is. As a result, spending more than a little time getting pattern into the story is worthwhile because your story ultimately is about character building.

A good pattern may reveal already-existing traces of what will create the complication, which are really just an offshoot of the tension or conflict (refer to the "Upping the ante: Complication" section for more information). The pattern needs to show the beginnings of those tensions that lead to major plot concerns for the main character. For instance, a kid gets bullied every day at school. Everyone knows what's going to happen in that story. One way or another, he's going to find some way to stop it. Maybe he'll hire a bigger kid to help him (the movie *The Bodyguard*), learn karate (*The Karate Kid*), or get a gun (my young adult book, *Unlocked* [Walker Books for Young Readers]).

The following are the easiest ways to deliver pattern to your readers:

- ✔ **Flashback:** Depicting entire scenes of the past can be quite revealing if used sparingly, so as not to jeopardize the forward momentum of the story. (Visit Chapter 6 for ideas on when to use flashback or not in your memoir. Overusing flashback can create problems so use this judiciously.)

- ✔ **Exposition:** Let the narrator do the work by explaining the character's history. (See Chapter 13 for tips on how to use exposition well.)

- ✔ **Dialogue:** What characters say and how they say it can suggest a lot. (Refer to Chapter 9 for how to effectively use dialogue in your memoir.)

- ✔ **Detail:** Properly chosen details can help get readers in the loop with a character's past. (See Chapter 7 for insight into how to use details to great effect.)

Evolving: External change

Knowing the normal trajectory of your character's life can also help your readers see how the external change redirects that trajectory. In other words, *external change* is when your character's story breaks out of the pattern that's been so much a part of his life. Daily life doesn't have all that much importance. It's the rare things that are different from daily life — death, love, adventure, violence — that often hold the most meaning.

How important is an external change in a story? To exclude an external change would leave the story in the realm of pattern, which is the regular day-to-day stuff of a life. No one wants to read a few hundred pages of the humdrum, normal stuff in a life.

You can introduce external change in several ways:

- **Change in location:** A change in location is simply that — a physical coming or going. This type of external change can be as familiar as the old Western motif: A stranger comes to town. Or it can be a kid moving to college, leaving home for the first time in his life.

- **Social environment changes:** Losing a job, being booted from a house, or winning the lottery will most certainly change a character's circumstance and thus change their pattern meaningfully.

- **Emotional or physiological changes:** One way to launch a story out of the daily routine is a significant interior or exterior change to the body. Suffering a serious injury or emotional damage are two clear ways to raise the stakes and send the story in a new, more impactful direction. For a very unusual version of this method, check out Mary DeMuth's *Thin Places: A Memoir* (Zondervan), which is a moving spiritual journey prompted by childhood abuse.

- **Action:** Readers love action, and that's why so many stories start with it. Action is often part of the external change. Starting with action is okay, although you still have to work in pattern somehow. (Refer to the earlier section for more on pattern.)

In medias res is the Latin term that means "in the middle of things." It's a narrative technique that launches the reader right into the thick of the matters, often with action and high stakes. If it's done well, the reader won't mind not knowing the characters or situation beyond the obvious action at hand. They'll figure the rest out later. A few examples of stories that start in medias res: *The Godfather, Star Wars, The Odyssey, What Is the What* by Dave Eggers (Vintage), and *The Time Traveler's Wife* by Audrey Niffenegger (Houghton Mifflin Harcourt).

Three examples of clear external change in memoirs are as follows:

- *Swallow the Ocean: A Memoir* **by Laura Flynn (Counterpoint):** Flynn realizes her mother is a paranoid schizophrenic.

- *Beautiful Boy: A Father's Journey Through His Son's Addiction* **by David Sheff (Mariner Books):** A bright, athletic, "beautiful boy" succumbs to drug addiction.

- *Memoirs of a Goldfish* **by Devin Scillian (Sleeping Bear Press):** Yes, this is a picture book, but even here the poor fish has an external change: Intruders come into his bowl and their very presence ticks him off.

Upping the ante: Complication

After the initial tension arrives, a *complication* occurs, which are problems, snags, and setbacks your character encounters. For your own memoir, you need to think about the obstacles that got in your way, which are the complications. Some will be minor inconveniences, which aren't worth spending a lot of time with. The bigger ones, though, are where the meat of your story exists. How you overcame them (or didn't) is what will engage readers. Readers want to see the struggle, the woman- or man-versus-self/woman/man/society stuff unfold.

You can see how complication plays out in this scene from an old West style story:

> **Pattern:** A former gunfighter retires to a sleepy, peaceful backwater Oklahoma town to run a saloon.
>
> **External change:** A gun-toting, dangerous-looking stranger comes to town looking to make a quick buck.
>
> **Complication:** The stranger is determined to take over the only profitable venture in town, the saloon, and he'll do it by any means necessary.

See how the complication ups the ante? If the dangerous stranger simply wanted to get drunk and chase women, he's no bother to the innkeeper. But the stranger's greediness puts the two characters in direct conflict. Like Clint Eastwood did in the movie *The Unforgiven*, the innkeeper in this hypothetical story has to decide whether to bring back the wild gunfighting days he promised to forego, or lose his livelihood and be called a coward by the stranger (and lose the respect of the town as well as himself).

 A novel or memoir can juggle a number of complications over the course of its many pages. In the preceding example, what if the innkeeper was in love with Penny, who deals blackjack and plays the piano? Imagine now that the stranger is Penny's long-lost brother? Now what does the innkeeper do? As a reader, I would certainly be invested enough in this story to find out.

Complication matters enough to give you one more example, this time from my own life. I was a very good baseball player in my tween years. Then I developed asthma. Then I got run over by a car and was on crutches for months. If my next memoir were called *My Life in Sports: The Ryan Van Cleave Story*, writing at length about how I persevered in the face of these physical adversities would be interesting and useful to readers. I wouldn't spend much time — perhaps none at all — on how I got an F in an Intro to Logic class at college, how I cracked a front tooth by diving into the shallow end of a pool, or how I ruined a friend's clutch by trying to teach myself how to operate a manual transmission. In this hypothetical memoir, I'd stick with the important complications that speak to the larger idea(s) my book is trying to cover (that is, sports and sports- or competition-related stuff). Some of the other problems in my life were indeed bummers, but they were low stakes plus they don't connect directly with the main complication and my main story.

Guiding the story: Internal change

Stories bring characters to a place where internal change can happen. Internal change doesn't refer to superficial changes, but rather significant, fundamental ones. *Internal change* is basically the outcome of the story and the guiding light. It usually affects the character's psyche, altering how he or she sees the world. It may well change how he or she thinks, acts, and feels.

If your manuscript didn't include internal change, you wouldn't really have a story. Stuff would've just happened on the page. Some might call internal change the entire point of the story and why you're sharing your story (and writing your memoir).

Internal change is tougher to show than external change because it doesn't have as obvious of an outward appearance. The transformation Ebenezer Scrooge undergoes in Charles Dickens's *A Christmas Carol* is at one extreme — a rather hard to believe one, at that. Most internal change is subtle, and as such, the clues that it has occurred need to be similarly subtle — a different way of talking about something, a different from usual action taken, a different answer to a question they've been asked before. After your readers see that small change, they can put the pieces of the story together to recognize that an internal change has happened.

A few examples of internal change include

- ✔ *Three Little Words: A Memoir* by Ashley Rhodes-Courter (Atheneum Books for Young Readers): After spending nine years in 14 different foster homes, Ashley lets go of her anger and finds the courage to begin her life anew.

- ✔ *Lies My Mother Never Told Me: A Memoir* by Kaylie Jones (William Morrow): After battling against alcoholism, a self-absorbed mother, and the stress of having a famous father, Jones finds purpose and satisfaction in earning a black belt in Tae Kwon Do with her daughter.

Some characters are presented with a situation where they have every opportunity for change, but they choose not to take it. Although there's no obvious change, they committed to a lesser path, a lesser version of themselves (such as a coward, a passive person, or a lonely person, choosing to stay that way versus risk rejection or pain by taking a chance in a relationship.)

Seeing Your Story as a Pyramid

Many writers have an easier time understanding the idea of a story if they see it visually rendered on the page. A pyramid illustrates the most common terms or parts of a story.

A couple of hundred years ago, a German guy named Gustav Freytag invented *Freytag's Pyramid* (also known as *Freytag's Triangle*) to use as a tool in understanding ancient Greek drama and the plays of Shakespeare.

You may see different terms than I use in this section if you did an online search for Freytag because this well-known idea has a lot of people using and writing about it. Everyone means the same thing. Freytag's Pyramid (check out at `www.ryangvancleave.com/freytag.pdf`) identifies the five main dramatic parts of a story. After you master it, you can start seeing it in sitcoms, movies, books, and plays.

Although Freytag's Pyramid is a useful way to see your story's narrative arc, it's not enough to come up with the five parts and say that you're done. Freytag's Pyramid works best in

- Helping regular people talk about stories
- Helping writers get the big strokes right, which can save a lot of time by keeping them from going in the wrong direction

It's *not* a plug-and-chug, paint-by-numbers formula that guarantees success. It is, however, a very useful way to just get started.

Starting the story: Exposition and inciting action

Two things happen around the start of your story. *Exposition* is the information given at or near the start of a story to show the normal life of the main character. Exposition happens when things change, so readers can see that more distinctly by knowing what it was to begin with. In many ways, exposition is similar to pattern, which I discuss in the preceding section, "Building your character's history: Pattern."

Exposition also shows readers, by contrast, why a story is being told. Stories are about important periods in a life. If they're about a rotten day at school, readers may think "So what?" Everyone has rotten days at school or work. If your story is about a murder or about finding true love or teaching yourself quantum mechanics while caring for a dying mother, then readers get it, and it's worth talking about. The story answers the "So what" question for readers. It's not your day-to-day, slice of life stuff.

At the beginning of the story, the inciting action also shows up. The *inciting action* is the change that happens that launches the story. *Incite* means "to start up," "to urge on," or "to provoke." Those definitions all work well in this structure. Because of the action that happens at the start, a story is provoked or incited into being. And that story will take your main character away from his regular world and a situation/environment where change is possible. Whatever the main story of your memoir is about, there's an inciting action there somewhere that got it going.

A few examples of exposition and inciting action include the following:

- *Harry Potter and the Sorcerer's Stone* by J.K. Rowling (Scholastic)

    - **Exposition:** Young Harry has a lousy life with the Dursleys who dislike magic and treat him horribly.

    - **Inciting action:** Harry receives his invite to Hogwarts, and he enters the world of wizardry.

- *Lucky: A Memoir* by Alice Sebold (Back Bay/Little, Brown & Co.)

    - **Exposition:** Alice has a fairly typical life as a student at Syracuse University.

    - **Inciting action:** She is raped when walking through an off-campus park.

In these two examples, take out the inciting action and you have a regular, normal life that's not worth writing an entire book about. For your memoir, take the time to find the inciting action of *your* story. Do that and you have a two-for-one — you know what your story is really about, plus you know where it starts.

Increasing the emotion: Rising action

Rising action is the long, gradual heightening of emotion, suspense, and tension. This part should represent the largest segment of your story. It takes awhile to set everything up right for the climax! In fact, well more than half of your story is probably rising action. In a particularly exciting tale, the rising action may be 60 to 70 percent of the entire page count.

Rising action achieves heightened tension by introducing (or expanding on already-existing) conflict. You can easily pick out a number of instances of it in any memoir or novel. The main characters are striving to reach their goals but they find obstacles in the way. Although the antagonist may be responsible for those obstacles, the ultimate showdown is still to come.

To put it another way, the main character has a goal, and the rising action is about the challenges or obstacles that keep that goal unattained.

With a memoir, the rising action is probably those parts of your past where you now say, "If only I knew *then* what I know *now*!" But you didn't know how to circumvent those problems and people and obstacles that kept you from success. That led to drama, and that drama leads to reader entertainment (and hopefully a good bit of well-earned reader empathy).

Some examples of rising action in stories, or moments where the stakes are upped, include

- ✔ *The Great Gatsby* by F. Scott Fitzgerald (Scribner)

     Rising action: Nick realizes that Daisy's husband, Tom Buchanan, has a mistress in the city.

- ✔ *Falling Leaves: The Memoir of an Unwanted Chinese Daughter* by Adeline Yen Mah (Broadway)

     • **Rising action:** Adeline's father never gets over the death of his wife. As a result, Aunt Baba quits her bank job to help watch the five children.

Reaching the emotional peak: Climax

Also called the *turning point*, the *climax* of the story is the emotional high point. In terms of Freytag's Pyramid, it's at the apex. The climax is also the opportunity for the greatest change in both the story and the main character. Here is where the main character confronts the antagonist/villain. Because the tension and intensity is so high for a climax, these parts of a story are necessarily short.

Although many climaxes contain a defining physical battle, a climax can also be an emotional or spiritual struggle. Through the main character's actions and decisions, she can help determine her own fate. Having a character controlling her own life versus just reacting to stuff that happens is far more rewarding, although in a memoir, you have what you have. You need to stick with the reality of what happened to you. In a novel, you can make adjustments so the climax is more impactful.

A few examples of climaxes are as follows:

- ✔ *The Return of the King* by J.R.R. Tolkien (Mariner)

     Climax: Frodo gets to Mount Doom and intends to throw the Ring of Power into the lava, destroying it forever. Gollum intends to stop him.

- ✔ *Battle Hymn of the Tiger Mother* (memoir) by Amy Chua (Penguin Press)

     Climax: The daughter smashes a water glass on the ground in a confrontation with her mother.

Starting to resolve: Falling action

If rising action is about heightening the tension and emotions in the story, then *falling action* is the exact opposite. The loose ends are starting to be tied up. The problem is that the antagonist/villain often has the upper hand here.

The outcome of the climax may suggest one ending, but there's still hope for another. The major conflict of the story is finally being resolved.

A few examples of falling action:

✔ *Macbeth* by William Shakespeare

> **Falling action:** Macbeth discovers that his wife killed herself; he still believes his misunderstanding of the witches' prophecy, thinking he can't be killed, so he heads out to fight Macduff.

✔ *Angela's Ashes: A Memoir* by Frank McCourt (Scribner)

> **Falling action:** Frank finally earns enough to go to America, the place he was born but never really knew since he returned to Ireland with his family at age four; he says goodbye to Ireland.

Wrapping up everything: Resolution

Also called the *catastrophe* (if it's a tragedy), the *resolution* of a story is where things finally get figured out — at least enough to satisfy most audiences! Conflicts are finally settled, which allow for the release of all built-up tension from the story. All that happens here is typically a direct result from what happened in the climax.

That released tension brings up a fancy Greek word, *catharsis*, that Aristotle first used in reference to storytelling in his book *Poetics*. The term basically means "cleansing" or "purging." In essence, the resolution of a story purges the audience of any emotional worries they had over the happenings of the story. Ideally, it's a therapeutic, if not entirely pleasurable, experience.

This part of the story is sometimes called by the French word *dénouement*, which literally means "the untying of a knot." In this case, it indicates that all the complexities of the story — the knots, as they were — are now managed and done away with. The dénouement can continue past the resolution of the story.

Thinking of the resolution as a happy occasion would be wrong. The resolution certainly can be, but as you can see from the following examples, it's often a moment marked with sadness, regret, or damage.

- ✔ *Raiders of the Lost Ark*

    Resolution: The Ark of the Covenant is boxed up and hidden away in a spooky US government facility with thousands of other boxes marked TOP SECRET.

- ✔ *Wasted: A Memoir of Anorexia and Bulimia* by Marya Hornbacher (Harper Perennial)

    Resolution: Marya survives her battle with eating disorders, though there are serious health consequences — osteoporosis, infertility, and a heart murmur.

Plenty of contemporary stories don't have a clear resolution, which may be because people no longer believe in wrap-it-up-in-a-bow endings. Another reason may be that if an author has a hit on her hands, she always like to leave room for a sequel so she can keep the financial gravy train rolling. That's not usually an issue with memoir, however.

Looking at an example of the pyramid structure: Little Red Riding Hood

To see Freytag's Pyramid in action, I take a look at how it works in a very simple story: *Little Red Riding Hood*.

Exposition: Once upon a time, there was a dear little girl who was loved by everyone.

Inciting action: Grandma gets sick and Mother sends Red off with a basket of goodies for her. She warns Red to stay on the path.

Rising action: Red goes through the dark woods to Grandma's.

More rising action: She meets the Big Bad Wolf.

More rising action: He convinces her to take a different route so she can pick flowers. He hurries ahead to Grandma's.

More rising action: He eats Grandma and dresses up as her.

More rising action: Red arrives and doesn't realize it's the Wolf at first.

More rising action: Red notices Wolf's big ears, eyes, hands, and teeth.

Climax: Wolf eats Red.

Having an epiphany

James Joyce popularized a term, *epiphany*, for use in talking about stories. Epiphanies — sudden bursts of realization/insight, or "aha moments" — occur as a result of the climax, falling action, or resolution. Some refer to it as a "revelation," considering it a separate point of Freytag's pyramid.

You can see how it happens. In moments of great duress, people often have great insight, such as: "My gosh, I really do love her," "I take it all back — I don't really want to die!," or "I've been a horrible, horrible father, and now that my kids are adults, it's too late to fix that." The epiphany isn't generally considered to be a true part of the Freytag Pyramid structure, though it often works hand in hand with the end of any good story.

Falling action: A woodsman comes by and hears Wolf snoring. As soon as he figures out what happened, he cuts open Wolf and frees Red and Grandma. He takes the wolf skin home. Red and Grandma eat the treats.

Resolution: Red learns never to leave the path again.

Part of why Freytag's Pyramid resonates with many people is that it echoes so many fairy tales and children's stories they loved when they were little, just like this one. Readers appreciate structure and clarity. Freytag's Pyramid delivers that in spades.

Eyeing the Importance of Plot

I discuss plot again and again in this book. In this discussion on basic story structure, *plot* is a series of cause-and-effect — linked scenes deliberately arranged to create drama and action for a character over the course of a story, which ultimately leads to thematic significance. Quite simply, plot is the main story arc that occurs in a memoir.

To clarify even more, story is what happens. Plot is the point-by-point happenings of the story . . . and unless audiences see the connection between each of those points, they aren't happy. They expect a kind of logic to govern the story, whether it's a memoir or a novel or even a video game.

A memoir has the added complication of what really happened, so it may seem confusing to define plot as "scenes, deliberately arranged." Sometimes life arranges the scenes in a very inconvenient way. The memoir doesn't always follow an orderly, Freytag Pyramid plotline. But you can still strive to find elements of the conventional plot in your own story. When inciting action, rising action, climax, falling action, and resolution can be identified, you would do well to take advantage of the opportunity.

Chapter 4

Researching and Remembering: Gathering Enough Material

In This Chapter

▶ Retrieving "lost" memories

▶ Tapping into stories and other people's memories

▶ Diving into research about yourself

▶ Seeing why honesty matters

*W*hether you're 29 or 99, you already have enough life material to write a memoir (and then some). The key? Don't get bogged down with the research and remembering part because doing so keeps you from actually writing. This excuse is too convenient for stalling your project.

The reality is that just because you lived an experience doesn't mean that you have everything you need available to write convincingly and effectively about it. That's what this chapter is about — getting those key, relevant memories and experiences to resurface. In many ways, this process may be the most fun part of the memoir creating process, so enjoy it. This chapter starts with helping you tap into your own memories so you can remember moments to write about. I also discuss how you can use external information, such as photographs, yearbooks, scrapbooks, and vital records, as well as other people to spark your memories.

Whenever you start remembering events in your life, you also want to represent those memories like they happened and not embellish them, so I provide a section on the importance of being truthful. Like with the other chapters in this book, I also include some exercises at the end to get your creative juices flowing.

You may not use everything that emerges during the researching and remembering that you do, but it will all help provide the context for your story. That's worth its weight in gold.

Tapping into Your Past: Unlocking Your Memories

Murphy's Law states that "anything that can go wrong, *will* go wrong." That's just as true for memoir writers as anyone else. You sit down to write your book, and a sudden attack of temporary amnesia sets in. What's my name? Where did I go to high school? When did I get a Shih Tzu? I worked for whom? When? And for how little money? I actually wore that?

Okay, so maybe your amnesia isn't quite that bad, but memory is a fickle thing. The human mind has an unusual way of remembering events, and a major psychological event or even just a little stress can impact your mind in ways that you didn't even know. As a result, you may have trouble recalling even the smallest details, like what you had for lunch. You can use the following ideas to help you kick your brain into high gear. Here I help you fire up those neurons and get the memories flooding back to life. Without your memory bank fully engaged, that memoir is going nowhere fast.

Coloring with crayons

Who knows what crayon makers put in them, but crayons smell great. Sniff a few and you'll be transported back to the days of napping on carpet squares, listening to stories, and drawing flying purple cat vampires on huge sheets of paper that's ripped off a giant roll. Why? Just because you can. A pretty magical effect for a three-cent stick of colored wax, wouldn't you say?

Crayons actually can help you recall and remember different times from your past. I suggest you buy a box of crayons, sit down, and try these different activities to help remember. If you have children or grandchildren, you can make this a family event where everyone participates:

- **Draw a self-portrait with your favorite color(s).** You don't need artistic skill. In fact, the less skill you have, the more fun and useful this exercise can be.

- **Write down your first memory involving crayons.** Sketch your first memories with crayons. However you choose to proceed, explore this memory deeply. Often, this is a powerful moment where you first discovered the appeal of creativity.

> ✔ **Draw the block you grew up on.** Add people, plants, and other details that you remember. Then write one of the many stories that you recalled.
>
> ✔ **Get a coloring book from one of those dollar stores.** Color outside the lines, use the wrong colors, and be as wild as needed, or even when not needed. Unleash the creative five-year-old within you.

These types of activities can launch you out of the malaise or frustration so many writers experience when they first come to the blank page. They can get you remembering what it was like to be deeply in touch with your creative self. That's a wonderful thing for a writer to recall, even if these moments don't actually appear in your memoir.

Practicing deep thinking and breathing

With life rushing past everyone at breakneck speed, people can easily just stay in a superficial state of reacting to things. To help you remember past memories, I suggest you take a moment to stop and practice some deep reflection. Doing so can help you understand and appreciate what has happened to you in the past. In other words, reflection is a crucial part of the learning process. Readers certainly want to see some of your experiences delivered in great detail on the page, but they also want to get a sense about what you discovered and what those experiences meant to you. That's what deliberate, careful reflection can offer you and your readers.

 Studies have shown that people remember better when lying down, so find a good spot to get comfy. Stick to these steps to help you slow down and grab hold of those elusive moments from your past. Try the following to put yourself in the best frame of mind to be open to your own past. It may not work right off, so be patient.

1. **Find a quiet place by yourself with no distractions.**

   A bed, couch, or well-carpeted floor will do. Turn off your phone, your TV, and your computer. If you have any children or pets, find a place where they can't disturb you for at least 20 minutes.

2. **Shut your eyes and focus on your breathing.**

   Recent studies show that closing your eyes and staying calm — giving yourself a little downtime — can help people remember more than any other method.

3. **Take in a long, deep breath through your nose, and then hold it in.**

   Most people use less than 20 percent of their total lung capacity with regular breathing, so you want to breathe deeply, starting with the bottom part of your lungs and then filling them all the way to the top. You'll know you're doing this right because you can feel your chest expand more than you might expect. All that extra oxygen will do your brain good.

4. **Slowly release the breath through your mouth.**

   Repeat. Repeat again.

5. **As your body feels more and more relaxed, start to think about the past.**

   As soon as it starts to happen, don't give up on it easily. Follow through on memories. Remember the context of every story, but also relish in the sensory details of your past.

   Let the flickers of memory burn brighter in your mind. Let one memory lead to another, and then to another. Some will center on people, places, relationships, and happenings. Others will have a focus that's harder to identify.

6. **After 20 to 30 minutes, slowly get up and in some fashion capture the most memorable moments you just had.**

   You can jot them down in a notebook or fire up your computer and type about what you just experienced. Don't worry if you can't recall every single thing. Something that slipped from your mind just now will surface later on its own.

Some psychologists claim people have better long-term memories in the evening. Consider doing your deep thinking a few hours after dinner for the best results. Perform this exercise a couple times a week over the next few months.

Putting on Your Researcher's Cap: Uncovering Vital Info about Yourself

When you think of the word "research," you may have nightmares, thinking of times studying in high school or college. Well, you can relax. I am not talking about generating a shoebox full of note cards or spending weeks reading a book you didn't want to only to write a report you never wanted to write on a subject you don't care all that much about.

Although the research may require some library work, you have a real stake now. You aren't researching academic papers to help you create an essay on Shakespeare's use of the semicolon in *King Lear*. The common denominator of everything you're finding out in your research is you — your favorite subject (or at least it should be for as long as you're working on your memoir)!

Of course, the memoir is about more than you — it's about your family, your community in which you lived, and the world you inhabited. All those things provide useful context, but the common thread through it all is you.

These sections identify different sources you can research to uncover more clues about the deep past. One of the best places to start? With images.

Examining childhood photos and home movies and videos

No matter whether you have photo albums, shoeboxes, manila folders, or a hard drive full of photos from your younger years, you can dig in and start to peruse photos to help you recall memories.

As you examine the photos, I suggest you consider the following:

- **Pay special attention to your facial expressions.** If you had to describe each in a single word, what would it be? Inspired? Worried? Safe? Morose? Bored? Ecstatic? Whenever something particularly speaks to you, jot down your reaction.

- **Study the photo and write up the situation in the picture to the best of your knowledge.** Even if you're not sure how this situation may fit with your memoir project, writing down your initial thoughts can be valuable at some point.

- **Be on the lookout for "Aha!" moments.** These moments may be people, things, or situations that you have forgotten or powerful moments that rush back. If you experience an Aha! moment, stick those pictures aside so you can return to them as needed for inspiration as you write.

   I have a snapshot of myself in a Cub Scout uniform looking about as sullen as is humanly possible for a ten-year-old kid. Any time my writing requires me to enter the mind of a bored, "Whatever!" teen, I yank that picture out and instantly channel my past sourpuss to great effect.

Don't forget about home movies and videos. They can be very useful sources of old, misplaced memories. You may be from a generation of the silent home movie or your father may have had a VHS recorder permanently strapped to his shoulder. Watching these home movies can help you recall the flavor of a particular moment in time and place. If you have really old movies that play without sound, don't worry — they may actually be more useful than movies with sound. More than one Hollywood director has said that you should be able to turn the sound off and still follow the story. Plus not having sound forces you to really pay attention so that you can pick up on nuances that you may otherwise not notice.

Although getting nostalgic is perfectly okay, don't spend too long combing through old pictures or watching VHS tapes. Anything that keeps you from actually sitting down and writing should be kept to a minimum. Get whatever inspiration and memory nudges that the pictures hold, and then get on with it.

Reading old newspapers, books, and magazines

One of the best ways to discover interesting historical pieces of information is to flip through old newspapers, books, and magazines. For instance, have you ever seen one of those "So you were born in 1945?" birthday cards that goes on to detail the major events of the day? Writers who want to accurately capture a certain moment in history look for any type of information they can.

Consider the following sources from the year you were born or also from certain eventful moments in your life:

- ✔ **Read the titles of the *New York Times* bestseller list for that year.** The nonfiction list in particular can tell you a lot about what mattered to people during that year.

- ✔ **Read the *Time* "Person of the Year" (if you go back far enough, it's called "Man of the Year").** This is the hero of the day, someone who probably reflected contemporary values and social mores in a powerful, influential way.

- ✔ **Flip through your town's local newspaper.** The headlines, the advertisements, and the comics can all help give a flavor of the time.

- ✔ **Hit up Wikipedia, which has extensive month-by-month information for each year.** Search for the year you were born. Look up "1972" — the year of my birth — to see what I mean. I obviously don't remember any of these things, but if I were to write about what my mother was worried about in the world, here are dozens of options: a national dock strike in Britain, a train crash in Mexico that killed 208, and the Yellow River dries up for the first time in known history.

- ✔ **Examine an almanac.** Whether you have a print version or a digital one, inside you can find such major topics as economics, medicine, religion, science, technology, sports, awards, geography, and government. That's an incredible amount of information from nearly every important area of human achievement.

Although some of this information may fit in your memoir, more than likely most of it won't. Regardless, it often helps to know what was going on in the world during key moments of your life. If you're at all like me, the first 18 years of your life are pretty much a blur beyond the walls of your house, car, or classroom. Reading what other people were thinking, worrying, and fighting for/about can be extremely helpful for creating the appropriate context for your story.

Most periodicals have an online archive that you can access for free or a nominal fee. If you have time or are nearby, you may want to spend a few afternoons in your public library going through bound copies or microfiche.

Seeing what's been saved in scrapbooks

In my family, my father kept things in a scrapbook of sorts — mementos, participation ribbons, snapshots, movie stubs. In your family, maybe your brother Robert or your Aunt Myrtle did it. Someone surely has a collection of odds and ends that's chock-full of memories and family history. Find out who has that stash and make use of it.

Some of these mementos may trigger memories. Beyond that, combing through a scrapbook may get you thinking about what's not in there and why. For example, I have a high school scrapbook where I've taken out any reference to a girl who dumped me in a horrifying, public manner — let's call her "Evil She-Devil." I ran across this scrapbook recently and while I spent an hour poring old variety show tickets, concert band programs, fuzzy snapshots, and napkins from dances, it's what wasn't in the book that had me thinking for days after. Ironically, what was left out of the scrapbook made a stronger memory than anything I once put in there. That just goes to show you that you rarely know what's important while you're knee-deep in the bushes. You don't have the perspective to see what's what yet.

Flipping through your school yearbooks

School yearbooks are wonderful ways to immerse yourself in a single calendar year. Since the 1930s, people have signed each others' yearbooks, and in the 1960s, the trend went from signing to including an often long-winded personal note. You can read through them for ideas about old relationships and what was important to people during that period.

You can also look through your yearbooks for other distinct features, such as a remembrance page, original class songs, calendar of events, humor, student art and literary works, and an alumni listing.

Checking vital records

Because so many documents are now digitized, checking vital records is easier than ever before. With a little patience and determination, you can find out a lot of revealing family facts. Here are a few sources often worth checking out:

- Canceled checks
- Cemetery records/headstone information
- Church records
- Deeds

- ✔ Divorce records
- ✔ Estate papers
- ✔ Hospital bills
- ✔ Immigration/naturalization records
- ✔ Licenses
- ✔ Military records
- ✔ Passports
- ✔ School records/transcripts
- ✔ Wills

Be aware that researching vital public and private records may bring up information you didn't expect. A student in my memoir class found out from legal records that she was adopted and her parents hadn't told her. Having that kind of revelation isn't likely, but it can happen so be prepared for an unexpected jolt of truth if you decide to rummage through records and documents.

Although knowing what year your relatives arrived on Ellis Island may be interesting, don't get bogged down in a slew of numbers and dates. You want to get the bulk of the information you need to write your memoir. Figure out what you need and then get on with the writing.

Student writers often ask me, "How do I know what I need until I need it?" Great question. Trust your gut. Jot down the dates, the quotes, or the information you think you'll need (or at least that interests you at the time). Then move on. If it turns out you need more later, you know exactly where to go back for more information. If you're filling page after page of notes and data, you're probably going overboard with the gathering part versus the writing part.

Using Others as a Mirror to See Yourself

Peoples' lives don't occur in a vacuum, so don't expect a memoir to function that way either. In other words, when writing your memoir, your interactions with other people (and what they think, feel, believe, and say about you) matter. Using that knowledge can help you assemble more material for your writing.

To tap into other people's thoughts, feelings, and beliefs about you, you can make a list of people who've been more than a fleeting part of your life, including bosses, coworkers, classmates, friends, neighbors, family members, ex-family members, and so on. After you compile this list, decide who's had the most meaningful interactions with you, and start by talking to them. Sometimes the best way to learn about you is to talk to someone else.

Thanks to Facebook and other social networking sites, you can easily find and reach out to people who may have been absent from your life for years. The ability to see lists of friends of your friends may also remind you of other contacts you should make.

Starting with others' stories

Even though a memoir is your story, it's not just about you. As a result, you want to find opportunities to weave in a few of those wonderful family and neighborhood stories that you grew up with, that helped make you who you were. Part of how you know some of the most important elements of humanity (love, sacrifice, humor, and so on) comes from these stories.

For instance, when I think about persistence, I think about my great-great-great grandfather Hiram Van Cleave, who made it from New York City all the way to San Francisco 160 years ago by playing his fiddle on wagon trains. He didn't have a cent to his name, and it took him more than a year, but he got all the way there because he promised himself he'd do it. And he did. The real reason I probably remember this story so clearly is because my father brought it up again and again, so in my mind, this story is more about my father telling me what to do (which was usually followed by a lengthy list of what not to do) than some long-dead ancestor.

One story can lead to another story, and that second story is really about you after all.

Or when I think of strength of character, I think of a third-grade classmate, Marc, who was the sickliest kid I've ever seen. He had inch-thick glasses, used an inhaler a dozen times a day, and popped some three dozen pills daily "just to keep me trucking along," he once explained. When he saw a pair of second graders being bullied by a fifth grade jock, he stepped in to stop it. Dozens of people had witnessed the bullying, but only Marc did something about it. He got the crap beaten out of him, yet he later said it was the best experience he ever had.

Consider working a few of these gems into your own tale not just because they're colorful and fun, scary, exciting, or whatever, but because they helped make you who you are. And that's a lot of what a memoir's job is — revealing you.

Using personal interviews

You can also rely on personal interviews to help figure out how others think or feel about you. In this case, the word "interview" simply means you're seeking information from others who knew you at some point in your life. To interview, you can purchase an inexpensive audio recorder and talk to people face to face, send an e-mail, or call up people who knew you.

Start with close relatives, if you're feeling a little shy. Ask them a couple of open-ended questions (not closed-ended questions that require simply a yes or no answer) and take down their answers. Listen for revealing anecdotes. Don't interrupt them. Just let them talk, remember, and share. Be sure to ask if they have any special photos you can look at and hear the stories about. After you get more at ease interviewing, move on to friends, coworkers, and so forth.

Here's something I realized from doing dozens of interviews over the years. Start with questions about them. Then start asking the questions you really want. Why? Because people are always eager to talk about themselves. So start with:

✔ How is the world different today than when you were a child?

✔ Have any recipes been passed down to you from family members?

✔ What did your family enjoy doing together?

✔ What is the one thing you most want people to remember about you?

And before long, shift to what you really want to know, such as:

✔ What's your first memory of me?

✔ What's the strangest thing I've ever done?

✔ What do you think was the most important decision I've ever made?

✔ If you had to describe me to a stranger, what would you say?

✔ In your opinion, what's the biggest mistake I've made in my life? Why do you think I got it wrong?

✔ What are three moments from my life that you think my memoir should include? Why?

Some people are awkward about being interviewed, whether you're recording the conversation or not. Try leading with a throwaway topic — feel free to keep the audio recorder off for this one — just to get them warmed up. Sports, current events, or movies all are great fluffy topics that can get them talking. After things are moving along nicely, flip on the recorder and keep asking away.

Sticking to the Truth: Avoid Embellishment

Every story has three sides — your version, the other person's version, and the truth.

Although no one has a perfect memory, you need to keep as close to the facts as you can when you remember. Some families keep memoirs around for generations, relying on them to offer an accurate sense of their own history. However sometimes those memories can be stretched or changed, which can result in legal problems when untrue statements are made about people, groups, and businesses. (Chapter 17 offers more on this potentially thorny subject.) Published memoirs become public documents. You don't want to decide that Aunt Cathy would be funnier on the page if she were a drunk. Even if she doesn't choose to sue you for libel, embellishing the truth is bad practice.

If you want to make stuff up, get *Writing Fiction For Dummies* by Randy Ingermanson and Peter Economy (John Wiley & Sons, Inc.) and dream up a story that's entirely made from your imagination. But because you want to write a memoir, you need to stick with just the facts. Readers come to memoir with the promise that the book is going to be truthful.

If you break that promise, readers will remember that you're an author not to be trusted and that everything you say and write is suspect. Worse, they'll discount your memoir no matter how well it's written or what beautiful stories you have to share. (See the nearby sidebar for a perfect example.)

Although more and more authors seem content to bend the rules of memoir by deviating from reality, I can't recommend that option. If you want that kind of flexibility, write one of those novels that's based on a true story. A memoir is a promise to the reader about the heat of truth's arrival. Anything else is dishonest to both writer and reader.

Lying in real life: James Frey versus Oprah

James Frey's 2003 bestselling memoir about drug addiction, *A Million Little Pieces* (Anchor), was named to Oprah's book club in September 2005, an honor which helped him sell millions of copies. The hubbub occurred when news later broke that the brutal story he told in his memoir was untrue. It wasn't untrue in the sense that a couple of facts were finessed, as Frey admitted at times; it was untrue as in most of it didn't happen, such as an incident with police that resulted in only a few hours in jail versus the 87 days as he wrote in the book. He vastly overstated numerous things for a desired effect, and he also simply made up stuff to make it a better story. To put it plainly, he revved up the facts to make the book sell better.

The outcome of this was Frey losing a two-book, seven-figure contract. His literary agent dropped him. Oprah blasted him multiple times on TV. He went on to have more success with other books, though many readers and critics still don't trust him or his work. He's the poster child for dishonest memoir writers, and more than a few memoir writing teachers bash him regularly for besmirching the name of honest memoir writers everywhere.

Identifying the difference between truth-truth and story-truth

With memoir, the idea of truth is incredibly important, and what makes it particularly tricky to deal with is that many writers acknowledge multiple types of truth. There's *truth-truth*, which is along the lines of the transcript taken in a courtroom or what a historian endeavors to document. Then there's *story-truth*, which is less concerned with 100 percent accuracy of what happened and more concerned with getting the experience accurate.

For example, if you're writing about your experiences in a combat zone, you may be able to read enough documents and interview enough soldiers to figure out who fired first, who fired second, and who did what to whom in what order. That's commitment to *truth-truth*. But as you can imagine, it likely won't make for good reading. A different rendering of this same scenario may not bother to distinguish who shot first, second, or third, because all that really matters — the *story-truth* of the moment — is that the main character was in a firefight, bullets were flying everywhere, and he was scared as heck despite wanting to be brave.

It's important to note that *story-truth* doesn't ignore *truth-truth*, but it also doesn't have the same sense of obligation to include an onslaught of historical facts just because you know them. Be choosy and include only what's important. For most authors, it's the experience of the moment versus the fact that it was December 13, 3:37 a.m., and there was an 80 percent chance of rain and the temperature was 48°. Sometimes you do want that kind of level of detail because it helps you create authenticity, but often it's better to write, "That December morning was cold enough to make my fillings ache," and then get to what really matters — the first time you were shot, or the first time you saw your future spouse, or the first time you felt like leaping off the Golden Gate Bridge.

Grasping why honesty matters

As a memoir writer, honesty is important for a few reasons:

- ✔ Publishers won't publish a memoir that is knowingly or even accidentally (if such a thing were possible!) dishonest. You may even be liable to cover their financial losses, which can be substantial.

- ✔ Readers will feel deeply cheated if a memoir turns out to be based in falsehoods.

- ✔ You're writing a memoir so people can get to know you and your story. Don't compromise on that. Let them get to know the *real* you, not some idealized, romanticized version of you.

Stretching the truth can ruin your memoir and your writing career

Other authors have flat-out lied and embellished the truth to sell their memoirs. Here are a few of the most infamous memoirs that turned out to be fakes, just like James Frey's book. Make sure your memoir doesn't show up on this list.

- ✔ Henri Charrière's *Pappillon* (Castillian): While the author wrote about being convicted for killing a friend and escaping from a French penal colony, much of the other wild adventures in this book are considered to be embellishments and cobbled together by stories shared by other prisoners.

- ✔ Anonymous's *Go Ask Alice* (Simon Pulse): The book is now classified as fiction, which tells you all you need to know about its authenticity.

- ✔ Margaret B. Jones's *Love and Consequences: A Memoir of Hope and Survival* (Riverhead): This private schooled Caucasian suburbanite tried to pass herself off as a gang member in south-central Los Angeles. If you want to see how upset readers will be when the truth comes out, read a few of the ever-increasing number of one-star ratings for the book on Amazon.com.

- ✔ Herman Rosenblat's *Angel at the Fence: The True Story of a Love that Survived:* Upon learning the story was fake, the book was cancelled. A children's book inspired by this story, *Angel Girl* (Carolrhoda Books), immediately went out of print and readers were offered refunds.

When a memoir is revealed to be false, some people will argue that the emotional truth of the story is still real, and therefore valid. My claim is simply this: truth matters. If you have an emotional truth in your story that isn't based in reality, appropriately call it fiction. If the truth is actually that powerful, your book will affect readers as fiction, and the exchange won't be based in dishonesty and deception.

Writing Exercises to Jumpstart Your Memory

Your memories aren't always at your beck and call. You may remember a few things, or what you remember has holes in it. Or you may completely have forgotten frightfully important moments. These exercises can help you try to recover the most useful memories in order to have them available for when you're working on your memoir. These exercises, too, may help you remember better in general.

❏ In your journal or on your computer, finish each prompt in as much detail as you can. Skip the ones that don't excite you.

   ❏ My first paid job was

   ❏ The best things about my first job were

   ❏ The first time I understood what love really meant was

   ❏ What I learned was

   ❏ The person I most looked up to was because

   ❏ The five things that mattered most to me when I was young were

   ❏ The five things that matter most to me now are

   ❏ The most influential book on my life was

   ❏ I liked the book because

   ❏ When I was young, I was really good at

   ❏ My first encounter with death was

   ❏ What I took away from that experience was

   ❏ The three best friends I ever had were

   ❏ When I think of politics, I think of

   ❏ And when I think of that, I think of

   ❏ My favorite crayon color was

❏ Find and play one of those "Hits of 1974" CDs, though select a year where important things happened in your life. While listening, write about whatever memories emerge. Take the best of these and see if they fit usefully into your memoir manuscript.

❏ Try talking your way into your memories. Get a digital audio recorder, hit record, and just start talking about your past like you've made a great new friend and are filling him or her in on the most important details of your past. When you realize you have any surprise or well-rendered moments captured, go back and transcribe them. See if they may help flesh out chapters of your memoir.

Chapter 5

Developing Ideas like the Pros

• •

• •

he *New York Times* reports that 81 percent of Americans surveyed feel that "they have a book in them," which they haven't written yet. Why *aren't* these people writing all these books? Because writing a book is darn hard work. Some just don't know where to start. Some are too busy. Others give it a shot and quickly surrender to what seems an insurmountable task.

If you're thinking of writing your own book, particularly a memoir, I have some great news for you. This chapter (and book) gives you what you need to know to help you start and eventually finish your book . . . and do it well. Rome wasn't built in a day, and no good book worth reading was either. So what's the best way to move forward? Looking at the experts — published authors — is an obvious place. Who better to give insight on how to write your book than folks who've done it before?

That's exactly what this chapter reveals: tricks, tips, ideas, and techniques that writers from Stephen King to Anna Quindlen to David Sedaris all use. Here's more good news. The very same things they do — from how to get the ideas flowing to keeping a journal to carving out writing time to getting past writer's block —are things that you can do too. So, dear reader, get ready to begin the book inside of you.

Summoning Your Muse: How to Get Inspired

The reality is that writing is plain hard work. In many ways, writing isn't a lot different from building a garage, overhauling a '67 Chevy, or making a prom dress from scratch. You probably won't hear anyone claim that the reason their hot rod is still up on blocks in the front yard is because their automotive Muse is MIA, right? Don't let it become an excuse for you to quit working — or worse, not even start — your memoir.

The Muses were goddesses from Greek mythology who inspired all the creative (yes, including literary) arts. Many considered them to be the source of all knowledge. It's no shocker then that writers who got a burst of inspiration claimed to have *found their Muse*. Those that didn't feel moved to write? They've *lost their Muse*.

Something professional writers know that you probably don't is that this whole Muse business isn't real. For far too many writers, the whole Muse idea has become an excuse for not writing. If you're truly committed to writing your memoir, get over the idea of some magical being fluttering into your room at night, sprinkling literary genius dust over your head and motivating you so you'll wake up bursting with stories and inspiration and Shakespeare-quality greatness. Writing just doesn't work that way.

If you insist on believing in your own Muse, make sure he/she/it is on call 24/7. If not, kick that one to the curb and find yourself a new one. The goal is to find ways to be inspired, not find excuses not to write, right? You just don't have time for anything except a high-powered, always ready-to-go Muse.

Finding and recognizing inspiration

Some people see a blank page and feel the irresistible compulsion to fill it with words. If that's you, just do it. Let it rip. If you're like most people, though, the challenge of getting inspired falls somewhere between stretching before a 100-yard dash and dropping by the dentist for a root canal.

One way to get inspired is to try some warm-up exercises at the start of a writing session. Give one or more of the following a try:

✔ **List every pet you've had.** Or write about all the pets you *didn't* have but wished you did. Or write about your neighbor's or friend's or relative's pets. (Did your town have one of those creepy cat-collecting widows?)

✔ **Assign people that you know the animal you think they're most like.** (Or the fruit they're most like. Or the book. Or the kitchen utensil.)

✔ **Write about rain.** The feel of it on your face. Your first memory of rain. The first time you ever had to trudge home in the rain. The coldest rain you've ever experienced. The taste of it on your tongue.

✔ **Focus on what you would do if you were someone famous.** Complete the following: If I were President/Michael Jordan/Oprah, I would . . .

✔ **Think of a song you've heard a lot recently.** Write a response to that song (through song lyrics, a poem, a story, an essay, or any form you choose).

How do you recognize when you're inspired? Your brain will seem super-charged and your body will be in "go!" mode. The idea of writing a single page, five pages, or even fifteen pages of your manuscript won't seem that daunting. You may feel so energized that you don't even appreciate how much you've written until after you're done, and then you may wonder how you did all that, and how you can make it all happen exactly like that again.

Look at inspiration in another way. After hitting six three-pointers in the first half of the 1992 NBA finals, Michael Jordan confessed that the basketball hoop looked about as big as a laundry basket. In other words, huge. Professional athletes call it "being in the zone." When you're in the zone, everything comes easily and effortlessly. It's the highest level of performance.

Let me give you a writing example: Jack Kerouac sat down in the spring of 1951, typing out *On the Road* (Penguin) on a continuous 120-foot roll of paper during a three-week burst of creativity. That's being inspired. That's being in the zone for a writer.

Watch for cues on when you find inspiration and perhaps get into your own writing zone. Here are a few common situations where ideas often spark to life:

✔ **The moments before sleep or just after waking:** Keep a notebook or laptop handy for when your brain's transitioning toward (or out of) sleep.

✔ **Listening to music:** Classical music or jazz is popular, but some people need Pink Floyd, the Dixie Chicks, or the heavy pounding beat of a band like Metallica.

✔ **Doing menial tasks:** Washing dishes, gardening, vacuuming, or doing laundry. Keep your body active but give your mind the freedom to roam.

✔ **In the bathroom:** Go ahead and say "Ugh!" if you want, but a steamy shower, a long shave, or even a few quiet moments on the toilet might do the trick.

✔ **During a commute:** Use a voice recorder app on your smart phone while you drive. Do you use public transportation? Get out a pen and a small notebook and jot down your ideas while someone else does the driving.

✔ **Writing group meetings:** Whether you choose to share your own work there or not, just hearing what others are writing and thinking about can jumpstart the excitement and ideas for your own work again.

In *On Writing* (Scribner), Stephen King explains that there's no magic place, no store, no secret island, where all the great ideas are located. You have to find them yourself. What he's confessing is what we all fear: It's up to us. But here's where the memoir writer gets the edge over King, Stephanie Meyer, John Updike, J.K. Rowling, and Sherman Alexie. They all have to make stuff up. Memoir writers just have to recount stories that, in a sense, have already been written.

If you had a choice, which option would you choose? The blank slate or the mind full of memories?

Location, location, location

Although a professional athlete may need special clothes, shoes, and other supplies, a writer can survive with a pen and notepad or a bare-bones computer. (Even if you don't own a computer, public libraries have plenty that you can sign up to use.) Perhaps most importantly, a writer needs a place to write — a place that's dedicated to writing and a place that's yours. A place that's available and inviting and comfortable and relatively distraction-free.

You need a space that you can return to for each writing session so you can develop some momentum without wondering, "Hey! Who wrote a shopping list on my chapter outline? And where's my favorite pen? Who put twenty episodes of *The Smurfs* on my hard drive?" You want your brain and your body to be trained well enough such that when you enter this good work environment, the immediate reaction is: "Hey, it's writing time!" And you're ready to roll.

For some people, this space is a converted closet or attic. But if you don't have an attic, closet, bonus room, or part of your garage that you can set off, or you prefer a situation with some controlled crowd noise and activity versus massive amounts of quiet, consider working at a library, which is a popular choice of writers for obvious reasons — so many delicious books!

Willa Cather and Herman Melville wrote at the New York Society Library. The famous Reading Room at the British Museum knew such literary luminaries as George Eliot, George Bernard Shaw, and Virginia Woolf. Perhaps your local library will one day have the claim to fame of you having written your memoir there!

What do writers say about the Muse?

Here are some of the most useful things that writers have said about this whole Muse business. As you can see, they don't wait on a Muse to give them inspiration. When it's time to get writing, these pros get writing.

- ✔ I can only write when the Muse is here. That's why I keep her locked in a cage in the basement." –Virgil Suárez

- ✔ "Health is the first Muse, and sleep is the condition to produce it."–Ralph Waldo Emerson

- ✔ "O! for a Muse of fire, that would ascend the brightest heaven of invention." –William Shakespeare

- ✔ "There is no place for grief in a house that serves the Muse."–Sappho

- ✔ "What brings on the Muse for memoir? For me it's photos. Home movies. The taste of foods I enjoyed a long time ago, like Pop Rocks or rye bread from a special bakery. Then there's the smells of forgotten worlds — the eucalyptus groves I passed on the way to junior high each morning, the Old Spice soap-on-a-rope I gave my dad each Christmas. And lastly, there's a slow walk through the old neighborhood. Those are the things that open memory in Muse-like ways."–Todd James Pierce

- ✔ "The loveliest Muse in the world does not feed her owner; these girls make fine mistresses but terrible wives."–Alfred de Vigny

If a library isn't your thing, but you're aching to get out of the house to do your writing, here are some other low-cost options:

- ✔ **A coffee shop:** Don't get too jacked up on the caffeine, though.

- ✔ **A fast food restaurant:** Enjoy the free wi-fi but watch the waistline.

- ✔ **Church:** During the week, it can be amazingly quiet and contemplative.

- ✔ **Parks:** Bring a cushion for those oh-so-hard benches. No benches? Bring a blanket and spread out on the grass.

- ✔ **The car:** Make sure you have a fully-charged laptop, and please only write while parked or when you're the passenger.

- ✔ **At work:** You get breaks and lunch time, don't you? Turn your work desk into a memoir writer's desk.

Refer to the nearby sidebar to see where some famous authors found their alone time to write.

If money isn't a real problem and you're concerned about being interrupted when you work at home, consider renting out a small office near where you live. Leave for "work" at 9 a.m. and come home by noon or 3 or whatever your writing plan requires. This tactic works well for a lot of freelance writers and journalists; it helps keep them in the "writing is serious business" kind of mentality.

Finding your favorite writing getaway

When you have a hankering for a burger, you probably have a half-dozen different fast food joints within easy driving distance. On one level, they're all about the same. On another, there's a world of difference between the burgers from the Golden Arches and the King, right?

Writing environments offer the same variety and there's no perfect "one size fits all" option. Find out what works best for you by trying a few different ones until you feel the right fit. Need some ideas to get started? Here are a few writing locations that worked well for others:

- Ben Franklin wrote in a bathtub.

- Legal thriller writer John Grisham wrote longhand in a yellow legal pad on the train to and from work every day. That's how he wrote his first novel, *The Firm*.

- When her children were small, Toni Morrison got someone to watch them so she could write in the peace and quiet of a motel room.

- Ken Kalfus writes from the moment his family leaves the house in the morning and quits when they return. The only other thing he does? Unplug the Internet cable so the computer functions as just a fancy typewriter.

- Marcel Proust wrote in bed.

- In an NPR interview, Alice Hoffman said, "I used to get up at five and work for several hours before I went to work, or before my kids woke up. Now I write wherever, whenever. I don't need an office anymore, or space, or a window. Just my laptop and time."

- Simone du Beauvoir had a regular table at the Café Flore.

- Robert Frost claimed to have never written at a table. He often used a writing board, but supposedly even wrote against the sole of his shoe.

If you use reference books when you write, keep them handy in your writing space. Nothing breaks up one's rhythm like having to stop writing, walk downstairs or to another part of the house, and yank a book off the shelf just to look up a word or check a fact. Life is distracting enough. You don't need any more distractions, such as stopping for a sandwich, chatting with a family member, or taking the dog for a long walk.

Protecting your time to write

The moment you really start cooking with your writing, the world needs you. The kids are starving. The spouse has a critter emergency. The kitchen is unconscionably dirty. The furnace starts to smolder. It never fails. The only thing you can count on is being unable to count on the world to leave you alone while you're writing.

Resist. Your friends and family (and your furnace) might not understand, but you are a writer. Whatever time you've carved out of your own busy life to write is exactly that: writing time. Keep it sacred. Keep it safe.

No one will take you seriously as a writer if you don't take yourself seriously. So do so. Start by valuing your precious writing time. This time is like gold dust running from an hourglass into a dumpster. Make it count.

You may want to choose to hang a "Beware: Writer at Work!" sign on your door. A good deadbolt may also come in handy.

Dealing with (or creating) distractions

Although you may like to write in a quiet place with no distractions, unfortunately no man (or woman) is an island as writer John Donne wrote. When distractions come your way, you can get flustered and stop writing or you can use them as potential inspiration.

The Internet is one of the biggest distractions. You check e-mail, read how your favorite team did last night, and post on your friends' Facebook walls. If you want Internet play, that's fine. Just set aside a certain amount of time. When it's time to write, you write.

Many computer programs are available to help keep your Internet use under control. Some of the more popular programs include

- ✔ **Freedom:** A program that locks you away from the Internet completely for an amount of time that you set.

- ✔ **SelfControl:** This open source Mac program blocks access to the Internet as well as e-mail servers. You can blacklist it all, or just the ones that are your own digital nemesis.

- ✔ **Anti-Social:** This program blocks all the social media elements on the Internet. (This means, gasp, no Facebook!)

- ✔ **Net Nanny:** This program controls the amount of time spent online. (Set boundaries with this and you *will* stick to them.)

In fact, a growing number of writers are killing their Internet when it's time to write because even all its benefits, such as being able to look up words, find images, fact-check information, and so on, don't outweigh the many distractions it presents to keep around. You may want to consider these two examples.

- ✔ My pal Scott Ciencin has written more than a hundred books in less than three decades. How does he do it? When he's on a deadline or is just really into a project, he goes into "unplug mode," where he doesn't spend any time with e-mail, Internet, TV, or phone. He just writes, writes, and writes.

✔ Jonathan Franzen, the author of *The Corrections*, famously wrote portions of that book while wearing earplugs and a blindfold. You probably don't need to go that far, but do make your environment one that's conducive to serious writing and good work.

Don't think that all distractions are bad. For some people, they provide much-needed breaks from the intense focus of serious writing. For example, a former professor of mine likes to write with his office door open so students can (and will) interrupt him. He's a people person, so every exchange gets his creative juices flowing again. When the students leave and he returns to the writing, he says that he's always recharged and ready to roll.

Although this situation may sound like a nightmare for writers who prefer to hide from the world when they're working, a distraction now and again can be useful. Even the most creative brains need a few moments of down time. Plan a short interruption every hour or two. Enjoy a granola bar and stretch your legs. Walk the dog. Splash water on your face. Throw in a quick load of laundry. You'll be surprised how much more effective your writing is after you return after that dreaded interruption.

Keeping a journal

Regularly writing in a journal can be a great way to record your ideas and to find your own voice. To start, pick up a fancy vellum one or use one of those elementary school notebooks office supply stores sell for 10 cents every fall. All that matters is that your journal is handy with tons of blank pages. Fill them. Doodle. Sketch key scenes from your memory. Recreate dialogue. Paste snapshots or pictures you've clipped from magazines into it.

Keeping a journal or diary is a strong start toward writing a memoir. Writing in a journal can help you:

✔ **Remember key events from your past:** You can probably do a lot less prewriting memory exercises. You may also be fortunate enough to have captured lovely lines of dialogue you otherwise would have had to make up.

✔ **Have the habit of writing:** Many would-be writers don't have this skill. The ability to sit at your desk with regularity and work on your writing is something to be envied. A number of famous writers have been attributed to saying that you aren't really a writer until you've written a million words. With that habit of writing, you're going to get there much more quickly — and with much less grief — than those people who procrastinate or wait around for the Muse to arrive.

Writing a journal is meant to be private. In your journal, you can vent, be random, leave out things, and even lie. It has a clear function. Just don't mistake a journal for a memoir. Although they share the same bloodline, they're cousins, not twins. When you read your own journal, you know what you meant, so your brain fills in the blanks. With a memoir, all the reader has is the words on the page, so you have to make sure the scenes and characters and moments of importance in your life are accurately and fully rendered on the page.

One way to make sure you're not lapsing into this journal mode is imagine that someone finds your writing after you're dead and gone from this world. What will they get from it without you there to interpret and explain things? If you have doubts about what they'll take away from the reading, go back and make the writing do more work.

Even if what you're doing in your journal doesn't seem to directly relate to your memoir, that's okay. Your brain is always making more creative connections than you're consciously aware of. Give it some free rein. What you're doing here is finding your own voice, which is crucial for telling your own story.

Staying away from booze and drugs

Name a half dozen famous writers, and odds are likely that more than one of them has or had a reputation for drug or alcohol abuse. Although most of this chapter suggests you turn to the professionals for advice and a model for your own actions, now is one area not to do so. Don't follow in their footsteps.

Real inspiration comes from a sharp mind, an open heart, and an eagerness for stories. Don't fall into the trap of thinking that to be as famous as Hemingway, you have to drink like Hemingway did. The reality is that most of those famous drunks wrote better when they weren't drinking. Worse, think about how many masterpieces the world never saw because Hemingway died at 61, Jack Kerouac at 47, F. Scott Fitzgerald at 44, and Dylan Thomas at 39? While Stephen King didn't drink or snort himself to death, he openly admits that he would've done better work had he simply stayed sober.

Want some Champagne or wine to celebrate when you're done with your book? Great. But keep the cork in the bottle until then.

Giving Yourself Some Structure

Okay, the ideas are coming. The inspiration is here. It's time to write. All you need is to focus on all that good stuff. That's where structure comes in — it keeps you aimed at the target all the time. The following sections point out some specific ways many writers before you have tried to find some structure. They're also great for you and your writing.

Put yourself on the Stephen King plan

Once, when asked by a reporter how often he wrote, Stephen King admitted that he wrote every day except for Christmas and his birthday. But he later confessed that those days weren't off limits — he actually wrote every single day. He just gave that first answer so he didn't sound too obsessive about his commitment to writing.

His daily goal? 2,000 words. If he finishes by 10 a.m., great, the rest of the day is free. Yet even though he's wildly prolific, he sometimes struggles and has to work long past lunchtime to hit his goal. But hit it he does or he doesn't leave his workspace.

So put yourself on your own version of the Stephen King plan. No, you don't need to write 2,000 words every day. Set your own daily standard — 200 words a day is fine. So is 500, 50, or 5,000. Establish a goal that you feel comfortable with and bang it out every day until you're done. It's that easy (and that hard!).

Take a writing class

Some writers require deadlines and a support system to flourish. Others put more time and effort into something they've paid for. Enter the writing class, which combines all of these elements. A writing class may be a perfect way for you to find some structure to your writing. You can find writing classes at community centers, YMCAs, high schools, community colleges, and universities. (Visit www.ryanvancleave.com/bonuschapter.pdf for more information.)

You don't need an instructor with *New York Times* bestseller credentials; a college degree and a few publications is just fine. What you do need are deadlines, assignments, quality feedback, and the literature-loving, pro-writer environment a good writing classroom provides. Although all writing classes are designed to offer these things, some classes (and some instructors) fall short, so ask around for recommendations before enrolling.

You can be the beneficiary of a new trend in higher education — giving away the lessons for free. Check out MIT's OpenCourseWare (OCW) initiative, where you can get lecture notes, videos, and suggested reading lists for undergraduate and graduate level creative writing classes. Other schools offer options, too: Utah State University, Purdue University, Wikiversity, and the University of Massachusetts-Boston, to name just a few. What is one of the coolest options with these online programs? Some of them can earn you college credit just by taking and passing an online exam after completing the course.

Join a critique group

Going to a critique group is another way to keep you focused on your writing. A critique group provides much of the benefits of the writing class — namely peers who are interested in writing and generous feedback on your manuscript — without the cost or the obligation of an attendance policy. In some ways, a critique group is better than a writing class because it's usually smaller, made of seriously devoted writers, and has the clear goal of publication-quality writing. It's also far more common to find published writers in a critique group than in a writing class. Critique groups are such an important part of many writers' lives; see www.ryanvancleave.com/bonuschapter.pdf.

Join a professional organization

Although in many states many professionals such as teachers need to belong to a professional organization, such as a union, to work, a writer doesn't have any such obligation. However being part of a professional organization has its benefits, so you may want to consider joining a professional organization. Some of the benefits are as follows:

- ✔ It can make you feel like a professional.
- ✔ You can read their group's newsletter and/or magazine for inspiration.
- ✔ You can attend the group's conferences.
- ✔ You can make relationships with other serious writers and ask how they maintain focus and structure when writing.
- ✔ You can interact with and ask questions from those who have written and published before.

No two groups are alike. For example, the Fellowship of Christian Authors is nothing like The Author's Guild. The Writers Guild of America is a far cry different from a local, regional, or state writers association. Before you send in any dues, spend some time online searching or speaking with current members to find out the best fit for you. Some groups don't allow new members to join unless they have significant publications already. (You can target that group after your memoir is published.)

Subscribe to a writer's magazine

If you don't already know about them, you may be surprised to discover that writers write about writing. These writer's magazines offer a lot of practical advice, inspiration, and guidance for readers. Consider reading a few issues of *The Writer, Writers' Digest,* or *Writer's Journal* at your local library. Or even pick up a subscription and comb through it in the comfort of your own home.

Don't feel as if articles and interviews on topics other than memoir writing are useless. Good writing is good writing, and any information on how to be a better writer can be beneficial. Sometimes just reading about how others succeeded in their own writing pursuits is just the inspiration you need to rev up your own creative engines.

Find an ideal reader

An *ideal reader* is a person who looks at your work, sees all of its weaknesses, but also recognizes its strengths. Most important, this person honestly tells you about both things. Ideal readers are rare and precious. They're sometimes not even writers themselves, but they all have this knack for offering the most useful advice a writer could ever want. That's priceless.

If you're lucky enough to find someone who is a careful, thoughtful reader and is willing to read what you write, thank your lucky stars. And thank your ideal reader too. (I recommend an occasional slice of strawberry cheesecake along with your latest draft of a chapter.) Even if you can only get your ideal reader to read a few chapters, that's better than nothing. Though if you can get him to read the entire manuscript, then do it!

If you can't find an ideal reader or you prefer to go with an expert — a book doctor or experienced freelance writer — that's fine. Just understand that these professionals won't work for a "Thank you!" and some strawberry cheesecake, no matter how the cheesecake is. It'll cost you money. For more on how to find these talented folks and work with them, visit Chapter 16.

Breaking Past Writer's Block

You've never heard of surgeon's block, or plumber's block, or teacher's block, right? So why do people insist there's such a thing as writer's block? Good question. Some people claim *writer's block* is a powerful, near-mystical force that quite literally keeps them in a state of being unable to write. Their hope is that it one day goes away on its own such that they can once again write with ease. But no one promised that writing is easy, so when you hit a little lull in your writing, resist the urge to say, "I have writer's block — time to go mow the yard."

Easier said than done, right? Well, read these sections for advice on how to make writer's block a thing of the past.

Checking your ego at the door

You're not William Shakespeare, Ernest Hemingway, or Kurt Vonnegut. Stop trying to be. Yes, being able to sit back, crack your knuckles, type as fast as you're able as if you're taking dictation from God and creating a masterpiece would be awesome. But that's not how writing works for most people. Leave your ego out of your writing room and eat some humble pie. Writing does take hard work, and you will make mistakes. Look at the good news: You will get better at writing the more you do.

Silencing your inner critic

Nearly every writer has a little voice in his or her head that pipes up every now and again and says, "Hey, you're not a writer! Who do you think you are?" Questions about grammar, your lack of the right college degrees, and a host of other concerns usually follow. Ignore this voice while you're finishing the first draft. Listening a bit to this voice when you're revising your manuscript, though, isn't the worst thing. At that point, the voice may be helpful in order to keep yourself from being blindly in love with your own work.

To silence the voice, try playing some loud music as you write. Try meditating before writing sessions. Try writing as the very first thing you do in the morning, perhaps before your little voice fully wakes up and gets going. There's no one surefire way to get that little voice to be quiet, so ask other writers for their own tips, too. They've had to deal with it as well.

You've lived your life well enough so far. That's all the qualifications you need to get started with writing your memoir and telling your story. You're good enough. You know what to say. Your little voice is just plain wrong.

Writing a zero draft

Writer's block often happens because you're worrying too much about your readers. What will my Aunt Martha think? She's a college professor and she can't stand grammar mistakes. One trick to get past this fear is to write as a *zero draft,* meaning a draft that isn't even good enough to be called a *first draft.* This draft is going to be so bad that carrion birds won't even bother with it.

A zero draft is *supposed* to be lousy. So with that low of expectations, how can you possibly go wrong? You're not going to even show it to Aunt Martha or anyone else until it's gone through as many revisions and edit sessions as the text requires. Then, and only then, will others get to see it.

So go write your own crappy draft. All professional writers do it. It's how they get past writer's block. The difference between professional writers and a beginning writer when it comes to crappy drafts is that the pros finish their crappy draft and then edit, edit, edit until it looks like a good draft. The beginners type "The End" and mail it to publishers.

Focus on writing, not on publication

Having a book on your shelf with your name on its spine is intoxicating for many would-be writers. So much so, in fact, that quite a few writers would rather skip the book writing part entirely and just be someone who already has written a book.

Stop worrying about publication. Don't think about literary agents or publishers or editors or readers or book reviewers. Don't hire someone to create cover art or take professional PR photos. Don't fret over who's going to play you in the movie version of your book (clearly Brad Pitt!). Don't even start making space on your bookshelf yet.

You can worry about all those concerns later, after the book is written and revised and then revised again. For now, focus on the writing. Enjoy it. It's your story, after all. Revel in making those moments come alive on the page.

Part II

Telling Your Story with Pizzazz

The 5th Wave   By Rich Tennant

"If you must know, the reason you're not in my memoir is because you're not a believable character."

In this part . . .

*J*ust like an engine has a slew of crucial moving parts that work together to power a car, so too does a story have a bunch of things all working together to power a memoir. In this part, I go a great deal further into narrative structure, looking at some nuts-and-bolts writing techniques — including tips and tricks novelists and Hollywood screenwriters use — to draw your readers in and keep them hooked.

I take a very detailed look at setting, scene, and character, because all three help create a vivid, believable world that readers will remember long after the book is closed. Next, I examine voice and dialogue, as well as point of view; together, these elements help make up your writing style and work to give each book its own characteristic voice. Finally, I explore some of the best ways to start and end your story, both practical and thematic.

Chapter 6

Giving Your Story Some Structure

· ·

· ·

Structure is the spine of the story. Without it, you have about as much chance of success as my Shih Tzu does of climbing on top of the fridge and opening a fresh bag of cookies without assistance.

Consider for a moment what happens to a human being with a spine problem — a slipped disc, cracked vertebrae, or other issue. Although 90 percent or more of the spine is in good shape, the 10 percent causes immense grief and suffering and makes the 90 percent ineffective in doing its intended job. The same is true with story structure. It needs to work top-to-bottom or readers will suffer.

This chapter breaks down the various organizing principles for your memoir, as well as presents the 4-1-1 on outlines, which can help you develop and concretize whichever organizing principle you choose. No single structure is better than another because no memoir is exactly like another — each case is vastly different, even if they both are, say, drug addiction and recovery memoirs. To that end, there is no magic bullet one-size-fits-all secret to handling story structure. You have to just understand what each structure option offers and weigh that against how your story suggests that it ought to be told.

Although other structure options exist beyond the ones I discuss in this chapter, the majority of memoirs being published today subscribe to one or more of the following. That's a pretty good recommendation for following one of these tried-and-true paths, though I'm not against you blazing your own trail. Just be sure to watch out for pitfalls, cliffs, and cookie-stealing dogs!

Going in Chronological Structure

People live their lives chronologically, so structuring the memoir that way makes a good deal of sense. With a *chronological structure,* you pick a point to start and proceed with what happens next, and then what happens after that. First this happened, that happened, and then this happened. A chronological structure is a clear, logical, linear method of following events. In fact, even a lot of art — music, dance, theater, and film — has this sense of chronological linearity to it. An element of time is built into the art form (as opposed to those forms that don't, such as painting, photography, or graffiti).

As you may imagine, the chronological option is a very popular choice for any type of storytelling, but especially for memoir. Because people's perception of their lives is a linear, straight trajectory, slicing out a part of it and then recounting it moment by moment on the page seems reasonable.

Just because you're choosing a chronological structure doesn't mean you need to include everything that happens after the first scene. For instance, if my memoir starts with me at age 8, I might then have chapters or sections with me at age 11, 18, 21, and then 23, which is still chronological. It isn't, though, if I squeeze age 45 in there somewhere. Skip the years/parts where nothing happens that relates to the overall story or theme. Readers won't be confused by those exclusions, just as they're okay with movies or books that skip showing people sleeping, eating dinner, or going to the bathroom.

To incorporate a chronological structure to your manuscript, start with the first relevant moment to your main story — your inciting incident (review this idea in Chapter 3). Then proceed with all the important scenes that happen after. Take as long as you need to fully develop each scene, using good time-related transition words to reinforce the chronological nature of the events. A few good options: "after," "as soon as," "before long," "finally," "meanwhile," "next," and "then."

Causality is something readers look for in stories. The chronological structure should play into that perhaps better than any other structural option. Because something happened in chapter 1, something else happened in chapter 2 as a direct result of what happened in chapter 1. Because this happened in chapter 2, something else happened as a result in chapter 3. And so on.

Let me give a clear albeit hypothetical example. In chapter 1, I got angry at work and quit my job. In chapter 2, my wife — who's been fed up with me and my temper and our lousy financial situation — walks out on me. In chapter 3, because my wife left me, I agreed to meet up with my sketchy high school pal, Bill, who has a "great opportunity" for me to make a lot of cash quick. Readers can easily see how trouble is likely forthcoming for this character. This chapter-by-chapter structure is a long yet linked chain of events that all starts with chapter 1; it makes a tight, believable, effective story.

The downside is that the effect of this relentlessly forward-moving motion can get a bit monotonous. Readers may long for a change of pace. The clarity and simplicity of this format, however, is hard to knock.

A few memoirs that powerfully use a chronological structure include

- *My Detachment: A Memoir* by Tracy Kidder (Random House)
- *Fat Girl: A True Story* by Judith Moore (Plume)
- *The Coldest Winter: A Stringer in Liberated Europe* by Paula Fox (Picador)
- *My Best Friend Is a Wookie: One Boy's Journey to Find His Place in the Galaxy* by Tony Pacitti (Adams Media)

Taking a Semi- (or Anti-) Chronological Structure

You may want to take a few liberties and fall into a semi-chronological structure. A *semi-chronological,* also called an *anti-chronological* or *nonlinear* structure, tells stories in a fragmented manner. This structure acknowledges that a perfectly chronological structure doesn't allow enough options to fully develop your story. With this type of memoir, your story will, at times, go as the clock and calendar do, but you can make some significant tweaks to the chronology of the story to make it more meaningful, interesting, or fun.

For instance, you can stop the narrative to talk directly at your reader or meditate for a whole chapter or two. Perhaps you do other things that make rule-following memoirists and novelists cringe. But you have a plan, so it's okay. A semi-chronological narrative often makes use of flashbacks or flash-forwards to quickly move to other points in the story.

With this structure, you do a lot more modifying of your story, which may also reflect the way your brain makes sense of the past. Memories come in chunks, in fragments. This structure mimics that better than straightforward chronological ones do. In short, this structure very consciously works against your typical idea of time.

You can stop moving chronologically forward and jump to another spot in these instances:

- When the drama or tension starts to ebb, you can jump to a moment where it's high stakes again.
- To make your story purposefully nonlinear, you can change the scene and setting with each chapter. Doing so is less potentially confusing to a reader because section breaks and chapter breaks give readers a chance

to reset, to get caught up. If you're concerned you may lose them when chapter 1 is in 1975, chapter 2 is in 1990, and chapter 3 is 1987, and then use a time/date header at the start of each.

Don't go the semi-chronological route just to be different. Some of these types of stories stay relatively true to the chronology of a life, though a few move around in place and time fairly quickly. Only be as nonlinear as you need to be to create tension, generate drama, or expand and develop themes.

The semi-chronological structure has a lot of advantages. It's close enough to how most TV shows, movies, and books work, so readers won't have to struggle to figure out how the story is being delivered, which is a plus. Simplicity and straightforwardness are assets to any story. It also can generate reader interest in that readers may know something is going to happen later, but they don't know how or why. TV shows like *Lost*, *The Firm*, and *Damages* have worked in a semi-chronological format for exactly this reason.

A few examples of memoirs that use a semi-chronological order include the following:

✔ *Stop-Time: A Memoir* by Frank Conroy (Penguin)

✔ *Paula: A Memoir (P.S.)* by Paula Allende (Harper Perennial)

✔ *Jeneration X: One Reluctant Adult's Attempt to Unarrest Her Arrested Development, or Why It's Never Too Late for Her Dumb Ass to Learn Why Froot Loops Are Not for Dinner* by Jen Lancaster (NAL)

Going with an Episodic Structure

Episodes are smaller incidents or events that, when taken together, form a larger work. So if you choose to use an *episodic* structure for your memoir, you probably have each episode make up a single chapter. An episode has its own beginning, middle, and end. It even has its own narrative arc, including a climax of some sort, though it's nowhere as meaningful or strong as the main story's climax. (See Chapter 3 for more on story climaxes and narrative arcs.)

For example, perhaps the easiest way to think about this structure is in terms of TV episodes. Each hour-episode of *Matlock* or *Castle* has a self-contained narrative. It links up to a larger, ongoing narrative, but you would still be satisfied (at least in terms of structure and story) if you only watched the one episode. The better TV shows offer a much richer experience if you watch them season by season, in the correct order.

Even a single TV episode has scenes within the larger story. What helps give closure to scenes are the commercials. As a memoir writer, you instead use section breaks and chapters purposefully as your section breaks.

These sections provide more insight into the episodic structure. Here I explain how you can utilize this structure and what benefit using it can give your memoir.

Grasping the power of bite-sized scenes

An episodic structure keeps readers wanting to know what happened to characters (real or imagined) that they've come to care about. Certainly, chapters can do this, too, but many stories — many episodes — run several chapters in length to properly develop.

The episodic structure adds power to a memoir by keeping scenes short and self-contained, but it links multiple ones together by theme or repeated imagery. To put it another way, an episodic structure is a lot more like a slide show than a movie. It asks the reader to do more of the work of putting the episodes together and making sense of it all — making readers active versus passive — by the very way it's delivered.

Ending an episode in the middle of an intense, climactic moment is called a *cliffhanger*. TV shows do this a lot at the end of a season, believing that viewers will be more likely to tune in for the following season if characters they care about are left in peril for months. Memoirs that utilize this form also feel structurally right, even if they play around some with the concept of time.

Using an episodic structure also makes figuring out how to handle the chapters terribly easy. You just start a chapter at the beginning of an episode, and end when that episode is done.

If the episodes are compelling, you may even be able to order them any way you choose, like magnetic poetry. Although you may easily be able to defend a random order of an episodic memoir, I do recommend thinking about how each episode interacts with the one immediately before and after it. When you write your memoir, think about how each episode speaks to the episode directly before and after it. Some memoirists choose to forego the cause-and-effect obligation most writers feel, in which case you don't have to worry as much about the order of your episodes. For those who do want that linkage, think of each episode as part of a much longer conversation. Make sure there's enough similarities in each for the conversation not to falter.

A few examples of memoirs that use some type of episodic structure include the following:

- ✔ *Eat, Pray, Love: One Woman's Search for Everything Across Italy, India and Indonesia* by Elizabeth Gilbert (Penguin)

- ✔ *The Goldfish Went on Vacation: A Memoir of Loss (and Learning to Tell the Truth About It)* by Patty Dann (Trumpeter)

> ✔ *Trespasses: A Memoir* by Lacy Johnson (University of Iowa Press)
>
> ✔ *Over Time: My Life as a Sportswriter* by Frank Deford (Atlantic Monthly Press)
>
> ✔ *Girl, Interrupted* by Susanna Kaysen (Vintage)

Considering the unexpected publishing benefit of an episodic structure

If the individual scenes or chapters (the episodes) you write are self-contained — meaning they have a beginning, middle, and a strong sense of a conclusion — then you have the option of publishing them before trying to publish your entire book. In fact, in Chapters 19 and 20 I discuss that having part (or parts) of your book published is a great way to generate interest and perceived value in your manuscript from a publisher or literary agent. In other words, having some of your memoir already published in print form may help you publish the entire thing as a book.

 You can use asterisks (the *) between sections as a useful tool to show a bigger break or pause than you'd have between paragraphs. The asterisks aren't quite as drastic as a chapter break, though.

Certain book structures don't lend themselves as well to this kind of excerpting — episodic (and thematic, which I discuss in the next section) structures do. (Chronological structures can work, but they often build off the context of so many other chapters that making any of the pieces self-contained is a lot more work than most writers choose to do.)

Sticking with a Thematic Structure: Focus on Connective Threads

Theme (your memoir's main point) obviously is an important thing in a memoir. Although a novel or movie may touch on a handful of themes, most memoirs zero in on one or two key things that resonate throughout the book. A *thematic structure* works only if the theme is well-developed, deeply considered, and worthy of book-length exploration.

Using this structure is a tricky way to write a memoir because you have to know clearly your theme before you start to order things. As Chapter 14 points out, theme sometimes doesn't fully emerge until you've written dozens or hundreds of pages. However, if you can pull off this structure, your memoir will stand out as an impressive feat of writing, thinking, and organization.

A thematic master: Joan Didion

See how Joan Didion focuses on one or two themes to great effect in her book, *A Year of Magical Thinking,* which revolves around the period after her husband suddenly died. It jumps around a ton, but the guiding principle is the main theme. The memoir is so different that you'll probably want to reread the book to better see how it works.

Didion is a master of understatement. Watch how she is Hemingway-like with her avoidance of adjectives. And her deadpan funny delivery and repetition is powerful, lasting stuff. She's a master whose keen sense of observation is poetic.

If you want to use thematic structure, you need to stop thinking about plot and instead focus on how you wrote argument papers in high school or college composition classes. In the beginning of both your paper and your memoir, you need to introduce your theme. The middle of each requires you to develop the theme and showcase new spins on it than what's been said before. The end needs for you to do far more than just provide a summary — you should push to explore further, plumbing deeper to find the most elusive (and rewarding) of meanings. And then, as with a good argument paper, a sense of conclusion or a nod back to the beginning is appropriate. Thematic structures focus more on theme development versus character development as happens in a chronological story. In a very real sense, theme is your character, and your role as author is to follow and explore that.

A thematic memoir wouldn't likely be as successful for topics like getting on the honor roll at Harvard or finding your soul mate via eHarmony. (Of course, as I write this, I'm thinking that each of those might work thematically if you got beyond the personal and involved social commentary and critique.)

You can compare a work of music to this type of structure. Although some composers range fairly far afield with the many sections of this type of piece, they always bury hints and nuances and echoes of that original melody. By the end, the original melody returns as promised. They include the middle sections to create interest and variety. And those are two great reasons for memoir writers to do it, too.

A few examples of memoirs that use a thematic structure are

- *A Year of Magical Thinking* by Joan Didion (Vintage) (see the nearby sidebar)

- *No Right to Remain Silent: The Tragedy at Virginia Tech* by Lucinda Roy (Harmony)

- *Frankie's Place: A Love Story* by Jim Sterba (Grove Press)
- *On Writing: A Memoir of the Craft* by Stephen King (Scribner) (This book is so easy to read and useful for student writers that I often make it the only required book in my freshman composition classes.)

Recognizing Unconventional Structures

If you think the tried-and-true methods that I discuss previously in this chapter don't satisfy you, or you're simply game to try something unorthodox, here are a few ideas on different story structures that may get you excited:

- Cookbook/recipes (*Julie and Julia: My Year of Cooking Dangerously* by Julie Powell [Back Bay Books] is a great example)
- To-do lists
- Scientific/psychological structures (*The Rules of Inheritance: A Memoir* by Claudia Bidwell Smith [Hudson Street Press] shapes her experiences around the five stages of grief)
- Catalogues
- Postcards
- Series of e-mails, text messages, blog posts, or social networking communiqués
- Photos
- Astrological signs, charts, or patterns
- Songs
- Top 10 lists
- Diary entries (Okay, this one isn't all that unconventional, but it's worth mentioning somewhere!)

The real beauty of using an unconventional structure is that it frees you of preconceptions of how the book has to be. This option is fine to try when you're just starting out. See how it goes. What type of energy are you generating? You may end up going back to something more typical, but the insight you get from trying any of these options may be worthwhile.

Some memoirs and most biographies include documentary evidence, such as photos or legal documents. No rule says you can't run with that idea. Consider including parts of the preceding list as needed, such as the recipe for your grandma's famous spiced rum cake, photos (only if they're great quality) of relevant settings, people, or places, or the postcard that says, "I hate you. We're getting divorced."

In my own memoir, I included a scan of a crayon drawing my three-year-old did of me. Including it may sound self-indulgent, but in a story about video game addiction, seeing my daughter draw me as she knows me — in front of a computer — was revelatory. And it helped change the course of my life. Of course it needed to be in the book.

Developing an Outline that Works for You

Writers fall into two categories: those who outline before embarking on a writing project and those who run screaming from the room like their hair is on fire when the idea of an outline is even mentioned. No matter which camp you belong to, here I discuss how writing an outline for your memoir may make sense.

An *outline* is a general plan of how you're going to go about writing something. An outline is also how to draw or trace the outer edge of something. That's a good way of thinking about an outline — your general plan simply describes or guesses at the rough shape of your entire piece. It's a draft, a sketch, a guess. It's open to change, but it at least gives you some perspective on the project as a whole, and best of all, it gives you a clear place to start.

Writers assure me that outlines are too difficult or too stymieing to use. They're wrong. For a memoir writer, outlines are a must-have for the simple reason that unlike with fiction, you can't just follow your main character wherever your imagination takes him. You're grounded by facts and historical truths. To manage all the things that your memoir needs in order to tell your story, you have to do some planning. You wouldn't start building a house after the lumber and steel girders arrive, would you? You would create— or pay an architect to create — a blueprint that gives you the best shot at a quality outcome.

That's what every writer wants: a quality outcome.

To help you reach your quality outcome and get more comfortable using an outline, I explain how you can create one, use one, distinguish between different types of outlines, and throw away your outline when you don't need it any longer.

Creating a basic outline: No painkillers required

Outlines aren't scary. In fact, they can be both easy and useful (two of my favorite things!). You can easily create an outline that you can use to write your book in the following way:

1. **Start with a title.**

   If you don't have one, at the top of your page just write something like "My Memoir." You can update it later in the writing process.

2. **Decide what the best, most dramatic moment of your story is.**

   That's chapter 1. If you don't fully involve a reader in chapter 1 (on page 1, really), the rest doesn't matter. To remember what chapter 1 is, write a sentence or two that describes what's going to happen there.

3. **Decide what the second most dramatic moment of your story is.**

   Make that your final chapter — for this purpose, call it chapter 10. Write down a sentence or two for that, too.

4. **Lay the trail to get from chapter 1 to chapter 10 in any way that makes sense to you now.**

   Select one key moment, scene, or idea to cover for each chapter, write down your note for that chapter, and then move on to the next chapter. When you're done, you'll have a twelve chapter outline all laid out, ready to go.

You don't have to stick with your initial outline. In fact, you probably don't want to go with this one because first thoughts aren't always the best ones. After you have something on the page, though, you can start to see the connections and the disconnections. You can also more concretely see what's missing from your story. You can then adjust as needed. When you're satisfied that you have a workable outline, follow the path you've laid out.

For example, here's a hypothetical story of the type you may read in someone's memoir and how you can turn it into an outline.

- ✔ I met Lindsey.
- ✔ We married.
- ✔ She developed a serious illness.
- ✔ We realized she was pregnant.
- ✔ We had to decide — the baby or her.
- ✔ She chose the baby.
- ✔ I'm a single father now, coping with loss, guilt, and new obligations.

Even bestsellers use outlines

Bestselling author Scott Ciencin didn't outline his books at the beginning of his writing career. He approached storytelling "organically" (freefalling through the story page by page, letting one scene lead to another, one character action spawn another) rather than "mechanically" (planning it all out in advance). It wasn't an issue until he was writing book two of his *Vampire Odyssey* books, a part of a trilogy. Halfway through writing that book, he realized the error — at the start of book two, the main character did one thing when she should have done another.

"That one character action would've led to the trilogy concluding at the end of book two," Ciencin says. "With a three book contract, that's a no-go! From then on, I studied and mastered three-act structure and outlined every time out." Since then he has written and published more than 100 books in a 20-year period and has never had to toss out even a partial manuscript and start over. "Whether I'm working on a novel or a nonfiction book, an outline keeps me on track. I also have the confidence to know in advance what the potential problems are in a book before I even write it. In fact, I once sold a seven-book series to Random House based on a 100-word pitch because the entire series was outlined in my mind and I was able to compactly convey all the key plot and marketing points." Talk about an endorsement for using an outline.

These seven sentences can show you the entire arc of the story. Give each bullet point a chapter, with perhaps two chapters on the illness and the decision, and you have something close to a full chapter-by-chapter outline. I know it's rudimentary, but it's enough to know which chapter your incident about baby food on the ceiling goes.

Using an outline: Take advantage of the benefits

An outline isn't a legal contract. In no way is it binding, so if you have a hot mess of an outline and it's too confusing to keep working with, then no big deal! The benefits of using an outline, though, are hard to ignore.

The main advantages to using an outline are as follows:

- ✔ **You don't get lost.** With an outline, you always know what's coming next. No guesswork or second-guessing yourself.

- ✔ **You see whether your story will work before you write.** Nothing stinks more than writing 40,000 words only to realize you focused on the wrong subjects, or the book you hoped to write isn't working. An outline can identify those problems without the months of wasted writing. Best yet, it can help you correct the flaws before you even start.

✔ **An outline creates a sense of unity.** Outlines help you see the big picture all in one glance. An outline allows you to focus on individual elements, but you always have the entirety. You can take it all in with a single glance. That large/small combination gives you much-needed perspective that gives you flow. You're also less likely to write unneeded scenes or chapters.

You can actually have multiple outlines, depending on the complexity of your story. For a Young Adult novel series I'm working on, I needed three different outlines. One focused entirely on the coming-of-age arc of the young main character. The second detailed the book-by-book development of Joseph Campbell's hero's journey. The last was the chapter-by-chapter happenings that most people think of when they hear "outline." Although you don't need to have more than one outline, I did, and it helped immensely.

Identifying the different types of outlines

These sections outline some different ways to do outlines. See if one of these ways works for you. Odds are that you'll find a method that you never considered. If none of them work for you, invent one that does. Each outline method here has a fine literary pedigree, having been used by many writers to produce lots of published books.

Even if you think you have a strong outline already, you may want to try a second or third type. Sometimes the structure of a different style of outline offers you insight into new story possibilities. Spending an extra hour or two on it is worth your time if the end result means your book will be better. I'd never recommend that someone write entirely different versions of an entire book, but to write two or three different outlines may indeed pay off.

In addition to the following methods, you also can check out *Writing Fiction For Dummies* by Randy Ingermanson and Peter Economy (John Wiley & Sons). Ingermanson uses an outlining system he calls the Snowflake Method. Although this method is designed to help you write a successful novel, you can easily shape and develop a memoir, too. You can also check out www. advancedwriting.com for more information.

Flowchart outline

The *flowchart outline* is great for visual people or people who like logic problems or want to see the clear relationship between story scenes, themes, or elements. A flowchart outline (see www.ryangvancleave.com/outline example1.pdf for an example) shows the order in which things move, the function of each part, and the ultimate outcome, which is useful stuff for a memoir outline.

Scientists used to design super-easy computer problems with flowchart outlines. Today, IT people and tech designers still use them to visually illustrate the flow of data through a processing system.

Note card outline

This outline sounds self-explanatory. With a *note card outline,* you get yourself a package of 100 note cards and start thinking about all the scenes your book needs to include. For each scene, jot down the main idea of that scene, which can be as simple as writing "Mom and I run out of gas on the way to Florida." Don't worry how big or small each scene is; just keep filling the note cards. If you need another package of note cards, no problem. Fill 300 if you have to recall that much.

If you've been traumatized by a high school teacher who made you work through mountains of note cards on research paper projects, skip the note cards. Use sticky notes. Use digital notes. Use scraps of paper. Use full sheets of paper. Use envelopes. Use the back of receipts. All that matters is that you have each individual element on a separate, movable thing. This allows you to easily reorder everything and anything as you see fit.

After you've exhausted your mind of every moment you think you want to write about, lay all the cards out on the floor. You then start grouping similar cards. Keep moving the cards around, and eventually, you'll have a line of a bunch of note cards in a specific order that you chose, and that order likely was suggested by narrative or thematic connections. Go with it!

Montage outline

The word "montage" literally means "putting together." The *montage outline* appeals to writers who like scrapbooking or consider themselves an arts-and-crafts person. With this type, you keep putting things together using whatever connective logic you choose. Eventually, you'll have nodes of connection that may start forming chapters for your memoir.

In film, *montage* means a very specific thing — a series of shots that fade from one to the next. For your purposes, a *photomontage* makes sense, where you create a composite photo by joining a number of other photographs together. (Refer to `www.ryangvancleave.com/outlineexample2.pdf` for an example.)

In a practical sense, you can create a photomontage outline by following these steps:

1. **Get a couple of poster boards.**

2. **Fill the boards.**

To fill them, you can

Cut pictures from magazines that remind you of things you want to include in your book.

Use copies of your own real photos.

3. **Jot down a few words with a marker, if you want.**

This type is rather free-wheeling and abstract. For some people, it's a Godsend. For others, the best course is to try a different outline option.

Wagon wheel outline

The *wagon wheel outline* (check out www.ryangvancleave.com/outline example3.pdf for an example) works a lot like a mind map, which is a graphical way to represent ideas or concepts. For a memoirist, a mind map can reveal all the associated ideas, scenes, and people associated with the story's main theme. You can also make a mind map for subthemes, individual chapters, or even characters from your memoir. If you can't get enough spokes to fill your page, either think harder or consider that what's in the center of that wagon wheel doesn't justify a lot of coverage in your book.

To create a wagon wheel outline, stick to these steps:

1. **Put a main idea (of the entire book or perhaps limit it to a single chapter) in the center of a piece of paper.**

2. **For each idea that your main idea brings to mind, put a spoke off the middle circle and add that idea.**

3. **Keep adding ideas and more spokes.**

   If you feel so inclined, add spokes to your other circles. Let the connections keep branching out.

You can access free software to help you digitally create a wagon wheel outline, if you prefer that over pencil and paper. Try FreeMind.sourceforge. net or TheBrain.com. If you choose to invest a little money to get a program with more bells and whistles, try www.smartdraw.com or www.xmind.net.

Knowing when to throw out your outline

A time will come during the actual writing of your manuscript that you'll realize you're not looking back at your outline any longer. Furthermore, if an outline ever gets in the way of you telling your story the way you want to — or need to — dump it. If you hit a wall or get confused about what should come next, revisit the outline. You can always create a new outline later, if needed.

Writing Exercises on Story Structure

Story structure provides the framework, the habitable environment for a story to live and thrive. To help you get better control over your own story's structure, here are student-approved writing exercises:

❑ **Write down the six most important things that ever happened in your life.** Be as specific and as detailed as you choose. Next, look over your list. If you see clear connections between those things, a thematic structure may work best. If you see a lot of self-contained events, perhaps an episodic approach makes the most sense. And if the idea of time is a big factor, then a chronological structure may be the way to go.

❑ **Make a list of all the topics and events that you may want to write about.** They can include people, places, ideas, whatever. Shoot for at least two dozen items. Your list may soon look something like this (or perhaps completely not!):

   ❑ Crush on my first square-dancing partner in P.E. class

   ❑ Asthma attack in high school

   ❑ Playing hockey with flaming tennis balls

   ❑ The girl with dental headgear who lived with her grandma

❑ **Make columns for each decade you've lived.** If you don't have enough decades to make lots of columns, go with five- or even one-year increments. Fill in the major events for each column. Whichever column has the most entries — or the most interesting ones — is probably where the heart of your memoir lies.

❑ **Start a timer at eight minutes and write "I remember . . ." as fast as you can, filling in the blank with what comes to mind.** Let the words just flow. Don't get bothered by grammar or spelling. The key here is volume. If you get stuck, write "I remember . . ." again and again until you can finish the sentence with a memory or thought. You'll think of something. When the time is up, odds are that some of what you wrote will feel honest or stand out as meaningful. Hold onto those for what they likely are — key moments in your memoir.

❑ **Write your obituary.** An obituary is an official notification that someone has died. In obligations, it's common to include the significant events and accomplishments of the deceased. Writing your own obituary may sound uncomfortable, but give it a shot: though keep it no longer than 300 words. Feel free to examine real-world obituaries for models. Also feel free to skip the parts about the actual funeral arrangements, unless you want to include that too for kicks.

Chapter 7

Establishing the Setting and Scene

. . . .

In This Chapter

▶ Understanding how a scene can be powerful

▶ Seeing the possibilities of setting

▶ Creating atmosphere

▶ Handling exposition

▶ Utilizing narrative summary

. . . .

*H*ave you ever read a book and felt like the author somehow, almost magically, created a blockbuster movie in your mind? It's because that author spent a lot of effort on making the setting look, feel, smell, and taste real. The setting probably played a huge part of what made the book enjoyable.

If your setting feels too small of a word for such a big idea, you can try *milieu* or *world of the story*. *Milieu* means "sphere, setting, background, and/or sur-roundings." (*World of the story* is essentially synonymous, but far less preten-tious.) Beyond the physical area, it also includes social and cultural forces. It's a pretty comprehensive thing when you really consider that setting is the entire environment your story takes place in!

In one sense, you're always working on setting because how characters speak, how people act, and what the cultural attitudes are all become part of setting. This chapter, though, spends a good deal of time making clear how you can manage those things versus hope they work out, which is sadly what many writers do.

As for scenes, they're the basic building blocks of stories. Consider how you'd build a stone fireplace. You have a stack of big stones beside you ready to go, but you don't just grab them willynilly. You examine each for its own shape and let its nuances suggest which would be the best fit next to those you've already mortared into place. The same is true for scenes.

In this chapter, I suggest ways to get the most out of both setting and scenes. Spend some time here thinking about ways to utilize these two story elements to make *your* story vivid, powerful, and memorable.

Maximizing the Power of a Scene

Scenes are the delivery system for your story. Scenes are action *in action,* not just stuff that has happened that you summarize for the readers. The emphasis is on what's happening in a single place at a single time. If you have a new place and new time, then you have a new scene.

Scenes have the goal of moving a story forward. They do so by presenting some type of goal that the main character wants to achieve. As long as this goal is important to the character, it matters to the story, even if it's a seemingly small goal. In essence, each scene is a smaller story within the framework of a larger story, or one stone in a big fireplace.

These sections show you how to manage the elements within a scene to ensure each scene contributes as powerfully as possible to the overall narrative. These following ideas and techniques also have the benefit of providing strong connections from scene to scene and ultimately upping the interest level of readers.

Facing resistance to reach a goal

Every scene in your memoir has to demonstrate how a character reaches for a goal. Most of these goals will be smaller goals, things that incrementally help the character toward the larger story problem.

Every goal has to have some resistance. If the character can just achieve the goal with no resistance, it's boring. It's not a challenge. It's uninteresting. Real goals come from effort and focus. Take the time to reflect deeply on the scenes of your story to figure out what each goal was. Then identify what conflict, resistance, or tension was there. After you have those things identified, you have all you really need to make those scenes work in terms of the larger narrative puzzle that is your entire memoir.

For example, a scene goal may be to extricate a character from a dinner with a boring couple. It's clearly a small-time goal, but it speaks to a larger truth about the character. In your hypothetical story, the main character has no patience for others, which starts to explain why his marriage is going to fall apart later. In light of that future disaster, doesn't the inclusion of that awkward dinner make more sense? The resistance may be when the host says, "If you don't stay for dessert, I'll drop you from the Smithers account!" And the solution — or at least one solution — to the character's dinner dilemma?

"Ooof . . . the fish . . ." he says, then runs out the front door, hand over mouth, faking the loudest retching noises he can.

Thinking about sequels

By bringing up sequels, I don't mean *Saw IX* or the last book of the *Eragon* series, but rather the sequels to each individual scene. By this, I mean to say that you don't want to put a goal-oriented scene back-to-back with another goal-oriented scene. Although this may sound contradictory to what I previously said, you need to do what you need to make your point and deliver the goods to your readers, even if it means breaking the rules you've come to know and trust.

Some writers will call a sequel scene a *transition*. That's a fine way of thinking about it — you help your readers transition to another goal scene. To tease out the meaning and tension of a goal-oriented scene, you need a *scene sequel* that is the outcome, the (physical, spiritual, emotional, or cultural/social) fallout, the aftermath of the goal-oriented scene. Remember that the goal-oriented scene likely ended poorly (novelists may call it a *disaster*). Up until the final scenes of a book — where the story resolution takes place — the main character typically meets a series of setbacks, disasters, or problems, despite having goals driving them. You need sequels where there's reactions to those bad scene outcomes.

Here is what happens in a sequel (call it a *sequel scene* compared to a *goal scene*, if that helps clarify things):

1. **Your characters react.**

   Imagine that after a heated argument over whether you're going to watch your action-packed TV show or her slow-moving drama program, she says the marriage is over. *Pow!* That's your goal scene for you. Your sequel scene comes next where you weep or feel pain. If goal scenes are about action, sequel scenes are reactions.

2. **Your characters make a choice.**

   From that choice comes a new goal, and with that new goal comes a new goal scene. Say you decide to make her fall in love with you again, so you rush to the grocery store and bring back her favorite flowers and a somewhat expensive bottle of merlot. Your goal is to woo her with your charm (and your bribes).

   What's the tension? She's ticked at you. She's angry over a million arguments in the past, much more so than the recent TV argument, which was simply the straw that broke the camel's proverbial back. The outcome is the same type of outcome — that 90 percent of the goal scenes in your memoir probably generate more problems, which will lead to another sequel scene.

Call me a pessimist if you want, but writers tend not to write about the periods in their lives where everything went right. Why? Take a psychology class or three to find out. Or have a frank talk with a dear friend who knows you well but will tell you the truth if asked to do so. Just know that using goal scenes followed by sequel scenes followed by goal scenes is a time-tested pattern that has made gazillions for novelists and screenwriters. Go ahead and use it too. I give you permission.

Using story beats

You can also toss this gem that novelists and Hollywood screenwriters use into your bag of literary loot: story beats. *Story beats* are an even smaller unit of story than a scene. They're important because how many you include in a goal or sequel scene — and what order you deliver them — is often the difference between a great dramatic moment and a blah interaction between characters that may potentially lull readers to sleep. Beats can help you organize your thoughts and make your memoir more coherent without needing as many exploratory drafts along the way.

You can think of a story beat as a heartbeat, because in that constant lub-dub that keeps you moving forward on this planet, it's your story's heartbeat.

The idea of story beats is a pretty in-depth, complicated one. If you want a more thorough explanation of it with plenty of examples, check out Todd Klick's *Something Startling Happens: The 120 Story Beats Every Writer Needs to Know* (Michael Wiese Productions).

The following sections dig more deeply into what a beat really is, because you're not going to find a boatload of discussion about them in writing classes or writing how-to books. Why? Good question. It's probably because they're pretty elusive little things worth discussing.

Beating in action or dialogue

A beat is either action or dialogue. The best scenes (either goal or sequel scenes, it doesn't matter) strike a nice balance between them, whether the beats are small or big.

Here's an example of a short scene that uses three beats (note that in your memoir manuscript, you wouldn't identify beats like I've done here for illustrative purposes — you'd just have the text on the page as seven very short paragraphs):

Beat 1

"What's happening, Jane?"

"About as much as your love life."

George said, "Very funny. Painfully clever, sis."

Beat 2

He went to the kitchen and returned with a tray of cookies and two beers. He flipped one of the beers to her. She ducked. The picture window of their parents' Tucson vacation home exploded. They both cringed.

Beat 3

"Jeez, didn't you play varsity softball?"

She shrugged. "People threw 12-inch yellow balls back then. Not beers."

"A beer's bigger. Harder to miss."

Why are these three story beats versus, say, one or two? Because each is a separate, distinctive element that together make up this short scene.

TV and film writers create *beat sheets,* which are documents that detail all the major happenings of a single episode. Think of a beat sheet as an outline for a scene or chapter. You can create beat sheets for your memoir to see if it helps you move from idea to writing execution.

If I were to create a beat sheet for the preceding scene (or part of a scene — I might choose to draw it out longer in a memoir), it may look something like this:

✔ George's deficient love life is revealed.

✔ Window breaks.

✔ Neither takes blame.

Now this beat sheet doesn't include everything that this little exchange does. You know their relationship (sis). You know a bit about her history (she played high school softball). You know some about their parents' economic status (vacation home in Tucson). You may also assume that they hang out together (they're in the vacation home, seemingly with no one else), but they don't really know each other all that well (the missed toss and catch).

That's a lot of stuff in a few lines. Don't forget the scene has to have action — exploding windows are always fun!

Creating your own beats: The how-to

You can create your own beat sheet to serve as a kind of outline for your primary story. At its biggest level, it showcases the main events of your story. The confusion about story beats exists because beats can be big, medium, or small. A big beat is made up of smaller beats, and many of those smaller beats are made up of yet smaller ones.

To get your head around the idea of beats and a beat sheet, think of those old high school composition paper outlines that use Roman numerals like this

> I. First Main Topic
>
>   A. First subtopic of I
>
>   1. First detail of subtopic A
>
>   2. Second detail of subtopic A
>
>   3. Third detail of subtopic A
>
>   B. Second subtopic of I
>
>   1. First detail of subtopic B
>
>   And so on.

A major story beat is equivalent to the I, II, and III parts. A medium story beat is equivalent to the A, B, and C parts. A small story beat is equivalent to the 1, 2, and 3 parts. Thinking of it this way, you can easily see that a major story beat (I) is made up of A, B, and C, but also the 1s, 2s, and 3s that make up each of those parts. You can follow story beats down to almost a paragraph level if you want, but typically three levels is enough to provide writers with a good enough handle to write a great, coherent, connected story.

If you're a writer who needs rules, go with this: A memoir should have between six and ten major story beats. A scene should have between three and six story beats. Each of those scene-level story beats should have three small story beats within them. There will be exceptions, but in general, these rules hold true far more often than not.

For instance, a beat sheet for the first part of your memoir may easily look like this:

✔ Introduce the setting

✔ Introduce the main character

✔ Reveal the main character's profession

✔ Show tension

You have conflict (tension) that the character strives to overcome. Your readers have learned something about the character (profession). Your readers have met the main character — always a good thing at the start of any book! And you have the setting, which is enough to get our story rolling. You did it in four story beats that equaled one initial scene in your book. Now just add another 30 or 40 scenes and you have what you need to make a book-length memoir.

Defining Setting: Where It's All At

Setting doesn't just happen on its own on the page. *Setting* is a mood-setter, it's props, it's context, it's evocative, and it's alive. Properly done, setting becomes another character who plays an important part of the story. If you don't take the time to carefully craft setting, you're essentially asking all the characters to stand on a blank stage.

Let me clarify a bit more. Setting has a number of crucial functions, such as the following:

- ✔ Adding vividness, beauty, and memorable sensory moments — Alexander Frater's travel memoir *Chasing the Monsoon* (Picador)

- ✔ Influencing and affecting character — Augusten Burrough's *Running with Scissors: A Memoir* (Picador)

- ✔ Developing plot — Sebastian Junger's nonfiction book and film *The Perfect Storm: A True Story of Men against the Sea* (W. W. Norton & Company)

Tall order, huh? That's okay. These sections detail some of the best ways to make setting work for you. It provides the right frame of reference for readers to smoothly enter the story.

Including the natural world

Setting is more than just the props you fill the "room" of your story with. It's also everything else in the background or natural world. Think about flora, fauna, and the sky above. Consider the chilly October wind, the sound of cricket song, and the funnel spiders nesting way up in the attic rafters. Include these details and your readers are going to appreciate how much more spirited the setting becomes in their minds.

Look at this example of how the natural world can help create setting:

> Starlight leaked through the canopy of leaves and fell across the face of the pond. An El Niño breeze kept the bougainvillea moving. In the distance to the east, a single cicada thrummed against the overpowering quiet that filled the empty park.

Just add a boy and a girl, and you have a powerful love scene ready to go.

Consider matching weather to a character's mood. I don't mean make it storm when it was a bright, sunny day, but rather don't focus overmuch on weather when it doesn't add much more than scenery. But if you have a huge argument while the thunder is banging away outside, then by all means, don't forget to keep the weather part of that scene.

Dialogue your way into setting

Another way you can clarify a scene's setting is through the use of dialogue. You want to include dialogue that real people use — it's often in front of people. For example, see how smoothly this exchange gives you numerous setting details:

> "I hate crab puffs," Carinda said. "Any party with crab puffs should be outlawed."
>
> Nathan whispered, "Then eat the mushroom eggrolls. Seriously. If your whining gets us kicked out of here, I'm never going to forgive you."
>
> "As if you've never been to a fancy-pants, look-how-big-my-bankroll-is soirée before."
>
> "Not at the Rutherland Club, I haven't."

Try a little culture

You can also add some culture in your memoir. *Culture* encompasses all human phenomena, including language, customs, and human capacity to interact.

Culture has become an umbrella that covers areas such as etiquette, gender issues, literature, politics, racial issues, and social class. If you can cover one or more of these topics in some depth, your book will be richer, more complex, and more lasting. On a selfish level, a book that includes a healthy amount of culture is more likely to be taught in classrooms and appear on approved lists for book clubs, which means more sales. But it also means that your book may have a longer life because classrooms and book clubs are always looking for new books to cover important issues and ideas throughout history.

In other words, if you don't allow your characters to live and breathe in a world that acknowledges the power and influence these forces have on their lives, then they're operating in a clearly fictional world. For a memoir, the moment a reader stops believing in the authenticity of a work is the moment the whole thing is over. Good writers react to and include the context of cultural/societal forces in their books.

Pop culture and brand names are two options on creating authenticity. Mentioning a few brands here and there works just fine. Just be careful. Too much and it can get gimmicky if all your characters drink Diet Coke, wear Jordache jeans, and sport Ray-Bans. (It can also feel like a bad '80s TV show!)

Don't forget music. More than a few people mark the important periods in their lives by the songs that were popular then. Give your readers a nostalgia ride and include them in the soundtrack of your life, which is likely similar to the soundtrack of their lives.

If you don't remember what it was like during a certain time frame, go ahead and do some research. For instance, a book written about the 1950s that completely ignores race relations in the United States is missing a key component to the setting. If you rely on memory alone, you're likely to have a very biased, filtered account in your book that will end up feeling one- or two-dimensional to readers. Weaving in cultural elements is a great option to, as my younger students tell me, "keep it real."

Creating a Sense of Place

Psychologists have proven that people rely a ton on their eyes. It makes sense, then, that writers typically handle setting via visuals. If you focus only with sight, you're missing some of the other evocative things that make scenes come alive. Utilize the entire sensory range to create scenes and settings that feel real enough for readers to step into.

Think about smell, such as a wet dog, new car, freshly-opened oranges, and bread baking. With touch, imagine bitter December wind that raises goose-flesh, the scratchy warmth of Grandpa's flannel shirt, or the roughness of old bricks that were used to make a lake house patio.

Read these sections for other ways to make setting emerge with crystal-clear surround sound quality onto the page. Remember: The more specific and concrete your description, the better results you'll have.

Adding dimensions: Physical space

Taking the time to establish scale and proportion can help readers more easily see things in their minds. How big do things appear? From what perspective can the character see it?

For example, "The single elm tree stood in the field behind the house like a titan had shoved a spear straight into the earth. Were someone to climb to the top, they'd be able to see the ocean for sure."

Scale and size are things you first note, so make sure you make an observation that comes early in the scene. No one stands around talking to a woman for five minutes only then to have the sudden realization: "Zowie, she's as tall as a giraffe!"

Describing setting with movement

This technique helps you keep the action going while still giving information on setting. In movie terminology, it's like panning (moving) the camera to follow the character. As your character moves from room to room, place to place, readers naturally focus on the things your character would likely be noticing, such as a moldy carpet, an echoey basement, or a gold-plated doorknob. This technique works like a first-person shooter video game. What the character sees, your readers see. When the character turns away from something, the memoir's narrative "camera" — the writer's focus through language — goes with them.

When you bring in setting details this way, they're interspersed with action and perhaps dialogue, which makes them more palatable.

To change up things so you're not always writing about what the character is looking at, you may have him react to something. An example: "Xenon had to turn sideways to squeeze past the stacks of old newspapers in Mrs. Jamison's kitchen." It's a nice change from "Newspapers were stacked in high columns throughout Mrs. Jamison's kitchen."

Noting familiarity with surroundings

Each character's point of view and how familiar she is with her surroundings can also create a sense of place. Consider who your point of view person is in each scene and accordingly adjust her perception of setting-related details.

Characters who come into a new setting notice far different things than those that are regulars. For instance, think about going back to your parents' home. What do you notice? More than likely, the new TV stand or the missing plates of the china set stick in your mind. Your eyes roll right over the same pictures on the mantel that have been there for years. You're blind to what's right in front of you. (This is also why you have to be careful when you proof-read your manuscript; your eyes may gloss too quickly over things you've seen many times before.)

Don't get too bogged down trying to nail this technique at first; you can effectively do it during the revision stage of your writing process (check out Chapter 15 for more information on revision).

A person's profession can also greatly affect how she sees things. An architect or mechanic may see the structure and machinery of a building whereas an artist may be entranced by the color and angle of the light streaming in from a bay window. Perhaps a beautician may notice the faint odor of jasmine leaking in from an unseen open window.

Memoirs that contain moments from childhood hold a special challenge. Remember that what you noticed about a place or a person at age six was likely different from what you would notice at your current age. Plus you were a lot shorter. Capturing how the world looks to a small child is another way of making your memoir both interesting and accurate.

Noting the time

Time is also a way to make a clearer setting in your memoir. *Time* includes both time of year and time of day, and the historical time (such as 1960s Greenwich Village). Whether you include references to season, days, or actual hours on the clock in dialogue, narrative summary, or exposition, your readers will appreciate it. To make the memoir experience effective, your readers need to be able to readily create the visuals needed to accompany the action. Dusk in July in the Midwest. Midnight in the salt flats. High noon in Times Square. It's the element of time that alters the way your readers envision those settings.

When you're using this method, think about light and shadow. Think about weather. Think about mood (I'm pretty cranky past 10 p.m., and odds are, your characters are too). For instance, a lakeside park where a romantic interlude takes place creates a very different ambience at 2 a.m. in July, noon in December, and anytime in 1942 America.

If the time period you're writing about in your memoir is anything other than the here and now, tell the reader right away. Just get it out there. If using a time/date header for a chapter or just coming out and telling the reader in the first paragraph feels right, do it. Nothing is to be gained from having the reader get 26 pages into the book only to realize they've been imagining the entire thing wrong because it's 1952, not 1992. Or that it's wintertime versus summer.

Working with Atmosphere

Atmosphere is the effect that a setting has on a reader. The physical details of a story setting generate a kind of emotional impact on the reader when reading the words on the page. This emotional response gets a reader empathizing with the main character. It can also get the reader recognizing that the story feels mysterious, melancholy, joyful, or frightening, to name just a few of the options.

For example, consider Edgar Allan Poe's setting of "The Fall of the House of Usher," which is an ancestral mansion on the edge of a mountain lake. The atmosphere is gloom, despair, and profound sorrow. The way Poe writes, the setting could've been a suburban house near New York and the words he chose still leave a reader breathless, afraid, and fearful.

Academics might argue that "mood" and "atmosphere" aren't the same. For these purposes, they're similar enough to be used interchangeably. Either is simply the emotional effect a setting has on the reader. (If you must know the nuances of distinction between mood and atmosphere, drum up your local English professor and ply him with a couple of pints of good beer at a nearby pub. Two hours later, you'll have your answer, but it won't help you in any practical way with writing your memoir!)

The next sections reveal the main ways to create a robust, compelling setting through less tangible things than place and time. Being able to effectively manage the following techniques is what often makes one writer's settings more potent than another's.

Intensifying mood

Atmosphere can serve as a mood intensifier. Your readers already have a sense of things from what the characters do and say (see Chapter 8), as well as some of the plot details (refer to Chapters 3 and 6). Layer in the emotional resonance of atmosphere now and you're really cooking. You can work with setting and atmosphere to help intensify the experience of your memoir. You need to be able to create and, when needed, intensify that atmosphere because it's a convincing way to create emotional resonance and striking scenes.

To create intensity, you can be choosy in how you decide to portray the setting and the atmosphere of a scene. I'm not suggesting that you move your verbal showdown with your ex-spouse from the Laundromat to a crashing airplane to make it more dramatic. Like the Poe example from the previous section, Poe didn't have to place the mansion up in the remote part of a mountain, but doing so helped heighten the solitude, the loneliness, and the dread. With a little care, you can have a Poe-like effect in even the most mundane of settings (which sadly is where much of people's lives take place — office cubicles, grocery stores, and the like). Use your writer's eye to spot the right details that will suggest the effect you want to create for the reader.

Foreshadowing: What's to come

Readers appreciate story logic. Story logic comes from a causal relationship between the parts of a story. One way to make this happen later is to set it up earlier by foreshadowing. *Foreshadowing* basically is a literary device where an author includes characters, things, or details that prepare the way for later events to occur. It's been around for hundreds of years — Shakespeare, Chaucer, and Dante all used it.

Foreshadowing creates dramatic tension and anticipation while readers wait for things to unfold as you've promised, hinted, or suggested. Foreshadowing works particularly well with early scenes setting up later conflicts.

Foreshadowing can be fairly obvious (such as when Romeo and Juliet talk about dying) or far more subtle (such as a man feeling a "terrible joy" upon first viewing a woman, because he's going to fall in love with her, but that love will ultimately bring him unending grief).

A few clear examples of foreshadowing include the following:

- ✔ **Shakespeare's *Macbeth*:** How the witches at the start suggest evil events will follow (or just that the story starts with witches suggests trouble, no?)

- ✔ **The movie *Bambi*:** How Bambi's mother warned Bambi about the threat of men and their guns

- ✔ **The memoir *Night* by Elie Wiesel (Hill and Wang):** How the author recalls Mrs. Schächter's frightening vision of fire

- ✔ **The memoir *Marley and Me: Life and Love with the World's Worst Dog* by John Grogan (Harper):** How the author is sad that no one has thrown him a birthday party

Correctly using foreshadowing is challenging in an early draft unless you have a fairly good outline. (Refer to Chapter 6 where I discuss putting together an outline.) Even then, you still may not see all the opportunities until later drafts. Either way, don't worry about it. You can most easily use foreshadowing in the last few drafts of your story, when you can see all the chess pieces on the board.

Tackling Exposition: Keeping on Task

Exposition is information that isn't so much part of your story, but rather something that helps readers understand your story. In other words, exposition is background, context, and the past. It's also the current situation that your character is in. Often, it's part of setting, atmosphere, or story tension.

Some writing teachers talk about exposition being primarily found at the start of stories, but this isn't true. Exposition can be found anywhere in your memoir to develop plot, provide character background, establish setting, and further the story's theme(s).

When you use exposition, focus on the task at hand. Readers need to know what's important. By spending too much time in the past, they may start asking "Why are we in the *now* if the *past* is so darn important?" And that's a valid reason to get fed up with a memoir.

You can deliver exposition in your memoir in a variety of ways:

- ✔ **Dialogue:** There are plenty of opportunities where one character tells another character about the past or an event they reasonably don't know about but that the reader needs to know. An example: "You should've been at the company picnic last year, where Stein drank a gallon of spiked lemonade then tried to swim home." (See Chapter 9 for more details on the use of dialogue.)

- ✔ **Direct narration:** This is the telling side of the showing/telling dichotomy. Telling, or direct narration, is exposition. (See Chapter 16 for information on showing and telling.)

- ✔ **Expository devices, such as flashbacks:** Jumping back to show scenes from the past can be useful, as long as you don't overuse them. (See Chapter 6 for structure-related ideas.)

- ✔ **Other unique options:** These include sections of a cookbook, a travel guide, official documents, or other nonfiction elements that a memoir may include alongside or even within the general text. (See Chapter 6 for options like this.)

Exposition is almost always telling versus showing. Chapter 16 discusses the maxim of showing and not telling. Exposition works against that maxim, which is good reason to use it sparingly. If you give too much exposition in one chunk, readers will more than likely skip it. The reason is simple: Readers like action, and exposition is the opposite of action.

Readers always focus on the main story. Moments (or, gasp, entire chapters) of exposition aren't the focus; they're a detour, which means the key to successfully using exposition is to handle it swiftly.

Here's an example of properly used exposition:

> "Love the Smurfs, do you?" asked the saleslady as she rang me up.
>
> "Daughter's birthday," I said.
>
> "Oh, how old?"
>
> "Six," I said, then winced. Of course she wasn't six. She was six when that shrew took her to live in France with her shrink/lover. Little Mindy was eight now.
>
> "They're precious at that age, aren't they?"

Compare it to this version where the main story takes too much of a backseat to the exposition:

> "Love the Smurfs, do you?" asked the saleslady as she rang me up.
>
> "Daughter's birthday," I said.
>
> "Oh, how old?"
>
> "Six," I said, then winced. Of course she wasn't six. She was six when that shrew took her to live in France with her shrink/lover. Little Mindy was eight now.
>
> Things had gone sideways without warning. An early return from a meeting only to find an extra car in the driveway. But it's a shrink, and one kind enough to do at-your-home sessions. Who'd ever think the a-hole was boinking Wendy and still charging ninety-five bucks an hour, which I was stuck paying? I had considered contacting the American Psychiatric Association when the divorce papers arrived — I knew I could ruin that fool's life, or at least his career. But try as I might to ignore it, I couldn't get past the fact: I loved Wendy.
>
> That's the type of fool I was. A hopeless one.

See the difference? The second version loses the momentum of the initial scene. You almost forget about the saleslady and the bag of toys. All that stuff about how the breakup occurred? Don't throw it out; just find somewhere else to ease into it — ideally in small doses.

Incorporating Narrative Summary: Knowing When It Makes Sense

Narrative summary is when you deliver information but don't reveal all the ins and outs of what happened. It's a shorthand way to deliver less important material to your reader quickly. Although it's quite useful at times, this technique can go wrong if used haphazardly.

Like exposition, narrative summary does what it purports to do: summarize. The problem with narrative summary is obvious. Readers would rather experience something themselves rather than read a summary of the same story. The ability to summarize is a good skill to have. You'll need it in your memoir from time to time. However, if your entire book is summary, most readers would rather pick fleas off a mangy alley cat than read it.

That's not to say that you should avoid narrative summary at all costs. Sometimes you need to convey information to a reader, but using fully developed scenes to do so doesn't pass the cost-benefit analysis, so narrative summary is the better choice.

Here's a quick example of how you can wisely use narrative summary to deliver much-needed information, but make sure you keep the reader firmly rooted in the now of the main story arc.

> "How could I not be your type?" I said. "We belong to the same church. We're both Harvard grads. We both hate the White Sox. I mean, c'mon. Jeez."
>
> Ruthie shrugged. She got up to leave. I moved to follow her but found myself stuck in the booth, my belly wedged too tight between the seat back and tabletop. Her eyes fell on my stomach, telling me all I didn't want to hear.
>
> For the next three months, I didn't drink soda. I cut sugar to a minimum. I even power-walked twice a week through the park. Twice I even joined the high school rowing team in its workouts on the waterway.
>
> The week before Christmas, I stopped in to see my cousin Lisa who worked the perfume counter at Macy's in Woodfield Mall.
>
> "Eighty bucks an ounce?" I asked when she showed me the newest celebrity-powered fragrance. *Oui Oui*, by Britney Spears.
>
> Lisa said, "It's all about the marketing."
>
> "Excuse me," came a voice from behind them. I froze. I'd recognize that voice anywhere.
>
> Ruthie drank in my freshly dyed hair, slim cut Hilfiger shirt, and new goatee. Then she took a step back. "Jethro?"

See how that small bit of narrative summary keeps readers from spending too much time on the physical makeover Jethro underwent? Readers knew his motivation was significant; he lost the girl, after all. Readers know what type of things people do to lose weight and improve their appearance. Narrative summary works here like shorthand. You can trust the reader to fill in the details.

Making History Come Alive Through Using the Present Tense

Most writers believe that the present tense is more immediate and powerful than using past tense. Memoir writers, too, want to convey the intensity of the past to readers, and past tense feels, well, like the past. Like old news. It's understandable for memoir writers to want to have the here-and-now feel that present tense provides. The stories being written about are personal. Is it wrong for the writers to locate the reader square in the middle of the action as it seems to unfold around them? This act is called the *historical present*, meaning that a writer writes about past events in the present tense.

If historical present is so terrific, why not just write the whole thing in present tense? I don't recommend it because memoirs work well when the context — typically created through narrative summary and exposition. How are you going to go back into the past when you're locked into the present? Are you going to jump back and forth? That sounds inefficient at best, and confusing at worst.

Writing Exercises on Creating Effective Scenes and Settings

Scenes and settings are two fundamental parts of writing a memoir that do a good job of sharing your story with readers. Make sure your scenes feel purposeful and richly developed. Setting, of course, plays a big part in making that happen. The following writing exercises can help you get a firmer handle on being able to craft strong scenes and effective settings no matter your writing task.

❑ **Think about a book or movie with a profoundly powerful setting.** Some examples include the movie *Alien,* the Gulf War memoir *Jarhead: A Marine's Chronicle of the Gulf War and Other Battles* by Anthony Swofford (Scribner), or *Talking the Wild Dik-Dik: One Woman's Solo Misadventures Across Africa* by Marie Javins (Seal Press). How many details about it can you visualize when you shut your eyes and return to that world of the

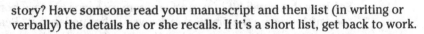

story? Have someone read your manuscript and then list (in writing or verbally) the details he or she recalls. If it's a short list, get back to work.

❏ **Select a short passage of narrative summary from your manuscript.** Expand it to a full scene; give it a page or two test-run. Which way works better? Adjust your manuscript as needed.

❏ **Spend a few moments outside, just observing.** When your gaze and attention finally focuses clearly on something specific, spend three minutes writing a paragraph or two of good, concrete description. Now write a descriptive paragraph or two of the same exact thing, only this time from the perspective of a person who just was offered his dream job or who just met his soul mate. How would he convey the same visual target(s)? How may emotion infuse his perception and word choice?

(Hint: Coming out and saying "I'm so happy. I just met Martha. I'm look-ing at a brown tree!" is boring. See how subtle you can be and yet still generate the same emotion that the speaker feels in the reader.) Try this one more time, only let this last person have the perspective of a parent who just learned her only child isn't coming back from the war in Afghanistan, or who just learned she has aggressive, inoperable cancer. How might she view that same tree, person, car, or whatever subject you chose for the first two descriptive passages? (I'm guessing a good deal differently. And again, be subtle, not "Oh, I'm dying. I'm so sad. And there's a stupid brown tree.")

❏ **Go through a single scene from your manuscript with colored pencils or crayons in hand.** Assign each of the senses a specific color and then mark each usage on the page. (For example, use red for sight, blue for sound, and green for scent.) Are you utilizing the whole spectrum or do you have, say, a ton of blue? (Ask someone else to do this for you so you're not tempted to cheat.)

❏ **Take a scene from your manuscript and rework it in a different tense.** If you wrote it in the past tense, try the present tense. Does it offer more immediacy to use what's called the *historical present*? Does it make the past feel more alive?

❏ **Tease out the tension.** After many writers have built the tension to what they feel is the maximum, their first impulse is often to release it as soon as possible. In a moment of high tension in your book, don't give in to that impulse. Hold out for another three pages. If you've set things up well, you're foreshadowing the tension's resolution there for the read-ers. They'll *know* it's coming. Make them wait. See how that scene reads with the tension deliciously teased out longer than you ever expected to go.

Chapter 8

The Character of Characters

Think about the word, "character," as in someone's character (such as being trustworthy or selfish or foolhardy). There's more than just one's attributes that make up a person. More than a single word descriptor ("jerk," "jock," or "cheerleader") sums up a person's life. Your challenge is to find the best, most effective way to make the people in your life and world come alive on the page as living, breathing, realistic characters.

Many memoirists who run into problems with making their book work do so because they make the mistake of only focusing on events. What makes those events meaningful to write about is how they link up with and affect characters. Without sufficient attention on characters and character building, a memoir will feel weak, hollow, and plodding.

The people in memoir are still called "characters" even though they aren't made up, which can be confusing for writers. The people in a memoir are real, but the reader has never met them, so they must be built up on the page detail by detail, just like an imaginary character in a movie script, short story, or novel. Just because it'd be more dramatically interesting to have your crazy Cousin Justin be millionaire movie star Cousin Kristine doesn't mean that's a real option for your memoir. Check out Chapter 17 about the ethical and legal concerns about making sure you truthfully represent your characters.

Think about the best memoirs (or novels or films) you've encountered. What do you remember most about them? You probably don't remember the who-does-what-to-whom plot stuff, but you remember the wild obsession of Ahab from *Moby Dick* or the frightening intensity of Hannibal Lecter from *The Silence of the Lambs* and the amazing in-the-trenches resiliency of Ann Hood in her tragic memoir *Comfort*, which centers on the death of her five-year old daughter Gracie. Readers don't invest in plot. They invest in characters.

So how do you handle creating and developing characters in a memoir that are so well depicted that they're seared into your readers' brains? That's what this chapter covers. Read on to discover how to work with the idea of character in a memoir, such that your past and your stories weave a powerful spell on your readers.

The art of creating characters in memoir is a challenge even for established writers because it's hard for many people to see what's familiar. You have to figure out ways to see the familiar anew from the perspective of an outsider.

This chapter is a crash course in the basics. My first recommendation on figuring out how to tackle characters in memoir is simple: Read a lot of great memoirs. See how other authors do it. Read

- *One Writer's Beginnings* by Eudora Welty (Harvard University Press)
- *Shock Value: A Tasteful Book About Bad Taste* by John Waters (Running Press)
- *The Woman Warrior: Memoirs of a Girlhood Among Ghosts* by Maxine Hong Kingston (Vintage)
- *Black Boy* by Richard Wright (Harper Perennial Modern Classics)
- *The Windward Shore: A Winter on the Great Lakes* by Jerry Dennis (University of Michigan Press)

Reading books like these can help give you samples of how to develop great characters, create compelling storylines, and generate reader interest. Each of them handles these tasks in a different way. But the end result is the same: a fine memoir that shows how high the bar of success can be set.

Understanding What Makes a Good Character

What makes a character memorable is important to writing good characters in your memoir. You need to think about what are the most crucial things that you can deliver on the page that will convey a good sense of the characters. These sections give you the real scoop for making that magic happen.

Dealing with desire

Like human beings, characters in stories *want* something. They desire. They yearn. They covet. From this desire nearly everything else unfolds. By knowing what characters desire, your readers know what matters to those characters. Desire can help your readers connect with characters. It helps them know what makes your characters tick. It makes the story more powerful and more real.

For your characters to ring true, you have to include the sense of desire with them. Don't mistake that for saying that all characters are clear and understandable. Anything but! Humans are a complex mess of contradictions, but humans do have goals — money, power, love, status, perfection, beauty —and they constantly strive for them. Your obligation as a memoirist is to uncover what the driving forces of desire are for your characters (that includes yourself!), and make those forces apparent to the reader. If it's clear what your characters yearn for, your readers will root for or against them. Either way, your readers suddenly care a bit more.

For example, when I was thrust into the role of teaching freshman composition for the first time in my life, I had a large class of eighteen-year-olds at Florida State University. I wanted those budding writers to feel a sense of camaraderie and kinship, so on day one I had everyone stand up and introduce themselves by giving their name and their major and anything else interesting.

A few kids plodded through this exercise with half-heartened enthusiasm. Then the biggest kid in our class stood up. He was African-American, maybe 6'7", 350 pounds, and thick as a house. He said, "My name's Larry and my major is the NFL." He wasn't joking. At a football powerhouse like FSU, having kids who took their future athletic careers this seriously wasn't all that unusual.

Halfway through his first season of playing for Coach Bobby Bowden, Larry (not his real name) blew his knee out and never played football again. For most people, blowing out your knee would suck, not withstanding that it's inconvenient and hurts. But it wouldn't get in the way of my desire to be a *New York Times* bestselling young adult author. It wouldn't get in my friend David's way of being a celebrated French chef. It wouldn't get in the way of my wife who has a master's degree in education and longs to return to the classroom.

But for Larry? Having that injury was about the worst thing that could happen *to him* because really huge offensive linemen rarely come back from a devastating total knee blowout. Larry didn't. And so when you hear this story, because you know his deep desire, you're profoundly saddened by what happened to him.

Everyone does things for a reason — even if the person doesn't realize it. This is what psychologists mean when they say, "There are no accidents." Unconsciously or consciously, everyone is striving for specific outcomes that they desire. For Larry, it was ultra-clear. For others, it may be much less so, but it's there nonetheless. Taking the time to figure out the desires of the characters in your memoir is a must.

For instance, check out these examples of character actions, and some of the potential reasons/desires that fuel those actions:

- The girlfriend who says on a third date, "I want to have a big family."

  She secretly enjoys being alone. Or maybe having her friends feel sorry for her. Or she's scared of commitment so she drives men away by saying this too early in a relationship, long before anyone has the chance to make a real connection with her.

- The guy who becomes a psychology major.

  He wants to have the knowledge to fix himself after suffering a brutal childhood. Or he wants the power to break people down and manipulate them.

- The wife who keeps bringing home stray dogs.

  She uses them as a replacement for the child her husband won't let her have. Or that her damaged uterus won't let her have. Or she has a good Samaritan complex.

Getting physical

Unless you have identical twins, characters look different. They dress different. Their haircuts, eye color, waist size, and degree of tooth whiteness are different. So describing someone so that they do seem different from others is a balancing act. Too little and what you imagine your character to look like may not match what your readers think, but give them too much and your readers can get bored.

Beginning writers feel obligated to give a head-to-toe description the moment a new character steps on the stage, which tends to stop the action and the movement of the story. This level of description feels unnatural. Select one or two telling details that suggest the essence of the character's appearance and let the rest slide for now, or possibly for good.

Don't feel like you have to deliver all the appearance details of a character at one time. Let them accumulate over time as the narrative progresses. For the best effect, find ways to attach them to meaningful action or scenes.

Here's an example.

I'd been bellying up to the bar most of the afternoon, doing my damnedest to try to forget Heather. Wasn't long before the meathead stopped serving me. I just sat there, staring at the game on TV, not caring who won or lost.

Sometime around nine, in walks this woman who looks dressed for the opera. In a craphole like this, heads turned. I couldn't get enough of that slinky yellow dress. Nearly the same color as the Miller Light sign burning up neon on the back wall.

"Buy me a drink?" she said, her dress wisping up against my leg as she sat beside me.

Wow, that woman is sexy, isn't she? Here's what you know about her. She's dressed well enough to go to a super formal event like an opera. And she's wearing a slinky yellow dress. That's it. Not a thing more. Nothing about her hairdo, her makeup, her breasts, her eyes, her height, her weight, her age. But don't you get a pretty good sense of the punch this woman packed? You can tell because of how everyone else around her reacted, including the narrator.

Another great way to deliver information about appearance is to use metaphors or similes. *Metaphors* are a type of analogy that compares two seemingly unlike things by finding a point of similarity between them. *Similes* do the same but specifically use *like* or *as* in the language that compares them. Here, see for yourself:

- ✓ **A straight description:** Curtis stood 6-foot-3 and weighed 230 pounds.
- ✓ **Simile:** Curtis was built like a Chicago Bears linebacker.
- ✓ **Metaphor:** Curtis is a monster. Get him angry enough, and he could tear his way out of a bank vault.

Which did you find most effective? Think about it the next time you need to describe a character in your book.

Giving your characters an age

You can just come out and announce your characters' ages. "Walter Bloom was seven years old." It's factually accurate, but it doesn't do much for a reader in terms of involving them or painting a picture. The better way is to use details to suggest that age.

For example

Walter leapt off his bicycle and ran howling around the cypress tree, glancing behind him every few moments as if he were being chased by a horde of space aliens. He tugged off his Spiderman shirt and whipped it around his head like a lasso. Then he suddenly stopped. "Freeze tag!" he yelled, sticking a finger out at nothing.

Marnie came out from behind the house and said, "Freeze tag with Invisible Bob again? You're such a loser, Walt."

Walter smiled. "Unfreeze," he said. "Go get her, Bob."

If you had to bet on guessing his age, you probably could get it within a year or so without the writer stepping in and blurting it out with the evidence the writer gives you — the bicycle, invisible friends, playing freeze tag, Spiderman shirt, imaginative play by himself. Add this together and you get a pretty young kid. He's not ten because he's probably too old for Spiderman and freeze tag. He's not four or five because he's articulate and allowed to play alone in the yard. This all happens in a flash in the reader's mind. This example is a great way to involve your readers in the story by helping them make easily made assessments, judgments, and evaluations. Offer them 1 + 1 and they'll happily shout, "Two!"

You can also follow up this scene in a later chapter with information that confirms his age. When Marnie sees Walter licking mint chocolate chip ice cream off the kitchen floor, she can say, "Walter, you're the dumbest seven-year-old I've ever met!" It reveals that info, but completely in the development of a scene versus some kind of data dump.

Adding patterns of behavior

Every time I come home, I toss my keys into the metal dish on the hall table, kick off my shoes, and then take our Shih Tzu, Ladybug, outside for a five minute walk. Night or day, rain or shine, I do it. I don't really think about why I have that pattern or where it came from (other than when I'm writing a chapter on patterns of behavior in characters, that is!).

People like routines. They develop patterns of behavior. Knowing what those patterns are for your characters will not only allow you to depict them more realistically, but also to understand them better. Take the time to pay attention to the real-world counterparts and see what they do again and again. These routes are often quite revealing about who they are and what they're about. For instance, what do you immediately get from the following passage?

I scrubbed at the sink with a scouring pad. I added more cleaner and then started working it to a thick foam on the stainless steel.

The door to the garage banged shut as my husband, Jim, came in. He gave my shoulder a little squeeze as he moved to the table to get a cookie from the jar. "Tough day at work, honey," he said between bites. When he finished, he added, "I'm going to go wash up for dinner."

The moment he left the room, I got the dishrag and wiped the kitchen table free of crumbs. Then I turned the glass cookie jar so the "God loves us. The proof is in the cookies!" placard faced north. The way it always faced.

Do you get a sense about the "I" character from this passage? She's that type of wife who probably mops the floor behind her husband the moment he comes in from the snow. And she's oddly particular about things being in their place. You also get a sense about his character, too. He's a bit more laid-back, by comparison. He also doesn't go out of his way to cater to her super-cleanliness or he'd have cleaned up after himself or perhaps eaten over a plate or napkin, right?

See how much you can get out of a few carefully rendered moments of inter-action between your characters? You witness a few patterns of behavior that clearly suggest long-standing elements of their relationship and psychology. That's the stuff readers want because it gives stories depth.

Getting inside their head

Having access to someone's mind is a great way to characterize him or her. With a memoir, so many writers get stuck in the idea of "It's my story, so I have to do it all from inside my brain." Feel free to do whatever makes the story better. If you need to change the *point of view* (the the writer's choice on which character's eyes will be observing the story) for a chapter, do it. Don't feel restricted by so-called rules if they get in the way of a good story. (Refer to Chapter 11 for more information on point of view.)

For instance, what do we know about the man in the following passage?

> *She's going to leave me. I know it*, Harry thought. He stared at the black-top parking lot near the football stadium. He wiped sweat from his fore-head — the stupid custodians couldn't keep any air conditioning in the building running right. *But at least they don't go around divorcing people at the drop of a hat. You just can't trust women.*
>
> "Principal Turtleson?" came his assistant's voice over the desk intercom. "You have a Samantha Evans on line 1. She's got a complaint about the new after-school tutoring program again."
>
> "Put her through," Harry said. And if she thinks she's getting anything from me, she's in for a world of disappointment. A universe of it.

Harry is a jerk. Or at least he's the type of guy who takes his problems out on other people. He's upset about his wife, for sure. Even though I don't know the full story there, I'm intrigued by it. Did he cheat? Did she? Does she resent him for not making enough money? Did he let his appearance go? Whatever the beef is, it's enough for him to live in fear. Without more access to his mind and the constant worry there, you don't know much about him. Although his external actions are pretty mundane, his thoughts create the tension here.

Portraying action

One of the most important ways that you can reveal character is to let us see what a character does, in other words, action. And as the old saying goes, "Actions speak louder than words." Adding action is fairly easy. Just share with the reader the things you or someone else did. Big, medium, or small actions, it doesn't matter that much because all that you do stems from who you are.

For example, if you have a young father with three kids roughhousing all the time, he may talk a good game about not losing his cool. But when one of them breaks the case holding his signed Sandy Colfax baseball and Dad instinctively raises a clenched fist? That says something. It's when people are most pressured that they show their true colors. Make sure to allow your characters to honestly present themselves in your memoir.

Sometimes inaction is a powerful thing to point out too. Think about how different *Hamlet* would be if Hamlet decided in Act II to just whack the dude who killed his father? Paying attention to inaction, such as when a mother ignores child abuse going on under her own roof, is a very powerful thing. Don't flinch when action or inaction really connects with the major themes of your story.

Identifying Character Archetypes

One way to think about your characters is to examine the character *archetypes* — long-standing patterns that are common across culture. You know the following characters because most of the stories you grew up with involve variations on many of these figures. They're familiar to you (and your readers) in all the right ways.

Of course, plenty of other character archetypes exist, though the following are the most common. You don't want to hew too closely to these alone when writing about your characters or you'll have problems being original.

The rest of the chapter gives you ways to personalize each character in meaningful ways. Sure, every character is different just as every human being is different, but I certainly know certain types. Thinking about your characters in terms of archetypes that are familiar to readers can help you better understand other story issues such as theme, conflict, and plot.

The story's hero

Also referred to as the *protagonist, main character,* or *focal character*, the popular hero archetype has seemingly been around forever. Noble, virtuous, courageous, and bigger than life, he (or she) is the story's central character. He steals the show when he's on stage. He overcomes obstacles and achieves success more often than not.

Some famous heroes in literature include

- Emma Woodhouse in Jane Austen's *Emma*, Atticus Finch in Harper Lee's *To Kill a Mockingbird* (Harper Perennial Modern Classics), and Max in Maurice Sendak's *Where the Wild Things Are* (HarperCollins)

- Barack Obama in his memoir, *Dreams of My Father: A Story of Race and Inheritance* (Crown), who is presented as an honorable, dedicated person who may well deserve being President one day

The nemesis

Also known as the *villain* or *antagonist*, a *nemesis* is the opposition and counterpart to the hero. That doesn't mean the nemesis is sociopathic, selfish, evil, or mean, though he often is those things. The nemesis's function is to be in the way of the hero achieving his goal.

I prefer the term "nemesis." "Antagonist" sounds too technical (and an antagonist doesn't have to be human, such as the weather in Jack London's short story "To Build a Fire"), and "villain" makes me think of over-the-top evil Disney figures.

You may recognize these famous nemeses:

- Iago in William Shakespeare's *Othello*, Sauron in J.R.R. Tolkien's *The Lord of the Rings* series, and Robert Lovelace in Samuel Richardson's *Clarissa*

- Dwight Hansen in Tobias Wolff's memoir *This Boy's Life* (Grove Press), who stole the hero's happy childhood right out from under him

Antihero

Just like it sounds, the *antihero* is the opposite (or the *anti-*) version of the traditional hero you see in books, films, and plays. This guy or gal is still the protagonist, but he or she isn't the sort of hero your mom would brag about.

Morally ambiguous, vulnerable, cowardly, lazy, even cruel, these people are somehow still a lot of fun to watch in action. They're profoundly imperfect and often buy into the "ends justifies the means" thinking. Yet something is admirable (perhaps his unwillingness to compromise or his ability to puzzle out the truth) or likeable about antiheroes despite their many flaws. If not, why would readers continue with the story?

Some memorable antihero examples include the following:

✔ Rip Van Winkle, Holden Caulfield in J.D. Salinger's *The Catcher in the Rye* (Back Bay Books), and Dexter Morgan in Jeff Lindsay's *Dexter* book and TV series

✔ The lovable rogue Han Solo (*Star Wars*)

✔ Myself in my book *Unplugged* (HCI) where my exploits are anything but heroic and bigger than life; I'm a lot more like Charlie Brown than Hercules.

Mentor

The *mentor* (also referred to as the *counselor, guide,* or *teacher*) provides much-needed wisdom and guidance for others. This character has a profound effect on people and plays a significant role in directing them on the journey of their lives.

Some examples of mentor characters include

✔ Yoda and Obi-Wan Kenobi from *Star Wars* and Aldus Dumbledore in J.K. Rowling's *Harry Potter* series

✔ Morrie Schwartz in Mitch Albom's memoir, Tuesdays with Morrie: An Old Man, a Young Man, and Life's Greatest Lesson (Broadway)

The fool

These free-spirited, wild figures provide comic relief, to be sure. The *fool,* also known as the *prankster, buffoon,* or *jester,* also represents or serves the causes of common sense, honesty, and truth. To that end, their advice is often deceptively important though not always well-received.

Here are some examples:

✔ Gimpel in Isaac Bashevis Singer's "Gimpel the Fool", the Fool in Shakespeare's *King Lear,* and Mr. Harley Quin in Agatha Christie's *The Mysterious Mr. Quin* (William Morrow)

✔ Dory in the animated movie *Finding Nemo*

✔ David Sedaris in his memoir *Me Talk Pretty One Day* (Back Bay Books)

Sidekick

This person is an inseparable, necessary companion to the hero. The *sidekick* is usually the same gender as the hero, and his qualities fill in the gaps and complement the abilities and knowledge of his "bigger" partner. Also known as the *partner, companion,* and *confidant,* more than a few sidekicks provide comic relief, too.

Famous sidekick examples include

- Phineas in John Knowles' *A Separate Peace* (Scribner), Horatio in Shakespeare's *Hamlet*, and Samwise Gamgee in Tolkien's *The Lord of the Rings* series.
- Robin Quivers, the longtime sidekick to Howard Stern, who is writing a memoir about her struggles with weight and health. Although she's the main character of the book, professionally, she's a sidekick.

Making Characters Three-Dimensional

Some stories have characters so thinly developed that you almost wonder: If they turned sideways, would they vanish? For your memoir, you want all the important characters to come across as real, living creatures. They should look and feel solidly three-dimensional.

This section covers some of the key ways to make readers believe in your characters' authenticity. You would think that was a given in memoir. Not so! You have to earn that kind of trust and belief. Read on to find out how to do exactly that.

Utilizing backstory

You have to know a character's backstory to know their current story. *Backstory* is simply the stuff that happened prior to page one. Your characters don't spring fully formed out of nothingness, so you need to be aware of the trials and triumphs and joys and sorrows of their past.

Ernest Hemingway believed in the Iceberg Theory. Just as only 10 percent of an iceberg is visible above water, only 10 percent of a story is above water. The rest lurks beneath, fundamentally attached to the rest, but unseen. He was referring to an entire story being like that, but the theory holds for characters too. A reader will likely only see the 10 percent of your characters. As a writer, you need to know the other 90 percent.

Fiction writers need to do a lot of dreaming and guesswork in advance. For memoir writers, you need to conduct some research, pay attention, and ask lots of questions. Both have their own set of challenges. Ignore backstory, though, and you miss out on giving your story a sense of complexity and completeness that'll make it stand out. (Refer to Chapter 4 for how you can dig deep and find more backstory. And Chapter 12 offers ideas on how to use backstory to rev up a reader's interest in your characters and story.)

Backstory can quickly turn into a data dump. You know that it's important so *bam*, there it is. Dumping too much backstory to a reader is a lot like trying to eat a whole ice cream cake alone. You can do it for about five minutes, but then you feel a little bloated and end up moaning all afternoon on the couch with your pants unbuttoned. Okay, perhaps not that extreme, but close enough. Just like the ice cream cake, though, give backstory in small slices and everyone will end up happy and satisfied.

Avoiding stereotypes and clichés

When creating your memoir's characters, you want to stay away from using stereotypes and clichés. The memoir is yours and yours alone. Let it really reflect your thoughts, ideas, and life. Don't let the language and ideas of others tell your story.

You know what the stereotypes in your family are already — you've likely been victim to them from teachers, classmates, neighbors, and strangers. You're African-American. You're from Russia. You're smart. You're stupid. You have a New York accent. You have a Louisiana drawl. You're short. You're fat. You're an angry woman. You're a clueless man.

Whichever of these may apply to you, you know there are a ton more to whom you really are. Don't fall into the trap of limiting how you see your other characters. Yes, Uncle Willie drinks a lot, but don't let him become The Drunk Uncle. Give him his due. Not only is using stereotypes a dull read, but it probably isn't that true. Really think about it. Is that all Uncle Willie is or does?

Even if you don't let your characters fall into stereotypical roles, you may still deal with them in clichéd ways. For instance, do you have any variations of the following in your manuscript?

- ✔ _____ had a heart of gold.
- ✔ The acorn didn't fall far from the tree with _____.
- ✔ _____ was on an emotional roller coaster.
- ✔ Her eyes danced with merriment.
- ✔ _____ touched her alabaster skin.
- ✔ _____'s heart started pounding.

Taking the time to discover fresh ways of talking about characters can get you away from clichés and help you avoid stereotypes. Anytime that you sense the words easily falling into place, step back and look. Oftentimes those sentences or phrases that come so easily come so easily because you've heard them a million times before, such as

- ✔ Neck? Swan-like.
- ✔ Breasts? Heaving.
- ✔ Eyes? Twinkling.
- ✔ Fingers? Elegant.

Put one word down, its partner-in-crime just leaps right into place.

Making Sure Your Characters Change

Stories are about character change, or at least the opportunity for change. Why are people so obsessed about change? For one thing, change is interesting. How excited would you be to read a memoir about a drunken professor, who drinks at the start, drinks throughout the book, and then is still a drunk at the end? Writers call that a "zero to zero" story. Readers vastly prefer a "zero to hero" or even a "hero to zero" story. They both have change and draw in readers.. The zero to zero feels static.

Readers are fascinated by the idea of change. They want to witness the coming-of-age of another person or the coming-into-wisdom that's so rare in their own lives. From it, they may learn a bit more about themselves and what it means to be human.

Take a look at some of the clearest examples of change in a character throughout the course of a story:

- ✔ *How The Grinch Who Stole Christmas:* We know how bad the Grinch was at the start. But by the end? He's as sweet as they come.

- ✔ *Rain Man:* Tom Cruise's character is selfish and ruthless at the start. By the end, he turns down money and realizes the importance of family.

- ✔ *Turning White: A Memoir of Change* (Momentum Books): Lee Thomas's memoir about the mental and physical battle with vitiligo (a skin disorder that literally is turning this dark-skinned man white) leaves him sensitive to issues of appearance and identity in a way he never was before.

Does your memoir demonstrate real change? Does it come organically from the story's plot or is it kind of tacked on? These sections can help you really get a handle on a character's ability to change. They also discuss how some characters ought not to change, and why to include those in your memoir, too.

Comparing static and dynamic characters

Dynamic characters are capable of change. Your main characters need to be dynamic characters. They're the opposite of overly familiar, cardboard, boring characters that you've seen a million times before.

To be clear, the types of changes your main characters undergo are significant. A change in understanding ("Aha, I really do hate that girl I used to torment!"), a change in commitment ("Lucy, I've been a fool — will you marry me?"), a change in values ("I was wrong — we will allow unmarried couples to stay at our bed and breakfast from now on."). What's at stake for a dynamic character is his own character (his nature).

On the other hand, *static* characters don't change in a story. They're waiters, distant cousins, dog walkers, passersby — people who are part of the backdrop to the real story. Think about extras in movies. It doesn't matter who does those roles because they don't matter. The director just needs some warm bodies to stand there and look like people. Static characters play supporting, minor roles.

Presenting change: The how-to

You can use the same kinds of techniques that a novel writer does and find ways to indicate that change is upon you at the end. You can show change through the following means:

- ✔ **Your character's physical appearance:** A new tattoo may show a new rebellious attitude, for example. Someone who decides to move out of his parents' basement and grow up may throw out the T-shirts and start wearing shoes with tassels.

- ✔ **Your character's thoughts:** This method is more subtle. The defeat of bigotry or prejudice, for example, may not have an outward reality but when given access to the character's mind, your readers can powerfully see the different worldview at work.

- ✔ **Your character's speech and actions:** Events in the lives of your characters will precipitate changes within them, and often these changes will become evident through what they say and do. Two real-life situations reflect this type of change.

  - A young man going off to war.

  - A juvenile delinquent going to kid boot camp or jail.

In both cases, the experiences each of those environments provides will change the person, and quite likely for the better. Many current and ex-military people are very courteous and polite, even if they were hellions in their youth.

For a memoir, you're the main character. You're the hero. It may feel a bit self-conscious to say, "And now I realize that I have to take charge of my life and make better decisions or I'll continue to live on the streets of Boston and snort crack cocaine until I'm dead before I'm thirty." That might indeed be true, though it feels a little hokey, doesn't it?

Although stories are about the main character creating change or being faced with the opportunity to change, other characters in the story can change too. Minor characters don't, but important, well-developed relevant ones can and do. In fact, other characters' change may be the catalyst needed to jumpstart change within your main character.

A younger person can more easily experience massive change than an older one. Why? Because they're still learning about the world and are more open to new experiences. Older people become set in their ways. Just try to convince your grandparents to change political parties, change to a new peanut butter, or learn to love the spouse you have that they detest. You'll quickly see how calcified the elderly can be.

Creating some motivation

Everyone does things for a reason — even if the person doesn't realize it themselves. Part of that comes from the character's desire. In other instances, motivation by threats, promises, and bribes, cause a character to do something. When creating your characters, make sure they have clear motivations, which may include one or more of the following:

- Achievement
- Companionship
- Fear
- Greed
- Hate

- Helping others
- Love
- Money
- Personal growth
- Recognition

"If I had a million dollars, I'd do _____" my students often lament to me and anyone else who'll listen. What they're saying is that they're not moving forward in their lives by acting on their true desires, but rather out of other motivations — paying rent, supporting a partner, fear of failure, seeking a parent's approval.

Readers want to know about motivation. Without it, they see characters doing things that elicit a collective "huh?" Keep readers in the loop. If a character is under pressure at work to do better or be fired, inform readers so they can worry along with them And readers will hope that he'll figure it all out soon so he can get back to working on writing his award-winning cookbook that will be ten times better than *The Joy of Cooking*.

Dealing with Minor Characters

Your important characters don't populate an empty world. Your memoir also has the minor characters, such as neighbors, police, teachers, bike-riding kids, people driving cars that make up the traffic jam, and pilots flying those planes overhead. You can't ignore them, so don't. Let minor characters have minor roles. It's okay. They won't complain.

Minor characters are simply part of the milieu (the world of the story). They have a function, and after that function occurs, they tend to vanish out of sight. You may possibly have minor characters in your story who stick around through many scenes. I have a security guard who drives around in a golf cart at the school I teach at. I nod at him every time I see him; he nods back. I don't know his name; he doesn't know mine. But when I locked myself out of my office one day, he let me in. That's about the extent of our relationship. If I were to write another memoir that focused on my experiences on various campuses as a college professor, he'd be a minor character in it.

Just don't make the mistake of spending too much time on them, either. As Chapter 7 discusses, what you point the narrative "camera" at needs to matter. The longer you point it at something, the more that something matters. So if you just pan that camera along the street and briefly show a half-dozen folks, the audience knows, "Hey, the author would've zoomed in on any of those people if they were important. I won't spend time worrying about them."

Where writers can go wrong is thinking that because description and detail can be good things, they need to include description and detail for everything, including minor characters.

Consider the following example, which uses an omniscient point of view to get inside the minds of more than one character (see Chapter 11 for more details on point of view):

> Sammy yanked the handle and let in two old ladies who bickered about the weather the entire time it took them to clamber up the steps, drop their money in the slot, and shuffle to an empty seat. He couldn't stand the old ladies. He grew up with his grandparents, and the house always stank of eucalyptus and menthol, and Grandpa Joe cranked the TV to the max. It's a surprise that Sammy survived living with them for five years after college when Alexandra came out of nowhere with that divorce so she could move to Paris to be a landscape painter. Lord, that hurt. But at least Boston was good to Sammy now. The change helped soothe his pain. Driving a bus wasn't his first choice of career options yet it paid the rent on his one-bedroom apartment that overlooked the harbor.

> Now if he could only figure out how to avoid picking up so many of those old biddies. . . .

With that much detail about Sammy, readers would expect him to play an important role in the rest of the story. They would be surprised and a little irked if he never appeared again.

Writing Exercises on Creating Effective Characters

Turning real-life people into characters in your memoir is challenging but fun. The following exercises help give you ideas on how to do that. Some just focus on the techniques of creating effective characters, and some directly work with the idea of translating real-life people onto the pages of your memoir. Have fun with them.

❑ **List at least ten ways that you can suggest a character's age.** Reading glasses, crow's feet, and forgetfulness are a given. Now you come up with ten more of your own. Don't forget to try a mix of internal and external things.

❑ **Act like Oprah and interview your characters.** Write down the questions you'd most like answered, and then in the voice of the character, answer them as your characters would, both yourself and the other significant characters in your memoir. Try these to get you going.

> What's the worst thing that happened to you? What did you learn from it?
>
> Describe your ideal day.
>
> What are two things others say about you after you first meet them?
>
> Who is in your dream golf foursome, living, dead, or imaginary? You and which three others?
>
> What do you like most about yourself? Least?
>
> What job would have suited you better than your current job?
>
> If God exists, what do you suppose he'd think of you?
>
> If you were in trouble, who would you go to for help?
>
> What words would you like on your tombstone?
>
> What do you lie to yourself about? Why?

❑ **Create a basic character inventory.** Include the following details:

  • Full actual name

  • Nickname/diminutives/terms of endearment

  • Personal history (family and backstory)

- Physical appearance (height, weight, age, looks, and clothes)

- Personality (both the good and the bad)

- IQ and schooling

- Talents, skills, and gifts

- Shortcomings and flaws

- Mannerisms and tics (sayings, habits under stress, and special personal objects)

- Main goal

- Secondary goal(s)

- Fears

- Secrets

❏ **Make an inventory of flaws.** A person's flaws make them distinctive and interesting to a reader. Make a list of the main three flaws the characters in your memoir have. Does your manuscript acknowledge and share those flaws with the reader, or do you hide those out of respect, fear, or some other reason?

Chapter 9

Making the Most of Dialogue

*W*hen people talk about "voice" in regards to writing, they mean one of two things:

- ✔ **Dialogue:** The actual words that come from a speaker's mouth and typically occur within quotation marks, such as, "Hey! Can anyone hear my voice?"

- ✔ **The voice of the narrator:** The "voice" of the entire book, which is more or less everything else on the page. Check out Chapter 10 that discusses the author's voice.

These two things comprise a lot of a memoir's power. If the dialogue and the narrative voice aren't working, the book simply isn't working, no matter how great your story is.

In this chapter, I deal exclusively with everything that comes from a character's mouth one way or another. This chapter gets into the nitty-gritty about all the related elements regarding dialogue and how you can use them to your advantage.

Managing Memoir Dialogue Differently than Novel Dialogue

A memoirist writes a good memoir only by utilizing the storytelling techniques a novelist has. But the obligation to tell the truth has to come before anything else. Dialogue creation can be an issue for a memoir writer. Unless you're writing solely about events that are fresh in your mind, you'll have to ask yourself: How much do I trust my memory? Is it okay to let my mother speak on the page because I remember her usual expressions and ways of speaking even if I don't remember an actual conversation? How do memoirists like Mary Karr, Frank McCourt, and Cheryl Strayed who all create such great dialogue handle these issues?

You can't just skip dialogue because you can't remember every single word said to you by your father 30 years ago. Dialogue creates a real sense of the here and now readers expect with any good book. And paraphrasing everything distances readers and gets boring quickly You can tackle these unique issues related to dialogue use in a memoir in the following ways:

✔ **As a historical transcription:** Readers come at memoir dialogue — and memoirs themselves, to a degree — with the idea that it's true, as in historical document, court-stenographer accurate. Although it's crazy, it's a reality memoir writers have to accept. You're not the only one struggling to work through the tricky issue of using dialogue. Even accomplished memoirists like Anna Quindlen have the same problem, as she talks about quite powerfully in her May 1997 article from *The New York Times Review of Books* entitled "How Dark? How Stormy?" All you can do is be faithful to your story and your sense of the truth. It's how the other memoirists manage it. It's how you'll ultimately have to manage it too.

✔ **As the truth:** How can you handle ages-old arguments, discussions, or chit-chat, knowing memory is hard to rely on? Many memoir writing how-to books gloss over this very challenge because the answer can feel quite unsatisfying. You do the best you can.

The dialogue transcribed right out of real life doesn't make good reading on the page. You can feel entitled to minor tweaking of dialogue, such that it works better in the story. What's the distinction between an acceptable amount of tweaking and too much of it? If the essence of what was said remains faithful, you're okay. If you start putting words into peoples' mouths that changes the meaning of what's being said, that's where problems arise.

Chapter 8 provides some exercises that may help you a lot with creating believable, honest dialogue. If you take the time to really get to know your characters, you'll know the type of response they'll give in most any situation. You'll also know their speaking habits, their inflections, and their favorite expressions. Add in your own memory to that and you're much more likely to remain truthful. The writing exercises at the end of this chapter, too, also help you get a handle on making dialogue work properly in a memoir.

You can also *paraphrase,* meaning to put the dialogue in your own words but without using quotes. Doing so clearly communicates that the dialogue isn't verbatim. Paraphrased material is nowhere near as specific or interesting as directly quoted material, but if your manuscript has exchanges that you feel especially uncomfortable recreating, you always have this option.

Recognizing What Good Dialogue Should Do for Your Manuscript

Dialogue has a number of important functions in a story, be it a movie script, fiction, or nonfiction, including a memoir. It entices a reader to be a participant in the story. It informs readers what characters say while simultaneously suggesting what they don't.

Well-written dialogue is nearly invisible. It doesn't draw attention to itself. It does what it has to do while propelling the readers forward with the narrative spell intact. Clunky dialogue (often called *wooden dialogue* or *writers with a tin ear*) stops the reader cold, breaking the spell of the story. The reader ends up asking "Has this writer ever listened to human beings before?" just before irritatingly turning the page on the story forever.

Good dialogue also has its own pacing. It's rarely like a ping-pong ball, bouncing from speaker A to speaker B equally. A *Seinfeld*-style rapid-fire comedy may have ping-pong dialogue, but a memoir unlikely doesn't. Be comfortable with awkwardness and silence.

Read the following sections to see what you can expect your dialogue to do and do well. If your dialogue doesn't do this, summarize it, paraphrase it, or skip to only the parts that manage to do this. Dialogue isn't just window-dressing — it has to justify its inclusion by doing more that just capturing words people said.

Providing action

Action is anything that physically happens in a story. Most people enjoy action in books and movies because it's exciting. Action is why actors like Tom Cruise and Jason Statham make millions and authors like Tom Clancy and Vince Flynn sell books by the truckload. Action, though, isn't just machine guns firing and karate kicks — it's also making and serving a Thanksgiving feast, having a serious head-to-head bowling match with your sister, and someone fixing a broken car radiator. Action is what happens when the main character isn't sitting around thinking or when the author has stopped the story to describe a lot of things (see Chapter 7 for more on how to handle description while still creating engaging scenes).

To use dialogue as action, think about the visuals that accompany what's being said. Rather than show all the details of a brotherly scuffle, you can simply use dialogue as this example does:

> "Stop poking me."
>
> "I wasn't — Ouch! Now you're the one poking."
>
> "Yeah, right. Ouch! Mom! Aww!"
>
> Mom arrived, eyes drawn. "The next person to poke anyone gets a crack from the dishtowel." She fired a warning shot over our heads. Serious stuff.

If this dialogue clearly communicates the action that's accompanying, then dialogue is pulling double duty, which is good stuff. Some other areas beyond brotherly scuffles where what's actually said between the quotation marks can persuasively show a reader action include lovemaking, bullying, teaching, dancing, and exercising.

For instance, check out this bit of text:

> I dodged the satellite TV dish as I opened fire on the rooftop. The black-masked intruder took one in the shoulder. It wasn't enough to stop him. He threw a gleaming knife that tumbled end-over-end at me.

You want to read on to see what's going to happen. You can't deliver your entire book in chunks of descriptive prose like this. For variety's sake, you can use dialogue to keep the action cooking, too.

Here's how. Even though readers are drawn to two men in a bar fight or a rooftop shootout, they're equally (or more) drawn to a tense argument. It allows them to witness the conflict of two opposed minds, not just two opposed bodies. Make sense? Consider this action:

> James closed in on me. "I always knew you loathed me," James said, "but to frame me for your wife's murder?"
>
> "Take your hand off me," I said. People from the nearby desks were starting to stare.
>
> James's eyes raged. I realized I'd framed the wrong man. Who knew that this mild-mannered playboy had iron in him?

James didn't release his crushing grip on my hand. He leaned in close to the me and whispered words that I'd remember for the rest of my life. "I'm not going to the police. Know why? Because jail is too good for you. I'm going to take my time and enjoy destroying your world, piece by rotten piece. All of it. Everything you have and everything you love."

A heated moment like this can give your readers goose bumps. It's bubbling with emotion and the threat of violence is omnipresent. The most powerful thing, however, is the depths of James's fury and need for revenge against the narrator; readers can glimpse his soul and it's righteous, yet dark as a category 5 hurricane. Know what I mean? You can watch any Hollywood blockbuster, and you're likely to see a couple of gunfights. A scene like this is much rarer and in many ways, much more memorable.

For some great examples of dialogue as action, visit

✔ *Lucking Out: My Life Getting Down and Semi-dirty in Seventies New York* by James Wolcott (Anchor)

✔ *Wasted: A Memoir of Anorexia and Bulimia* by Marya Hornbacher (Harper Perennial)

Advancing plot

A dialogue should escalate the plot. Dialogue moves things forward and ups the ante of what's at stake. It reveals things that through cause and effect advance the plot.

Banter has no escalation, no build, and that's precisely why it has no place in your memoir. Banter is like riding an exercise bike — no fun, and you never go anywhere. Dialogue is not banter.

To advance plot through dialogue, choose to include verbal exchanges where people are meaningfully discussing the main story tension. Even if clear advancements aren't made in terms of pure plot, the context of knowing more about how plot matters can help readers. In that way, it advances plot. It expands on what readers know about plot.

Here's a short example of how dialogue can advance the plot in a hypothetical memoir about adoption.

I sipped at the steaming oolong.

"What?" Brenda finally said.

I didn't answer.

"C'mon."

I took another sip, then said, "I'll just never know who I am unless I do this."

"Do you mean it this time? I refuse to get worked up if you're just going to drop this again. I don't have that kind of—"

"I mean it," I said, realizing it for the first time.

And here's how well-used dialogue can advance plot in a very different type of situation.

"I don't know why you just can't be nice to him," Theresa said. She pedaled harder as the exercise bike moved into mountain climb mode.

I took a long drink from her bottle. I'd stopped pedaling awhile back.

"I *am* nice to him."

"Oh, come off it. You turned him down so many times that I swear I see boot prints on his head."

I smiled.

Theresa hopped off the bike and sat on one of the benches. Who knew regaining your breath got harder the moment you turned 30? I joined her.

"Isn't he sweet as a cupcake?" Theresa said.

I said, "If you like that sort of thing."

"Gotcha."

I drained the rest of my water bottle in one long glug. I said, "Okay. I'll go with him to that thing at the marina. But God knows I don't have a clean black dress to wear."

Theresa said, "Problems, problems, problems."

Theresa wasn't as sharp as my other friends, which is why I liked her. The point about Miles being sweet was spot on. Worse, he was exactly the sort of guy I could see myself falling in love with.

Dialogue precipitated the narrator's — Janice's — realization that she could fall in love with Miles. Readers also get the bonus of learning that since Theresa recently turned 30, Janice is likely around that same important milestone age in a young woman's life too, which probably explains her reluctance to fall in love. Another bonus is that readers learn a little about Theresa (she's not terribly smart and she's probably fit — she stays on the exercise bike longer than her friend did). Readers also find out a bit about their relationship — Janice is the smarter, dominant one, and Theresa seems okay with that, or she's not smart enough to notice. Either way, that information is useful to readers.

This example is clearly a love story of some type. It may be a love story where Janice denies love for other reasons (work, duty, fun, and so forth). Or she may go head-over-heels and get married and have a house with a white picket fence and 2.5 kids. For these purposes here, all you need to see is that this dialogue exchange moves that love story farther than it had gone before. To be clear, it advanced the plot forward because she *admitted* to herself that Miles may well be the love of her life. Her next step may be admitting it aloud to someone, although not likely Miles, which comes later. The large narrative arc isn't a race. It's a slow escalation, which is what makes the payoff of the story's climax so delightful and rich.

Showing character depth and values

One of the easiest ways to reveal what characters *really* think and believe is to let them chat for a bit. Journalists know this. They turn on the recorder and then ask the interviewee a few softball questions that are easily answered. Then they ask, ask, and ask some more. Eventually, the interviewee starts feeling comfortable and lets down his guard.

Showing what your characters think and believe happens — or should happen — in your dialogue in your memoir too. People can't help but say what they really think and mean, so let them. To do so, revisit those conversations you engaged in or overhead where people really let their guard down and revealed their character. Some of the most likely venues for this type of exchange to take place are churches, funerals, weddings, birthday parties, and hospitals. After you recall those conversations, make sure to include the most pithy, trenchant moments of that dialogue so the reader, too, can witness these moments where a character is stripped to their essence. Readers love to be let in on these private, revealing times.

Doing so is much more effective than to write something like this:

> I stared out the window as the moving truck rolled to a stop. Two burly black men got out. I held my breath. When I realized that they were wearing work uniforms and were there to unload, I released it in a rush.

You can actually use dialogue to provide more depth to your characters, like this version:

> As starlight began to pepper the night sky outside, I entered the living room and poured my father some coffee. The TV blared away in the corner.
>
> "Make it the right way?" my father asked from the couch, not looking up from his paper.

"You bet."

"None of that sugar or milk you fill those six-dollar drinks with at fancy restaurants. Wussy stuff."

"There's nothing wrong with a latte."

My father snorted. "Marry a New Yorker and look what happens to you. Regular joe isn't good enough anymore."

That's revealing information. Readers know exactly how the old codger feels about this daughter-in-law (and New Yorkers), and his son (the narrator) for marrying her. They also get a sense of the disrespectful, distant relationship between father and son, although the son is trying to be a dutiful kid (he gets his father coffee, after all).

Dialogue works in a memoir the other way too, where it reveals positive values in a character. Here's an example.

"I'm here to tender my resignation," I said, slumping into the chair across from my boss.

"What on earth for?"

"I lost the Snipson account."

When Mrs. Brockmeier raised her arm, I flinched. Just a head scratch, though. Yet she had that type of ferocious reputation. No wonder she ruled a Fortune 500 company at age forty-something.

When she spoke, her voice was softer than I expected. "No one loses their job today."

"Why not?" Instantly, I regretted it.

She said, "Because it's my birthday. No one loses their job at my company on my birthday."

"Oh my God," I said, stumbling at trying to shake her hand and back out of the room at the same time, all before she changed her mind. Finally, I was behind the door and rushing for the stairs. That's when it came to me: Her birthday was six months ago. The senior officers threw her a small party just before Christmas.

Providing some relief from the wall of text syndrome

Dialogue can help give readers some reprieve from long amounts of text. Every semester, I give my students an anonymous questionnaire about reading and writing so they can feel free to answer honestly without penalty or prejudice. The No. 1 confession was they skip pages when it's wall-to-wall text. When asked why, they say the skip it because it's just description, and/or the real action occurs in the skinny parts.

White space on a page is where the most action is. White space is also less intimidating to readers. It gives them a sense of airiness, of spaciousness like an open field on a quiet, sunny afternoon in Vermont.

So try it out.

Just see how nice it works?

Give it a try.

Try this for yourself. Go get a copy of Amin Maalouf's *Origins: A Memoir* (Farrar, Straus, and Giroux) and look at the first few pages of chapter one of this 400+ page book. Or just think about the last doorstop-sized book you read. Odds are, there are plenty of sections with text that makes you think, "Jeez, maybe I'll just jump ahead to where something actually happens."

Identifying the Four Types of Dialogue

Most writers have a very limited understanding of their true options when conveying what characters say. The following sections showcase all the options and reveal how each offers benefits worth considering the next time one of your characters needs to utter words.

Summary

Summary dialogue does exactly what it says: it presents the dialogue, but only a summary of it. You never get access to the specific words that were said because it covers a lot of material fast. Summary dialogue doesn't offer much texture, but it works.

Summary dialogue is appropriate when you need to tell the reader something but the language used wasn't all that exciting or when the relevant parties said it in a terribly roundabout, reader-unfriendly way. You can also use summary when you only know the gist of the conversation. In any of those cases, you simply sum up what was said like you're writing the CliffsNotes version of it, and that's what you go with. Short, sweet, and focused will be your result.

Check out this example:

Anthony told his mother he needed to skip the party that night.

This example is about as efficient as it gets. It communicates information to the reader without burdening them with too many details — almost no details in fact. Remember to use this type of dialogue sparingly because it rarely has the level of imagery most readers prefer.

Indirect

Indirect dialogue gives the reader a sense of the words, phrases, and rhythms, although what was exactly said isn't reported verbatim. It's essentially a more involved version of summary dialogue that appears in the narrative versus inside quotation marks. Indirect dialogue is a fine choice when the reader already knows what you've covered or if you're writing an especially long conversation or windy speech. Indirect dialogue also has an effect on pace (it speeds things up whereas a lot of "he said" "she said" talking can gum up the narrative's engine and slow the story down).

Using indirect dialogue is very similar to how you create summary dialogue, except instead it's more detailed. If indirect dialogue is about an argument, the summary version may just say who was fighting, what they were fighting about, and who won. Indirect dialogue, though, may go a level deeper by giving an example or two of the types of evidence they used to argue or the style each utilized to duke it out verbally.

For an efficient example of indirect dialogue that doesn't draw out the scene more fully, try this

> Anthony burst into the room. Mom swept him into a hug and tried to coax away the tears. He burbled about how his teacher hated him, how she had it out for him, and how no one else in the class had to redo the book report.

If the exchange isn't that important, then move things along quickly via summary or indirect dialogue to get readers to what matters. Readers get the gist of the conversation and don't need a blow-by-blow account of it. For instance, if the point is that he now has to miss a cute girl's party because of the extra schoolwork, then that's what readers need sooner than later. Taking all the time to detail the exact instances of whining and complaining and calming him down will take pages. Knock it out in three lines and then take your time showing how he handles missing the party he promised everyone he'd be at. And what if he learns that instead of him, it's a classmate who gives that pretty girl her first kiss?

Direct

Direct is the most common type of dialogue. When people say "dialogue," they almost always think about this kind. It's very useful in that it's the most precise of the options; you get *exactly* what the person says. Direct is the easiest option to do (if you remember the conversation) because you're essentially taking dictation. It's more than that, though, because you may need to pare down what people actually say — cutting the umms, errs, and burps, for instance.

You should use direct dialogue in the following situations:

- ✔ When a character says something worthy of a bumper sticker
- ✔ When you want to reveal character (which won't come through in summary or indirect versions)
- ✔ When your character says something that is lovely, profound, or interesting

Each of these are appropriate times to let your characters carry the story for a bit.

Direct dialogue is wonderful. It's vivid, it reveals characters, it's colorful, and it's easy for a writer to do. Too much of it, though, can get unwieldy on the page. Experienced writers know that readers like the variety of different types of dialogue delivery. These writers also know the best way to stay in control of the text is to make the best choices with each of the story elements. Each type of dialogue brings certain pros and cons with it. Successful writers not only use each option, but they take the time to figure — through thinking it through or trial and error — the best option for each specific place in the memoir.

Read this example to show how direct dialogue can explain what your characters mean:

> I rocked in the chair, the Florida sun hot on my face. I said, "I could use a lemonade."
>
> "We're out of lemons?" asked Xenia.
>
> We rocked a bit more.
>
> "I thought we used the powder," I said.
>
> "No," said Xenia. "The Publix on Fruitville Road stopped carrying it a few months ago."
>
> "What's wrong with the Publix on Bee Ridge?"
>
> Xenia sighed. "Too many left turns to get there."
>
> "What's wrong with left turns?"

"I don't like making them, that's what's wrong with left turns."

"Nothing's wrong with a left turn," I mumbled.

"Nothing's wrong with a whack to the head either, when someone's asking for it."

Readers can hear every word the characters vocalized. As a result, readers can justifiably say a bit of disconnect exists in the relationship between these two. The narrator doesn't know much about the day-to-day workings of the house (or at least the kitchen). And Xenia is pretty darn set in her ways. She also doesn't take any guff from her man. Readers can almost hear the unspoken, "And you open your fool mouth about my left turns again, I *will* hit you!" after that last line.

Combination

Also called *intermixed* dialogue, *combination* dialogue is where the other three types (summary, indirect, and direct) are used together in the same passage. It allows you to highlight certain parts of the conversation while downplaying others without ignoring them completely.

Blending these three main types effectively can cover a lot of ground and give readers a great feel for the conversation without having to include every single word, which most readers don't need anyway. I find this method especially useful for the key scenes of each chapter. You want to let the characters get their own words in, but you also want to keep the pace brisk. This option lets both happen simultaneously.

You can switch from one type to the other in a same section of combination dialogue based on your taste. Some writers love to let characters speak their own words, which is fine. You also need to realize that there's time to skip the action ahead by de-emphasizing dialogue as indirect or summary versions do. Think about the conversation itself having a narrative arc (visit Chapters 3 and 6 for a fuller understanding of story structure and narrative arcs). Depending on what type of dialogue scene climax you're driving at, you may want to speed things up (summary or indirect) or really tease out the tension (direct) and let the reader wait for it. If you don't nail it the first time, no problem — that's why I have a chapter on revision (Chapter 15) and one on editing (Chapter 16).

Here's the combination dialogue version of poor Anthony's story from the previous sections:

Anthony listed his teacher's faults — too pushy, too hard of a grader, too unfair with assignments. "And she's about as friendly as a cobra," he said. When Mom asked if he had anything more to say about Mrs. Kenton, he brought out a sheet of paper with writing up and down both sides and began reading.

Managing the Mechanics

Maybe quotation marks are spooky, but for whatever the reason, writers who are perfectly competent in other aspects of the book fall apart when handling the grammar and punctuation and formatting of dialogue. If you fall into this group of writers, this section can help get all those hard-to-digest issues under control. For the rest of you, it's a nice refresher.

Using commas correctly

Commas go wrong in two main ways. Here are the two ways and how you can use them correctly.

Tagging dialogue

Some writers incorrectly use commas with *dialogue tags,* which are those phrases used to establish who is the one speaking. The most simple form of this is

John said, "Get lost, pal."

Though dialogue tags can also be more richly described, as in

"I hate green beans!" snarled the lady who wore the yellow pinstripe jumpsuit.

In each case, the dialogue is "tagged" with the information a reader needs — who said these things. Just as a dog tag contains the important information about a soldier whose neck it hangs on, so too does a dialogue tag convey important information about the dialogue itself.

Using the comma in sentences with dialogue

Some writers misuse commas in the dialogue sentences. Just as you do with text in other parts of a memoir, you need a comma with every direct address. You also need them with a conjunction (but, for, nor, so, or yet, for instance) to connect a pair of independent clauses. And you also need a comma at the end of a sentence of dialogue if a dialogue tag follows it. These rules are easier to see in operation than in the abstract, so read on for examples.

The following are the ways to correctly use commas in dialogue and examples for each.

- ✔ **Place a single comma inside the second set of quotation marks.** "I wish I understood the rules of the comma better," said Gregory.

- ✔ **Set the direct address of a person off by commas.** "Laura, will you come help lift this chair?" asked George.

  "I have to confess, Jimbo, that I hate your name."

- ✔ **Use a comma either before or after the word when directly addressing someone.** Tad said, "The last thing I want to do is hurt you, Heather."

Commas really aren't a big grammar thing. To ignore them though can create confusion, and confusion can lead to reader frustration. Use this section to make sure you don't trip up with them when writing dialogue.

Verifying quotation marks

Part of the confusion about using quotation marks is that you see them misused all the time online and in print, so when you need to use them, you remember those incorrect cases as often as correct examples. Another reason it's confusing is that people from Great Britain utilize a rule that makes more sense than the American rule does. For them, end punctuation goes at the very end of a sentence, no matter what.

A sample using British English rules:

Sir James said, "I think the ghost went that way".

The American English version:

Sir James said, "I think the ghost went that way."

Thankfully the Brits and Americans agree on a few things, such as a semicolon and colon don't belong inside a quotation. Unlike a comma, both don't feel right about sticking one of these high-powered grammatical markers inside quotation marks unless it was there to begin with.

Here is a correct example for both British and American English:

My roommate and I have three meanings for "commitment": a desire to raise a family, trying not to get smacked for eyeballing other girls when on a date, and regularly updating my Twitter page.

Drafting Speech that Sounds Real versus Real Speech

What you're going for with dialogue is *verisimilitude*. It's a fancy German word that means "lifelike" or "realistic," which isn't the same as "real," and that's a crucial point. You want what's on the page to seem real, not be a literal transcription of what comes out of peoples' mouths.

This section can offer advice on how to make dialogue more efficient and effective than what you do in real life through speaking. Because dialogue is a big part of what makes scenes work, I provide plenty of examples here to really show the way.

Working in sentence fragments

Sentence fragments (also known as incomplete sentences) can be a lovely change of pace from regular dialogue. They create a nice change of pace. They can also add a sense of urgency or importance. Above all, they do a good job of replicating how real people speak because real people don't always use full sentences.

Do keep the option for using a pithy sentence fragment or two around for those key moments where you want the dialogue to sing. Like any other writing technique, don't overuse it or it might become gimmicky.

Some examples include

- ✔ "The heck you talking about?"
- ✔ "You copacetic?"
- ✔ "Not a beautiful woman."
- ✔ "Ugh. Just ugh."

Using umm, errr, and huh

Although having speech that sounds real is great, real speech is full of verbal tics and nonsense. When writing dialogue, don't feel like you need to include it. Take out all those "umms" and "errs" and "huhs" and your dialogue will read more smoothly.

Here's an example to show how it detracts from the sense of the passage.

"Hey, John? I was thinking . . . ummm . . . maybe we should . . . err . . . you know . . . give that new pizza place a try."

And here's a revision without the verbal tics:

> "Hey, John? I was thinking we should give that new pizza place a try."

The second example sounds better to my ear. If the wishy-washiness isn't a fundamental and important character trait but rather just verbal tics, cut it.

Using can't or cannot

The choice between "can't" and "cannot" seems like a minor point, but it matters. There's a world of difference between someone who says, "I cannot let you in!" and "I can't let you in." Do you hear the difference? A lot of what makes dialogue "right" or "wrong" is how it passes (or doesn't pass) the ear test. When writing, figure out what sounds right and what clangs like a dented cowbell. The difference is that the character who doesn't use contractions sounds like the Queen of England, or at least a very educated and proper person, perhaps even an intellectual snob. The other way sounds like 98 percent of Americans do.

Most people speak in contractions. Even if the rest of your narrative is relatively formal, what appears in quotation marks shouldn't be, unless, that is, you have a very specific type of character. Think of the uppity professor who says, "I will not be accountable for the acquiescence of the hoi polloi who cannot think for themselves." Yeah, I buy it for that bozo. He doesn't use contractions. Me? I don't leave home without them.

Writing Less Is More

Americans love big things — big sandwiches, big cars, big sports stadiums. Many American writers also like big dialogue passages. When you're writing your memoir, you should resist the urge to fill page after page with talk-talk-talk-talk-talk.

Think of that person in your life who gabs nonstop. You know who I mean? Imagine spending a whole afternoon with him. That's what it can be like if you have too much dialogue in your memoir.

Some writing teachers and coaches suggest that you should never have more dialogue in one place than your index finger is long. So hold your index finger up against a single-spaced page of text and see if the dialogue runs farther than your finger will stretch. If it does, see if all the dialogue really needs to be there, or if you can trim some. (I call this a good "rule of thumb," but that doesn't seem exactly right, so consider it a good rule of finger.)

These sections provide more insight on how you can write dialogue with care by paying close attention to meaning, silence, and causal relationships. Beginning writers tend to overlook them to the detriment of their memoirs.

Avoiding oh-so-empty vacuous speech

All people are lazy speakers. In fact, that's where the word "vacuous" enters the equation. It means "empty" and "purposeless." When you're writing dialogue, make sure you steer clear of including any pointless chatter where nothing happens.

Here are some examples. How often have you heard some variation on the following in real life?

"S'up, Dan."

"S'up."

"What'cha doing?"

"Nothing. You?"

"Not much."

"Later."

"Yep."

This kind of exchange may feel familiar and true to your own experiences. However, give this type of idle chit-chat to readers and you'll squash any interest they have in moving farther into the book. It's a signal that the writer doesn't know what to focus on and what to ignore. Don't include this type of dialogue exchange in your memoir.

The need for silence

Want to understand the power of silence? Ask a musician. The crescendos, the fortissimos, the allegro moments all have power and energy. But the power of a tactical moment of quiet can be deafening. When writing dialogue, sometimes a no response — silence — is incredibly potent and meaningful. Use silence in key moments for a big effect. Find opportunities to lower the boom in dialogue — just do it quietly.

Here's an example of a well-used moment of silence in a dialogue exchange.

"Jennifer, you're driving me crazy," Mom said. "Running around with boys at all hours of the night, sneaking out? It's too much. Too much!"

"Just keep your pants on," Dad said.

Mom snorted. "I'm not the one you should be worried is keeping their pants on or not."

"Don't talk about my daughter like that."

"Your daughter? Are you trying to say that you have a uterus, that you spent nine months waddling around like an orca with feet?"

"I'm just saying give the poor girl a chance to speak."

"Okay, okay," Mom said, turning to me. "Speak."

"Woof," I said.

"Oh, very nice. You clearly learn your manners from your father."

"Don't blame me!" Dad said.

"Why not? It's your fault that —"

"*Stop it!*" I yelled.

My parents looked at each other. They looked at me.

"The two of you don't know anything about anything. And you certainly don't know anything about me." I had my hands on my hips now, staring my two parents down. "For one thing, I'm not a virgin. I haven't been since I was fifteen."

No one spoke. Dad had a kind of alabaster sheen to his freshly shaven face. Mom looked as if she just swallowed a lobster, carapace, claws, tail, and all. I smirked. Then I gave a little curtsey and left to go sleep at a friend's house. Amanda, maybe. Or Caitlin. It didn't matter. Anywhere was better than home.

Did you catch the silences? This passage actually has two — one was Jennifer's nonparticipation in the back-and-forth between the parents and where she floored her parents with the revelation that she was sleeping with boys. That silence was more potent than if her parents had started screaming at her. That silence said they were dumbfounded, literally speechless. That's far more powerful than a screaming match, isn't it?

Questioning but not answering

Another way to make dialogue sound real is to mimic how people don't always have a linear or cause-effect conversation in real life. In your memoir, as in the real world, Q&A doesn't always mean a question followed by an answer. Sometimes that non-answer is more revealing than what one expected to come.

For instance:

"What's going on?"

"Good."

(A different throwaway answer, but to the wrong question. The proper answer was "Nothing," or the question should've been, "How are you?" But that's not the way things work, is it?)

Or try this one:

"What are you crazy? No one goes into that water without a wetsuit."

"I'm perfectly fine."

"What were you thinking?"

"I'm good. Really."

Considering Accents and Dialect

In an effort to accurately portray the speech of your characters — which you've no doubt heard in real life plenty of times — you may feel inclined to capture their speech with unusual punctuation and spellings. These sections explain your options with accents and dialect that can help and which are more likely to help than hinder.

Avoiding accents: Righty-o, Guv'nor!

Even if you have a friend who's fresh off the boat from merry old England and speaks like he's ripped from the dusty pages of a Dickens novel, the best option is to treat the character like you'd season a pot roast — a dash of this, a pinch of that. If you drop an occasional "lorry" or "flat" into the conversation, those subtle nudges will remind readers that your character has a British accent without hitting them over the head and potentially distracting your readers.

Furthermore, letting your character mention the accent and direct readers' attention to it that way is loads more effective than writing something and hoping readers can puzzle it together.

Remember those old WWII movies that have Germans speaking English? The same trick works there. Toss in a "bitte" and "Entschuldigung" now and then and readers are all on the same page. It's "German," but without subtitles or the reader bothering to learn German to figure it out.

Staying away from phonetic spellings

Resist the urge to use a lot of phonetic spellings. Although it may make sense to try to clearly demonstrate to a reader just how your Grandpappy Slim said

"Wellya dun lit up da barn wit yous stoopidutee," doing so is more likely to cause more problems than it's worth. You may also have claims of racism or elitism leveled at you, too.

The reason you may feel a need to use phonetic spellings is to acknowledge dialect, which is a particular variation on a language used by a group of people that shares geography, socioeconomic factors, and/or belief systems. Even though some authors like Mark Twain used it in *The Adventures of Huckleberry Finn,* using phonetic spelling is distracting. You're writing your book so people read it. If they can't figure out what your characters are saying, they'll more than likely put it down. I'd rather have my readers be thinking about deeper meanings of the book than scrutinizing dialogue for the sentence-level sense of it.

Most readers prefer a subtler approach to dialect such as syntax and idioms, which I discuss in the next section. If you absolutely have to have your Bostonian say "cawn" instead of "corn," then by God do it. Just use it sparingly.

Using idiosyncratic expressions

Idiosyncratic expressions are those strange ways that certain people have of saying things. You can use them in your dialogue because they help your readers differentiate one character from another. They also help give each character a distinctive voice that comes from his unique way of seeing the world.

For example, if my grandmother got ticked that you couldn't locate her heart medicine fast enough, she might say, "You're so blind that you couldn't whack a pig in the ass with a banjo!" (For those of you who didn't grow up on farms, pig's asses are large, as are banjos.)

Think about the truly memorable sayings the people around you have offered. If you can't remember, ask others for their favorite memories, expressions, and sayings. Odds are, you'll find that most people have about a half-dozen things that are their pet sayings. Eavesdrop on my family, and you'll gather this collection before long:

✔ Time to get cracking.

✔ Does that suit your fancy?

✔ You've done gone lost the whole shooting match.

✔ Onwards and upwards.

Ask your family about yours, and you'll have a whole different list to work from, even if you grew up outside Chicago and studied English, music, and philosophy as I did. Language reveals who people are and were, and it's always so much more than people's background and DNA. Let those curious, weird, or funny ways the people in your world have of speaking fill your pages. Your readers will appreciate it.

Being Aware Where Dialogue Goes Awry

Because dialogue has the potential to be so useful, writers tend to have a lot of it in a book. Yet if you're not careful, it can go wrong. Really wrong. Here are a few of the most common pitfalls with dialogue that can leave readers dissatisfied, confused, skipping pages, or shutting the book for good. Keep track of these mistakes so you can avoid using them in your dialogue.

Talking heads

Sometimes, dialogue just flies at you out of nowhere, with no context or clear indication of who or what is happening. It's disconcerting for a reader to encounter. Writers have struggled with the balance of dialogue versus non-dialogue forever. Don't just add in an action or image just for the sake of doing so. Make each of them count.

For example, check out this bad example:

> "I can't believe you did that."
>
> "Did what?"
>
> "Did *that* to him."
>
> "He deserved it."
>
> "Oh yeah?"
>
> "Absolutely."
>
> "Well maybe this will change your mind."
>
> "Don't tell me . . ."
>
> "Too late."

This dialogue is very confusing. It's the sort of thing I see from student writers who want to start their story off with dialogue. There's nothing wrong with that impulse, but without a scene or visuals or any kind of situation, it's just two floating heads in the vacuum of space. Are they talking about murder? Feeding a dog chocolate muffins? Firing a second chair trombonist for being an alcoholic? Are these even humans or perhaps just talking chipmunks? Or aliens? Or paramecia? Sentient LEGOs?

Readers won't know what's going on unless you cough up a little context. If you don't set up the speakers at first with a "said Yosef" or two, they'll be lost, and then they'll stop reading.

Check out this revised version:

> "I can't believe you did that," I said as we zoomed along I-75 toward Key West. We passed the thirty-third McDonald's we'd seen that day. I knew — I'd been counting. Ever since I promised myself I'd get under 250 pounds, I kept track of every fast food restaurant I didn't go into.
>
> "Did what?" Beckyann said.
>
> I snorted and went back to nibbling on a rice cake. "Did *that* to him. Pointed out his bad math in front of the class."
>
> Beckyann shrugged. "He deserved it."
>
> "Oh yeah?"
>
> "Absolutely."
>
> We drove for awhile, passing through the traffic of Fort Myers. I eyed the Arby's off the highway the way a cheetah eyes a gazelle.
>
> Finally, I said, "Well maybe this will change your mind." Then I handed Beckyann the hardcover book I had on the back seat.
>
> She eyed the words "New York Times #1 bestseller." And it was written by *him*. Her ex. The jerkiest, good-for-nothing professor in the entire English department. "Don't tell me . . ."
>
> I offered her a weak smile. "Too late. He's rich and famous."

This version gives the appropriate context for the dialogue to be meaningful. Without it, the situation conveys no specific image to a reader, and it's confusing — both aren't good choices for writing your memoir. Remember that dialogue isn't just dialogue and dialogue tags. It has a lot more going on, as you can see in this example. Keep up the action, the visuals, and the plot.

Getting caught up in the "said" dilemma

After writing a few pages of dialogue, writers start to worry: Am I repeating "said" too much? On one hand, repeating any single word too much is generally a poor idea. However, you want to stick with "said," and when it's a question, use "asked." That's going to suit readers for 96.8 percent of the time.

"Said"" is a magical little word. It's accurate, but best of all, readers read right past it like it's not even there. It's almost invisible. Toss an "enjoined Ernie" and it's anything *but* invisible.

If you don't stick to said, it leads to an even worse outcome as you spend too much time in a thesaurus finding synonyms for "said," which leads to:

> "I love you," Barbara cooed.
>
> Nathan purred, "I love you too, sugar."
>
> The doorbell rang. Nathan went to answer it. "Who is it?" he barked.
>
> "It's your damn brother. Open the door!" growled a voice from outside.
>
> "Open it," dissuaded Barbara, "and I'll beat you silly with my shoe."

Pretending to be dialogue

As authors, you know more about the story than the reader does. Your impulse to quickly get that information to them so they can understand the context and the complexity of things can lead you to poor decisions. Oftentimes authors bury important information-giving exposition in dialogue. Make sure you don't fall victim to this pitfall. Here's what it looks like:

> "Why Bentley, though we've been married for twenty-two years and have survived a hurricane, a robbery, and your scare with colon cancer six months ago, I'm not sure I'm in love with you any longer," I said.
>
> Bentley put down his toast and gazed into my eyes. "I almost left you once for that topless waiter in Daytona back when you were in the hospital while your father recovered from hip surgery, but it would've been a mistake. I am in love with you, Doris. Completely. Even if your father-in-law dislikes you enough to write me out of his will."

Nobody would dump facts like Doris and Bentley did in an everyday conversation. Think about your own life. How often do you summon the past like this in regular conversations? Unless you live in an extremely strange world populated by forgetful people who need to be reminded of events they lived through, not very often.

Worse, what should be a crucial turning point for their relationship — which could go either way, breakup or not — turns into a dossier of the past two decades of their life. It defuses any emotional impact. The result is artificial-sounding dialogue that not even my Shih Tzu, Ladybug, would believe.

Killing readers with the name game

Although clarity is a good thing, dialogue tags and common sense go a long way toward making meaning for a reader. Some writers, though, end up with name overkill. They bludgeon readers with names in ways that don't happen in real life.

In real life, how often do you call your spouse or partner, your friends, or your family members by name? You don't need to at all in your memoir. Set it up with a pair of dialogue tags and you're off. Trust me — readers can keep track of a two-person conversation that's often little more than a back and forth. Do it right, and you can manage a three-person conversation with nearly no speaker attribution, too. Here's an example:

> "Hello, Bill," she said.
>
> He said, "Hey there, Jane."
>
> "I've been thinking, Bill, that while your expertise might be in selling commercial real estate, you surely could help me sell my vacation home in Jacksonville."
>
> "Why, Jane, I bet I could," Bill said.
>
> "Thanks, Bill. I need to get out of that thing. The extra mortgage is killing me."
>
> "You got it, Jane. Anytime."

Other than that the scene is decidedly dull, the big problem is the sheer volume of names.

Writing Exercises to Help Your Dialogue

As you can gather from the range of issues covered in this chapter, dialogue isn't something to just be lazy about. For some writers, it's the hardest part of writing. The following writing exercises can help make dialogue one of your strengths, no matter what your relationship with writing dialogue is today.

❑ **Sit in a public place — a busy pizza parlor, a bus station, or shopping mall bench — and listen to the conversations around you.** Yes, I give you permission to eavesdrop. Record as accurately as possible a few exchanges of actual, real-world dialogue. Then go back and look at them again. How well does that transcript of conversation read? (More than likely, it's boring, slow, and meandering.) How may you better render these exchanges in writing? What type of choices would you need to make?

❑ **Revisit an existing scene from your memoir manuscript that includes a lot of dialogue.** However you chose to handle it, change the type of dialogue (direct, indirect, or summary). How does it change the pace of the scene? The meaning? Try a combination dialogue approach, where you use all three of your main options. What happens to the text now? Remember that you're in control of the dialogue at all times. Make good choices for the book as a whole and the scene in particular. Make the words sing.

Chapter 10

Realizing the Power of Voice

*V*oice can be a powerful element of any story. I'm not talking about the type of voice that happens in dialogue, but rather the writing itself. In essence, voice is the accumulation of words throughout the entire book and the lingering tonalities of a particular authorial voice that's distinctive from any other. It's you, your personality, your unique take on life, your universe.

I may have called this chapter "What we talk about when we talk about voice," because that's what I cover here — the makeup of the narrative element of voice. As you read this chapter, you can discover one of the great surprises of voice is that the more effortless and natural voice seems on the page, the more care and planning went into creating it. Don't assume that the voice that emerges when you start page one of your first draft is the best voice for your piece. Trial and error can help make a better match.

Grasping Voice: Your Manuscript's Soul

Although some writers refer to voice as *writing style, style,* or *narrative voice, voice* is more than just how you put the adjectives and pronouns and periods on the page. Voice also encompasses belief, desire, passion, and theme. To put your voice on the page is to be profoundly exposed, which is why so many writers avoid giving 100 percent of themselves into voice. What they don't recognize is that voice gives your manuscript substance, depth, and soul.

Think of voice in another way: Consider your favorite singer. Have you ever heard someone else do a cover version of one of his or her hits? Everything sounds more or less the same — the chorus, the music, the words, the instrumentation. But it somehow isn't ever as good as the real thing, is it? It may not be bad, exactly, but it's certainly . . . different.

That's what I mean when I talk about voice in writing. Take the same general characters, plot, setting, story, and conflicts of a piece that a lesser writer handles choppily, and a talented writer can make it sing. And no two talented writers can make it sing in exactly the same way.

Voice is a higher order skill in writing. Unfortunately it doesn't come easily. If thinking about or working with voice is challenging, that's fine. Do the best you can with it after reading this chapter and then move on. Some professional writers even have a difficult time talking about, thinking about, and working with voice. The following sections give you the ins and outs of voice so you can then start to discover how to master voice in your manuscript.

Seeing how voice affects your manuscript

Breaking down voice and then talking and thinking about it is important because voice is a fairly comprehensive element that affects so many other parts of your book. From the way you manage dialogue to the way you create atmosphere to the way you utilize point of view, your voice will come through. To put it another way, your voice is largely what makes your manuscript unique — no other writer will (or should) sound the same even when handling the same characters, conflict, and plot.

Before getting too detailed, allow me to make an important point. Every story is a *construct*. In other words, it's fake and not real, which means it's not happening right in front of you like watching a car crash, love story, or physical triumph. Although your manuscript details real parts of your life (and by its very definition is truthful), the pages themselves are silent. Voice is one of the ways that your story comes alive on the page. A piece without a strong voice will feel generic, the story wooden, and the characters bland.

How you deliver the story: Whispering in the reader's ear

The voice is the implied author who is telling the story to the reader. It's *implied* because the author isn't physically present (even when listening to the audio version), yet the author's voice is so powerful that the reader (or listener) *feels* like the author is right there, whispering the story into his or her ear. In the reader's mind, he or she perceives the implied author is the author, which is the opposite of journalism or textbook writing, which quite purposefully often feels robotic and authorless.

If you were to write three books, you may construct (remember that voice is something you consciously create) three different narrative voices, each appropriate to that story. Do you have the following people in your life?

- ✔ The know-it-all kid
- ✔ The hypochondriacal aunt
- ✔ The anti-government neighbor
- ✔ The bossy single mother
- ✔ The weepy ex-girlfriend

Imagine each of them telling your story. How would they play up, play down, edit, or embellish? What words would they use to describe you, your actions, your friends, your disasters? Which would be the funniest? The most serious?

Part of your voice is the manner in which you deliver the story. Just because you are you doesn't mean you're limited by the first method you tried to tell your story. The illusion of the story-reading experience (not the actual happenings of the book) is fake after all, so try a few different voices to see which one works best. Reach deep into your own personality and let it pour forth onto the page, uniquely you and uniquely yours.

You may resist this idea, saying something like "But I'm me! How can I be anything but me when I let out my voice?" Think about the many facets of you. You're funny. You're foolish. You're smart. You're bone-headed (at times). You're romantic. You're stodgy. Think of all the contradictory mishmash that makes up a person. You can highlight any one of those elements through your narrative voice. For instance, if the ultra-serious you isn't working, unleash your snarky side. You have it in you. If that doesn't work, you can get dreamy, wild, and free. You aren't being dishonest; you're simply isolating the best parts of your multifaceted personhood to most effectively deliver the stories that will make up your memoir.

Some people have the mistaken idea that voice is something they have or don't have. I am here to tell you that everyone already has voice. No matter how good yours is or not, you can develop your voice further after you know where to put the effort.

If the idea of voice interests you beyond what this chapter covers, check out a few entire books that are devoted to the subject:

- ✔ Thaisa Frank's and Dorothy Wall's *Finding Your Writer's Voice: A Guide to Creative Fiction* (St. Martin's Griffin)
- ✔ Les Edgerton's *Finding Your Voice: How to Put Personality in Your Writing* (Writer's Digest Books)
- ✔ Ben Yagoda's *The Sound on the Page: Great Writers Talk about Style and Voice in Writing* (Harper Perennial)

Being a Minimalist versus Maximalist

Some of a voice's power emerges from the quantity of words or the sheer density of words on the page. The two extremes are a minimalist and a maximalist.

- ✔ *Minimalist* writers use words like they have to pay for each one — they're amazingly economical. They avoid adverbs and ask the reader to draw a lot from the context. It's a challenging way to go because the writer has to know exactly how much to leave out. Take out any more than that and you're losing readers.

- ✔ *Maximalist* writers are at the other extreme. This type of writer celebrates richness and fullness by including a great level of detail throughout the text. It often leads to big, big books like Charles Sydney Frost's memoir, *Once a Patricia* (Vanwell Publishing), which is a whopping 564 pages. Other writers who are often called maximalists include Thomas Pynchon and John Barth.

Overall book length — and the sheer amount of words you give to handling the many tasks of the narrative — is your choice. Make sure that you consider your options, and go with the choice that best suits you and your story.

For instance, a minimalist goes for the diet plate and a maximalist believes in the six-course buffet approach. He used 50 words for what he could say in ten.

The following shows a hypothetical example of a minimalist and the way a maximalist may rewrite the same passage:

Minimalist: He sat and drank the beer. The beer was cold. And good.

Maximalist: George Winderson eased into the hard-backed, weathered chair that, if imagination and memory could collide, would tell a world of tales about this gin joint beside the gleaming blue face of the Atlantic Ocean. There, like a flame swirling up from the cold eternity of darkness, was a cold tankard of Red Eye.

At times you may want to purposefully alter your minimalist or maximalist approach for a desired effect. Be on the lookout for those opportunities. Just like a changeup pitch is sometimes the right choice in a baseball game, so too is this type of change in your writing in certain situations.

For action-packed scenes, a minimalist approach typically keeps things moving along swiftly, which adds to the reader's excitement. For scenes that are thick with atmosphere (think about the first page of Edgar Allan Poe's short story "The Fall of the House of Usher"), I recommend the maximalist approach. Yet feel free to use either technique whenever you feel it's appropriate for the page you're working on. Let the material itself always dictate your creative choices.

Using Tone

Tone is one of those tricky things that high school English teachers badger you about but most students never quite understand. *Tone* basically is the author's attitude toward the work. The tone may be grave, intimate, amused, ironic, formal, or condescending, for example. Every piece of writing has tone, even if the tone is working under the surface. You want to make the most of the tone with your memoir because tone can help create reader interest, empathy, and meaning. Sounds like a couple of good outcomes, no?

A few centuries ago, the writer Samuel Taylor Coleridge wrote about "the willing suspension of disbelief." He meant that a reader *knows* every story is a construct, but he's willing to disbelieve it (overlook it) in order to have a grand time enjoying a story. Unfortunately, most readers aren't that willing to disbelieve anymore. So how does a writer convince them to willingly enter the world of the story and "buy in" to it? Tone can do it.

Or have you ever gone to a fast food joint and had a bored pimply teen who mumbles and looks bored help you? The experience isn't as enjoyable, even if the food is fine, right? The same is true of some writing. Some writers don't believe in their own work. Adjusting the tone, however, can change that.

If you go with whatever voice (and tone) you dreamed up first, you may not have the necessary enthusiasm for your own story. Like the writers of ancient literature, you can remain oblivious to the idea of tone even though it's clearly there. Yet if you carefully examine what you have, then you can just tweak it a little as needed, then disinterest can suddenly become infectious interest. In other words, you know tone isn't working if the reader's (or Heaven forbid, the author's!) attention is wandering during a specific part of the story.

These sections investigate a few specific ways you can tackle tone in your memoir.

Reveal details

If you stop to consider that atmosphere is related to tone (see Chapter 7 for good information on atmosphere), you realize that you can create both with apt, careful details and descriptions. The key with adding details is not to just fire off a bunch in hope that one or two hits the mark, but rather use specific, concrete ones.

Remember that important details might be more than imagery — they may communicate values or judgments, too. Ultimately, the effective use of details is part of what makes a memoir compelling and believable.

For an example of how details can make a sentence do more than just describe, identify the difference between these two sentences:

> My father's house has been vacant for three years.

> The roof of my father's empty two-story has collapsed beneath the weight of snow, as if that soulless place is trying to swallow itself once and for all.

The answer is, of course, the second one because it's rich with tone and nuance. It's easy for a reader to feel how much anger and sadness the author has about the house. The other is perhaps factual, but it's as flat as a run-over soft drink can.

Come from a different angle

Although the facts of your story aren't up for negotiation, how you choose to tell them certainly is. One way you can engage unexpectedly with the material is to select an unconventional voice to communicate that story. By that, you should consider more than one tactic for creating meaning, which includes being open to your many tonal options, too.

For example, when telling a story about an inherently depressing topic like cancer or the death of a child, rather than tell it in a depressing way, approach it from a different angle. Think about how much tone is in the breakout best-selling "kids" book *Go the F**k to Sleep* or the TV show *Dead Like Me*, which has some of the funniest grim reapers ever on page or screen. Would it sell without the same level and type of tone?

Offer an unexpected treatment of your subject and your story will stand out. For instance, it took Frank McCourt years to distance himself from his story enough to write *Angela's Ashes: A Memoir* (Scribner) without being judgmental as one may expect him to be, and rightly so!

Stay consistent

Generally speaking, you're better off being consistent with your tone throughout the entire book. Let your first sentence make a promise about the rest of the memoir, and then deliver on that promise. If you find yourself drifting from the tone you began with, revise your manuscript until you get your tone back on track.

Tone can soften a sensitive topic

Mark Twain made good use of tone in *The Adventures of Huckleberry Finn* by juxtaposing Huck's (our narrator's) keen but uneducated sense of the world with Jim the slave's actions that, at times, make him seem foolish. But Huck's clarity of perception recognizes the nobility and humanity within Jim, which would've been a difficult sell in 1880s America where the primary readership was white people who mostly witnessed slavery firsthand.

Remember, too, that the story itself is set well within the period of slavery versus after the Emancipation Proclamation and the end of the American Civil War. In short, tone made Twain's book on race relations and moral injustice palatable versus sermony.

You may get away with changing tone for an entire chapter, if appropriate, because there's a natural break between chapters, which allows for shifts in time, place, and voice. Going from being rip-roaring funny for three chapters, for instance, to solemn and morose for one chapter, to goofy for a few more is jarring. Because memoirs are usually about one core incident, a single tone typically makes the most sense.

Take responsibility

The issue of being responsible is an issue unique to memoir. Fiction is all zero stakes because it's all untrue. On the other hand, in memoir, many writers still use deflection and denial to avoid taking responsibility, and these tactics are obvious to readers who roll their eyes and shut the book. Doing it is easier said than done, I realize. Readers want to see people own up to their own stories, no matter what those stories are. Own up to your story. Own up to your life. Own up to your memoir.

Not taking responsibility in your memoir is like that unobservant talky person next to you on the plane who blabbers about how difficult it is to keep three vacation homes up and running while still having an active social life by hobnobbing with celebrities. You want to kick him. If he were to change his snooty tone to one of self-deprecation, humor, and forgiveness, you may listen a bit more intently.

Creating Irony

Irony is what happens when what you get is not what you expected — it's usually the opposite. In writing, irony is when a writer achieves that same effect on a reader through that careful use of word choice. It's that delightful incongruity. In fact, the type of irony that you use (or choose not to use) helps create voice, and having a strong voice can help your memoir be memorable. Irony can also keep your memoir from being too straightforward or literal.

The most common type of irony is one that you probably encounter every single day. Sarcasm. You nearly smash into a pedestrian with your car while fumbling to change the radio channel and the person smiles and waves, saying, "You're a terrific driver!" Or your fairly unintelligent neighbor announces at a picnic that he's going to graduate school to study English literature and you can't help but pipe in with, "What a *tremendous* idea!"

The three primary types of irony that you can use include the following:

- ✔ **Verbal irony:** This is where the intended meaning of a word or phrase is different from what's literally on the page.

  Sarcasm shows up in this type of irony, although you can also see it in stories like Frank O'Connor's *Guests of the Nation* where the "guests" are actually prisoners. If you've ever said, "Sure, c'mon in, sweetie!" while muttering "jerk" under your breath, that's verbal irony too. (It's also not very nice!) Verbal irony isn't always negative, though it often is.

- ✔ **Dramatic irony:** Here's where you know something that characters are ignorant of. For instance, the reader knows that Juliet is moments away from awakening just as Romeo surrenders to grief and guzzles the poison. Dramatic irony creates suspense as the reader tries to anticipate what will happen.

- ✔ **Situational irony:** This type of irony is where you expect a situation to work out one way, and you get what you least expected. This one is less common in literature, but you see it in real life often enough, such as when Senator Larry Craig — with his longtime anti-gay rights stance — was arrested in 2007 for soliciting gay sex in an airport. A literary example is the O. Henry short story "The Gift of the Magi," where a young man sells his watch to buy combs for his wife's hair, while at the exact same time his wife sells her hair to buy a chain for her husband's watch.

Properly used, irony creates a memorable voice as well as a surprise or shock for the reader (depending on its intensity). Don't go overboard with this technique and you now have a powerful tool for writing stories. Be on the lookout for ironic situations in your own life and bring them to the page as needed to help make your voice (and your memoir) come alive.

Generating Humor

If you've ever read Dave Barry, David Sedaris, or Jenny Lawson, you know the power of writing with humor. After all, who doesn't like to laugh?

If you want to add humor to your manuscript, you can try these methods:

- **Be ironic.** Humor certainly can come from irony because of how it plays against a reader's expectations. I discuss irony in the previous section. An example of a very funny memoir (and a graphic novel, too!) that uses irony throughout to great effect is Alison Bechdel's *Fun Home: A Family Tragicomic* (Mariner Books). In the hands of a lesser writer (or at least one without a good funny bone in operation), this story of a young girl's issues with sexuality, suicide, and society's gender roles would be awfully dry stuff. Instead it's a total hoot.

- **Look for life's absurdity and silliness.** The funniest memoirs go beyond a little self-deprecation now and then to really revel in the existential angst that could otherwise bring everyone down.

  For example, how does Augusten Burroughs make a book on alcoholism — *Dry: A Memoir* (Picador) — funny? Because he knows to include anecdotes about how his stint in a Minnesota rehab facility included the use of stuffed animals in group therapy. Because he writes scathingly true lines like "Making alcoholic friends is as easy as making sea monkeys."

- **Be visual.** Humor works well if you can paint a funny picture with your words; just don't add in extra details unless they contribute fully to the humorous depiction.

- **Use exaggeration.** Make your point by multiplying your initial impulse by five. Instead of saying the gap between your front teeth is big, go ahead and say it's been given its own zip code.

- **Bring in pop culture.** Readers get a real chuckle out of someone who's lost their smartphone down a street sewer grating versus a wallet. Having either happen to you totally sucks, but the first is funnier by far — and it's more memorable, too — another plus!

- **Get literal.** The movie *Airplane!* did this a ton, which is why it was such a hoot. Remember the traumatized, hard-drinking ex-fighter pilot Ted Striker? At one point as he was holding a glass, he confessed that he had a drinking problem. He then spilled the liquid all over himself. Thus he truly had a "drinking problem." Like most funny things, it's far less funny when you explain it. But ask people for the top ten funniest movies of all time and *Airplane!* is usually in the running.

Whether you're known as Mrs. Chuckles or not, give humor a shot in your memoir using any or all of the preceding techniques. Run a section of the humorous text by a friend or writing peers and see what they think. If you get an actual out-loud laugh, you know you're on the right track.

Being funny in real life is difficult. Being funny on the page is even harder. If humor isn't your gift (and yes, it is a gift), I suggest that you find other ways to make your writing effective. As a matter of fact, plenty of real-life funny people I know can't summon a guffaw from a reader off the page. Live humor — comedy films, standup, and so on —generates most of the humorous effect from tone of voice, sounds, body language, and facial expressions. The writer is simply armed with words. Making those words work wonders on a reader's funny bone is a rare gift to have, which is why Sedaris and Barry and other humor writers are so beloved and successful.

Using (Yes, I Said "Using") Clichés

A *cliché* is a simile or metaphor that's so overused that it's practically dead. It's no longer interesting, memorable, or sizzling-hot writing. Every writing book on the planet insists writers run screaming from the page where clichés exist. But to them I say: Sometimes, a cliché is a great option.

Now don't step up to the plate and say you just can't put lipstick on a pig. Don't kill the messenger: Let me explain.

You can use a cliché as a tactic for humor in a couple different ways, including the following:

- ✓ **Use a changeup.** Take a cliché and change the final part of it. Readers will be expecting the usual and the changeup will surprise and entertain them.

    For instance, consider the following:

    > She sat at the bar, sipping her mai tai. Then in he came. He was tall, dark, and gruesome.

    You were *certain* it was going to be "tall, dark, and handsome." That changeup is what's funny. It ran against what you expected. It set you up for $a + b =$ and then gave you z. It's certainly memorable, which many writers struggle with creating memorable language.

- ✓ **Bombard the reader.** Don't just use the cliché once — bang the reader with it a bunch of times. Doing so isn't quite as clever or funny as the twisted cliché, but it still can work. David Letterman sometimes uses this same tactic on his show. He tosses out what he hopes is a snappy line, yet it ends up being a stinker. Most people would let it die a deserving death. Not so, Mr. Letterman! He resurrects it again and again. After a time, the effect is so over-the-top that it becomes ridiculous. And for an audience, ridiculous can equal funny.

You can have the same effect with an over-the-top range of clichés versus the same one being constantly recycled. The accumulated result of either case can have an audience grimacing but giggling. Absurdity can do that.

✔ **Use clichés in dialogue.** People use clichés all the time in everyday conversations. For instance, I have a friend whose answer to any problem — relationship or otherwise — is "there are plenty of fish in the sea!" It's almost become a running gag now after years of hearing that. You probably have someone in your life who overuses a cliché to the point that it's funny.

✔ **Follow through with the cliché.** In your exposition, you may speak about a profound disappointment by saying, "I should've been like a kid in the candy store that afternoon, but instead the door was locked, the lights were out, and the shelves were empty. And my sweet tooth hurt like heck."

You can also discover another good lesson in writing humor from TV comedies. Know when to bow and get off the stage, just like George Costanza learned in "The Burning" episode of *Seinfeld*. For example, you know what I mean if you've ever had a kid discover the magic of the word "poop." "Poop poop poopy loop poop doop *poop*!" he yells happily as he charges about the room. Laughing at him is difficult after he does it for three minutes. After 13 minutes? It gets annoying, but most jokes get annoying after 13 minutes.

Now, with apologies to Freud, sometimes a cliché is just a cliché. In those writing cases, dump it. A cliché used as a cliché is simply poor writing. Read more about poor writing and how to make it good writing in Chapters 15 and 16.

Writing Exercises to Help You Find Your Voice

Whether you're working on your first book or your 100th book, the following exercises can help you find or further develop your writing voice. You can easily lose track of your voice and just write. These exercises can help get you refocused and sounding like you again.

❑ **Write a fictional interview with yourself, a friend, or a someone famous.** Conduct it in the style of *Playboy, USA Today,* or *Seventeen.* Which was most challenging about doing this exercise? Why?

❑ **Have a friend read your memoir (or a part of it).** Don't ask "Did you love it?" Instead ask "What parts sound most like me?" You may follow up this last question with "Why?" though that question may stump him or her.

❑ **Read a chapter, story, or entire book from a favorite writer.** Get deeply into his or her head. Then write a page or two in the style of that author. The goal isn't to copy that author, but rather to loosen your own writing voice by trying on someone else's.

❑ **Get into a silly mood however you can and then revisit a favorite scene from your manuscript.** Get jiggy funny with it. Find the absurdity. Find the silliness. Discover the fun in the words you use. See if you can make humor work for you.

❑ **Make a list of your top dozen cliché similes.** They can be ones you use, ones you like, or ones you've found via research. Break the following cliché similes in half, so "big as a whale" becomes "big as" and gets listed on the left side of a page, and the "a whale," part goes on the right side. Now match up the first parts from the left side of the page with words from the right side in creative, surprising ways.

  • Big as   a whale

  • Cool as   a cucumber

  • Quiet as   a mouse

  • Sly as   a fox

  • Smart as   a whip

Some examples include

  • Quiet as a cucumber

  • Sly as a whip

Use this type of unexpected language with your similes and you won't be making clichés anymore, but instead you'll be creating interesting, exciting language. Some of it won't make much sense, yet some will be terrific. Feel free to try this with regular clichés, too, such as "drive a hard bargain" and "drink like a fish." Maybe those become "drink a hard bargain"? What about "The early bird catches the bargain"?

❑ **Try to sum your writing voice in five words only.** Want a real challenge? Try it in only three words.

Chapter 11

Handling Point of View

*P*oint of view (also called *viewpoint*) is the perspective from which the story is presented, or to say it another way, it's whose eyes the story is viewed through. You may think that as a memoir writer, you're stuck with first person because you are the subject of the story, but that's not necessarily so. In fact, limiting yourself to a single point of view may have you missing out on the benefits that other options offer.

Your point of view choice deeply affects how your readers respond to what your characters say and do. Your first choice may not be the best one. Before you make any decision, take some time to think it through. Consider trying a few pages of each option to see what feels and works best. This chapter takes a closer look at how the decisions you make about point of view can make your story work better.

Understanding Your Basic Options

Unlike some of the challenges of prose writing, point of view has only a handful of basic options. Each has its own set of unique intrinsic strengths and challenges. After you start really looking into the menu of choices, you may start to get overwhelmed, not from the number of choices, but from the fallout of those choices. How can the decision really be that difficult you wonder? It's just a memoir, after all, right? Why not just use "I" (first person) and run with it? Well, you can. But you may not want to use first person if for no other reason than the obvious first choice isn't always the best choice to make in any situation.

The following sections identify your options for the point of view in your memoir. Here I explain why a certain point of view may be better than another, depending on your memoir.

Choosing point of view is as important for a story as getting the right eyeglasses prescription is for your myopia. Point of view is the lens through which readers will see the story. Are you using a microscope, a telescope, or something else entirely?

Although this chapter covers all of your main point of view options, remember that *nearly all memoirs are written in first person*. To do otherwise is a very unusual choice. Still, in the interest of thoroughness and for those of you who may want to write one of the 2 percent of memoirs that don't exclusively use first person point of view, I detail all your options in the following pages. One other reason to include all of that information — understanding how the other options work and what the advantages and disadvantages are may give you insight into point of view in general. The more my writing students understand about point of view, the better they're able to manipulate it to good effect in their own work. It's my belief that what follows can help you whether you stick with first person or not.

First person

Writing in first person is the default for memoir writing. In *first person,* you use "I" or far less commonly, the plural, "we." The narrator serves as the eyewitness to the happenings of the story. First person isn't just an *eye*witness, though. The reader encounters everything in the story through the author's perceptions — smell, taste, touch, thoughts, and feelings. It's subjective and highly credible to a reader.

To use first person, you need to do more than just drop "I," "me," and "my" into your sentences. Effectively used first person creates a movie in the mind of the reader. It also reveals the thoughts and feelings of the narrator, which for a memoir is a very good thing.

With first person, you get a kind of shared consciousness with a reader, which may really work for certain kind of memoirs. For others, a little more distance may be more effective. After all, you're stuck in your narrator's skin, which means that unless the narrator is present, you don't have access to other characters, events, and conversations that readers may drool to encounter. You have to decide whether first person will serve your story best.

Identifying the pros and cons to first person

Using first person, just like the other points of view, has its upsides and downsides. The benefits of telling a story in first person include immediacy and emotional connection between reader and narrator. If the story is about *you,* why not let *you* be the ringmaster of the event? First person allows you to do just so. It also can help readers understand the logic and motivations for actions that may otherwise not be as evident.

With memoir, you have *ironic distance,* meaning that you're writing your memoir at a point in time where you're older, wiser, and more mature than when you were the wee lad (or lady) you're writing about. If you're careful, you can sneak in some of that current insight — just don't pass it off as the observations of a seven-year-old.

On the flip side, some of the downsides to using first person are as follows:

- ✔ **It can feel repetitive.** For instance, "I went to the fridge. I grabbed a beer and some cold turkey. I always did this when I got the munchies — I ate like I was in college again." Even if you dispense with all the I-I-I stuff, the I sometimes encourages authors to get too introspective, too long, too often. Limit the interior monologues.

- ✔ **It always feels a bit artificial to describe the main character.** This leads to tricks like the character staring into the mirror to offer that opportunity. A related issue is how to handle important things that occur when the main character isn't present, which requires a change of point of view, which can be jarring.

- ✔ **It's so commonly done.** That's not enough of a reason to go another route in and of itself, but it's a reason to carefully consider the limitations you're putting on the readers. If they're following you throughout the entire book, you need to make sure you present yourself as someone worth following. That can happen from both the plot structure (Chapter 6) and a compelling voice (see Chapter 10).

With first person, what you say may come across as bragging even when you don't mean to do so. Just be conscientious of it and watch for those parts of your memoir where it may be an issue. Perhaps have an unbiased reader give her opinion about that element.

Considering an example

What better way to illustrate what first person looks like than to show you an actual example? This passage comes from chapter one of my published memoir, *Unplugged* (HCI).

> I begin to slide the wrong way off the ice-shellacked railing, the Potomac suddenly a big, dark magnet and me, a huge lump of iron slag.

> One of my boots tears loose and heel-over-toes all the way down until it's lost in the swirl of wind-stirred water, frigid enough to kill a man faster than being shot in the gut.

It's not hypothermia that kills you, I've learned from one of those Discovery channel shows, but cold shock. You inhale the water which leads to heart attack, stroke, panic, gasping, and hyperventilation. Next on the agenda: rapid drowning.

Hypothermia operates on a scale of hours—cold shock, mere minutes.

Oh my God, this is it.

This passage wouldn't be as powerful if it was told in a different point of view.

Note that in the entire passage, I only used "I" twice. Watch out for the repetitiveness of overusing "I," such as "I ran upstairs, then I opened the door; I couldn't believe what I saw." The reader knows that it's you. Make sure you only use "I" when necessary.

Noting variations of first person

Not all first person points of view sound or look the same. You can still use first person and diverge a bit. Some first person stories have the main character talking to someone else, relating the events like he or she is chatting with an old friend, a policeman, or a parent. You may even set up a first person book as a series of letters, which are always written in first person. A few examples of these talking to/writing to options include

- *Bridget Jones's Diary: A Novel* by Helen Fielding (Penguin Books)
- *The Catcher in the Rye* by J.D. Salinger (Back Bay Books)
- *Portnoy's Complaint* by Philip Roth (Vintage)
- *No One Ever Told Us That: Money and Life Letters to My Grandchildren* (Business Plus) by John D. Spooner

Another variation of first person is where the first person narrator isn't the star of the story — he or she is a peripheral character. If someone near to you overshadows your life story, using this person as the main character might be a great option. You can be the observer. And the trickiest part is that you essentially get two stories — that of the person/event you're watching, and that of your own.

Second person

You grab a book on how to write memoir. You read it. And you come to the section on second person point of view. What then? What's second person all about? Well, you just witnessed it in action. Second person is the "you" stuff I just did on the page.

Properly done, using the second person draws the reader into the action of the story. It feels immediate. It feels intimate, too, just like a conversation. It also has the novelty of being something most readers don't see in books very often.

Although second person allows you to, in a sense, speak directly to the reader, it's the least commonly used of your point of view options. The danger with it is that if the "you" does something that the reader doesn't relate to or believe, then there's a strange disconnect. Also, it can feel like the reader is being instructed (like in a cookbook) or offered advice, which can be off-putting when all most readers want when they open a book is to be told a story.

Consider this example:

> You can't believe that Tabitha dared to show up at the Ferguson's Beach Party for the Blind fundraiser. She throws her arms around your best friend, Hank, and then blows you a kiss. You're not sure what irritates you more: that she crashed this party after the separation, or that Hank isn't working harder to extricate himself from her tentacles.
>
> You storm up to the pair. "I thought you were summering in the Hamptons," you say without trying to conceal the venom in your voice.
>
> She smiles. "I've decided to sleep with Hank."
>
> You slap her across her twice surgically-adjusted chin that you paid for. Dearly.

The reader: Whoa, no. I'd never slap a woman. And just like that, the story stops working for the reader. See the problem?

Second person lends itself well to tourism ads, self-help or how-to titles, and "choose your own adventure" books. Can it work in memoir? Absolutely. And when it does, it has this nice *Wonder Years* nostalgic feel to it that is engaging.

A few examples where second person does work include

- *Bright Lights, Big City* by Jay McInerney (Vintage)
- *An Italian Affair* by Laura Fraser (Vintage) (yep, a second person memoir!)

Jay McInerney and Lorrie Moore (who wrote a whole book of stories in the second person self-help mode) have pretty much cornered the market on second person. Tread carefully in these waters or you may come across as a mere copy of one of these well-established writers. If you want to give second person a whirl, try to find a way to make it uniquely yours.

Third person

Third person point of view is a very popular option for most types of stories. With *third person* point of view, you have the option of following just one person, or letting the reader follow multiple characters. Because the "I" doesn't have to be present for every scene in a memoir, the third person is an ideal choice for those moments. Furthermore, third person is usually fluid and flexible in all the right ways.

To use third person, you refer to characters by name and also bring in the pronouns "he," "she," or "they." If you do it well, it has the same level of closeness that first person can have. To give you two distinct examples, J.K. Rowling's *Harry Potter* series uses third person, while Stephanie Meyer's *Twilight* series uses first person. Both get readers in close with the main characters, but they go about it a bit differently.

Third person works for memoir, too, though it can feel a bit stuffy because you're talking about yourself in the third person. In real life, you typically only hear this sort of thing from ego-monster athletes. "Joe Plemmons is a star," says Joe Plemmons. "Joe Plemmons deserves six mil a year. Joe Plemmons likes the feel of hundred dollar bills on his bare skin." Furthermore, third person can leave the reader feeling a bit removed from the story's action.

Third person of any type is a curious and not-so-popular choice in a memoir. But it can be done! For a good example of how, check out Salman Rushdie's *Joseph Anton: A Memoir* (Random House). Not only is it written in third person, but this 656-page book also isn't delivered in chronological order (see Chapter 6 for more on alternative memoir structures like this).

Check out this example:

> Jane sat on the bench outside the Union Square Barnes & Noble. She couldn't believe she paid twenty dollars to hear Michael Skye III read from that horrid tell-all memoir about his affairs with the prime minister's wife. She had believed the hype, that it was a "glorious, rip-roaring good read." All it was, though, was sophomoric sex talk and vitriol.
>
> "Everything okay?" asked a passerby businessman decked out in Brooks Brothers.
>
> "I don't know," she said. "I just don't know."

Third person has some interesting variations on it in a way that first and second person don't. The following sections explain each and offer an example to show how they differ.

Objectivity isn't always a plus

In nonfiction, third person is preferred for its objectivity. Ever stop to think about why college term papers are written this way? The same is true for newspaper and magazine articles. It keeps the "I" out of the way. It keeps the focus on the subject versus the writer.

Memoir, though, is all about exploring the "I." Objectivity isn't an asset of most memoirs. Most beginning memoir writers suffer from too little authorial voice and personality. So make sure that whichever point of view option you choose, find a way to get inside of the life of the main character. Get subjective. Show the richness, the vibrancy, and complexity of the world which that character inhabits. As long as you do that, any point of view option is fine.

Allowing the author to pop into a character's head

Third person omniscient allows the writer to pop into whoever's head he or she needs to at any point. In other words, omniscient point of view offers writers the God-like power to be anywhere, overhear anything, and know anything in the story. For a memoir, this is tricky because knowing what other people are thinking is hard. Using this type may require quite a bit of research (see Chapter 4 for more on this part of the memoir writing process).

To use a third person omniscient point of view, just choose to follow the most important character for each point of the overall story. After the story moves ahead, choose a new character so you're always where the main action is. You aren't tied to any one character's experiences. Doing so may give your writing a breadth and depth that is hard to achieve with other point of view options.

Use the power of omniscience wisely. Even though you can enter any character's mind, give context for events, or show things the main character isn't privy to, you can also comment on the story itself as Milan Kundera does occasionally in his novel *The Unbearable Lightness of Being* (Harper Perennial Modern Classics). Choose it because you're going to make use of all that it offers in service of a terrific memoir. Also watch so that you don't jar your reader by jumping from one character's head to another's to another's — it can be a dizzying and unpleasant effect.

When using omniscient point of view, the challenge is in picking the right person to follow at the right time. You can choose a new one whenever you need to, or you can stick with one as your focus for the entire book but allow the reader brief access to things beyond that focus character's perceptions. How do you choose who to follow? You pick the one that's most dramatically interesting for each scene.

Limiting what the reader experiences: A rare choice for memoir

Third person *limited* is a very rare point of view choice for memoir. Third person limited is a lot like first person. If your viewpoint character doesn't experience something (through seeing, touching, hearing, and so on), then neither will your reader experience it. What the reader receives is filtered through the consciousness of this character (who may or may not be you in your memoir). One outcome is that this can create a sense of mystery because the reader is limited by what the focus character knows.

Limited is sometimes referred to as *third person singular point of view* or *limited omniscient narrative.* No matter what it's called, it's all terms for the same thing. With this point of view, you provide the reader access to your main character's thoughts and feelings. You may also choose to have access to other characters' thoughts as well, but not 100 percent of them — that'd be called third person *omniscient.* Most third person limited point of view stories focus on only one or two characters. Choosing this point of view option over first person gives you a bit more objectivity, but that's of more use for fiction writers than memoir writers.

Here is an example of third person omniscient point of view:

> Kiki considered taking just one lick of the chocolate chip ice cream. She knew that if she let herself do that, though, it'd be all over. She'd down the darn thing and find herself, fifteen minutes later, horking in the john.
>
> "Go ahead," Diego told her. He knew she was struggling with her weight again, ballooning and then shrinking away to nothing. Every day was culinary World War III for her. But she had stolen his motorcycle and then crashed it into a brick wall on a dare. "Eat that delicious Ben & Jerry's," he said. "Ummmmm. Yummy."
>
> "Enough!" Mom said when she came into the room and saw them ready to pound each other. What was wrong with those two? It made her want to start with the after-dinner vodka martinis again; they were so horrible these days.

See how that worked? I plunged into the mind of three different characters in three different paragraphs. It allowed me to guide the reader's interpretation of events. That's a real strength with omniscience. If I wanted to shift this to third person limited, I'd have to rely on my limited narrator noticing physical gestures or interpreting events.

Keeping everything objective for the reader

With an *objective* point of view (sometimes called *third person dramatic*), the reader has access to no one's mind. The writer simply tells what happens without stating more than anyone can infer from the happenings of the story. Readers don't ever know exactly what the characters think or feel — they remain a detached observer, similar to watching a movie. Readers see what the narrative shows them — nothing more. Readers are welcome to (they have to, in fact) form their own opinions.

As you can imagine, using third-person objective is difficult for many writers because getting readers to empathize with a character from such a distance is difficult. Third person objective doesn't lend itself well to a book-length memoir. It does, however, work well for certain types of short stories. To write from the objective point of view, you have to completely show and not tell. It's all external and visual. As such, creating a real sense of intimacy is difficult. But if you enjoy writing challenges, try it for a few pages. It certainly requires a lot from the reader and keeps the action coming. The real disadvantage is that it works against nearly everything a memoir usually wants to do.

Recognizing When "I" Isn't "Me"

Just because you're writing in first person doesn't mean you can't have some other character use the "I." In fact, doing so may be quite freeing for you. You may give this tactic a shot if you want to bring in another distinctive voice that has something to add to the overall narrative and/or theme. Sure, you can communicate this in your own words, but it'll sound different — perhaps more unique, more powerful — in their own voice. As long as you clue the reader in that this "I" isn't the same as elsewhere, he or she probably is willing to go for the unexpected ride.

The danger of this is in the reader losing track of who is the "I" that's speaking. My choice is always to be as clear as possible. To that end, if I wanted to bring in the voice of my mother, I may title a chapter "What My Mother Believed about My Addiction." Then using first person from my mother's point of view makes sense.

Another way to use the "I" for a different character in the book is to have a passage where that character takes his turn as the "I" character, but you do all you can to make sure it's clear the narrative torch has been passed. I'd endeavor to tell the reader directly in the text that this change was about to happen, but I'd also probably mark the different type of text on the page somehow, perhaps by using italics.

A few options for an "I" who isn't you:

- ✔ A scene from the point of view of your mother, before you were born

- ✔ A scene from the point of view of your nemesis

- ✔ A scene from the point of view of an inanimate object (particularly if one is present for most of the major scenes of the story)

- ✔ A scene from the point of view of God (or another supernatural figure/being)

When you use this convention, you want to maintain clarity. With a memoir, readers expect the "I" to be you, the author, in every case. So if you're going to change the rules, give your readers the new rules as early as possible and most readers will be willing to play that new game. How do you show that new rules are in operation? If you're going to shift who the "I" is, do it in chapter one or two. That way, readers are used to that convention. If it happens for the first time in chapter 25, readers may understandably experience a "What?!" moment.

Using Multiple Points of View in a Single Story

When writing your memoir, you don't have to use the same point of view throughout the entire manuscript. In fact, you don't even have to keep the same one in a single chapter, though you need to be sure that your shifts don't jar the reader. For example, most memoirs are written in first person. There are times, though, when it makes perfect sense to have access to someone else's brain. Well, that's third person omniscient. If changing up point of views makes the story more effective, do it. Don't feel obligated to a set of point of view rules you took away from a writing teacher or book.

To do so, you can simply shift the person pronoun, from "I" to "you" or "he/she/they." Of course that shift is only one small aspect of what the change necessitates. To embrace a new point of view, you have to reassess your own distance from and perspective on the story as the writer. You also have to use very strong scene cuts before changing point of view or else a reader can encounter a great deal of confusion.

You may want to use different points of view in your manuscript for different reasons. Doing so involves the reader more — the reader is no longer in the passenger's seat, going along for a ride with a single narrator. In that case, what other option do they have? With many narrators (many rides, as they were), they have choices. When using multiple points of view, readers also have to decide: Which version of events is more accurate? A reader can't just sit back and let him or herself be told what to think and feel, because he or she can get variations (sometimes contradictory) on that information. The reader has to get intellectually and emotionally involved.

If you want to see how multiple points of view work in a single book, I recommend visiting a number of titles that do it well. Here are a few:

✔ Ian McEwan's novel *Atonement* (Anchor)

✔ Dennis Lehane's novel *Mystic River* (William Morrow)

✔ Ann Brashares's novel *Sisterhood of the Traveling Pants* (Ember)

✔ Gregory Martin's memoir *Mountain City* (North Point Press)

The danger of using multiple points of view is that you lose the increasing momentum of a single narrative point of view. A single narrator provides clarity and a deepening relationship with that person. You have to decide if the benefits of slipping in and out of the lives of other narrators outweigh these drawbacks.

Creating Narrative Distance

The amount of *narrative distance* in a story, often called *distance* or psychic distance, is the distance between the story and the characters. Because the reader is at the mercy of the story, it's also the distance between the memoir's readers and the characters of a memoir. In other words, see how far you can go into a character's head, and how long readers stay there versus change to a different level of connection and observation. The effect of this directly relates to how close a reader feels to the characters.

Some different options for narrative distance include the following with examples to illustrate them:

✔ **Macro:** With this type of distance (also called the *long shot*), readers are so far away that they don't get much beyond general external details. This method is a popular way to enter a scene, starting from far off and slowly closing in until readers are sharply focused on our main character. Example: *The girl ran across the hot blacktop.*

✔ **Medium:** A medium length of narrative distance (or *medium shot*) has another level beyond what the macro distance allows. This is useful for getting the focus on a character but remaining far enough back to still have a clear sense of context. This is a very common, very comfortable distance to use. Example: *The girl ran across the blacktop, her feet aching from the stored-in Florida heat.*

🗸 **Micro:** This close up is where you can get deeply inside the subject and have full access to the range of thoughts, emotions, and experiences. This level of closeness brings readers practically into the skin of the subject. It's too detailed to use for long periods of time. But for a short while, it's an incredibly potent manner to draw attention to a character or scene. Example: *Every inch of skin under her foot aflame, she hustled barefoot over the blacktop, cursing the brutal Florida sun.*

To incorporate narrative distance in your writing, you want to stay at one level of distance for a chapter. Staying at one level for an entire book is like trying to look at one of those strange pictures you see for sale at shopping malls where if you stare at the stack of triangles long enough, a space ship pops out. Only in this case of staying at the same level, your readers can't see a space ship —just the awkward feeling of wrongness, of missing out on something.

You need to modulate distance to vary things up. The real challenge is to do it so smoothly that the reader never feels the story shift gears.

Readers are far more interested in zooming in for a closer look than pulling way back. Make sure that if you do pull back, you do so for a very good reason.

Although narrative distance functions largely like a camera zooming up or moving back from the subject, it's also related to time. The events of your story are all in the past, which is fine. But to give them immediacy, you may choose to write them in the present.

Here is an example past tense passage:

> I was thirteen and wishing I were done with school already. School sucked. Everything sucked. The only thing that didn't suck was baseball. But my mother didn't think I was good enough to play for the Tampa Bay Rays. She never believed in me.

The same passage made into present tense:

> I'm thirteen and I wish school was just a distant memory. School sucks. Everything sucks. The only thing that doesn't suck is baseball. But my mother doesn't think I'm good enough to play for the Tampa Bay Rays. She never believes in me.

And after a bit of tweaking that mostly includes smoothing out minor word choices such that the language sounds better in present tense, it becomes something like this:

Thirteen sucks. School too. At least there's baseball. Only Mom thinks me and the Tampa Bay Rays are like fire and ice, or maybe sharks and minnows. She doesn't get it. She doesn't get me.

Some memoirs that do a great job of writing the past in the present tense and creating narrative distance are the following:

✔ *Look Me in the Eye: My Life with Asperger's* by John Elder Robison (Three Rivers Press)

✔ *Lost in Translation: A Life in a New Language* by Eva Hoffman (Penguin Books)

✔ *The Boys of My Youth* (Back Bay Books) by Jo Ann Beard

 One of the best books on writing fiction is *The Art of Fiction: Notes on Craft for Young Writers* by John Gardner (Vintage). This thing is a warehouse stuffed with great ideas, but most relevant to this section is that he has a very clear section on distance that would be useful for writers of any type of prose, which means it's as useful for memoirists as it is for novelists. (He calls it *psychic distance*.)

Writing Exercises to Help Find the Right Point of View

Because point of view is something that many writers struggle with, I include a number of exercises here to help practice some of your most useful options.

❑ **Write two separate versions of the same lousy birthday party.** Have version one be narrated via first person from the perspective of the mother who paid for this lavish party her 16-year-old daughter couldn't care less about. Let version two be in third person. Give each version at least 300 words so you can see how the point of view alters the development, pace, and level of emotion.

❑ **Tell the story of a child lost at the shopping mall.** Tell it from his point of view. In another version, tell if from the frantic father's point of view. Try a third version that uses omniscience. Try a final one that's in second person.

❑ **Write a scene in which a person gets away with a heinous crime.** Select the point of view that best allows you to give a compassionate, empathetic rendering of the situation. Find out how to make this miscreant compelling. (Consider how well Thomas Harris does this for the serial killer Hannibal Lecter.)

❑ **Take a famous fairy tale and tell it from the first person point of view of a secondary character.** How does the story change as a result?

❑ **Use a scene from your manuscript and change the level of distance.** Bring it really close. Then try it further removed. (Remember that you're not just the writer, but the director. You decide how best to showcase every scene.)

❑ **Rework a scene from your manuscript in a new point of view.** For a few pages, try second person, or one of the third-person variations. See what kind of possibilities these unexpected point of view choices offer. Whether you include one of these versions in the final manuscript or not, you may get some perspective on the text that can prove valuable.

Chapter 12

Bold Beginnings and Fantastic Finishes

. . . .

In This Chapter

▶ Utilizing the three-act structure

▶ Making the most of the beginning

▶ Revealing four tips to start your story well

▶ Avoiding a muddling middle

▶ Finishing strong

. . . .

*W*hen I'm called in to work with someone on a memoir as a writing coach or freelance editor, usually one of two things has happened:

✔ The writer couldn't figure out how to get started.

✔ The writer did some (or a lot) of writing, but got bogged down before hitting the finish line. He or she ran out of ooomph. At page 25, 75, or 150, for some reason, they just plain stopped.

I include this chapter in the book to give you some extra encouragement and guidance to help you at both of the hardest parts of the memoir — the beginning *and* the ending. After all, Mickey Spillane explained exactly what's so important about beginnings and endings — he said beginnings sell *this* book and endings sell the next one. From writing prompts to strategies on hooking your reader to published memoirs that serve as good models, this chapter covers it all.

Even if you haven't hit a problem at either place yet, this chapter still can offer insight on how to handle these (or other) parts of your memoir. A good writing tip is a good writing tip, no matter where you are in the writing process.

Going with the Three-Act Structure

The three-act structure has a long and strong literary pedigree, stemming from the days of Aristotle and the plays of Shakespeare to the most recent Hollywood movies and bestselling books. Indeed, most writers in the past thousand years are aware of this structure, and many have used it to good effect.

The most simplistic way of looking at a *three-act structure* is this:

- Act 1 is the beginning.
- Act 2 is the middle.
- Act 3 is the ending.

But that explanation of structure is missing some of the key ingredients that make stories so powerful. After all, even a third-grader who writes a story would likely have a beginning, a middle, and an end.

These sections examine the three-act structure and the rest of this chapter then takes a closer look at each act so you can better understand this standard story structure.

Moving and changing

What the three-act structure emphasizes is movement and change. The story *moves* purposefully forward, and the main character experiences *change* as a result of the happenings of the story. In other words,

> Rule No. 1: Protagonist's goal + Obstacles = Dramatic conflict
>
> Rule No. 2: Repeat

These are the two fundamental rules of screenwriting and for narrative in a book, including a memoir. This structure keeps the audience wanting to know what's going to happen next. If audience members don't yearn to know, then they're bored or disinterested, which is the end of your story as far as the audience is concerned.

The three-act structure helps writers arrange a story's events in such a way that each conflict results in change. And each change then results in new conflict. I also discuss this cause-effect aspect in Chapter 3 because it's a basic lifeblood of good storytelling.

Although some writing teachers may recommend you avoid the three-act structure in part to push you to be original versus formulaic (they have the idea that a "formula" like the three-act structure will create repetitive stories), I suggest you stick with this structure. It's a winner, whether you follow it religiously or loosely.

Writing effective acts

Some rules need to be broken. Don't feel hemmed in by the three-act structure. The goal is to write effective acts, meaning an effective beginning, an effective middle, and an effective ending. Focus on doing so and you have yourself a book worth reading whether you painstakingly followed some literary blueprint or not.

Part of what makes an act effective is to give yourself enough space on the page to properly cover all you need to cover. For instance, here is the ratio for one of my favorite books, *The Hobbit*: Act 1: 30 percent, Act 2: 40 percent, and Act 3: 30 percent. This type of ratio has a long lead time to the real complication, and it also features a fairly slow end to the story after the climax.

Compare it to a Hollywood summer blockbuster that rakes in the dough but won't ever win any major awards and you can see the ratio adjusting to something like this: Act 1: 10 percent, Act 2: 80 percent, and Act 3: 10 percent. The screenwriter follows this because audiences want action, action, action (which is really code for drama, conflict, and complications). You don't see much of that in Act 3, so you frontload it all.

I am amazed how many writers don't stop and figure out the percentages on their own stories. I understand the resistance to following one of these ratios prescriptively, but you don't have to do so. Come up with a descriptive ratio so you can identify potential issues before agents, editors, and readers identify them for you.

I recently worked with an older man who said his memoir just "wasn't working." His wife echoed it. Every reader he showed it to agreed. The problem was that when we broke down the book into a ratio like this, he had: Act 1: 40 percent, Act 2: 20 percent, and Act 3: 40 percent. The moment I showed that to him, he immediately saw how he had misplaced his attention and lost focus. His memoir was lopsided. Every reader sensed it, but only when he took the time to analyze it that way did it become so obvious.

Beginning with the First Scene: Setting Up Act 1

You can use a number of synonyms to describe Act 1 — exposition, the setup, the catalyst. Act 1 is where things get underway and you realize the *dramatic question* (the major worry of the story that can be phrased as a question, such as "Will Sylvia overcome her fear of crowds and realize her dream of singing at Madison Square Garden?" or "Is Michael Corleone going to be able to save his family?") that will (in some way) be satisfactorily answered before the story's conclusion. Act 1 is where the reader sees the character start to struggle and assert some control over his or her future.

These are the crucial things to include in any Act 1:

- ✔ Your character and their world: Give us the relevant lowdown on their job, their aspirations, their worries, and their family. Immerse us in the world they're a part of.

- ✔ The inciting incident: This is the event that launches the story beyond the day-to-day happenings of the character's world.

- ✔ Their desire: We need to know what the character wants. Once we have that, we'll empathize with them more easily. It provides the context for their actions.

Although you more than likely are going to write Act 1 first, you probably will only find your writing voice after you've written some or most of your memoir. Once you've got real control of the voice, go back and rework Act 1, or at least the first few scenes.

Making first lines matter

First lines have to grab your reader. They set the tone. They create a mood. They reveal the writing style. They engage a reader's curiosity. They make a reader unable to put the book down.

To write a first line that sizzles, immediately establish mood, conflict, or character. If you can suggest the book's main theme, too, so much the better. Writing a winning first line isn't easy, so if it doesn't come to you right away, go with whatever you have and revise later. As my first-grade teacher wisely told me, the best way to start is simply to start. Writing the first line at the end works for many writers because after they've written the entire book, they know without a doubt what the mood, conflict, or character is.

Here are a few examples from recent books. For each, ask yourself what is it that does/doesn't compel you to read on? What promises does this first line make?

> From Mary DeMuth's *Thin Places: A Memoir:* "At four years old, long before seat belt laws, I crouch down on the floor of my father's dying Studebaker, pressing my left eye to the rusted floor where a convenient hole the size of my kneecap beckons."

> From Monica Holloway's *Driving with Dead People: A Memoir:* "It changed everything: a school picture printed on the front page of the *Elk Grove Courier*, the newspaper my father was reading."

Test out your opening lines by reading them aloud. Read them to others and carefully watch their response. Play magnetic poetry with them — move words, phrases, ideas, and images around to test out different possibilities. If you haven't test-driven at least a dozen first lines, you probably haven't arrived at your best first line yet, so keep testing them.

Eyeing your main theme to start your memoir

A reader entering a story is a lot like a swimmer entering an outdoor swimming pool. Some like to leap off a diving board and just plunge in, no matter whether the water is freezing cold or bathtub warm. Some like to go to the kiddie side of the pool and dip a toe in. Only then do they wade in, a few inches at a time.

Your memoir should follow either of these approaches. Which is better for your memoir? Well, your main themes ought to suggest that. If you have action and high drama and hookers and guns, then I suggest the diving board. If your memoir is mellower, I suggest the slow start and luxuriously work your readers in.

Every story is different, so don't feel obligated to follow some rule or advice if it doesn't suit your story. Like trying to sand wood against the grain, you have a tough task in forcing your story to behave differently than it wants to. Be open to possibilities and listen for opportunities.

Avoiding problems when starting your story

From looking at hundreds of student stories, I've identified some of the most common ways memoir beginnings can go wrong. To ensure yours doesn't go wrong, here are some suggestions you can follow to ensure you overcome those potential problems:

- ✔ **Too many people on stage** Don't crowd the first scene — start with your main character. Your readers experience the world of your story just as your main character does, so introduce them to that character and ease them into the mindset. After they have that, they'll know who to root for, what to worry about, and what to pay less attention to. Get too many people on stage at once and you have awkwardness, lack of focus, or just plain chaos.

- ✔ **A disconnect between the story's beginning and ending:** Think about some of the successful stories you've encountered. Many have a circular feel to them, where the ending is physically or thematically linked to the opening scene. A few examples include Suzanne Collins's *The Hunger Games* (Scholastic Inc.), the movie *The Wizard of Oz,* and Maurice Sendak's children's book *Where the Wild Things Are* (Harper Collins).

- ✔ **Too much revealed too fast:** My mother grew up on a little farm in Herndon, Iowa, so she knew all sorts of rural colloquialisms, such as "Why buy a cow when you can get the milk for free?" To tweak that for this purpose: "Why read the story, when the author gives away the ending in the first few pages?" I recently ran into this with a memoir about a family tragedy, where the author said on page one "There are no answers to a tragedy like this. Sometimes bad stuff happens." Oh boy. If that kind of bumper-sticker wisdom is all this memoir provides — and it gave it on page one — why read on? The solution: cut chapter one.

✔ **A flashback in the first chapter:** If you're already flashing back to a different point in your story, you haven't started in the right place (and time). Ground your readers in the here and now for a few chapters before leaping about in time and space or readers won't ever feel settled into your story.

Novelists and screenwriters typically spend many more hours on thinking about their opening scenes than do memoir writers. Go ahead and get what you can from them and their practices. A few good books geared toward novelists and screenwriters, but whose tips may be helpful to you include

✔ Nancy Kress's *Beginnings, Middles, & Ends* (Writer's Digest Books)

✔ Laura Schellhardt's and John Logan's *Screenwriting For Dummies* (John Wiley & Sons)

Moving to the Middle Scenes: Making Act 2 Work

Although this chapter is about beginning and endings, I need to also discuss the middle of your story because middles are the glue that hold starts and finishes together. They're a big part of what makes your book work (or not). These sections give the middle of your story its due and examine how to make your middle rock.

Meeting some basic obligations

If you're looking at your middle in terms of the three-act structure, you have some specific obligations for your story's middle. Here are the crucial ones:

✔ **The main dramatic complication:** You usually reveal it at the start of Act 2.

✔ **Growing tension:** You need to intensify the conflicts and complications in play. Typically, this intensity is a series of peaks and valleys, of rising and falling action that still remains an overall upward rising tension that leads to the story's climax (which happens in Act 3).

✔ **Darkest before the dawn:** Near the end of Act 2, you should beat down the hero to the point that the audience thinks, "Oh boy, he's toast. It's all over."

Middles are the soul of your story. It's where your readers really start rooting for the character because things get worse and worse for her. In other words, middles are an act of discovery in multiple ways:

- ✔ The reader learns about aspects of the main character's character as the story unfolds, because true character is best revealed in high-pressure situations.
- ✔ Readers discover depths to the main character that they didn't expect.

Examining why so many middles fail

Middles can be tricky to manage. Although a good beginning is a grabber and an ending usually has a lot of *wow* (and maybe some tears, too), a middle just has a lot of stuff going on. Not exactly the strongest selling point. As a result, you want to make sure your middle has action and energy. You need to keep readers enthralled in the story, not skipping pages or stepping out for popcorn. Middles should move the story forward meaningfully and purposefully.

Here are some of the main reasons middles sag, slug along, and suck the life out of an otherwise good story:

- ✔ **(Seemingly) less interesting to write:** Middles can feel like a chore because you're so excited about the ending — that's where everything is wrapped up, after all. And beginnings are as exciting as going on a first date. It's all fresh, exciting, and full of possibilities. To help keep yourself interested while writing middles, keep thinking about how great it'll feel when the book is finished.

    You can also step away from the story for a day or two, or even find inspiration by reading good memoirs and seeing how those writers handled their middles.

- ✔ **Lack of planning:** If you don't know where you're going, you can easily get confused, intimidated, struck numb, (insert adjective here) by all the possibilities that emerge the farther you get into a story. By the middle, you may have 200 different roads to take, which means you're not sure where to go. (Some writers call this writer's block; check out Chapter 5 for overcoming writer's block.)

- ✔ **Boredom:** Because some authors can't figure out what to do with all that space allocated to the middle, they settle on a linear narrative that reads like a grocery list. This happened. And then this happened. And then this happened. Don't settle on this sleeping-at-the-wheel tactic because you're bored. And don't bore the reader, either!

- ✔ **Unclear focus:** If your book has too many targets, you're not going to hit them all. By the middle, this problem will be painfully obvious, so the phrase "This is a mess!" may emerge, followed by the urge to quit. Go back to your original dramatic question and make sure the middle stays on target.

Raising the tension

Keeping the tension going is a challenge. Conflict is something many people avoid in their lives, which explains why so many manage to avoid conflict in their writing, too. Do the opposite of what you're inclined to do — up the ante wherever and whenever possible. If you don't want your readers mentally checking out in the middle, upping the ante and increasing the tension can help.

For example, I often tell my students to get their main characters trapped in a tree. Now open fire on them with rocks, preferably big ones. Then the author perhaps can set fire to the tree.

You may respond with, "Hey, I never got stuck in any tree, literal or otherwise! How the heck am I supposed keep the tension up?" You can increase the tension in your story in one or more of the following four ways:

- ✔ **The way you tell the story:** Use language to your advantage. Change how you write about scenes, characters, and events to best highlight their dramatic potential. For an example, just consider the differences between the following two passages about the exact same moment in a hypothetical memoir. Do you see the difference?

  "The longer I sat at the bar, the more I realized the woman next to me was open to something. Maybe anything. I was tempted but I was married."

  "Every time she went for a sip of her white wine, she turned her head a little so her long sandy hair flipped to the side, always brushing my arm resting atop of the bar. I signaled for another Dewar's. The ex-jock bartender slid me a new glass filled higher than last time. He eyed me, then the woman, then me again. Then he gave me the subtlest of nods as if the universe itself was saying, "Go go go go!" I'm sure I could've gotten away with it. On the west coast for six weeks per year, plus a week in Vancouver and a few more in various cities throughout Europe, I've had chances. Or at least opportunities. But here one was, and it wasn't me telling myself I was handsomer than I knew to be true, or that I'd have to fork over a wad of sweaty bills to some sex worker who'd as soon stick a fork in my eye as get it on with me. God, I wish Brenda had picked up earlier when I called, but she was so pissed before. So pissed. And rightly so."

- ✔ **What you reveal and withhold:** You can create reader interest by withholding certain information until the end of the story. Keep certain things to yourself at the start to keep the readers reading.

One memoir I worked on was about a boat accident in the middle of the Pacific where 31 lives may have been lost. The writer mentioned in the first few pages that no one died and they all were saved. Well, that's not very exciting now, is it? Withholding that information would've made the reader tense throughout. *Will they live? Will the boat make it back to shore before it sinks*? If you want to tell me that it's being manipulative, I'd say yes, but it's a fair type of manipulation, because the characters in the story didn't know what their outcome was going to be. Because the characters are locked in their struggle, having your readers share your characters' fears and uncertainty is quite reasonable.

✔ **Different stakes:** Not every story is life and death, nor should it be. What are the personal ramifications, the social ones, the religious, the career? To emphasize how a character's life will be impacted by the story is to create reader interest. Your readers see how the outcome matters. Getting readers to care is a great way to answer that dreaded "So what?" question, which is only asked when they don't care.

✔ **Giving your middle a middle:** One way to avoid the messy middles of memoirs is to take your middle and divide it up into its own beginning, middle, and end.

At some point, raising the stakes may lead you to go too far. If you're ascribing cosmic import to opening a jar of pickles, you know you need to scale it back.

Ending with the Final Scene: Closing Act 3

Have you ever been watching a movie that you've really enjoyed . . . right up until the end, when it all falls apart and ruins the experience? That's what you want to avoid with your memoir. Your book may be 90 percent great, but if the ending falls flat or rings untrue or gets plain silly or just kind of stops, readers will pound you with one- and two-star Amazon review ratings.

Your memoir as well as fictional books, plays, movies, and cartoons all need to have an appropriate ending that both wraps up all the significant loose ends and surprises your readers in a believable way. Endings enmesh your readers in the outcome (often to the point of readers having to stay up with a flashlight under the covers until 3 a.m. on a work or school night to find out what happened!). Endings may also connect with universal themes. They don't resort to gimmicks, tricks, or sermons (which unfortunately is a popular, but inappropriate ending for memoirs).

Endings have a tough job before them, but don't worry. These sections detail some of the key things to consider in making your ending be more like the *1812 Overture* than a slide whistle.

Making the last lines matter

The last line in your memoir is your last chance and final shot to leave an impression on the reader. Readers almost expect the last line to resonate with, sum up, and expand on everything that came before. A tall order, sure, but if you can nail it, your readers will remember it for days and days. They may even chat about it to their friends and coworkers.

Because a memoir isn't an autobiography (see Chapter 6 for more on this distinction), you can pick and choose where to stop. All that matters is that you go with an option that answers your story's dramatic question — the "What if?" that got your story started in the first place. It can be happy or sad, surprising or hitting a target revealed early in the story. It doesn't matter so long as your ending is the natural conclusion to what came before. Your story has a single right ending. After you discover it, you're set.

How do you know if you have the right ending? Read it aloud. Share the ending with a trusted reader and take in her feedback. Try out three others that are different in size, scope, or tone. You'll feel the rightness of the best ending in your gut. You'll be willing to fight to keep it that way versus go with another option. When you get to that point, stick with what you have.

Here are a few interesting endings. As you read each, ask yourself what readers may find appealing about each one:

> Ernest Hemingway's *A Moveable Feast* (Scribner): "But this is how Paris was in the early days when we were very poor and very happy."

> Tony Pacitti's *My Best Friend Is a Wookie: A Memoir* (Adams Media): "Instead I felt giddy, free from thoughts of the grown-up world outside our crammed little street corner. In that moment there was nothing more important than the images up on the screen and the fact that all of the strangers sitting around me were my friends for those brief couple of hours that we shared together under George Lucas's stars."

> Vladimir Nabokov's *Speak Memory* (Everyman's Library): "There, in front of us, where a broken row of houses stood between us and the harbour, and where the eye encountered all sorts of stratagems, such as pale-blue and pink underwear cakewalking on a clothesline, or a lady's bicycle and a striped cat oddly sharing a rudimentary balcony of cast iron, it was most satisfying to make out among the jumbled angles of roofs and walls, a splendid ship's funnel, showing from behind the clothesline as something in a scrambled picture—Find What the Sailor Has Hidden—that the finder cannot unsee once it has been seen."

Finding some closure

Everyone likes to have closure in relationships, in business deals, and in classes at school. You can bet then that people like to have it in books, too. That sense of finality, of a suitable and appropriate finality makes readers feel complete.

As a memoir writer, you should find a way to give the reader a sense of closure. Although you likely had a great deal of uncertainty when you were living through the events you're now writing about, you clearly came to a place where you overcame that uncertainty. Help your readers do that too. Give them the same trajectory — from confusion to knowledge and wisdom. Moving from a state of ignorance to one of knowing is one of the main reasons people read, after all.

While psychologists differentiate between numerous types of closure, *cognitive closure,* which is the desire for clear, firm knowledge on some issue, seems to be most relevant to memoirs. To gain it is to bypass or destroy ambiguity and confusion. You may think of cognitive closure as the lesson learned in a story, though I'd argue that any good story has multiple lessons.

Ending your memoir: Some helpful suggestions

Here are eight ways to effectively end your memoir. Some may be wildly inappropriate to your specific book, but here are your main options anyway. Choose appropriately!

- **Everyone wins:** In this type of ending, the main character comes out happy and on top of the world. Often other characters end up equally well. More than a few of Shakespeare's plays ended with everybody getting married at the end. Or think of winning as a big celebration, like the medals being strewn about at the end of Star Wars. Surprisingly, a fine memoir example of this ending is the addiction memoir *Heal Thyself: A Doctor at the Peak of His Medical Career, Destroyed by Alcohol—and the Personal Miracle that Brought Him Back* by Oliver Ameisen (Sarah Crichton Books).

- **Big dance number:** A big dance number doesn't have to be a dance number. A big celebration is fine, too. End with a party, a joyous get-together. Crank up your favorite upbeat song to set the mood when you're writing it.

- **Never-ending story/fade out:** You've seen this one plenty of times. You're clearly given what's going to happen next, then a fade out before you see it. It suggests that the adventure and drama will continue. This type of ending does a nice job of making the characters feel alive beyond the limitations of the page. One example is the end of *The Adventures of Huckleberry Finn* by Mark Twain where Huck "lights out" for the territories.

- ✔ **Full circle:** You can bring your characters back to where it all started, but because the main character has changed, this bringing together highlights that difference. One of the strengths of this story ending is its clear sense of finality. A clear example of this is S. E. Hinton's novel *The Outsiders*, where the story ends with the same line as it begins.

- ✔ **Off into the sunset:** Who doesn't love *Casablanca?* This type of ending requires you to wrap things up nicely a bit before the end of the book so the scene of the hero and a loved one walking off into the literal or meta-phorical sunset is the icing on that cake of closure, so to speak. Too few memoirs have this ending. If yours does, please let me know about it!

- ✔ **Hero wins, but emerges damaged or broken:** This choice is popular because lots of memoirs are about damage being done to characters. If you have a confessional story to share, I hope that you end yours this way. This version finds the silver lining behind a ton of storm clouds and lightning and soul-drenching rain. Without the silver lining, you have just too much lousy weather and that's no good for anyone. My own memoir, *Unplugged* (HCI) ends this way, with me cutting off an entire part of my life to try to rebuild the rest again. Joan Didion's *The Year of Magical Thinking* (Vintage), too, ends by her accepting her hus-band's death a year after it happened, and she returns to her regular life, though without a true sense of purpose or clarity (that's the damage).

- ✔ **Unresolved ending:** A rather unusual choice, this option doesn't resolve the main conflict but leaves it hanging there awkwardly for both the characters in the story and the audience to deal with somehow. If you like dissonance versus harmony, this ending may appeal to you. An example? Anne Frank's *The Diary of a Young Girl* (Everyman's Library), which simply stops with an unexceptional entry on August 1, 1944. On August 4, 1944, her family was betrayed to the Nazis and they were taken away, ending Anne's story for good.

- ✔ **Smashed fourth wall:** The *fourth wall* is that barrier that keeps the characters from a story from knowing they're in a story and that an audi-ence is following along. In this option, you break it down by stopping the narrative and stepping out and talking directly to the readers. Get real. Get intimate. This ending will get their attention for sure because readers don't see it that often in novels or films. But because so much of memoir involves *interior dialogue* — which is like the narrator speak-ing to himself and to the reader — this ending seems quite appropriate for many memoirs. In fact, the closeness and intimacy of memoir may well have you smashing the fourth wall throughout your book with clear addresses to the reader.

Tread carefully with deus ex machina

Fiction writers sometimes resort to a *deus ex machina* ending, which in Latin means "God out of the machine." It means that the writer let some extreme coincidence, unexpected bene-factor, or other God-like miraculous happening occur at the very end of the story to save the day. This ending is unsatisfying for a reader to witness because the main character wins without earning anything. This ending also feels really fake.

The good news: Memoir writers don't have to worry so much about this type of ending. If your story ends with a lottery jackpot that saves your house, your marriage, and the life of your uncle who needs an expensive heart transplant, so be it. Readers can't say it's fake because it really happened. If this type of ending suits your book, do what you can, though, to make sure you demonstrate character growth and change so readers feel satisfied.

Use any one of these, use a couple of them, or make up your own. Just be sure you do something that makes sense to both *you* and *your story*. If you listen hard enough, your story will probably tell you exactly how it needs to end. Listen to it. Your story is almost always smarter than you are.

Figuring out what to do next

Although your memoir may have a beginning and ending now, the odds of them being fully recognized aren't good. Until you've written the entire manu-script and then taken some time away from it so you can get a fresh perspec-tive on your memoir, you're not ready.

One of the best things you can do next is to write your next book. It doesn't have to be a memoir. Write the next bestseller, a picture book, or a bodice-ripper. Just write. The same writing skills you've developed during the writing of your memoir will serve you well no matter the literary task you set for yourself.

Writing Exercises to Help with Beginnings and Endings

A great way to figure out how to handle beginnings and endings is to engage in writing exercises that explore your options. Here are a few that students in my classes have found particularly useful.

❑ **Write three distinctly different endings to your memoir.** Read each in the context of the last few chapters that came before. Select the one that resonates best with the rest of the book, even if it's not the one you expected to use. The only caveat? Stick to the truth in every version. How you handle that truth, though, is entirely up to you.

❑ **Plot out your memoir from the end to the beginning.** If you know your ending early in the writing process — or even before you start — work backwards. Reverse plot the entire book, scene by scene, until you suddenly find where you need to start. Voila! You now have your beginning, ending, and most of the middle figured out.

Any time you feel bogged down in your own story, jot down at least five questions you have about your own story. Be as specific as you need to be, though don't ask questions that can be dismissed with a quick yes/no. Ask open-ended questions, such as why, how, and what. (Often in the course of doing an exercise like this, your subconscious will surprise you with an unexpected solution or two.)

❑ **Write a three-page beginning to your story.** Use first person, but don't use the word "I" more than once per page. Keep the focus on the external rather than the internal.

❑ **Imagine that your book's movie rights were just sold to Steven Spielberg for a staggering sum.** The only caveat is that he can't let the movie be longer than two hours, and your book won't get made into a huge Oscar-winning movie *unless* you can cut three scenes from the middle. Which three scenes from the middle of your memoir would you cut? Why? (And why aren't you cutting them in your manuscript right now?)

Part III
Revising, Editing, and Pushing Your Story to the Next Level

The 5th Wave   By Rich Tennant

"Do you use these 3x5 cards for anything other than charting your manuscript, or does the creature actually make a pineapple bundt cake at this point in your memoir?"

In this part . . .

No writer gets it perfect the first time, which is perfectly okay. In this part, I cover ways to fine-time some of the key parts of your memoir, such as structure, story, and theme. Next, we look carefully at the important differences between sentence-level editing and large-scale revision, with an eye toward when and how to perform each. For those who want some top-level input, I discuss how to locate, hire, and work with a professional editor. Finally, I tackle the idea of knowing what to write and what *not* to write, whether it's for ethical, moral, practical, or legal reasons.

Chapter 13

Adjusting the Big Picture: Fine-Tuning Structure and Story

In This Chapter

▶ Adjusting your story's size

▶ Arranging conflict and tension

▶ Utilizing pace

▶ Transitioning effectively

*I*f you asked publishers and literary agents to create a top ten list of ways that good memoirs go bad, a "weak story" and "poor/ineffective structure" would be near the top of the list every time. The good news: Generating a story is easy, and generating a structure is easy too.

This chapter shows you how by examining several ways to push your memoir's story and structure (the "big picture stuff") to the next level. This chapter also asks you to challenge your story. This type of hard-nosed scrutiny can mean the difference between your memoir being published or not and between a reader loving it or telling you, "Well, it was fine."

Skip this chapter at your own peril. Plenty of memoir writers have worthwhile life stories to share, but if they don't put the much-needed time in on story and structure, their book will just be something with potential versus something that's fully realized. Potential doesn't get a book deal. Potential is just a book that's not done growing up yet.

Sizing Up Your Story: Maintaining Proportion

Here's where you need to take off your writer's hat (also known as Oh-I-love-everything-because-I-wrote-it hat) and get critical. Your memoir is no longer about "my life"; more importantly, your manuscript is "a story." When you size up your story, you have to remove your ego from the picture. Tell your historian side to take a back seat — just because it happened doesn't mean it has to go in the book.

The main question to ask yourself when writing your memoir is whether the information you may include helps the story. That goes for the size of your sentences, your scenes, your chapters, and your entire book, as well. When you look at all these elements, you want them to have reasonable proportions. In a memoir, *proportion* means that you an adequate amount of the text on the pages devoted to the various parts of a story.

Proportion exists in more than just the big structural areas, like I discuss in Chapter 6. Here are some other places that your proportion may quietly be out of whack:

- ✓ **Internal versus external:** A memoir has a lot of interior moments — thinking, reflecting, and musing. Those are welcome but too much of it makes the reading go slowly.

- ✓ **Description versus action:** Sure the reader wants to have imagery to paint the visuals in. Just don't forget movement, action, and energy.

- ✓ **Dialogue versus exposition:** The past comes alive when scenes are happening right in front of the reader, which means dialogue is actually heard versus talked about. Exposition is that talking about. Use both equally. Visit Chapters 8 and 9 for more on how and when to use dialogue.

- ✓ **Showing versus telling:** Don't religiously follow the adage, "Show, don't tell." Sometimes telling is essential. See Chapter 16 for more on showing and telling.

- ✓ **Long sentences versus short sentences:** A long sentence is great because it can do a clear job of communicating so much in a single instance. Short sentences can too. Use them both as needed. Don't neglect either option.

Although there is no hard-and-fast rule that says all memoirs need to look alike, the proportion of narrative summary to fully-developed scenes, of dialogue to exposition, and of conflict to beauty are generally similar from book to book.

Don't worry too much about these things when you're writing your manuscript's first draft. Just write and get that full draft done. You can then scrutinize whether the preceding list of elements is proportional during the revision process. Enlist a careful reader friend to help, if you want, or do it all yourself. What matters is that each of your options is a choice that you specifically considered and decided upon. Don't just let something go because it's too much work to rework or because you don't see an easy way to fix it.

The preceding list of areas where proportion can be an issue may overwhelm you. Remember that you don't have to deal with them all during the revision process. In fact, the most effective editors isolate one specific concern and read for only that issue, adjusting and fixing as they go. That kind of attention takes real commitment, but the end result is a manuscript that's carefully crafted.

Revving Up the Story's Engine: Bring On Conflicts Big and Small

Conflict, the struggle between opposing forces, is the engine that drives your story. Without conflict, readers quickly lose interest in your story, and that's even if you do everything else about the memoir well. In fact, a writing workshop I once attended reiterated the three more important elements of dramatic writing are conflict, conflict, and conflict.

A reader may come to care about the main character of a memoir, but a good story needs characters who readers come to care for. And yes, good stories are about character change. But how does that change come — as a result of conflict.

During the revision process, ensure that your story has conflict. To do so, make sure your manuscript does the following. If it doesn't,

✔ **Reveal all the smaller conflicts that are simultaneously happening beneath, around, or alongside the major conflict.** Select the right ones and we'll be swept up in the high drama of what might actually be generally low-stakes situations. If you go back and look at the big changes in your life, they were probably heralded by smaller but important changes. Note that chain of events because it's relevant.

For example, a story where the main conflict is about coming to terms with your homosexuality may have a subplot conflict of dealing with a neighbor's Rottweiler that craps on your lawn. In the big scheme of life, that's a minor thing. A gigantic irritation maybe, but if you were this character and you could wave your magic wand to fix one thing about you and your world, you'd probably make yourself and everyone in your life okay with your sexuality versus stopping the dog doo-doo issue, no? Your sexuality and how everyone handles it is the main issue, dilemma, concern, and problem in your life, after all — the reason you're writing the memoir. But most people can relate to the small injustice of a dog turning his or her beautifully manicured green lawn into a toilet. Or they know of a similar small injustice (such as how someone drinks the last of the coffee at work but doesn't start a new pot, or how someone in your apartment building yanks out the coupon section of your Sunday paper each week before you get up) and can therefore relate. Working in a minor conflict serves as a useful contrast to the big conflict in the character's life.

✔ **Set up your character for change, and then show that change.**
Character change is powerful, and meaningful changes only occur from
conflict. Show readers the stages of how that happens.

For example, the preceding small dog poo conflict shows your character
being passive regarding this incident for some time. When the character
finally snaps, perhaps collecting all the dog's poo in a bag and emptying
it in the neighbor's open convertible, it signals a change. That change
may likely set the stage for a change regarding the major conflict in the
character's life. He is taking charge. He is no longer content with the
status quo. Today may be about the dog poo. Tomorrow, the character
may have the coming-out talk with his parents, followed by a Facebook
post that undoes a lifetime of repression and lies. Talk about change!

Adjusting the Pace

How fast a story takes place is called its *pace*. Some writing teachers mistak-
enly talk about pace when they mean story structure, and vice versa. There's
a huge (and crucial) difference. Structure is basically the mansion the story
lives in. Pace is the speed in which you go through the mansion. If the mansion
is well furnished, you're going to want to take your time moving through it.

Let me extend this metaphor for a moment longer to reveal one of the major
pace-killers writers use: flashback. If structure is the mansion, and pace is
how you move through it, a flashback is when you stop and talk about the
mansion as it was 20 years ago. Or a flashback may even move the reader to
a completely different place to show a discussion that the writer believes is
relevant later. See the potential problem? Be where (and when) you are, not
somewhere (or some time) else.

Flashback isn't the kiss of death to a story, but it does always adversely affect
the story's pace because the current story has to stop completely for the
reader to jump back in place and/or time to witness another story. For more
on story structure and flashback, see Chapter 6.

The following sections show you how to manipulate your story's pace to
make your story more powerful. They also discuss *when* to make these
changes to your pace to maximize its positive effects.

Speeding up or slowing down the pace

Listen to any piece of music that lasts for more than five minutes and you'll
quite likely hear different tempos (the musical equivalent of pace in storytelling). On the simplest level, "variety is the spice of life." In other words, readers enjoy change. On a more important level, you need to be in command of
the elements of your story. And to be able to keep a reader in a tense scene

longer or get them out of a low-stakes scene more quickly is a valuable tool in your writing toolkit.

Like most writers I struggled a bit when writing the middle of my own memoir. One day, my wife asked me why I was moping about and I sort of said to myself as much as her, "I need to pick up the pace." Without missing a beat, she said, "Write faster."

If you're like me, you get more of that type of advice than anything truly helpful. Let me remedy by offering a number of clear ways that you can use when writing your manuscript to speed up or slow down.

Picking up the pace

To speed up the pace of your story, do the following:

- **Jump cut/slam cut.** These movie terms refer to how some films simply leap straight forward from one moment to another, from one fast scene to another fast scene, completely ignoring the idea of trying to transition one to the other.

- **Use shorter words.** Writing with shorter words sounds like a small thing, but it can help to speed up your manuscript. Just read Hemingway to see how this kind of writing can zip you through a chapter. An important tip when using shorter words: Avoid commas. They're too easily used to make sentences longer.

- **Use cliffhangers.** Want to keep scenes and chapters trucking along? Leave readers with a *cliffhanger*, just like a good TV soap opera does every Friday. Leave your character in jeopardy and then move to a different scene. The entire time your readers are in that different scene, they'll be wondering about — worrying about — that character in jeopardy. It's a very efficient way to tease out the tension of a high-stakes moment in a story.

- **Use active voice.** Focus on action by using active voice, such as "Jimbo punched out the pint-sized mime," rather than "The pint-sized mime got punched out by Jimbo." Active voice keeps the focus on the subject, not the object of the sentence. It's also less potentially confusing.

- **Avoid description.** Don't get bogged down in adjectives and modifiers. Reading them is like stopping to smell the roses. Readers won't stop to smell what's not there.

- **Use words that readers know.** You don't want your readers to have to look up a lot of words. Throw a "paronymous" or "imbroglio" at them, and one of two things will happen:
  - They'll stop the story to go look up the word.
  - They'll skip it and read on.

  Both aren't great options. Using big words may also make you seem like a snotty author, the I'm-smarter-than-you-dear-reader kind of person regular people detest. Another bad outcome!

Slowing down

If you've been cooking along for awhile now, and you want to slow down, try these few options:

- ✔ **Use a wide viewpoint.** Extend the focus on the scene. If fast-paced scenes focus tightly on the main character, the slower scenes pull back and include setting, scenery, and other elements of their environment.

- ✔ **Write like F. Scott Fitzgerald or William Faulkner.** Go for it. Get as long and descriptive as you need to be (as long as you don't get ridiculous with it).

- ✔ **Let dialogue develop slowly.** Don't allow your characters to speak in sound bites. That's probably how they really spoke in those moments you're writing about, anyway. No need to have that punchy TV dialogue where everyone speaks like they have to pay for every word uttered.

- ✔ **Reflect and muse.** You have the time. Let characters think, pontificate, consider, surmise, and imagine.

Knowing when to take it slow

Pacing doesn't mean your memoir has to blaze forward at the speed of light. Readers can't take a nonstop blur of a story, no matter how amazing and exciting your life really has been. They need a breather now and then. That's why you want to slow the pace down once in a while.

The general rule of pacing is a 2:1 ratio. For every two scenes of high drama, conflict, and excitement, you can include one that's more domestic, slow, or introspective. If your book is especially zippy or fast-moving with high drama, go for 3:1.

For example, I recently took my daughters to Busch Gardens and they rode the Scorpion roller coaster with me. Afterwards, the oldest said, "Wow, that was fun." I said, "Want to go again?" They both said no. They had had enough. They wanted to sit on a bench and slurp Italian ices. But sure enough, within an hour or two, they were clamoring for the Scorpion again.

Readers are like that as well. Give them a break. Preferably with an Italian ice (which for a memoir may equal some lush description or even a funny moment).

Avoiding three pacing mistakes even good writers make

Pace is almost as important to your memoir as plot, setting, and conflict. Unfortunately many writers, even the good writers, get caught up with pacing problems and don't spend enough time to fix them. Here are three ways you can affect pace in a bad way so you can steer clear of them:

- **Starting in the wrong spot:** If the story is a climb up a mountain, you need to start close enough to the top to reach it in a timely fashion. Start too close to the top and you don't have anywhere to go for your ending (or even your middle!). Start far enough back that you have time to knock the character off a precipice or two, but still have the space for her to crawl back up and keep on going.

- **Letting the brain run overtime:** With memoir, you want to include what you thought. On the flip side, spend too much time in the thinking arena and your character suddenly isn't doing anything on the page. Standing around thinking isn't action. Standing around thinking isn't dramatic. If you're not doing anything but thinking, the pace has not only slowed, but it's completely halted, and your readers will stop reading fast, which you don't want.

- **Forgetting to think cinematically:** If you think about how a movie director would film each of your scenes, you can focus on what matters and leave out the rest. Who knows? You may even be more likely to have your book picked up as a movie!

Getting the pace right for a poem, a short story, or a memoir doesn't really help you with the next piece you write. There's no one-size-fits all pace. The more you write, the better you'll be able to guess the right pace early on in the process. Figuring out the right pace is like a doctor who after six seconds can guess that you have hypothyroidism, for instance, though he won't know until he runs a battery of tests. He's had enough experience to know he's probably right. More times than not, he hits the mark.

Using Transitions Effectively

Transitions are the words and phrases between sentences and paragraphs. Creating connections is also a great idea for scenes and chapters. When your scenes and chapters have a smoothness to them, the overall flow of the story is stronger.

Some common transitions you can use in your sentences are

- Additionally
- Although
- As a result,
- Equally important
- Finally

✔ First

✔ For example

✔ For this reason

✔ Moreover

✔ Similarly

Although this list of transition words works well enough for high school and college freshman essay papers, tacking on a "meanwhile" to a new scene isn't enough to expect to wow readers. Scenes and chapters need more. They deserve more, too.

The good news: The following sections help you take the idea of transitions beyond the sentence level. The result will be increased unity throughout your story and a more seamless experience for readers.

Examining scene and chapter transitions

Using transitions at both the scene and chapter level are important in a number of ways. By scene level, I mean the movement from one scene to the next. By chapter level, I mean how one chapter ends and the other picks the narrative up. Sure, there's a necessary sense of closure when either of those ends, but you have to keep the readers moving forward and wanting more. That's where transitions can help.

Transitions can help do the following at the scene and chapter level:

✔ **Offer description:** *Description* should appear throughout the manuscript, but at the end of a scene, a focus on it can help make a final strong image. It's equally useful to lock the reader into a clear, concrete situation at the start of a new chapter or scene. See Chapter 16 for more information on using description well.

✔ **Break (or increase) tension:** Tension is part of conflict, but readers don't want to experience it endlessly — it's exhausting. A chapter or scene change can shift things to a less intense pace and atmosphere. See Chapter 7 for more on creating atmosphere.

✔ **Slow (or speed up) the pace:** The opposite of the preceding bullet is also true. Readers aren't content to plod along through hundreds of paces. A natural place to shift gears to a higher speed is at the start of a new chapter or scene. To follow the metaphor through, moving the story into these new chapters or scenes can be like going from a residential road to an interstate highway. Speed is now a safe possibility.

- ✔ **Change location:** What better place to change location (setting) than at the start of a new scene or chapter? This is a far better, easier-to-follow option than shifting locations in the middle of a scene. Chapter 7 covers all you need on how to handle setting.

- ✔ **Have point of view:** A point of view shift can be confusing if you change at any other point except the start of a new chapter or scene. The transition of these story parts is a very good way to keep readers from getting lost by a point of view change. For more on point of view and point of view changes, visit Chapter 11.

You can also use transitions between scenes and chapters to skip periods of time. Your characters have lives in the story that run 24/7, but practically speaking you can't include it all. As a result, you use transitions to exclude anything that doesn't link up meaningfully with the story, like brushing your teeth five times a day or fetching a pre-dawn box of donuts. (Now if your memoir is about obsessive-compulsive disorder or weight issues, either of these scenes may merit inclusion. For other memoirs, transition right over them, just like you do for bathroom breaks, TV watching, sleeping, and day-dreaming, which are all things that probably happen in everyone's life, but we don't need to witness on the page.)

To transition from scene to scene, use the same philosophy as if you're transitioning for the sentence and phrase-level stuff. You have X and you have Y. You need something to connect the two otherwise you just have two random things, standing side by side. Check out the next section for how to actually use transitions in scenes and chapters.

It's like a sandwich cookie. Without that delicious creamy filling sticking the top cookie to the bottom one, you just have two darn cookies.

Applying transitions to your manuscript

Being able to effectively use transitions in your writing at different levels, ranging from the chapter and scene to the sentence level is critical. Here are some options to utilize transitions:

- ✔ **Use a teaser:** A *teaser* is simply when you reveal a hint of what's coming next. It teases a reader with a sense of humor, drama, or conflict, but to know exactly how it plays out, the reader has to read on.

  If you end with "I knew that botching a project like the Milligan account could spell the end of my career with McMasters and Sons" then you can start the next chapter right away with: "The next morning, I entered the McMasters high rise and nodded at Pete, the ancient ex-detective who snored away the afternoons. Next to a surprisingly alert Pete stood Jim, The Boss. And he looked angry enough to eat a hornet's nest." I'm suddenly quite interested in this new chapter, aren't you?

✔ **Re-center the reader:** When you have a shift coming, take the time to ground the reader in the new time and/or place. Here's an example that would be a fine way to start a new chapter for a memoir about a man who convinced himself that he fell out of love with his wife so he leaves her and New York for a life of adventure:

Six months of the Ensenada sun had turned my well-muscled body a deep bronze that drew the eye of most tourists as I drove busloads of them to Land's End to snap photos each day. While I overheard more than a few women comparing me to an Adonis, I couldn't stop comparing each of them — unfavorably — to Kalina. Even my new girlfriend, Babette, bored me when we weren't making love in the waves of a hidden Cabo beach.

✔ **Offer closure:** To get to something new, you need to get past the old. In story terms, if you feature a critical fight scene between a couple, get them to a point where there's resolution to their fight. Close that tension. It may be as simple as writing this exchange.

"Well," John said, eyeing me.

"Well, indeed," I said without a hint of mirth.

John let out a long, deep sigh. Then he said, "I'm moving in with Tommy." I snorted. "You think our boy wants his old man around?"

"He's got that couch in the basement. That'll do."

I frowned. "Always the martyr," I said, then held the door open for him to exit our home of thirty years like he's been exiting my life every day for as long as I could remember.

✔ **Show cause and effect:** If your scene ends with a cause, show the effect in the next one. For instance, one scene can showcase how a family decided to skimp one month on allergy pills because the father had been laid off. The next scene can show Little Todd having an asthma attack — one that could've been prevented. This powerful cause/effect combo links two scenes and involves a reader. Readers may even sense it coming, but they can't do anything about it except grow tense with worry (a good thing for writers to get readers to do).

✔ **Add dialogue:** A brief dialogue exchange can tie two scenes together well. The following example may start a new scene where the previous one left our 20-something woman on a bench outside a movie theater, having been dumped moments before by her jerky boyfriend:

"I've been up all night!" Sandra said.

I shrugged. My roommate was a worrier. "Sorry."

Sandra poured herself another cup of coffee. She frowned, but poured one for Juliet too. "Where *were* you?"

"Thinking."

"I get that. But where? I called everyone we knew. I even got in my car and circled the neighborhood near the theater."

I said, "I'm not sure. I had too much on my mind."

To show a break between scenes, use a centered XXX between the last paragraph of the scene and the first paragraph of the next one. Some publishers will print those XXXs to alert a reader to a transition. Others will remove it and add an extra space to do the same thing — tell a reader that a shift has occurred.

Although the rule "show, don't tell" is a good one in general (see Chapter 16 for more information), most transitions are instances of telling, which isn't a problem. You can tell as long as you get back to the vivid scene building and action as soon as you've effectively transitioned the reader.

Writing Exercises on the "Big Picture"

The following exercises can help you modify your memoir's structure and story by looking at the big picture. Work through them and see how your manuscript's pace quickens or slows down.

- ❑ **Go through a chapter of your manuscript with an assortment of highlighters in hand.** Assign each color to one of the things in this chapter, such as blue for conflict, green for transitions, yellow for fast pace, pink for slow pace, and so on. Mark the scenes accordingly. Feel free to mark things down to the sentence level. Which colors are most predominant? Does that surprise you? Are any of the colors disproportionately represented?

- ❑ **Take one of your favorite scenes from your manuscript and rework it to drastically change the pace.** If your manuscript is slow to start, speed it up like an NFL receiver. If it's already dashing ahead, toss a piano on its back. Carefully watch how adjusting the pace can affect every other element of the scene and story.

- ❑ **Create a scene where two completely made-up characters argue over something they both are certain about.** Don't let the scene devolve into a physical altercation; keep it all in the realm of language (both words and body language). Perhaps choose a setting that either is appropriate or quite inappropriate for such a conflict.

To slow down the pace, you may need more details than you can readily remember. Think about a scene that you want to slow down and then try some of the following phrases to jumpstart your brain and memory:

"I don't remember _____."

"I thought _____ but now realize _____."

"What I do recall is _____."

"Perhaps what happened was _____."

❑ **Write a short scene (two pages tops) about a past memory without using a single adjective.** How does your ability to describe handle this challenge? What type of language choices does this self-imposed limitation force you to make?

❑ **Write a descriptive passage about your mother.** Include whatever physical, emotional, or other details you want. When you finish that part, add your father to the stage. What types of conflicts suddenly flare to life? Which are external? Which are internal? Select one and write about how your parents struggled with that conflict. If this scene doesn't appear in your memoir, ask yourself why not? Does the way your parents interacted with each other inform how you engaged (or not) with the world?

❑ **List your life conflicts.** List the conflicts you had in your life during the period your memoir covers. List your childhood conflicts. Think about physical ones, emotional ones, social ones, external ones, internal ones, and so on. See if you immediately recall any drama and tension from your past. Are any or all of those conflicts represented in your book? If your memoir doesn't have a lot of tension or conflict in it already, consider adding one or more of these in to further raise the stakes.

❑ **Focus on the major conflicts in literature.** Which one of these best describes the conflict in your memoir? Do your major scenes address this type of conflict? Why or why not?

Man versus man

Man versus self

Man versus society

Man versus fate, destiny, circumstances

Chapter 14

Ensuring the Theme and Meaning Are What You Want

In This Chapter

▶ Reading between the lines

▶ Using imagery

▶ Using timing to great effect

▶ Making the most of your book's title

Going back through your manuscript to ensure that it's about where you hope it to be makes sense. Unfortunately, you may be surprised how often this isn't the case.

This chapter focuses on the part of the writing process that really isn't the province of revision (see Chapter 15) or editing (refer to Chapter 16). This chapter deals with seriously *deep* material — the stuff people will be arguing over in book club meetings and teaching to bored college sophomores in literature classes. This chapter is all about theme, pure and simple; in other words, *theme* is the book's meaning. I talk a lot about how to fine-tune and expand on your structure and story in Chapter 15, but this chapter lays the groundwork to get you started thinking about theme. Having thematic significance is what makes your book worth rereading, or even reading at all.

Spending an entire chapter to discuss the basics of theme and meaning is worthwhile because theme is where you can communicate something profound. Theme is also what enriches the reading experience. You may wonder why you address theme near the end of the writing process. Basically, you can't rush theme. Theme is an undercurrent that only surfaces when enough of the other parts connect properly. Focus on theme too soon and it's like playing checkers while being red colorblind. So read this chapter to see the best ways to approach theme and help your work have greater depth and meaning. And when you're ready, Chapter 15 is waiting to help you take your story to the next level.

Some writers consider the theme-story relationship to be like the chicken-egg one. Which comes first? If you choose to lock onto your theme targets early in the writing process and that works for you, fine. In my experience, though, having a cheat sheet to keep track of your different themes may have you over focus on theme versus story, and without your story being dynamite, you won't have readers. Without readers, who cares what the themes are, right? (But as with all advice in this book, go with what works for you, which may be different than what works for others. You won't hurt my feelings either way!)

Focusing on Theme between the Lines

When you review your manuscript to pinpoint the different themes, you can read the book line by line. What's really important though is what appears between the lines that speak most to theme. Perhaps it's more accurate to say it's what goes across the lines, such as the connections and repetitions that recur, and losses that echo other losses. Look for words, phrases, or dialogue that repeat. Identify things that hearken back to other things that came before.

These sections brief you on how you can identify your memoir's themes and meanings as you read your manuscript, line by line.

In general, theme works best if you do it with subtlety. Obvious themes in a memoir feel preachy and didactic. Generally, readers resist or avoid preachy books, so be careful that your book doesn't sound too "better than thou" or "I know more than you."

Staying on task (of story)

Staying on task basically means to keep the focus on where you need it to be, which ultimately is the story. This section asks you to review your manuscript carefully to see if what you've already written has that focus. If you're reading this chapter yet you haven't started writing, that works too. Consider the following to be bonus information about the marriage of story and theme that might save you some time in the revision process later.

Here's the challenge. Writers want to tell a story which engages readers and keeps the pages turning. Writers also want to communicate a theme, which is related to your core beliefs about how the world works. Theme is something that is dear and personal to a writer, something that fully resonates within them. Understanding that, it's easy to shift your focus to theme at the expense of story. What I mean is that it's easy to start pointing the narrative "camera" at things you believe will help create and develop theme, but as a consequence, you might then be losing track of your main story. Don't worry, though. Your story will still have themes whether you are consciously working on them as you write or not. And if they don't come through clearly enough, you can play them up or down as needed during the revision process (Chapter 15 covers this in great detail), or by using the ideas here to make the changes now.

To help create clarity, focus on what those themes are that you may be trying so hard to make come alive. Basically, I am talking about what your book is really about. So go ahead — identify three themes in your manuscript.

Now as you comb through your manuscript pages, keep a list of those themes taped to your computer monitor to see whether you're focusing too little, too much, or just enough on hitting those themes. Starting to write about Uncle Mikey's penchant for burning buttermilk pancakes at 2 a.m. and singing old love songs in Russian loud enough for the neighbors to call the cops is one way to start rolling with the quirky family stories. In a book about being the child of an alcoholic parent who can't quit? You have to tone down the extra stuff. You can keep some of it in, sure. That's what provides the unique context that makes the story yours versus a generic story about alcoholism. Yet if the reason to add something is just to create a bit of local color, then that's usually not enough to keep it in. As a writer, you need to stay on task.

Keep asking yourself, "What does this scene add to the overall story?" If the answer doesn't promptly reveal itself, consider cutting. Story has to be No. 1, even though theme feels so incredibly important to many writers.

Don't let your book become cluttered with random things, no matter how interesting they may be to you. Scenes, images, actions, and even people must earn their way into your book. They have to self-justify taking up room. They have to carry their own weight, both in terms of contributing to the overall story as well as the main themes. How do they do that? By the story losing something if you exclude them.

Looking for repetition

Because most memoirs will have 80,000 words, give or take, repetition is crucial. If you say something essential to your worldview and your philosophy only once, it will be lost beneath the sheer volume of other words. Say it twice, and a few readers may latch onto it. Say it three times, as Michael Cunningham does with his flower image in *The Hours* (Picador)? That's a lovely, memorable number. Talk about repetition done so well that most readers don't notice it consciously!

Good readers are much more attuned to reading for beneath-the-surface stuff, such as theme. You don't need to worry about them; they'll figure it out on their own. You have to think about the majority of people who will read your book. Carefully done repetition becomes road signs to guide the reader on the path you choose.

Notice that I don't say a gigantic, glowing neon sign. A road sign has useful information but it's unobtrusive and out of the way. If you're actively look-ing for the road signs, you can easily find them. If your attention is on other things (the pretty girl in the seat next to you, the iPod that won't quite con-nect right with the car radio, or a giant wolf spider that's crawling over your shoe, to name a few distracting options), you won't even notice a road sign. Yet when you need them, there they are.

If you find that you have too few or too many road signs, make some changes via revision. Chapter 15 has lots of practical advice on how to do exactly that.

Recognizing the main theme versus other themes

Every book has a single main theme. You (and your readers) can identify it because it's the one most naturally suggested by the dramatic question that drives the story and the ultimate outcome caused by the main character's actions and choice. But along the way, other themes emerge. Some are nearly as important as the main one, but they should never overtake it. If they do, you have started with the wrong dramatic question. Changing to a new dra-matic question is easy enough to do, though it's also fine to re-prioritize your themes.

You need to know which theme is more important than the others and then develop that main one more fully than anything else in the rest of the book. It sounds basic enough, but again and again I run into writers who tell me that their book is about X, but after I look through their manuscript, it's clear that the themes A, B, and C are far more pronounced. Either the writer is simply wrong about what the book is really about, or he's going to be disappointed when critics and readers all think the book is about something different. In either case, the writer would be well-served to do some revising to make sure the book works well for both the reader's and the writer's goals.

Addressing each theme

Another reason to create a hierarchy of your themes is to figure out how best to handle each theme. A main theme should come up again and again throughout the entire book, and you may be able to handle appropriately and adequately a subtheme in a single chapter.

To address theme — the idea or topic that connects meaningfully to important changes the main character will undergo — you must at some point look at your text and identify where theme is being developed. You can build it through a variety of methods to be effective. Make sure you're doing the following:

- ✔ Your dialogue interfaces with theme at some level.

- ✔ Your descriptions and scene setting do so, too.

- ✔ Your showing and telling also use words, phrases, and images that suggest theme.

To see an example of how a book uses the main themes and subthemes, read J.R.R. Tolkien's *The Hobbit* (Mariner Books). You'll immediately see the main theme is about good versus evil. Yet the book is also about courage, friendship, redemption, and love. And just when you stop your list of themes and subthemes, you realize that it's also about justice, loyalty, greed, revenge, and oppression, to name a few subthemes. None of those subthemes are as developed, pronounced, or important as the main theme: good versus evil.

Tolkien handles some of these subthemes at the chapter level, which means they're not major themes. They're important, sure, but not über-important. That kind of purposeful choosing regarding how and which themes are developed is useful to keep in mind when writing or revising your own book. Some of your chapters will focus on lesser but still important themes, which is okay.

Look at a memoir example. The third book in Mary Karr's memoir trilogy *Lit: A Memoir* (Harper Perennial) is first and foremost about recovering from alcoholism through the help of religion. That's the main theme and much of the book connects powerfully with that. Subthemes of this book include reflections on the first memoir she wrote, her literary life, and her family. Karr always tells a compelling story, which is her journey from disease to health, but the idea of rescue and purpose is built into everything, too. She clearly spent a lot of time figuring out how to wed story and theme to good effect, including dark humor, confession, poetic description, and surprise.

How often should you return to your main theme? You want to do so often enough that readers don't get distracted by other elements of the book. Certain types of books — such as addiction, abuse, and stories — can't help but be neck-deep in the main theme throughout, which is fine. For other types of memoirs, though, you have to make an effort to weave in the major theme every few chapters. As a result, you may have to alter the structure you chose to achieve this more easily.

If you don't mind rewriting hundreds of pages — as I had to with my memoir *Unplugged* (HCI), which necessitated two entirely new manuscript drafts to get back under control — then fine, write about whatever you fancy, however you choose. If you want to be efficient and end up with a better end product that has a commitment to story and also does a great job managing theme, then figure out your main theme as well as your subthemes as soon as you can.

Creating Key Images

At some point in the writing process, writers need to engage the right hemisphere of their brain to generate images. *Imagery* makes a lot of sense in terms of creating meaning for a reader. A picture is worth a thousand words, right? Well, that's true in terms of writing. Creating imagery on the page — remember that imagery isn't just visual, but any sensory data input, such as smell, touch, and taste — makes a scene memorable. It engages readers by subtly asking them to interpret what it means. One other function of imagery is why it's being discussed here in this chapter (and in the following sections): It helps create theme.

Comparing the types of images

When reviewing your manuscript, look to see how you've used images. Images come in two varieties:

✔ **Regular:** It's the sort of thing a writer includes in a story to evoke the senses. Although most regular images are visual in nature, readers appreciate it when you include images that use other senses.

For example, here are a couple regular images:

> That's when I saw her, lounging on a beach towel at the edge of the water, the western sun turning the lake the same hue of pink as her one-piece swimsuit.

> Janette moved through her grandfather's garden, running her fingers across the fat azalea buds, the cannas blossoms, and the orange-red of his prize begonias. Everywhere, she noticed the thick heady smell of peat moss and moist air.

Both are successful because they're descriptive and they easily help develop a scene. You have a slew of regular images throughout your story.

✔ **Key:** Also referred to as a *charged image* or *central image*, the *key image* is the dominant, theme-connected image of your story. The key image is a crucial, memorable piece of your larger narrative arc. It speaks directly to what your book is and is about. Most stories have a single key image.

You may not be able to completely grasp what a key image is. The following section provides a look at three of the most well-known images in all Western literature to see how each key image speaks to theme and meaning.

One way to help see how to create a key image is to look at . . . comic books. Pick up any comic book you choose from your public library, local bookstore, or comic shop and open to any page. You may notice that you're now looking at two sides at once, that they're full of smaller panels and one larger single image. The big image is a key image. Flip another page or two and you'll see a similar layout — lots of smaller image panels and one larger one. Although those are all important scenes, the No. 1 most important scene is the cover. It's always a full page in size, and it's nearly always the most vivid, impressive scene of the entire comic book. Also, it probably gives you a clear thematic sense of what the inside of the comic book will be about — love, betrayal, death.

So to help you with your own key image, think visually like a comic book illustrator about your memoir. Which scenes would be the biggest on the page? And now for the big question: Which is the cover scene? That's likely your key image for the entire book.

If you want to find additional avenues of seeing key image examples, consider my suggestions:

✔ **Go to your local movie theater and examine the movie posters.** The best of them often visually illustrate the key image of the movie.

✔ **Hit up your public library and look at a few good picture books.** Although you see a host of pictures throughout the book, likely one really stands out. It'll be bigger on the page, more vibrant, and more successful somehow. That's your key image.

Considering three examples of key images

A key image is the most powerful, dramatic visual that connects story and theme. It's what you see on a movie poster that tells you what the movie will be about and also urges you to spend your money to see the whole film. It's also what is typically on book covers, serving both as a teaser of the plot and a hint of what themes will be explored in the book. Although you may have a lot of important images throughout your book, it will have just one key image — one iconic visual — that best represents what your book is all about.

The following examples aren't memoirs, but they're texts you're probably already familiar with, and each clearly demonstrates the idea of the key image. Read on to see key images in operation.

If you want to see key images in memoirs, examine the hiking boot at the beginning of Cheryl Strayed's *Wild: From Lost to Found on the Pacific Crest Trail* (Knopf) or the recurring images of food and wool coats in Frank McCourt's *Angela's Ashes: A Memoir* (Scribner). Check out the various cover options of this National Book Award finalist for different renderings of the same theme: silenced rage and suffering.

Huck Finn's raft

In *The Adventures of Huckleberry Finn,* a book about slavery and freedom (among other things), Mark Twain put Huck and Jim the slave on a raft, moving down the mighty Mississippi. On the pure level of plot, the raft serves as a model of transportation that gets the characters away from trouble. For Huck, the raft is how he escapes the violence of his father as well as the civilizing that Mrs. Watson and the widow want to impart upon him (and he doesn't want!). For Jim, the raft is his way to escape a much more obvious type of slavery and lack of freedom.

What the raft is beyond that, however, is a home for each. On the raft, Jim and Huck have an emotional breakthrough and achieve a connection. After all, on the raft is where Huck decides to be truly free by making his own adult decision (which is contrary to society's view), and then accepting the consequences for his actions. His decision? Whether to turn Jim in or not.

If you're still not certain that the raft is the key image, let me ask you this question: What's the one visual you get when you think of this book? Odds are that you think of the two characters on the raft. Voila. The raft is the key image for you.

Gatsby's green light

The green light in *The Great Gatsby* isn't just a green light. The first time you see it (remember that authors repeat images of importance!) is at the conclusion of the first chapter. Nick Carraway, the narrator, sees Gatsby at the end of his dock reaching for it across the water. Soon enough, you discover that the green light is at the end of Daisy Buchanan's dock, and that regaining her love is Gatsby's singular purpose.

The mysterious green light comes to mean the following for different readers:

✔ Green is the color of hope and renewal.

✔ Green means wealth, and from this book's portrayal of the rich, you know that wealth corrupts, so green = wealth = corruption.

✔ Like a traffic light, green means go, and Gatsby indeed goes, goes, and goes relentlessly toward his goal.

- The light is "the green breast of the new world" (comparing Gatsby's dream of rediscovering Daisy to that of the discoverers of America).

- The light is Gatsby's "unattainable dream."

- The light is, for everyone else, the American Dream (which, too, is shown as unattainable, by virtue of the light first being, and then later remaining, "minute and far away").

That's just what I recall without cracking open the book again (though admittedly, it's a favorite and I've taught this terrific book enough times to have quotes readily available in my head). But if I had to, I could pick up my old copy of it and easily write a few dozen pages detailing the importance of this one specific image and how it connects with the major ideas, themes, and characters of *The Great Gatsby* to show how it's a key image in this classic book.

Don Quixote's windmill

In Miguel de Cervantes' 1604 novel, poor Don Quixote attacks windmills because he thinks they're giants. They dominate the landscape for miles and loom large and dangerous. What they really represent, though, is the practice of sheep farming for wool, which was displacing poor farmers. In essence the windmills represented the titans of industry who were squashing the lives and livelihood of peasants.

Beyond that, the windmills also represent the destruction of the past. They represent tyranny. They represent idealism versus realism. They represent man versus machine (much like our own John Henry legend).

This image is so powerful that it has come into common knowledge. People accuse you of "tilting at windmills," which means that you're attacking imaginary, powerful enemies, or engaging in a hopeless cause. It also provides the adjective "quixotic," which means the impractical pursuit of idealism.

What about how this specific image/action keeps coming up in popular culture?

- The band name They Might Be Giants

- The film, stage, and ballet production of Man of La Mancha (containing the song "The Impossible Dream")

- The 1998 book *Tilting at Windmills* by Clay Chastain (Leathers Publishing)

- The spinning of a finger at the side of our head to indicate madness (a windmill turning?)

Pretty strong evidence of this being a key image, wouldn't you say?

Using Timing for Comedic or Tragic Effects

Timing in terms of writing a memoir is about how and when you deliver key moments on the page. Part of how your manipulate timing is with tempo, rhythm, and pauses. In many ways, timing is quite similar to pacing (refer to Chapter 13 for more information). A key difference, though, is you use timing to make a moment funny or tragic. Pacing is a more general term that covers the general speed of a story's delivery through scenes, chapters, and the entire book.

Here's an example whose effect is changed by the timing of its delivery. See what I mean:

> Knock knock.
>
> Who's there?
>
> Interrupting cow.
>
> Interrupt . . .
>
> MOO!

My eight-year-old daughter thinks that's funny stuff. She's right. Why? Because the timing is dead on. Have you ever encountered that "funny" uncle who can't tell a joke to save his life? Those uncles don't recognize that it's not just what you say, but it's also how and when you say it that can make a world of difference.

That same type of timing works in your memoir. Readers want to experience a range of emotions. Figuring out how to deliver them is your job as the author. For instance, say your memoir is largely about your spouse succumbing to a brain cancer. You can't just start with *sad,* then go to *sad,* to have a middle about *sad,* and then drive to the end with a huge *sad.* Doing so would be like painting an entire portrait with only the color yellow. You have to know when the reader is going to need that changeup, that surprise, that thing which plays against their expectation.

Because movies do a very clear, visual job illustrating this, consider the movie, *Saving Private Ryan.* During one of the later battles with German forces, Tom Sizemore's character has an unexpected one-on-one encounter with an enemy soldier. When a rifle jams, the German throws his helmet at Sizemore, who chucks his own helmet right back. Then they both struggle to get their pistols out to finish the battle. Sizemore wins, shooting the other soldier, though he's then struck by a stray bullet from an unseen shooter. Furious, he throws his pistol at that unseen attacker.

Compare that to the final scene where Matt Damon's character is in Arlington Cemetery saying, "Tell me I have led a good life." One is unexpectedly hilarious and timed perfectly during a tense action sequence. It's funny and it also represents the absurdity that life sometimes smacks you with. The other is a delicious, poignant payoff after a slow, gradual build and the raising of the emotional stakes throughout the movie.

Your themes will likely have emotional resonance of one type of another. Remember to set up the big moments (the key image, the climax, or the reversal of the main character's fortunes) by using the full range of emotions and tensions in other parts of the book. Create a deep, complex web of experiences for readers to engage with, and deliver them at the best times. How do you know where the best spots are? They're where you recognize that you're playing the same emotional hot button with your reader too much. Give them those moments of release.

Recognizing Why Your Memoir's Title Matters

As the executive director of C&R Press, a nonprofit publisher, I often run across a manuscript I love that is saddled with the most blah title ever. Sometimes I can't get past the title and end up passing on an otherwise good book. A title makes your first impression.

A good title does the following:

- ✔ Sets up a key image, theme, or mood
- ✔ Generates an emotional response in prospective readers
- ✔ Creates a sense of curiosity in a viewer
- ✔ Works as a marketing tool (does it stop someone who's walking past it in a bookstore?)

In short, your title matters, so make sure you've given your title some real thought before going after a literary agent (see Chapter 18) or looking into publishing avenues (see Chapters 19 and 20).

A great way to find your title is brainstorm a long list of ideas, themes, and emotional response that you want your memoir to invoke in your reader's mind. Don't censor yourself. Use visual words. Use location words. Ask questions. Go back to key words for your outline (see Chapter 6) and see if any jump out as possibilities. Keep going until your list has at least 50 words or phrases. Now that you have this big list, go back through it and start looking for one-word titles. Look for a title that's simply one noun plus one adjective. Look for short phrases that could serve as a title.

Ask your spouse or kids for help. Ask members of your writing group. Go to your local bookstore and find at least two dozen books that similar to yours — not just memoirs, but a specific type of memoir, like travel memoir, addiction memoir, or school memoir. How did those authors handle their titles? See if you can utilize theirs as a template that you fill in with words from your list.

To ensure that your title will entice readers,

- ✔ **Be original.** Figure out a unique and creative title. If your story is about moving from New York to Los Angeles, don't call it *A Tale of Two Cities*.

  For example, I've recently been working with a first-time author who's writing about a family member who suffered a devastating injury in a car crash. The proposed title of this book? *From Tragedy to Triumph.* Yes, that is the book's general theme, but summing it up so clearly stole the delight of the ending. It nearly pre-empted the need to read the book. Worse, I did my due diligence and checked out that title and its close variations on Amazon. More than two dozen other books use that phrase as the title or subtitle. And when you count variations on those words, you add another pile of books that someone may accidently purchase when specifically looking for this book. People don't always remember an author's names, but they do remember titles. Because you can't copyright a title, don't make things harder for yourself by selecting a title that's been well-used.

- ✔ **Be clever or humorous.** If your memoir is straightforward and serious, don't bother with a clever or humorous title because it promises the reader that a similar sensibility will be inside the book, too. But if you have moments of fun or laughter inside, go for it with your title. Readers react to cleverness if it's not too silly or too over the top. Try wordplay or puns. Consider hyperbole, too. Augusten Burroughs's *Running with Scissors: A Memoir* (Picador) and Jennifer Niven's *The Aqua Net Diaries: Big Hair, Big Dreams, Small Town* (Gallery Books) are good examples. Compare those to R. Kelly's memoir, *Soula Coaster: The Diary of Me* (SmileyBooks), or John McManamy's *Raccoons Respect My Piss But Watch Out for Skunks: My Funny Life on a Planet Not of My Choosing That I Now—Maybe, Sort of, Not Really, Well Okay—Call Home* (McMan).

- ✔ **Be concise.** Short is good. Short is punchy. Short is easy to remember. Keeping a title concise forces you to select strong nouns and verbs, such as *Leading with My Chin* by Jay Leno (HarperTorch), or *I Am Spock* by Leonard Nimoy (Hyperion). Meanwhile Dina Kucera's *Everything I Never Wanted to Be: A Memoir of Alcoholism and Addiction, Faith and Family,*

Hope and Humor (Dream of Things) is a bit of a mouthful. Sometimes you can't do anything about this but if you can, try to keep it short.

✔ **Be aware of the book's website.** Check the .com URL of your title to see if it's available. If not, what will you use for your book's website URL? You want to select a title that makes marketing the book as easy as possible.

The following memoir titles do a good job of using the preceding characteristics of a good title:

✔ *Let's Pretend This Never Happened: (A Mostly True Memoir)* by Jenny Lawson (Amy Einhorn Books/Putnam)

✔ *Will Love for Crumbs* by Jonna Ivin (CreateSpace)

✔ *The Devil in Pew Number Seven: A True Story* by Rebecca Nichols Alonzo (Tyndale Momentum)

✔ *Are You There, Vodka? It's Me, Chelsea* by Chelsea Handler (Gallery Books)

✔ *Loud in the House of Myself: Memoir of a Strange Girl* by Stacy Pershall (W.W. Norton & Company)

✔ *Blown for Good: Behind the Iron Curtain of Scientology* (by Marc Headley BFG Books Inc.)

Imagine standing in a bookstore or surfing Amazon. Which of the preceding titles would you select from the shelf and start thumbing through or view certain parts? Ask yourself why. What promise(s) does the title make about theme, style, and content? What is it about these titles that pull you in? After you answer those questions, draft your title so it does the same.

A publisher will likely want to change your title, which is fine. A good title at this point, though, may help you get to the point where you actually *have* a publisher, so make your title count.

Writing Exercises on Generating Theme and Meaning

Theme and meaning are what your book is about. It's a big task to figure clearly your book's meaning, and it's equally daunting to manage theme throughout a book-length manuscript. The following writing exercises can help you get thinking about and looking at theme and meaning in other memoirs as well as in your memoir. You may even find your book's title from doing these exercises, as well.

❑ **If you've read this chapter before starting your manuscript, take the time to write the five main themes that you think your book will be about.** Decide which of them will connect most meaningfully with the main conflict. That's likely your primary theme. Be aware that you may be wrong, which requires you changing the text a bit. You may not real- ize it, either, until you have written an entire draft. A memoir never looks the same on the page as it does in your mind.

❑ **Read a favorite memoir and note any repetition — place, images, events, conversations, and so on.** Taken together, how do these things add up to something meaningful? What practical lesson can you take away from that reading and use to help you create meaning in your memoir?

❑ **After you identify the possible themes in your memoir, ask yourself of each theme: "Why should regular readers care about this theme, this message?"** If you have a difficult time seeing the possible impact it may have on their lives, consider how you can tweak your memoir to focus on other, more relevant themes. Trust me — your story has at least one huge, universal theme that most readers will care about. It may not be the one you would choose to write about, but that's the reality of a memoir — the events of your past won't change. If you still can't see what you feel are important things, enlist the help of unbiased readers. Get their input. You're under no obligation to go with their ideas, but a fresh pair of eyes often sees things as they are.

❑ **Watch an episode of one of your favorite dramatic TV shows online, recorded, or on DVD.** That way you can pause when you need to pause. Scene by scene, jot down a one-sentence description of what goes on in that scene. Then add a short description of what you perceive to be the point of that scene. After you complete the entire episode, go back to what you've written and see how each scene interrelates. What are the connections? What are the repetitions? How does each relate to the overall story of this episode and of the entire TV series? Can you follow theme this way? Do you understand what each scene means individually as well as in terms of the entire story?

❑ **List ten nouns that come to mind when you think about your book.** Then list ten verbs and ten adjectives. What words come to mind when you think of your major character, the action of the story, and the theme(s)? Using these lists as a starting point, come up with three new title options. Select the best and go with it as your title for now. Before showing it to a literary agent or publishing professional, reevaluate the title one final time.

Chapter 15

Making Revisions

- -

- -

A t this time, you take your full draft of your entire manuscript, although you can also use a completed chapter of a scene, and as my grand-mother used to say, "Make it pretty." Now is the time to do some revisions. If you're ready to revise your manuscript, you've come to the right chapter. Here you can find everything you need to powerfully revise your manuscript while still maintaining your intended meaning.

Comparing Revision and Editing: Differentiating between the Two

Many writers use "edit" and "revise" interchangeably, but there's a major difference with the two terms. *Revision* means that you're tackling the macro-level stuff. In essence, you're re-envisioning things. Meanwhile *editing* means you take what you have and work with it at the micro-level. Other words for editing include polishing, buffing, and tweaking — that sort of thing.

I visit writing groups all the time and one of the most popular questions is some variation of this one: What's the secret to great writing? The answer? Revision and editing. The following shows you the distinction between editing and revision:

During editing, you focus on the following:

- ✔ **Sentence level:** Here you break up overlong sentences and adjust lan-guage for rhythm and clarity.

- ✔ **Spelling, grammar, punctuation, and word choice:** This is the stuff that college freshman composition teachers insist that students get right, such as using commas properly, avoiding sentence fragments, and avoiding passive voice. It also includes finding the best word versus just going with an acceptable one.

- ✔ **Transitions:** *Transitions* are words and phrases (such as "frequently," "on top of," or "in addition") that make writing flow smoothly by bridging one idea to the next. You either add or improve them.

- ✔ **The manuscript as a product:** With this mindset, the big elements of the manuscript are set, and your job is simply to make it all better. Essentially, you're shining to a high polish what you already have.

With revision, you address the following:

- ✔ **Story elements:** Story elements include plot, conflict, character, and setting. You must carefully consider and reconsider them and then improve them as needed.

- ✔ **Big idea questions:** Here, you challenge everything that's a part of your story (beyond the story elements, which you've already handled). Some of the most useful things to reevaluate include using a consistent point of view, showing change in your main character, presenting and developing an interesting conflict, and using natural-sounding dialogue. You should also take a fresh look at elements like tone, voice, structure, and style.

- ✔ **The manuscript as a product-in-process:** With this mindset, nothing is set in stone. If you need to chop off chapters or flip flop plot elements to be more effective, do it. The entire piece, while existing as a complete manuscript, is just a draft. It's not a final piece that simply needs minor tweaking.

The rest of this chapter explains the most useful ways to engage in revision for your memoir. This chapter also asks you some difficult questions, too to help you see where your manuscript can be improved. From those answers will come clarity, focus, and quality.

Because so many writers confuse or conflate the two, here is a bit more clarity between editing and revision. I have created some sample text to work with and I show an edit of it and then a revision of that same text. Watch for the differences.

Here is the sample text:

Ichabod Andrews jumped atop the cafeteria table and yelled, "Food fight!"

He scooped up mashed potatoes and let fly. Zack Johnson ducked just as Mrs. Birkeback entered the lunchroom. POW.

Every other kid settled back into their seats, eyes cast downward.

"ICH-A-BOD!" she howled.

Here is the edited version of the sample text:

> Ichabod leapt onto the table. "Food fight!" he bellowed as he let fly with his mashed potatoes. Zack the nerd bent over to tie his shoe — the gooey glob sailed right over him. Mrs. Birkeback came into the lunchroom and got nailed in the face: ker*splat!*
>
> The masses settled, murmuring into their seats. One kid let out a long, slow whistle as Mrs. Birkeback wiped the buttery mess from her eyes.
>
> Finally, she opened her mouth. "Ick-a-boooooood!"

And here is the revised version of the same text:

> Three weeks in detention, and Lord knows how much grief my parents were onboard for as soon as they found out. Who knew Mrs. Break-Your-Back was going to stomp into the cafeteria right as I tried to start World War III with some airborne potatoes?

Can you see the dissimilar mindset a writer has with each version? The writer engaging in editing has a commitment to what's on the page and simply wants to tweak it. The writer engaging in revision can do anything — I mean anything — in order to make the entire book work better. The author can do anything from cutting a chapter, cutting characters, adding scenes, changing a present-tense scene to a flashback, altering the point of view, or switching up the style.

A reader looking at an edited text may not notice lots of differences between the edited text and the original. On the other hand, with revised text, the reader should notice plenty of major differences. A revised manuscript may be 50 percent shorter, twice as long, use a different point of view, or have a plot that went from chronological to episodic (see Chapter 6 for an explanation of different story structures).

Editing does *not* mean that your final version is shorter. Yes, writers often create flabby, bloated language in early drafts that are best improved by tightening. Often that's true because the flabby writing done in early drafts can easily be tightened. But for clarity's sake, sometimes you need to add things back in — thus, the additional length, as you can see from the previous sample. For more on editing, turn to Chapter 16.

Being Committed and Brutal to Your Text

When you revise your text, the bottom line is to be committed to the text and at the same time brutally honest with it. You must be behind it 100 percent during all phases — not just the initial writing of the first draft, but the entire process, beginning to end. At the same time, although you'll have a professional editor comb through your book to make a good book, ultimately it's your responsibility to make it a good book. So stick it out, and do the best you honestly can with the revision stage. Your effort is worth it. After all, who wants to write a book that no one wants to read?

No matter what your memoir writing goal is — self-publication, traditional publication, scrapbook publication for your family, Internet publication on your webpage, or something else — you need to be committed to the memoir being the best that it can be. If not, readers will be as excited to read it as people are when you ask them to look at your photo collection of birthmarks that look like presidents.

Cutting things because the words are yours and the story is yours isn't easy. You may feel as if you're cutting off your own arm. The revision process is the time to do so. You just have to ask yourself: Will these changes make the story more effective? For instance, if the strange neighbor girl with the whole-head dental gear isn't helping the story, she needs to go so you can focus on what *does* matter. Eradicating someone from your story during the revision process isn't disrespectful. You aren't blasting that person out of existence and denying that she ever lived. Your revisions simply are a matter of improving the story, which is always the benchmark.

Developing Your Revision Process (and Sticking to It)

When it's time to revise, most importantly, you need to have a process to follow — some way that you can actually ensure that you make your revisions. For me, I revise right on the computer screen. My novelist pal Michael does it into a handheld recorder. The science fiction guru Harlan Ellison claimed to do all revisions in his head. California writer Todd James Pierce often does multiple versions of the same scene one after the other in a single computer file.

If you have to read your text aloud in an echoey bathroom, fine. If you have to print up the entire thing and sprawl out on the guest room bed, fine. If you have to handwrite the first draft and do revisions as you type it into the computer, fine. The bottom line: There's no wrong way to revise, just as long as you do it.

When determining which revision method works best for you, here are some questions to ask yourself about the process and your relationship to it. Answer them honestly; you may discover a hiccup or two in your writing process. A few of these questions, too, may get you to see specific places in your manuscript that revision can help.

✔ What's more important — you loving your manuscript or readers loving your manuscript?

✔ Do you reread things before sending them out for publication?

✔ Do you reread things that are rejected for publication?

✔ Is there a difference between a piece being "done" versus "good enough"?

✔ Are there any places in the story where you skip when rereading?

✔ What is the best part of the manuscript?

✔ What part would you change if you had more time, energy, wisdom, or talent?

✔ How many people do you personally know who'd pay $25 to read your book?

✔ Do you work best in mornings, afternoons, or at night?

✔ What kind of environment do you create for your revision?

✔ Do you revise more than once?

Getting introspective about your writing process is always a good idea. Writing takes time out of your work, your family, your health, and your life, so make sure you revise your manuscript to make all the hard work worth the sacrifice.

Making Revisions: A Nine-Item Checklist

Many writers want nuts-and-bolts help when they're revising their manuscripts. If you're one of those authors, you've come to the right section. Here you can find a get-in-the-trenches-and-fix-stuff checklist to help you fully navigate the revision process. Ask yourself the following questions and honestly answer them. (You can use this list for anything you're revising, whether "it" be a character, a passage, a scene, or a chapter as you work your way through the entire manuscript, front to back.)

✔ **Does it advance the plot?** The plot needs to move forward at a clear, steady pace. Always be on the lookout for making that happen.

✔ **Does it reveal motivation?** Readers want to see why your characters do what they do. What motivates your characters?

✔ **Does it impart key, relevant information?** Make sure you give readers important information that explains what a character is thinking and why a character acts a certain way.

✔ **Does it characterize the main character?** Refer to Chapter 8 for more about characters.

✔ **Does it create new conflict or increase existing conflict?** You can swap "tension" for conflict if that makes more sense for you. Conflict is the engine of a story. Making it work more effectively is always a good idea in terms of generating and keeping reader interest.

✔ **Does it arouse the senses?** Who doesn't love vivid imagery? As long as you don't get carried away, see if you can focus what readers see via the words on the page.

✔ **Is it static or dynamic?** Something that is *static* is unchanging whereas something *dynamic* has movement, energy, life. You want as few static elements in your story as possible. Character description, scene details, physical confrontations, and heartfelt dialogue should all pop with energy. If the word "static" can appropriately be used to describe any of them, you have trouble.

✔ **Is it profoundly honest?** Readers want all books to feel honest, but with a memoir, it has to be unflinchingly so. If you're holding back, they'll know and they won't be happy. Look for ways to reveal and share meaningfully.

✔ **Is it going to inform the lives of others?** Think about what the audience will take away from your book. Find ways to make your story relevant. If you're unsure how, have trusted readers read it and give you some input on that specific thing.

If the answer to any of the preceding questions is "no," then strongly reconsider leaving those parts of your manuscript out. You have a lot more room to roam in a memoir than in a literary essay, but that doesn't mean you should roam. The further you get from the crux of your story, the less inclined you should be to include it. (If you absolutely love something, save it in a different file and use it for a different project.)

If you're an extensive outliner and like to plan everything before you begin a project, you may ask yourself these questions as you develop your book's outline and as you write the manuscript. Even so, you should still take one final, critical look at the entire thing after you've finished it. Call it your final pass. Don't skip it.

Incorporating Three More Advanced Revision Tactics

Talk to a dozen different professional writers and you'll get a dozen different tips on how to revise effectively. Call them "secrets," if you want. You may not have access to professional writers, so these sections examine three secrets that pro writers regularly employ. Use them as you choose!

Remembering the reader

When revising your book, you want to create the mindset where you're coming fresh to your story. If you're reading like a reader would, you'll more likely see the same shortcomings and underdeveloped areas that they would. To help me with this, I have a 3-x-5 note card taped to the wall beside my computer screen. On it, I've written: "What About the Reader?" Just having that in my line of sight helps me regularly remember that the memoir isn't just for me — it's for others, too.

The best way to remember the reader is to put yourself in the reader's shoes. Ask your significant other or a trusted friend to read aloud your manuscript to you. Switching the role from writer to reader helps you hear your story differently so you can then take notes of moments where you lose interest. You can then either infuse those boring moments with new energy or entirely remove them.

Acknowledging the power of change

You want your memoir to show how you've changed. Readers connect and enjoy reading about the incredible changes that people have gone through — ideally to be better people in the end. When you revise your manuscript, look to see whether the catharsis you've gone through is significant so readers can admire or empathize with you. If this change isn't obvious, you can focus your revisions to make this metamorphosis stronger.

As you revise, give your entire manuscript a holistic look regarding the main character's development. Is there a genuine change of some type? If not, then readers will probably ask "so what?" when reading about your character, and ultimately your story. You want them to care, and the main character's evolution, however shape it takes, is what readers care about.

In other words, Jerome Stern, one of my favorite writing instructors during my graduate school years, used to denounce the "zero to zero" story. What he meant was that a story about a drunk who drank throughout the story and ended up a drunk in the end wasn't all that interesting, and he's right.

A memoir that's a zero to zero story isn't interesting, or at least you and I can admit that figuring out *how* to make it interesting will be very difficult. Perhaps your manuscript starts at zero and ends at zero, but you have some deviation along the way. If you don't have a zero-to-zero arc, then the writing needs to be astute and brilliant throughout, so much so that readers overlook its absence.

The subject matter of memoirs

This issue comes up more and more as society brainwashes future generations to believe that they're unique and profoundly special — everything they do is just brilliant. Wearing that kind of blinders can be a death sentence for a memoir, even one with a seemingly interesting topic. Basically you want to ensure the subject matter of your memoir is shaped for a memoir.

I see this phenomenon in my memoir workshops. Writers are convinced everyone will love their story because they wrote it. Or they're convinced that just because they're writing about being a part of SEAL team six or turning around a failing auto company in five years by introducing a top-to-bottom administrative makeover based on Sun Tzu that it'll be a stunning hit. Unfortunately not so.

Any of the preceding ideas can easily become a strong memoir if the authors took the time to reflect and plan how to make their stories interesting and relevant to readers. If they have a compelling reason for looking back at that stage in their life and asking questions about it on the page, it probably will work well for them and the reader. If the authors are just dumping data or bragging, then they have a recipe for a book destined to end up in the remainder rack.

Give yourself sufficient time — six months, a year, whatever you need — to reflect before getting too far along with the writing of your memoir. If that sounds like too much of a delay, at least give yourself a long weekend of quiet introspection. Some workshop leaders insist that all material written for a memoir needs to be at least a decade in the past. If your subject stands the test of time, it's worth writing about. Plenty of writers think their subject matter was huge when they wrote about it, only to find that, years later, it was decidedly trivial. I say give it a year or two, but feel free to take notes along the way (or start with the deep past first).

What makes any subject matter worthy of being shaped into memoir form is when you

- ✔ **Are exotic:** If you can vividly show readers a world they don't know well — an Afghan combat zone, the world of XXX film stars, or the inside of a training room for professional European soccer teams, for instance — you'll have something many will want to know about.

- ✔ **Are perceptive:** Even if you don't have an exotic story to tell, if you can step back and find the extraordinary in the ordinary, you're going to please readers. Writers with a background in poetry are often quite successful at viewing the world in these interesting ways and also communicating it in exciting, evocative language.

✔ **Don't over share:** This seems to run counter to the idea that memoirs should be brutally honest. But remember that some scenes can be effective without the blow-by-blow barrage of details. Be judicious in how visceral you get.

✔ **Aren't self-congratulatory:** Few readers enjoy authors who toot their own horns. Trust that readers will be impressed by impressive things you've done without you making a big deal about it. Humility goes a long way here.

✔ **Aren't self-pitying:** Self-pity is never that interesting to anyone except the author (and possibly not even then). You can have a sad story but don't focus on that "Oh, poor me!" part of it.

Incorporating these characteristics comes with time, patience, reflection — and honesty.

Keeping Your Eye on the Prize: Wowing Others with Your Story

The prize isn't publication. The prize is having written a memoir that's smart, funny, touching, concise, memorable, and readable, which is really what this book is about. Make sure your manuscript adheres to these criteria, and you'll *wow* readers, whoever they are.

Writing a memoir is a way to interrogate your history and define your life. So many people are defined by what others think and say about them. Taking the time to revise your stories is the last chance to make your memoir a larger, more important experience. Don't cheat yourself of this opportunity.

Writing Exercises on Revision

Revision can be a challenge for writers of all experience levels. Let the following exercises prompt some general and specific ideas for you on how revision can help your manuscript. Feel free to follow one, some, or all of these prompts.

❑ **Take a single chapter of your manuscript, and for each paragraph, mark its function with a word or phrase in the margins.** Afterwards, go back and see how much redundancy you have. Do you have six paragraphs all serving the same goal? Do you need all six? Also look for what's missing, such as in a scene where there's a pair of lovers relaxing out in a field but you don't have a single paragraph devoted to creating that bucolic setting. Adjust as needed. (You can also use this tactic, chapter by chapter.)

❑ **Take a section of the memoir that you feel isn't working, then write about it, dialoguing with yourself on a fresh page.** For example, try your own version of this: "Dear Ryan — what I wanted to do in this chapter is show how the main character is resisting going home because he's afraid he may have to admit that leaving in the first place was a mistake. The intention was to present him sympathetically." Admit what you like about what you currently have, point out where you're holding back, and identify places that need to be developed as well as list specific ways to develop them. Ask (and answer) questions, such as "Why am I hung up on this part?" and "What writing strength do I have that could improve this section?"

❑ **Find a chapter or section that doesn't quite have that *wow* factor yet.** Add in a secondary (or even a primary) character. Now rework that chapter or section. How did the addition of that character affect things? So much of a memoir is about deciding what to exclude. Try including more for once and see what happens. (Just remember to adhere to the truth and you can't go wrong.)

❑ **Examine scenes where characters are interacting.** Ask yourself four important questions

- What does each character desire from this exchange?

- What's at risk?

- What is being withheld?

- What function does this scene serve to the larger narrative at work?

❑ **Write the back cover text for your memoir.** This text should serve as a teaser for your book and incentivize readers to take the plunge with you. Make it no more than 125 words. (If you have a hard time doing this exercise, you don't really know what your book is about, and/or you don't have a clear idea of the most exciting part(s) of your book yet.)

❑ **Put your manuscript aside and move on to a new writing project.** Come back and revisit this one with fresh eyes in a week, a month, or a year. When do you know it's been long enough to revisit it? When you don't fully recall everything you wrote. That makes the text feel new to you, and when rereading it you'll have much-needed perspective that has you viewing it like an ordinary reader encountering it for the first time.

Chapter 16

Streamlining Your Story with Sentence-Level Edits

· ·

· ·

*A*lthough plenty of authors debate about whether writing can be taught, teachers of writing and publishing professionals agree: Editing *can* be taught. But to really master it takes a lot of study and practice. For your purpose in writing a memoir, you don't need to master it. You just need to be competent.

Part magic, part mechanics, and part methodology, the art of editing is something to bring in at any stage in the writing process. *Editing* is basically getting into the text and fixing or improving things on a word, phrase, or sentence level, compared to *revision,* which focuses on larger scale issues like voice, structure, tone, and theme. (Check out Chapter 15 for more on revising your text.) However, many writers feel schizophrenic jumping between the role of writer to editor and back to writer. For them —for everyone, in fact — waiting for the editing until you've written a complete draft (of the book, of a chapter, or of a scene) is perfectly fine.

This chapter is a crash course in the basics of self-editing. You can't rely on others to do the editing for you. At some point, you need to take off your writer's hat and put on your editor's hat to take full ownership of your own work. No one wants to slog through sloppy, bloated, or imprecise text. Putting the time in to edit well can be tough, but the payoff is worth it.

Having a Firm Grasp on Grammar

Grammar is an agreed-upon set of conventions designed to clearly make meaning with language. As a writer and editor, your knowledge and use of correct grammar is paramount. Run against those long-standing conventions at your own peril. The goals of editing are to make the meaning of sentences clear and to do it as efficiently as possible. Simple as that.

One way to reacquaint yourself with the rules of English grammar that you studied in middle school and high school English class is to read one of those grammar rulebooks. Here are a couple I suggest you check out if you need a refresher:

- ✔ Strunk and White's *The Elements of Style* (Longman)
- ✔ *The Chicago Manual of Style* (University of Chicago Press)
- ✔ Lynne Truss's *Eat Shoots and Leaves: The Zero Tolerance Approach to Punctuation* (Profile Books Ltd.)

Your English teachers knew the rules and, more importantly, knew that they mattered. Here's one simple reason why.

The polar bear burst into the room and ate your lunch.

The polar bare burst into the room and ate you're lunch.

The first is a scary depiction of a hungry ursine. The second is a laugher and makes the writer look foolish. Which would you prefer? You can figure out both, but reading the second still makes the reader think, "Wow, that writer really sucks." Editing can keep that from happening.

Appeasing Your High School English Teacher: Avoid Wordiness

Many manuscripts face the problem of being wordy. When you're writing, you may just write whatever comes to mind. During editing, you can now review line by line and ensure the text is tighter and more concise without unnecessary fluff.

If you're wordy, I can relate. My high school English teacher was Mrs. Nixon. My classmates and I affectionately called her the Grammar Nazi because of her militant insistence for avoiding comma splices and for knowing the difference between you're and your and other rules like that. She also wrote long-hand responses to everything we turned in. In beautiful script with green ink, she wrote "redundant," "wordy," and "cliché" in the margins of my research papers, reading responses, and story writing assignments.

For a long time, I assumed she just hated me. That she hated all kids, in fact.

But she was right.

I was wordy. When one word would do, I used twenty ways, perhaps because we had minimum word counts. I ran on too long, repeated myself too much, and relied on tired, old expressions.

Mrs. Nixon won't grade your manuscript, but you still want to eliminate unnecessary words. If your manuscript is wordy, readers may skim it for only the essential elements. That's not good. I want to help you reduce your wordiness. These sections explain how you can tighten your text and be as concise as possible without losing meaning.

Using better nouns and verbs versus more modifiers and qualifiers

The English language has a lot of words — in fact, more than a million. No matter what you need to say, a word out there can do the trick in nearly every instance. If you pick the first word that comes to mind instead of taking the time to search for the best word, you'll have to do a lot of adjusting and modifying to get that sort-of-correct word right.

In the simplest terms, fewer words equals less wordiness. If you pick the type of nouns and verbs that don't require modification, you eliminate the need for adjectives, which equals less wordiness. A bonus is that you're likely to have created more precision, too.

Here's an example of the thought process some of my student writers go through when writing. Assume the assignment is to write a short description of a neighbor.

> "Woman." Well, she's more than that. She's old.
>
> "Old woman." Yeah, but she's been a total jerk since someone stole her mailbox. How do I convey that?
>
> "Mean old woman." She's also ugly as the rear end of that mangy mutt that follows her everywhere.
>
> "Mean, ugly, old woman." Give me my A, Dr. Van Cleave!

To which I may say, "How about just selecting a stronger noun and going with 'hag'? It makes the point efficiently, doesn't it?"

The same situation is true when you're dealing with verbs. Consider that neighbor lady from the previous example. How does she enter a room?

> "She walked into the room." Oh boy, this is functional, but as about as enjoyable as a hungry person eating a rice cake.

> "She shuffled into the room." This is better, especially if she uses a cane and moves rather slowly. You may want to consider "amble," "ease," "sashay," "lurch," or "swagger." You may also try "march," "wander," or "stagger," too.

Select a word that fits both that character and the exact manner in which she moves. Editing is all about honing your language to a diamond-like polish. You get that by using diamonds (the best word) versus semi-precious stones (the sort-of-okay words). Take the time to find the best word and your readers will appreciate it. Your stories will, too.

Clarity truly matters

I tell my writing students constantly: Clarity is job No. 1. If your readers don't know who is doing what to whom, all the greatest themes and metaphors and beautiful language in the world won't matter. Confusion equals the end of your story. Readers will move on to a story that doesn't confuse them.

To see a confusing situation in action at the sentence level, look at this example: "He took an ice cream bar from the freezer and ate it."

When you use "it," the word "it" should replace the noun that comes immediately before it. In this case, the sentence reads as if someone is eating a freezer. You can revise it to read, "He searched through the freezer, found an ice cream bar, and ate it." Which of these two sentences is superior if clarity is job No. 1?

Sometimes, clarity issues arise on a much more significant level, such as within an entire paragraph or scene. For example, here's the type of paragraph I regularly see in first drafts.

> She told her that she was looking to buy a Harley-Davidson. But she didn't have the money, did she? Marla was tired of the nonsense. It was all nonsense with her mother. She always hated this kind of thing.

Try to unpuzzle this paragraph and you may develop a migraine the size of Mt. Saint Helens. When you're writing, be kind to your reader and be as clear as possible. When in doubt, choose clarity over other options. I hear readers complain all the time about not being able to follow what's going on in a memoir, but I never hear anyone say, "Wow, that book really ticks me off. It's so clear! I always know what's happening in it! What's wrong with this author?"

To check that your manuscript is clear, read aloud everything that you write. And read it aloud slowly. Your ear will notice things that you simply miss when reading or re-reading silently to yourself. Having an audience may help. Enlist a friend, loved one, or even a pet for some sympathetic ears.

Resisting the Urge to Overexplain

You want your readers to get — I mean *totally* get — the point you're making, so make sure you really give it to them. On one hand, wanting to be super-clear makes sense. Just come on out and tell them everything. Explain every single thing you intend to mean so there's zero chance of confusion. If confusion is bad, then super clarity is super good, right?

Follow that mindset, however, and you're saying to your readers, "Hey, you aren't smart enough to figure out my meaning, so let me just treat you like a child." Maybe you didn't mean to, but it comes across that way. You have to give your readers credit for being able to figure things out on their own. If they can't get it, rewrite the scene, just don't explain.

Give the readers 1 plus 1, and they'll come up with 2. "But what if some of my readers don't get it?" you ask. They will. Resist the urge to overexplain what a reasonable reader will get on her own.

Want to see overexplaining in action? Here's one example of how an author may go overboard in trying to ensure that the reader gets it.

> Ted rubbed eucalyptus oil onto June's tired feet. Working the overnight shift at the diner really was heck on her heels, so this type of attention from her new husband was heavenly. When Ted finally finished, he planted a soft kiss on her forehead before heading to the kitchen to check on the raspberry crepes he was making for their romantic breakfast. She felt so content that she nearly purred. "I adore you," June whispered lovingly. Every day with him felt like heaven.

On the surface, this passage may seem okay. They're complete, coherent sentences. It has imagery and dialogue aplenty with even a little action. But it also includes phrases and entire sentences that simply explain things that readers already realize on their own.

Watch out for overusing *-ly* words. Writers primarily rely on *-ly* words (adverbs and adjectives) to explain emotion, such as "angrily," or in our preceding instance, "lovingly." Toss out those words and rework your scenes to evoke those feelings a different way. Let body language help. Let action do its work. Let dialogue matter more.

Two sins are at work here in the preceding passage, so make sure you avoid these same mistakes in your writing:

- ✔ Talking down the reader
- ✔ Lazy writing (or a lack of confidence in the writer's own writing)

The point of this scene is to show readers how the new husband Ted treats June well, and she likes it. That's all. So how can you best handle conveying that information to a reader? If you can temper the impulse to explain emotion and character motivation, your writing will tighten immediately. Every scene will be sharper. An added bonus is that your writing will flow better, too.

Here's a shorter, stronger version of that same scene, changed from one to two paragraphs.

> Ted rubbed eucalyptus oil onto June's feet after she'd finished another overnight shift at the diner. When he finished, he planted a kiss on her forehead before checking on the raspberry crepes he was making.
>
> "I adore you," June whispered.

Showing versus Telling

The "show, don't tell" chestnut has been around since the dinosaurs, or so it seems. The point with this "writing rule" is that showing is good and telling isn't. Can you just cut the parts where you're telling the reader things? No, because the reason you're telling is that you want to get something across to the reader. If you cut that, you're missing something. If you're not missing something when you cut a section that's all telling, well, you have a whole different problem now — writing about things that aren't important!

Showing makes a scene unfold right before your eyes. It's more powerful and vivid than just using telling. It's also a great deal more memorable.

Showing is built through imagery, meaning the use of sensory details. If you're including colors, smells, textures, or sounds, that's all in the realm of show-ing. If you're using words like "lovely," "ugly," "horrifying," or "embarrassing," that's telling. You can use imagery to communicate those same ideas to a reader, but that involves working hard to find the right sensory details to do so. Showing is harder, which is one reason some writers don't do it enough. They also don't trust the reader enough.

Try this example.

> An attention hound, Aunt Bertha entered the guest bedroom loudly. Jennifer whined that she needed more sleep. Aunt Bertha apologized but didn't mean it. She loved everyone to be looking at her all of the time.

From her dangly gold earring hoops to her cheap turquoise bracelets, she was all about glitter and showiness. There wasn't a conversation she couldn't find a way to turn her way.

Do you see how hard the author is trying to communicate that Bertha is all flash and little substance? The author delivers that idea quite a few times, yet the cumulative effect of this kind of repetition weakens the passage. Astute readers feel like a car stuck in the mud — no forward motion, just a lot of tire spinning.

Here's that same scene delivered with an emphasis on showing versus using vague claims (telling) to characterize this woman.

Aunt Bertha slammed the guest room door open.

"Hey, what gives?" Jennifer said, squinting at the sudden light.

"Oopsy!" Aunt Bertha said, not leaving. She toyed with one of the over-sized gold hoops in her ears. On her wrists clinked the trio of turquoise bracelets she bought at a garage sale because they reminded her of something Heather Locklear once wore in a movie.

Like most rules of writing, this one's not absolute. Sometimes telling is more efficient than showing. One situation where telling works better is when showing is going to be longer and/or more boring than telling. Never choose an option that's going to make a reader yawn.

Another situation where telling is a fine choice is with thought. Unlike a movie or TV show, a book can quite effectively get into a character's head. In a memoir, this likely happens many times. What would be the practical, actionable way to show what something's thinking? Go with telling in these cases.

For example, watch how this conversation goes.

"Hey, Amanda."

"Hey, Tom. Come on in."

"Thanks."

"Let me take your hat and beach towel."

"Sure thing."

"What's up with you today?"

"Not a whole lot. But if it gets any hotter, I might melt."

"I hear it hit a hundred again."

"Jeez, that's hot."

"No kidding."

"Let's sit under the ceiling fan and have a cool drink."

Wow, that's dull reading. Readers would rather get a root canal than waste their time reading such mundane prose. So how about you find a much more efficient way to convey that information through telling?

> Amanda let Tom inside. She cranked up the ceiling fan and settled onto the couch with him, offering him a frosty glass of root beer.

This passage is more telling than showing, but it's efficient. It gets the job done well. Now if this moment had any more significance — say Amanda is secretly in love with Tom — then the scene would need more showing. You could expand the moment with more sensory data to reveal the tension Amanda feels at being so close to her secret sweetie. But for the purposes of getting one character from point A to point B, telling works wonderfully.

Avoiding Amateur Constructions

Some sentences are grammatically correct, but they don't reach the potential level of sophistication and elegance that they could with a little help. Poorly-constructed sentences can occur when you get too simple ("The cat is yellow. The cat ran after the bus.") or unduly complex ("As quick as a Ferrari, John, who always wanted to be a professional baseball player, and who knew he didn't have the wherewithal to generate enough income to make up for the scholarship he lost when his brother got them both arrested for marijuana possession, and he never forgave him for it, signed up for the military"). One is far too clunky in its simplicity. The other? It's confusing and more than a little ridiculous.

When a reader encounters amateur sentence constructions, it's noticeable. Have you ever seen a kids' tree fort made by an enthusiastic but carpentry-challenged parent? It has splinters. It's crooked. It's ugly. It may even be dangerous to get inside. That's just how readers feel about awkward, amateur sentences. They're functional to a degree, but there's no sense of beauty, precision, or skill. Readers may well be fearful to enter.

One common amateur construction is the overuse of the -ing phrase, which can get in the way of good writing. Consider this sentence:

> Tearing a hole in the screen door, Fluffy went after the neighbor's cat.

This sentence sounds as if both actions occur at the same time, which is a physical impossibility. In addition, starting the sentence with the -ing phrase feels amateurish. Here are a few options on how to tweak that dog versus cat sentence.

> Fluffy tore a hole in the screen door and went after the neighbor's cat.

> Fluffy tore a hole in the screen door and then went after the neighbor's cat.

Putting an action like "tearing a hole in the screen door" and sticking it in a dependent clause makes it weak. (A *dependent clause* reveals useful information but can't stand on its own as a sentence.) It distances a reader. The action seems less important.

An *-ing* phrase like "Tearing a hole in the screen door . . . " is called a *participle phrase.* In the first case, "Tearing" is the participle, and "a hole" is the direct object, or the thing that receives the action of the verb. Participial phrases can do other things too, such as function as an adjective ("Girls interested in baseball early develop strong cooperative skills.") Share this bit of grammatical knowledge the next time you're having drinks with English professors and you'll be a hit! (You can also refer to the later section, "Fixing dangling participles" for more information.)

To see this concept in greater detail, check out this example passage:

> As he went into the garage, George tugged off his T-shirt. Already sweating, he was hot, hot, hot. And he hated the idea of going through his father's old boxes. Someone had to, though. He'd been gone six weeks now.

> Stopping at the army footlocker, George leaned against a bookshelf and mopped his brow. As he thought about the stories his father had told about the war, he wondered how many more he'd never heard. What secrets did his father keep? Now to find out, he thought as he opened the footlocker and started rooting through the past.

How can you avoid amateur constructions (and perhaps do some minor tweaking to make it all read more smoothly)? Try this:

> George went into the hot garage and tugged off his already sweaty T-shirt. He hated the idea of going through his father's old boxes. Someone had to, though. The funeral was nearly six weeks past.

> George paused at the army footlocker. He leaned against a bookshelf and mopped his brow. His father had told so many stories about the war, yet how many more had he kept to himself? What secrets did George's father keep? Now to find out, he thought as he opened the footlocker and started rooting through the past.

This version has the type of rhythm and clarity that you can incorporate into your writing. If you test out the language on the page in your mouth by saying it, and in your ears by reading it (or having it read to you), you can start to figure out what works best. Just getting rid of those "as XXX as" and -ing phrases can help tighten up things.

Steering Clear of Common Grammar Issues

You don't need to commit to love one of those Bible-sized grammar tomes most college students had to buy their freshman year. Those things are intimidating and seem to be written in the most un-fun way possible.

You still need a refresher on important grammar issues, so you can steer clear of potential grammar pitfalls. To help you out, I discuss in the following sections what really matters grammatically. The following are some of the most common grammar issues that cause editors and literary agents to say, "No, thank you." Make sure your manuscript doesn't have these issues and your odds of publication increase tremendously (even if you don't know the high-powered terms "perfective past," "nominative," or "modal verbs").

Fixing dangling participles

A *dangling participle* (sometimes called a *dangling modifier*) simply modifies the wrong noun. Usually the noun is just entirely MIA, as in "Wearing infrared goggles, the deer trail was more visible." What that literally says is the deer trail is the one wearing goggles. Not likely unless this deer is part 007.

Your spell-check won't catch these types of gaffes. Odds are, if you're not specifically looking for them, you may miss them too while editing. They're easy to troubleshoot, however, as soon as you know what to look for.

You can quickly fix a dangling participle by moving the proper subject in the sentence. Usually, it goes right after the participle or participial phrase. For example, to fix the preceding sentence, try "Wearing infrared goggles, I could see the deer trail." Or even "I wore infrared goggles so I could see the deer path."

Present (or past) participles are when verbs function like an adjective. You can easily identify them because they usually end with -ing. For example, "swim" is a verb, but "swimming trunks" uses the present participle version of "swim" to modify the work "trunks." Without the present participle, readers may think of luggage, elephant trunks, or something else.

Identifying homonym issues

Homonyms are words that sound alike, but are written differently. Editors, literary agents, and readers expect you to use the right word at the right time. When you're editing your manuscript, pay special attention to their misuse. If you don't know which one of these homonyms is which, look them up.

Here are 20 of the most common problem words:

- **alter/altar:** *Alter* refers to a change, while an *altar* is a structure inside a church where sacrifices are offered.

- **brake/break:** A *brake* is what stops a bicycle or car; a *break* is what you take after a long session of writing your memoir.

- **coarse/course:** Something that is rough is *coarse*. A *course*, though, is the path or route of travel. A *course* is also less often the main mast of a sailboat or a unit of instruction in a school (among other definitions).

- **counsel/council:** To *counsel* is to give advice. A *council* is a group of people called together for a discussion or debate.

- **hear/here:** You *hear* with your ears. The place you're currently at is called *here*.

- **its/it's:** (This is one of my great grammatical pet peeves!) *Its* is a possessive, as in "The dog licked its butt." *It's* is a contraction, meaning it + is. An example? "It's a shame more people don't know the difference between its and it's."

- **morning/mourning:** *Morning* is that time right after the sun comes up. If someone dies though, that period of sadness that friends and family feel is called *mourning*.

- **naval/navel:** If I were a sailor, I'd probably work on a *naval* ship. The word *naval* refers to things connected to the ships in general or the navy in specific. A *navel*? That's your belly button. It's also the center or middle of a thing.

- **passed/past:** If you're behind me and then zoom ahead in your car, you've *passed* me. *Past*, though, refers to the time that's not now but rather all that happened before.

- **peel/peal:** You can *peel* the skin off an apple. When church bells ring, they're said to *peal*.

- **peak/peek/pique:** The *peak* of something is its top. To *peek* is to peer or look, especially from a place of concealment or through a small opening. To *pique* is to provoke someone into acting through irritation or excitement.

- **principle/principal:** A *principle* is a general law or truth, or a rule of conduct. A *principal* is the person in charge of a high school. I'd expect most *principals* to have *principles*.

✔ **read/red:** To have *read* is to understand the meaning of something (like music, printed words, and so on). *Red* is the color of most roses. One of my favorite poems to read is William Carlos Williams's "The Red Wheelbarrow."

✔ **there/they're/their:** *There* has lots of meanings, but the main ones are in that place (as opposed to here) or at a specific point of a longer action. *They're* is a contraction for they + are, as in "I like Neil Gaiman and George R. R. Martin because *they're* both terrific fantasy writers." *Their* is the possessive used when the subject is they. An example? "They didn't believe that *their* home could be robbed so easily."

✔ **threw/through:** If you chucked a football at my head, then you *threw* it. If you missed and that football hit a car window and ended up inside the car, I'd say it went *through* the glass.

✔ **to/too/two:** *To* expresses a point of limit in time ("I eat lunch from 1 *to* 1:15.") or motion toward something ("The giant chicken came *to* the house."). *Too* means also, as in "I like you, too." It can also mean to an excessive degree, like "I ate far *too* much cake!" *Two* is the number after one.

✔ **wear/ware/where:** To *wear* something is to use it often (like a wig) or to have it on your body (like clothes). *Ware* is usually found in the plural, *wares*, and it means goods or services, or a specific class or merchandise. Here's an example of that last definition: "The silver*ware* is way too dirty to eat with." And *where* asks what place, what respect, or what position? "*Where* do you come from?", "*Where* will this new tax hurt me?", and "*Where* do you stand on the proposed gun laws?"

✔ **weather/whether:** Snow, rain, or sunshine are various examples of *weather*. *Whether*, though, introduces either one or two alternatives, such as "I'll go see the movie whether your sister comes or not."

✔ **whose/who's:** *Whose* refers to the one or ones belonging to what person, as in "*Whose* armadillo just ran through my living room?" It's also the possessive case of which or who used as an adjective. *Who's* is the contraction of who + is. "*Who's* the one who'll learn the difference between *whose* and *who's?* You!

✔ **your/you're:** *Your* is a form of the possessive case when you is the subject, as in "Where are *your* sneakers, young lady?" *You're* is the contraction of you + are. An example of how it's used is: "*You're* a fool for not marrying that wonderful man, Janette."

My teachers finally convinced me that I had a problem with it's/its. Here's how I finally figured out how to get it right every time. I memorized "it's" as "it + is." That's all. If "it + is" fit the sentence, I used "it's" and moved on. If it is didn't fit, I used the other its. In the grammatical situation where you run into an either/or, memorizing just one is half the work but can get you the correct result 99 percent of the time. The same trick works for you're versus your. (You're equals "you are.")

Lie versus lay

If you're at all like me, you probably just guessed at irregular verbs for years. They're confusing because some irregular verbs look like tenses with the same spellings, which is even worse than a homonym because they look exactly the same!

The verb "lie" means to tell a fabrication, as well as to lie back, or recline. (It's this second meaning that gets confused with lay.)

The verb "lay" means to put something down. If you think about it, this action requires something or someone to be acted upon. So you need an object or person connected to this. Your idea is incomplete without mentioning that object or person.

Correct examples of "lie" include

- **Present tense:** I lie here daydreaming about Julia Roberts.

- **Past tense:** I lay in bed the entire morning yesterday with my sick son.

- **Past participle:** I had lain on that grubby carpet before.

Meanwhile, correct examples of "lay" include

- **Present tense:** I lay the gun on the table after my partner handcuffed the crook.

- **Past tense:** I remember that I laid your library book down on the kitchen counter.

- **Past participle:** Randy had laid the dog's collar on the bed.

If you're still feeling stuck, jot down these six examples on a note card and keep it near your desk. Whenever you encounter the lay/lie issue, re-examine the examples. Eventually, you'll no longer lie around worrying about running into them anymore! No lie! You can lay down your lie/lay cheat sheet for good.

Maximizing the Active Voice

When editing, always consider changing passive voice into active voice. *Active voice* is more immediate and does a better job of creating a visual in your reader's mind. On the other hand, *passive voice* works against creating a clear image because it hides the actual subject performing the action of the sentence until the very end.

Verbs in the passive voice are easy to spot — they often have some form of "to be" paired with a past participle form of an action word, like "The gopher *was thrown* by Jasmine." Although both types of sentences are technically correct, active voice can help you get a book deal and passive voice won't. The passive constructions are typically longer, more awkward, and less precise.

To make a sentence active voice, you move the true subject to the forefront and use a strong verb right after it. This 1-2 combo provides the reader with directness and energy. Often they're more efficient than passive versions, too.

Compare these two example sentence pairings. In sentence No. 1:

- ✔ The feral monkey bit the boy. (Active voice)
- ✔ The boy was bitten by a feral monkey. (Passive voice)

And sentence No. 2:

- ✔ The dragon's fiery breath scorched the cathedral. (Active voice)
- ✔ The cathedral has been scorched by the dragon's fiery breath. (Passive voice)

Can you hear and sense the difference? Watch for the differences when you read professional writing. You can start noticing passive voice in newspaper articles, magazines pieces, and even other peoples' memoirs. The better writers avoid passive voice as much as possible except in two cases:

- ✔ When they want to make the active object more important: "The lottery was won by my Uncle Jackson!"
- ✔ When they don't know the active subject: "My purse has been stolen."

Bringing in a Professional Editor

You've done your best with editing, although you know the manuscript needs more help. You realize that your spell-check caught a few of the mechanical corrections, but you need more support and guidance. You need someone who is completely engaged with your writing. You need an ally with insight and subtlety who can help develop and polish your words until they shine like a string of freshwater pearls. It's time to bring in the ringer, also known as the professional editor.

No matter what shape your manuscript is in when you deliver it to a professional editor, you should be surprised at how much better it is when the editor returns it to you. A good editor's work has a *wow* factor.

These sections show you what an editor can do for you and how you can find the right editor for you and your memoir.

Making cuts before hiring a pro: The 10 percent rule

Just because you're considering hiring a professional editor doesn't mean you don't have work to do. Before you even start the process of finding one, see how much of the serious editing work you can do on your own.

Some writers feel better when they work with a goal in mind. If you're one of those writers, strive to cut 10 percent of the flab from your piece when you edit. Which 10 percent do you cut? That's for you to decide. It'll probably come from –ly words, lazy writing, clichés, redundancies, excess exposition, and off-topic sentences and scenes.

Cutting or trimming makes sense because readers want tight, taut language. Hold every page, every paragraph, every sentence, every phrase, and every word up to scrutiny. Challenge them. Insist on strong reason for their inclusion. If you can't immediately see that reason, cut, cut, cut.

After you've done this, see what you think. Do you still need that professional editor? If so, the following sections will tell you what to do. If not, then move on to the next chapter (though you should consider the exercises at the end of this chapter, which have worked wonders with many memoirists who've come to me for guidance).

Seeing how a pro can help

Good editors go beyond the basic mechanics of just proofreading your manuscript. They ensure that your scenes are vivid, your characters memorable, and your overall writing is effective. They also deal with both the forest (big stuff like structure, pace, organization, and style) and the trees (smaller stuff such as imagery, dialogue, and description). How they go about editing depends on the amount of money you choose to spend and the specific services they offer.

Remember *why* you're hiring a professional editor. Don't lose sight of the big picture, which is to help improve your manuscript. Never take edits personally and don't freak out if your manuscript has lots of changes and suggestions. The editor is simply doing her job — making the text the best that it can be.

The main reasons to hire an editor are as follows:

- ✔ You believe a professional edit can increase the chances that a publisher will accept your manuscript.

- ✔ A literary agent likes your manuscript but feels it needs more work before being submitted for publication. (The agent may not agree to take you on until this level of editing is complete. Or the agent may sign you but hold off on submitting the manuscript to a publisher until it's truly ready to succeed in a competitive marketplace.)

✓ You want your manuscript to be more professional, but you feel that this type of interaction could work like a private tutoring session.

✓ You think your manuscript is ready, but you want peace of mind that you're correct.

✓ A publisher offers a contact contingent on getting the manuscript professionally edited first.

✓ You intend to self-publish and want the end product to be as professional as anything a traditional publisher puts out.

Knowing how much an editor can cost

In general you can choose three different types of editing a professional editor can provide, from least expensive to most expensive. Note that the terms may be different, depending on whom you speak with, but the goals will be similar.

✓ **Critique:** A general, short evaluation of your project, which doesn't include copyediting. Rates range from $30 to $60 an hour.

✓ **Copyediting:** Editing at the line level for syntax, grammar, clarity, consistency, and formatting. This level of service often includes a very brief overall evaluation or summary. Rates range from $35 to $75 an hour.

✓ **Manuscript evaluation:** This edit includes a very close read with a detailed written response that outlines weaknesses and strengths (both small and large issues). It also includes clear, specific chapter-by-chapter feedback that can improve the work. This level of service often includes suggestions on how to troubleshoot some or many of the problems, and may even have a few paragraphs of pages reworked using those solutions as an example of how the writing can be strengthened. Rates range from $50 to $80 an hour.

Some editors prefer to charge a per-word rate, per-page rate, or even a flat fee. Any of these options is fine as long as you're confident you're getting your money's worth. For the per-word or per-page rate, consider seeing how much they can finish, say, for $75. Then either commit to the rest of the project, renegotiate the rate, or find yourself a different editor.

Finding and hiring a pro

Plenty of people claim to be professional editors, so not only do you have to locate them, but you have to check out their services and products.

Editors often specialize. Although any editor can likely help any text, look for editors who have successfully worked with memoirs before.

A few of the best ways to find qualified editors are

- Search online in your favorite search engine for "memoir editor" or "book doctor."
- Call the English department of a local university or college and ask for recommendations.
- Look on the Editorial Freelancers Association website (www.the-efa. org) for its job board and a listing of members you can directly contact.
- Scan the Professional Editors Network website (www.pensite.org), which has a searchable database and a useful resources section.
- Use LinkedIn, a professional social networking site.
- Use www.elance.com, a freelance professional website.
- Investigate independent publishers to see if their editors do freelance work on the side.
- Ask your writer friends.
- Scan the acknowledgment pages of memoirs you like to see if the author thanked the editor. Even if the editors have a full-time editing job, a kind request may impress them enough to take you on as a moonlighting situation.

After you locate some potential candidates, you want to check their editing credentials. Get a list of past clients from any prospective professional editor, perhaps even including testimonials. If not, move on to the next editor. You want someone with a track record of making writers happy; the editor should welcome the chance to share this information. Expecting to see the editor in action is also reasonable. You can ask him to edit a page or two of your text for free or show you a few pages that he has edited for someone else.

After you find someone you feel can help, get the entire arrangement in writing first. You shouldn't have to offer too much of a deposit upfront. You also should have an out if you decide along the way that you're a less good match than first expected.

An insider secret to editing

Editing is more than just improving the mechanics. Something profound and powerful happens during the process of editing a memoir. You learn exactly what you have to say as you make conscious choices on how best to say it.

In other words, the process of revision and editing is the process of story-making. All the pro writers know it. More than a few have been credited with saying, "There's no such thing as writing; only rewriting." And editing is a crucial part of that.

Take joy in the process. Come at it like it's a new opportunity to improve your writing ability, learn more about yourself along the way, and make your manuscript better. Three birds, one stone.

Don't put too much stock in a sample edit. The few marks delivered on a sample edit can't reveal an editor's true expertise beyond surface-level grammar issues. From such a limited sample, you can't see whether the editor is gifted at dealing with deeper story issues.

Additionally, you want to look for verifiable work experience, association with quality publishers and authors, and past jobs in the publishing industry. With any of them, you can be surer of your editor's skill than by examining a few pages of sample edits.

Working with a pro

Just because you hire a professional editor doesn't mean you can wipe your hands and sit back, expecting the memoir to magically become perfect while you catch up on past seasons of *Lost*. Unless you only pay for a simple line edit where the editor solely corrects the language and grammar, you're going to get the manuscript back with a nice to-do list. The key is to ensure that your to-do list covers all the significant issues with the text.

Making sure that your editor does all you need him to do starts with communication at the outset of your professional arrangement. Let the editor know what your needs are before the editing starts. Talk about your desired outcomes (*New York Times* bestseller, self-publishing, or something else). Inform your editor of the challenges you had in writing the book. Share your specific desires for improvements. In short, the more guidance and context you give, the better the results will be.

Having worked as a ghost writer and freelance editor for more than a decade, I have discovered three things that can help make your partnership with a professional editor a success. They are

- **Turn in the best-edited manuscript you can.** The better shape your manuscript is in when you pass it to an editor, the better shape it'll be when you get it back. And really, do you want to pay good money for someone else to fix things that you're entirely capable of handling yourself?

- **Request as many comments and explanations as your editor is willing to give.** You'll be making better informed decisions as a result. You'll also have more opportunity to learn the craft of writing better.

- **Inform your editor of your concerns with your writing.** Don't assume that your editor will catch everything. If you help narrow his focus on issues you know are there, you'll get better feedback and possible solutions. Don't worry — just because you say, for example, that you've had problems with the development of Aunt Marnie, the editor won't skip evaluating the narrative arc, the dialogue, or the fight scene from last Christmas where everyone ends up soaked in cranberry sauce.

Some editors offer a significant discount for a resubmitted piece. Ask your editor about this possible discount in advance. If you suspect that you may want to do more than one round with an editor in order to make your manuscript as good as it can be, this upfront arrangement may help you limit your options of choosing an editor in a useful manner. In short, if the editor will work cheaper on more drafts, that's a good option.

Some professional editors prefer to be called *book doctors*. Other terms include *manuscript developer, book consultants, manuscript editors,* or *freelance editors*. Generally speaking, they all mean the same. But do check their credentials to see what they've done and how they do it.

Writing Exercises on Effective Self-Editing

Some writers get stymied when looking at their own writing with a critical eye. To help practice the craft of editing on someone else's text, I provide a passage in this section that you can work on and improve. The other two exercises ask you to take your editing skills and apply it to your own memoir. See how much of a difference you can make with some careful attention to detail and judicious pruning.

❑ **Take a single page of your own memoir and reduce it by 10 percent.**
How you choose to handle that kind of cut is up to you. Now here's the
real bonus challenge — cut *another* 10 percent. What kind of decisions
did you have to make? How much unseen fluff was lurking just beneath
the surface? How difficult was it to let go of some of those words?

❑ **Examine the following passage and rework it according to the principles of sound editing.**

Roger charged me with his bicycle. He came at me like a hurricane.
I leapt to the side at the last second, wondering what I'd done to
have forced him into such a violent reaction. He'd always been the
quietest kid on our baseball team. You could pick on him for hours
and he'd just sit there, taking it.

"Hey, Roger," I howled. "What gives?"

"I'm gonna punch your lights out," he snarled angrily.

"What did I ever do to you?" I asked.

"Just like you not to know," he said.

Confused by his erratic behavior, I shrugged. What the heck was
he talking about? I debated trying to run away. He was too fast
for me, though. On foot or on a bike, he'd run me down. He was a
strong kid.

So I went toward him, my hands raised high in surrender. "I give
up," I explained.

He smiled guiltily.

The next thing I knew, his fist was rocketing toward me. Then my
mouth exploded.

❑ **Take a chapter of your memoir and scour through it for instances of
active and passive voice.** For every sentence with active voice, put a
check on a note card. For every passive voice use, put a check on the
back of that note card. When you're done going through the entire chapter, tally up the marks on each side. Which has more? If it's active sentences without a doubt, reward yourself. If you have an equal number
(or more) of passive voice usages, get out your red pen and get to work.
Consider doing this with every chapter unless you've already mastered
the use of active voice.

Chapter 17

Saying the Unsayable: Knowing What to Include or Exclude

· ·

In This Chapter

▶ Handling unpleasant moments from the past

▶ Considering whether to use family secrets

▶ Uncovering missing information

▶ Thinking about ethical issues

▶ Considering the law

· ·

*J*ust because you have freedom of speech doesn't mean you should write just anything. You need to balance the reasons for writing a memoir against the possible pain and problems it may cause for yourself and others. On the other hand, your stories inevitably overlap with others so you really can't write a memoir that never mentions other people. No one lives in a vacuum. So how do you walk the fine line between telling the full truth and potentially secrets without hurting yourself or others?

This chapter details some things you need to think about and do before writing or publishing a book that could have disastrous outcomes for others. Some topics you may want to tread carefully about are outing a closeted gay relative, revealing family secrets, disclosing how someone committed a secret crime, sharing how a friend had a mental collapse, and so on. Read on to know what to consider before making such choices.

Tackling Painful Memories

When telling your story, writing about painful memories can be extremely difficult. People generally avoid pain, yet experience tells me that healing comes from writing about difficult memories. To write something is to order it, shape it, and understand it.

Natalie Goldberg, one of the most prominent writing teachers working today, believes that truly potent writing comes directly from a person's emotional, spiritual, and existential core. Writing like that is authentic and powerful. Gathered and shared in a memoir, these well-wrought, authentic writings make social connections and life affirmations. To me, those sound like valuable outcomes for writing a memoir.

When you're putting your story on paper, don't avoid your painful past. Contradict the inner critic who says, "You're not good enough. You don't deserve success. You're not a writer. You're nothing." Face the darkest parts of you on and drag them into the healing power of the light, whether you decide to ultimately include them in your book or not.

When you do encounter painful parts of your past, here are a few tips at handling them:

- ✔ **Distance yourself from them.** Do so by using third person ("she" or "he") versus "I," which can make the main character feel less like you. If it helps, go so far as to give them a name that's different from yours — anything is okay if it helps get the writing done. (See Chapter 11 for more on your different point of view options and what they can do for you.)

- ✔ **Give yourself permission to write about your darkest and brightest experiences.** Admit that no one is perfect and it's okay to have made poor choices, had bad luck, been foolish, or been amazingly fortunate. Nothing is wrong with you. Tell yourself that it is okay to write about those things along with the rest of your story. It's your life you're ultimately writing about, so own every bit of it. How do you own it? Don't flinch when it's time to write about these extreme moments. Write with generosity, perspective, and vividness. Take the reader into the essence of these moments through your careful use of language. Make these times come alive.

- ✔ **Make a list of the tough things you want to write about but can't yet do so.** A list is important. Putting things down on paper is powerful and a commitment of sorts. It can help you refine your focus and goals, and it can help you start to see how to move forward. Making your goals visible increases the likelihood you'll actually achieve them. Plus when you write them all down, there's no real chance of your forgetting one, is there? See Chapter 6 for story structure ideas that can easily incorporate the elements of a list.

- ✔ **Recognize that truth is truth, no matter how you hide it.** To hide something admits that you're ashamed or embarrassed by it. Everyone has scars, figurative or literal. Hiding yours doesn't make you any less scarred. Be proud of what it took to get you to where you are today. It's the truth of your past, it's the truth of your present, and it's these truths that, taken together, will make your memoir feel authentic. Let the reader witness the truth of your story.

✔ **Writing about your pain gives you power over it.** The act of putting your painful memories on the page gives you control over them. You decide when to bring them into the narrative, how long to write about them, and when to move on to something else. You're in charge.

If you're still having trouble writing about distressing moments of your past, feel free to change what happened so that things turned out better. Write about everything around the painful memory except the actual painful memory. Write what you think another writer may write about this memory. Do what you need to in order to get writing. When you're fully ready to confront the past, you can match your writing up with history as you prepare this text for your memoir.

On the most practical level, to not write about that which pained you is to exclude the reader from some of the most meaningful moments of your past. To put it more plainly, if you can't write about pain, you can't yet write a memoir.

Avoid overusing emotion words and phrases — such as "weep," "heart," "tears," and "soul" — when writing about those difficult times because they defuse the power of your story. Using them is weak writing and keeps your experience at a distance. Distance is okay if it helps you write, but distance is to be avoided for what ends up on the page of your memoir. In order to share your pain, truly verbalize it in your own powerful language versus relying on clichés or generalities. Own your past. Take charge of it.

Many memoir writers have struggled with depression, destruction, and despair in their lives, and some rightfully choose to share those moments in their memoirs. Although you can write a recovery circle narrative where the mere spilling of a tale is enough for praise and support, remember that the general public isn't looking for that kind of book. They want a story that they can relate to or at least empathize with. Make sure that there's more to your memoir than pain and suffering. Even Anne Frank's amazing *The Diary of a Young Girl* (Everyman's Library) has instances of childhood wonder and joy.

If you want to write a recovery memoir, Karen Casey's *My Story to Yours: A Guided Memoir for Writing Your Recovery Journal* (Hazelden) is a good how-to for that specific kind of project. Another option is Louise Desalvo's *Writing as a Way of Healing: How Telling Our Stories Transforms Our Lives* (Beacon Press).

Touching on the Taboo: Family Secrets with the Living

There's a tension between wanting to tell the most complete, honest story possible, and being faithful to secrets and private shame, particularly when they deal with other people who are still alive. Keeping secrets takes a lot of energy and focus; secrets can hold an amazing power over you. To remain silent can make you complicit. But do you have the right to share other secrets with the world?

If you do decide to write about secrets and they involve other people who are alive and recognizable, you owe it to them to let them read those passages. Remember that writing about others and disclosing their secrets can carry severe consequences, such as losing friends, being exiled from your family, damaging reputations, and even facing potential lawsuits (see the last section in this chapter about lawsuits).

You have to make the conscious choice with great patience and empathy. Depending on how the family secret links up with your themes and stories, it may be the underpinning of major moments in your life. To ignore them would be to tell only part of a richer story. If you're still set on writing about them, you may want to obscure their identity by swapping out any identifying characteristics, from their name and city to their physical description, job, and mannerisms.

If you want to handle a secret in your writing, you can consider one of these two suggestions:

- ✔ **Write two versions of the relevant scenes.** In one scene, reveal the secrets and share what you will. In the other, keep things private. After you're finished, see which one has more energy. See which one tells a more faithful story. To decide which to go with for the final version of the memoir — the public one — use the ideas that are throughout this chapter. Make the best, informed decision you can that requires a cost-benefit analysis. Only you can decide what is the best way to move forward.

- ✔ **Write a fictionalized version of it in a novel.** Shandi Mitchell did exactly this with her grandfather's life in her novel *Under this Unbroken Sky* (HarperCollins). She told about how he spent two years in prison for stealing grain after defaulting on a homesteading contract, and how he struggled to provide for his destitute family. The story is a novel because she included made-up elements in the story, but the core comes from her family's secrets.

If you're self-publishing (see Chapter 20 for more about this option), you can't be too careful with these issues concerning the disclosure of secrets. A traditional publishing house (see Chapter 19) has people who scrutinize your manuscript for places where you may be sued. If you self-publish and no one checks for these issues, you may be creating a massive problem for yourself beyond losing friends and family. Read the later section, "Laying Out Your Legal Issues" for more on the legal issues involved.

You may be tempted to use the memoir as a forum to get back at people. I warn you: Doing so isn't worth it. You end up looking like a jerk for doing it, even if you're 100 percent in the right and the other person is a chump.

Dealing with the Dead: Unclear or Missing Information

"Dead men tell no tales," growls every peg-legged captain in cheesy pirate movies. And dead people don't complain about what you've written about them in memoirs, either. But that doesn't mean you can say what you want without fear of repercussion. Even if you're not worried about getting sued (see the last section in this chapter for more on that), you still want to do right by people, whether you knew them well or not.

You can possibly upset descendents with what's published about their ancestor. The safest path is to treat the dead as you would the living. Make smart choices, and if you're not sure, ask your editor, agent, writing group, or family for guidance. This is one aspect of memoir writing where the saying "an ounce of prevention is better than a pound of cure" holds quite true.

Filling in the missing information can sometimes be a problem when writing about dead people. People die, and the people still living sometimes forget. Add in that many people never bothered to record their lives, and you may encounter a gap in your story that you simply can't fill. The data isn't there. The hard drives are blank.

That problem is less serious for living people today. Nearly everyone documents their lives, by taking photos on their smartphones, blogging about their hopes and dreams, and sharing everything they do online with their Facebook, Twitter, and other social networking accounts. Your kids or grandkids will easily be able to reconstruct the major (and far too many minor) moments of their lives, if they choose.

In the meantime, what do you do with MIA information? If it's not crucial, you can skip it and move on. You have to make choices about what to include and what to exclude anyway, so you can skip the missing information if it's not crucial to your story. If the missing information is crucial to your story, you can accept those vacant spaces as part of your story. One of the great strengths of the memoir is its acknowledgment that memory is elusive and that nothing is ever for certain. Let there be gaps. Or fill them in imaginatively, fully admitting that's what you're doing.

An example like this may work:

> I don't truly remember what my brother Eddie did after our fight that Christmas morning, but I imagine him up in his room, slamming his fist into the mattress again and again as he cursed my name. Eddie always overreacted when we fought, even though I'd always forgive him within minutes of the last blow. It usually took him days to cool off.

Make sure you speak to others who may know the information that you need. Ask a few good, open-ended questions, and then be sure to shut up and listen. People often know more than they admit at first. You may be able to sleuth out what you need if you're patient and persistent enough.

You can also check out Mary McCarthy's *Memories of a Catholic Girlhood* (Mariner Books). In the story, she fact-checks everything, which is an interesting way to share one's tale. Read to see how she compares her memory to what her research provided and what sense she makes of it all.

Looking at the Ethics of a Memoir

Most people don't have a sound definition, though, for what ethics are. My students often think that ethics are how one feels about something. A few tell me that ethics are merely what one does to follow the law. Still others say ethics come from religious beliefs. If pressed, most of them would readily admit that they aren't all that sure what ethics specifically are, but they're certain that ethics are important.

Ethics are the long-standing, well-reasoned standards of right and wrong. They may be in line with the law or religious edicts, but that's not necessarily the case. Allow me to clear everything by showing the other elements that play into ethics:

- ✔ **Values:** These are one's fundamental beliefs, such as honesty, respect, or honor.

- ✔ **Morals:** They're the values attributed to a belief system. These systems (such as religious or political) provide a higher level of authority than that of an individual. Many moral values are in line with what one's personal values are. For instance, I believe it's good to be compassionate, and so does the Methodist church I attend.

✔ **Ethics:** They're the choices or actions you take that are either consistent with or work against your morals.

Ethics comes from a Greek word, *ethos*, which means "character." You can easily see why the choices or actions you take will define your character. Not only are those choices in line with your morals and values (which are about what you stand for), but it's how people know you. To them, what you do and say is your character. (For more on how to define character in the characters of a memoir, see Chapter 8.)

Making an ethical choice is often not about right versus wrong, but rather two competing rights. As a memoir writer, you need to worry about the ethical considerations of writing a memoir because memoirists encounter more ethical dilemmas than most other types of writers. This section examines some of those dilemmas and helps you see the best ways to deal with them versus ignore or avoid them.

Thinking like a journalist

Now that newspapers are going the way of the dodo, universities and colleges are offering fewer journalism programs and classes than ever before. In those programs, students have to take at least one class on journalistic ethics. A few of the general things students study are the following:

✔ Diligently seek out and report the truth even when it's unpopular to do so

✔ Test for facts and information for accuracy

✔ Never plagiarize

✔ Show good taste versus pander to lurid sensationalism or curiosity

✔ Show compassion for your subjects, especially children

✔ Always disclose unavoidable conflicts of interest

✔ Admit mistakes and endeavor to correct them

If you abide by these guidelines when writing your memoir, you can avoid coming across as arrogant in person or in writing. You'll also likely end up with an accurate, responsible memoir that you can be proud of, regardless of how well it's received by the world.

Nearly all journalism ethics classes cover the Society of Professional Journalists with special attention to the SPJ Code of Ethics page (www.spj.org/ethicscode.asp). There, it breaks down what's expected from professional and responsible journalists into four main parts.

What most journalism students realize at some point is that you can do a very good job at getting at the truth of something and presenting that truth on the page, and still be a very good person. The same is true for a memoirist. Some people think all memoirists are monsters who seek to exploit the past. That doesn't have to be the case.

Mattering beyond the "I"

A memoirist needs to assume a role of heightened responsibility to the social function of a memoir. Like it or not, readers are impacted by a memoir because the form itself promises facts not fiction. Readers come at it with different expectations than they do with the fiction. Because truth matters, what you say — and how you say it — will be taken as truth. Those are stakes far beyond the ones a fiction writer faces in terms of how to tell a terrifically engaging story.

Here are some ideas that can provide a good framework for your weighing the possibilities of your ethical dilemmas:

- **Utility:** Which option produces the most amount of good? The least amount of harm?
- **Rights:** Which outcome is most respectful to anyone who is affected?
- **Justice:** Which version treats people equally?
- **Virtue:** Which choice moves you forward toward being the person you desire to become?

Ultimately, every choice you make about your memoir is exactly that: a choice. You're the one who has to accept any consequences, so you're the best one to make those choices. Often, the most useful way of thinking about how to handle ethical dilemmas in a memoir is the Golden Rule, which is to do unto others as you would have them do unto you. My aunt from Iowa has her own version of this: "What's good for the goose is good for the gander."

Laying Out Your Legal Issues

This section may be the most important one for budding memoirists. If your story is a tell-all or one of abuse, tragedy, or illegal behavior, you need to know if you're setting yourself up for legal nightmares down the road. Anything you include in a memoir can and likely will be used against you if someone brings a lawsuit to your door. These sections outline some potential legal issues you may face and how to avoid them.

Harming someone's reputation: Libel

Libel is when you damage another person's reputation by what you write in your book. Libel or slander (of a product or a person) can cause big trouble. To be clear, you *slander* someone or an entity by what you say to others that is presented as truth but is in fact false. Libel is when you damage a person or entity through what you put in printed form (which now includes the Internet) that is presented as truth but is in fact untrue.

Most courts now include audible media as libel, too. Both libel and slander are specific instances of the broader term defamation. Because libel is far more likely to be a possibility in writing your memoir than slander, look at this example.

> I worked for Don McMeaney for three years as his administrative assistant at McMeaney and Associates out of their main office in Scranton, New York. Just between us, he's the biggest crook I know. He scams his clients and skims a portion of every employee's paycheck. He should be in prison.

To identify someone so clearly and specifically and then make a claim that alleges illegal activity is very dangerous for your memoir. Even if you're 100 percent accurate about this information, look to see what value it really has in your memoir. You may want to go with something more like this passage:

> I worked for years as an administrative assistant in the world of construction. To my utter shock, I found that dishonesty was the norm here. Over-reported stock loss, under-reported profits, unpaid pensions — I had to wonder if my own paycheck was even accurate.

Both passages make the same point, but the second version is far less likely to get Mr. McMeaney to phone up his lawyers. Be smart about how you present material, and you'll be able to avoid legal troubles in almost every instance. If you're not sure what may be libelous, just flip the situation. If someone wrote the exact same thing about you, how would you feel? Wronged? Misrepresented? If you're at all unsure, play it safe. No memoir is worth being sued over.

When someone accuses you of libel, you may face a wide array of possible outcomes:

✔ **If you're fortunate, the person may demand only an apology.** Whether it's a formal, written apology or something informal, strongly consider doing it — it's the easiest way out of a potentially very problematic situation. You didn't mean to hurt someone, so why not apologize if you accidentally or inadvertently did?

✔ **If you're not as fortunate, the person may use legal means to stop the publication of your book and even seek financial damages by suing you.** This is unlikely to happen unless you share the book with this person, or they learn about it through hearsay or reviews published in advance of the book coming out. Can they literally stop your book from coming out? You bet. A court order or legal letter to the publisher can stop the process cold.

If you're writing about a person or company that has a lot more money than you do, they may choose to sue you despite having a weak case because they can outspend you. This scenario is very serious and can cause you grief. They can make your life miserable and bankrupt you along the way, just for kicks.

Don't think that your publisher will cover your butt if you get sued. Your publisher may help only if you're published by a huge commercial publishing conglomerate with a team of in-house lawyers. Most standard contracts put the libel issue back on the author.

As a result, you want to take libel seriously if you're writing a memoir where it may even remotely be an issue.

For more information on libel, examine *The Associated Press Stylebook*'s "Briefing on Media Law" section. The AP is one of the world's biggest news sources. If anyone knows how to reveal tough topics and inflammatory stories without getting sued, it's them.

Invading someone's right to privacy

Whether you realize it or not, every person has a right to privacy. Although the US Constitution doesn't guarantee this right, most legal minds infer this as an implied right. Right to privacy exists in three versions of the law:

✔ **The publication of embarrassing information:** The word "embarrassing" is misleading because you may think about nose picking or other small stuff. A better phrase is "highly offensive to a reasonable person."

✔ **The publication of false impressions:** Also called presenting someone in a *false light,* this is where your words damage a subject's dignity with reckless disregard. This can only happen to a living person, and if what you write is perceived as giving that person a distasteful perception.

✔ **The intentional intrusion on a person's privacy:** This is the paparazzi-style stuff, such as telephoto snapshots, Facebook stalking, and trespassing on someone's property.

The guidepost is if a reasonable person thinks that you infringed upon any of these three rights, you have problems. The best defense against any of these problems is to stay accurate and truthful.

If you don't want to run afoul of the right to privacy, you want to avoid using the following in your memoir:

✔ Financial data

✔ Journals and diaries

✔ Medical records

✔ Private e-mails or letters

✔ Sexual behavior (or orientation)

If you get signed permission to use any of those things, fine. If not, avoid them even if they're the juiciest stuff around.

Protecting yourself: Bring in the lawyers

When in doubt, have your subjects sign a release. A release form (www.ryangvancleave.com/releaseexample.pdf for an example) is a legal document that releases you from any liability of claim. You can find dozens of sample releases easily online, or you can use an online service, such as www.rocketlawyer.com for free legal forms to use. A release doesn't guarantee that you won't have unhappy people down the road or that you won't be sued. But if those things happen, you're on much sturdier legal ground than you may otherwise be with signed releases.

The only way to be 100 percent certain that you're on safe legal ground is to pay an attorney to look over your entire manuscript. If you use a traditional publisher, the publisher may have someone vet your book for potential problems, though that's not enough for you to feel 100 percent secure. Sometimes the publisher may only have an intern check. If you want to be certain you're in the clear, hire a lawyer to pore through it for legal landmines.

The easiest way to not worry about libel and lawsuits is to write a happy memoir about happy things. So many writers focus on pain and misery and suffering. We all could use a little more sunshine. Go that route, and the legal woes vanish in a blink. Yes, it's a bit unrealistic, but it's an option for some people. Consider this a simple reminder of your available options. Check out this example: Gretchen Rubin's *The Happiness Project: Or, Why I Spent a Year Trying to Sing in the Morning, Clean My Closets, Fight Right, Read Aristotle, and Generally Have More Fun* (Harper Perennial).

Writing Exercises on Saying the Unsayable

"Saying the Unsayable" is a pretty tall order, I realize. But writers have managed it before and future ones will handle it equally aptly, too. The writing exercises here are ones that my students have found helpful in getting their stories out of their memory and their manuscripts done. See how they work for you.

- ❑ **Focus on negative things that have happened to you.** Write down the most awful thing that ever happened to you. Include every emotion, feeling, and pain you experienced. Spill it and then step away for a day before looking at it again. Now try writing the same scene again but through the lens of a neutral observer. Which feels more like therapy and which more like a powerful scene from a good memoir? Make sure that writing for therapy stays in journals.

- ❑ **Focus on the Doubting Thomases in your life:** On a sheet of paper, write the name of the person who told you that you couldn't do something — couldn't write, couldn't love, couldn't succeed. Crumple up that paper and throw it as far as you can. If you have a fireplace, burn it. Free yourself from the limitations others have put upon you. Write down more names on other sheets of paper and deal with them as you need to.

- ❑ **Journal for a week.** Write about your painful past as many different times, as many different ways as you can. Vent the rage, and let it rip. Curse, scream, howl, and swear. Give yourself complete freedom in this journal. After you've written it enough times, you probably feel purged of that experience (or at least the deep pain of it). When you get to that point, try to tackle it effectively in your memoir. Does it even seem like it fits now? Sometimes, the answer is still no.

- ❑ **Forecast the worst-case scenario.** Imagine that you spilled every bean you could in your memoir, every secret, every mistake, every no-no you know about. Now imagine every character in your book reacted horribly. Write down the worst-case scenario with each real-life person. How bad could it really get? Just seeing this end of the potential responses may show you that even if things go wrong, you can live with it. That knowledge may free you to write more honestly or include more than you might otherwise choose.

Part IV
Sharing Your Story: A Publishing Primer

In this part . . .

At this point, you should have a full-length draft of your manuscript, so I can show you what to do next. First I look at the pros and cons of using a literary agent with some practical examples and guidance on how to woo one.

The next topic I cover in depth is traditional publishing. I look at its challenges and benefits, but also reveal the right way to submit your work for publication to prospective publishing houses. Next, I explore the new publishing options that have emerged thanks to new technologies: various models of self-publishing and e-publishing. I talk about what type of writers and books these options might best suit, and also discuss how to make the most of any of these avenues. Lastly, I explore how to promote and market your book no matter which publication path you went with.

Chapter 18

Locating and Landing a Literary Agent

You've been slugging away and writing alone for awhile now, but maybe you want to get someone in your corner. Enter the literary agent. The literary agent takes care of all the business stuff, while you, the writer, can take care of all the writing stuff.

You don't have to use a literary agent. In fact, writers like two-time National Book Award finalist Stephen Dixon sold hundreds of short stories and more than a dozen novels on his own. But he's an exception. Many writers don't have the moxie or business savvy to work the business end while still writing. Sometimes the worst advocate for a writer is the writer himself.

This chapter covers all the ins and outs of literary agents, from finding one, asking the right questions before you sign with one, helping your agent sell your book, and knowing what to do when things go wrong.

Seeing What a Good Literary Agent Can Do for You

The ideal agent/author relationship is symbiotic, which means it's built on mutual gain — that win-win thing that was so hip to talk about in the 1990s. When a relationship with a literary agent is working well, it's the best thing in a writer's life. When it's not working well, it's a lot like having someone around that you've been dating for a decade. The following sections outline the role of a literary agent and help you figure out whether you really need one.

Eyeing an agent's role

A good literary agent can do a variety of things for an author that she represents, but here are the top four in order of importance.

- ✔ Quickly get your manuscript into the hands of a decision-maker at a publishing house. (This means you get a prompt response too!)

- ✔ Work with an interested publisher to develop a book contract that maximizes your earning potential in ways writers don't always see or even know about.

- ✔ Help sell additional rights that earn you money (film, foreign language, audio, and merchandising, to name just a few).

- ✔ Develop your writing career beyond your current book she's selling for you. This may mean sequels, other books, *work-for-hire* projects (writing done for someone else who pays you for the work but more than likely doesn't give you any credit or ownership of that work), speaking gigs, or other opportunities.

A good agent is part sales representative, part business manager, part friend, part confidante, and part literary consultant. Not too bad to have someone like that working for you around the clock!

Some literary agents also help with editing, developing your manuscript, and finding authors freelance work. In short, a good agent provides access, knowledge, and guidance. A good agent is like your own personal literary Yoda. Can't you just hear the wisdom? "Write successful memoir, or do not. There is no try."

Determining whether you need an agent

A literary agent can be a powerful ally in your quest to get your memoir published. She basically serves as a book broker. If she agrees to represent your memoir, she'll try to sell it to a publisher. She'll use her industry insider knowledge to find the best match with an editor and publishing house. She may even sell movie rights, book club rights, or foreign language editions.

You don't need to decide if you need an agent until you have something to sell, so don't sweat this decision now if you don't have a finished manuscript. A lot of beginning writers ask me if I think they need an agent. The answer is this: Unless you're sure you don't need one, you probably do need one. It's not easy to get one, either, so after you've decided to chase one down, start early, be patient, and stay persistent.

Having an agent does have a cost. If your agent is successful in getting your book published, she takes a certain percentage of your book's income — from both the *initial advance* (the money you get before the book comes out) and from *royalties* (the percentage you receive from all book sales) — for the entire time that your book is in print. She also gets that same cut for movie deals, foreign rights, audio versions, and other ways that your book reaches the world.

Although you may think that sharing future profits on your memoir with a literary agent is a poor idea that costs you money, working with an agent has many more pros than cons, like I discuss in the previous section.

If you think that the fairly standard agent fee of 15 percent of everything is too much to pay an agent, you may want to hire an entertainment lawyer instead who can review your contracts and deals to ensure they're sound. Paying the lawyer $150 an hour, compared to paying an agent 15 percent, may end up being a bargain for a book that sells more than a few thousand copies, not to mention books that hit bestseller charts or have movies made out of them. In other words, the bigger the deal (or sales numbers), the bigger the savings for using an entertainment lawyer versus a traditional literary agent.

Finding an Agent Who Meets Your Needs

More literary agents are available now more than ever before. The reason is simple: If you're an editor at a big publishing house and you acquire a book that ends up selling a million copies, with a 15 percent commission, you net a year's salary or more. It's like playing Literary Lotto, only with much better odds!

Having a few strong clients can allow an agent to sit back and just maintain her career versus having to chase down a ton of new business. This means some established agents aren't actively looking for — or even considering at all — new clients.

Plenty of mid- or early-career agents are actively trying to find new authors. These sections examine the best ways to find and court these writer-seeking agents.

One great trick to find an agent is to look in the acknowledgments page of memoirs you enjoy. Many authors thank their agents there by name. With that information available, you can write to that agent and say, "I'm writing to you because you represented (insert book title here) and I love that book." Not a bad way to introduce yourself and your writing to someone, is it?

Referrals rule

One of the best ways to connect with an agent is the same way most people land jobs — personal recommendations. Agents who are told by a current client "Hey, you really need to check out this person's book!" find that a very persuasive thing. Hearing from a client — someone who she respects — demands her attention and increases the chance that your manuscript will get a very thorough look. What more could you ask for?

If you're fortunate enough to already know a published writer, you may kindly ask him for a recommendation on literary agents. He may request to see a sample of your work first. Don't worry. It's not an insult. A writer shouldn't lightly give a recommendation without first being familiar with a person's writing.

An easy way to drum up new relationships with writers is to get involved with writers' blogs, writing critique groups, and online communities for writers (see www.ryanvancleave.com/bonuschapter.pdf) for more information on these opportunities). Really invest in those authors whose work you admire. If you're in a big city, you can do this in person at literary readings and other book events. In a small city like Sarasota, Florida (where I live), more than four dozen *New York Times* bestselling authors live within an hour's drive. Hitting up local events is sure to encourage chance meetings with one or more of them. Do the same in your own hometown.

Don't e-mail or Facebook stalk random writers and ask for favors. It's a waste of time, it comes across as spam, it's unprofessional, and it's rude. Successful recommendations have to come out of a genuine relationship that can take a year or more to develop.

To get to know potential writers who may give you an agent recommendation, you may want to take a weekend or weeklong writing class with them. Most writers teach these master classes or workshops from time to time at community centers, colleges, or bookstores. Sign up, go in there, and wow them. The class will have many other eager writers so make sure your writing sizzles on the page so you truly stand out. Then later, if it seems appropriate, humbly request the instructor's assistance in finding a literary agent for your manuscript.

If the writer declines, don't take it personally. Some well-known writers get asked multiple times a week for things like agent hookups, editor introductions, blurbs for other people's books, and so forth. They simply can't do it all, nor should they be expected to. So if you do get some help, be darn sure to sincerely thank them!

Agent listings and databases

These extremely useful agent listings used to be solely print publications, but no longer. The real plus with so many of these listings and databases being available for free or for a small cost on the Internet is that they're often more up-to-date than their print counterparts. Agents tend to move (both physically and from job to job), so having a current list saves everyone time and money.

Here are the most popular options for finding the contact information and submission guidelines for literary agents:

✔ **The Writer's Digest annual *Guide to Literary Agents* (Writer's Digest Books):** Edited by Chuck Sambuchino, this thick book is available at nearly every public library and bookstore in the United States. If you know of an agent who isn't listed here, more than likely the agent isn't looking for new clients and has asked to be excluded. Or the agent is too new to be included, which may or may not be a good thing.

✔ **Chuck Sambuchino's *Guide to Literary Agents* blog:** Hosted on www.writersdigest.com, this literary agent blog is considered the best, bar none. It has interviews, deal information, useful articles, and tons of links to web resources. Best of all, it's free. And you know it's authoritative because Sambuchino is the editor for the Writer's Digest guide.

✔ **Jeff Herman's annual *Guide to Book Publishers, Editors, and Literary Agents* (Sourcebooks):** With more than half a million total copies sold, this book has helped many aspiring writers find the road map to publishing success.

✔ **Agent Query:** This free-to-use website (www.agentquery.com) advertises itself as the "largest, most current searchable database of literary agents on the web." It's how I found one of my own agents.

✔ **Publisher's Marketplace:** This site (www.publishersmarketplace.com) claims to be the "biggest and best dedicated marketplace for publishing professionals to find critical information and unique databases, to find each other, and to do business better." This is a good place to find an agent, locate a professional editor, or learn more about a publisher.

A great free resource from this site is the free e-mail service called "Publishers Lunch," which shares some of the newest book deals. More than 40,000 publishing professionals read it daily, and with good reason because it's a fast and easy way to stay in the loop.

✔ ***Publisher's Weekly*:** The most current book deals are reported here in both the print and online versions of this weekly periodical. If you want to really understand how the publishing world works — and who the major players are in it — this is the Bible.

- ✔ **Association of Authors' Representatives (AAR):** To qualify for AAR, an agent has to meet the professional standards and ethics listed on this website, `http://www.aaronline.org`, so you know these agents are worth working with. You can find a lot of terrific information here for writers (such as agent blogs and discussion forums), plus a good database of sound, professional agents.

- ✔ **Media Bistro:** Although the main site (`www.mediabistro.com`) houses various blogs and job listings for journalists, the subscription service AvantGuild has a lot of insider information on publishing, literary agents, and writing.

Conference your way to connections

Agents read manuscripts at work. Then they go home and read more manuscripts at night and on their weekends. Yes, they love it, but it doesn't do much for their social lives. So not surprisingly many leap at the chance to attend writer conferences where they can have a drink with fellow literature lovers and perhaps serve on a panel or two. Going to a conference is a chance to get away from the Mt. Kilimanjaro–sized stack of manuscripts they need to read but still stay professionally active.

You have a great opportunity to interact with literary agents at writers' conferences. I suggest you consider attending a writers' conference that features an agent or two. Even if you don't manage to catch a minute of face-time with that agent, you still have a great opportunity to stand out from the crowd. You can write to the agent after the conference and reference something specific that she said.

Here are a few reputable writing conferences among hundreds (see a much more comprehensive list at `http://writersconf.org`) where you can get quality information about writing and also encounter an agent or two. You may even make a writing friend from the other attendees.

- ✔ Antioch Writers' Workshop (`www.antiochwritersworkshop.com`)
- ✔ San Francisco Writers Conference (`www.sfwriters.org`)
- ✔ Sanibel Island Writers Conference (`www.fgcu.edu/siwc`)
- ✔ Writer's Digest Conference (`www.writersdigestconference.com`)

Some writers' conferences allow attendees to sign up for short manuscript critique sessions with editors or agents. Doing so isn't cheap but it's often worth it. Surely the agent can remember you if she gives you advice, you follow it, and then you officially submit it to them down the road.

Hooking the Right Agent

Not all agents are created equal, which is why if you want to hire an agent, you need to make sure you diligently research and find the right agency for you and your memoir. As you make your final decision, make sure you're selective.

Some agencies prefer to specialize in a certain literary area, which means that your memoir may not be a good fit for every agency. For instance, Agency X may only want, say, romance novels. Agency Y may be a better fit if your memoir is about overcoming addiction, because the agency's website says that the agency "loves triumphant true-life stories of overcoming great obstacles despite the odds." Some of the larger agencies have someone there for any topic, but that's not the same as saying any topic will work with any agent.

Although agents do sell books, they do it via relationships that they have cultivated over the years. Even though you may think an agent could sell any book, that's simply not the case. Make sure that the agent you're targeting has sold books like yours before and that she is actively looking for new clients. If the answer to either of those points is no, you're wasting your time and energy with this agent. Move on to the next one on your list.

These sections walk you through several pointers and tips as you work to hire an agent. Here I explain the importance of following the agent's submission guidelines, discuss what agents vehemently dislike from writers, and share some insider secrets to help you catch the agent you want.

Do you want Stephen King's agent? Although it sounds very cool, the reality is that King's agent has his hands full with super high-profile writers like King. Even if you could hook this big fish, you're the guppy in a deep, deep pool. Expecting a lot of time and energy from this agent is unlikely at best.

Sticking to the submission guidelines

Because of the sheer volume of submissions that flood into literary agencies every day, they have to have some kind of policy guidelines in place. Whatever the guidelines are, show that you can follow directions and be professional. Standing out in a crowded publishing market is a must, yet now isn't the time to be different. Let your story be different. Let your prose be noteworthy. With your submission, do what the agency requests. It's the only way in the door.

For example, a common guideline these days is to send manuscripts via electronically. Some agencies even have their own submission uploader that they insist you use versus general e-mail.

If the agency website says the agency is currently on hiatus or not reading until a specific date, listen. You may be tempted to think that now is the perfect time to submit something because no one else is. Don't do it. At best, your submission will be boomeranged back with a rejection after not even having been looked at. At worst, the agency will add your name to its "Never Work With" list.

Understanding what literary agents hate from writers

Literary agents can lead crazy lives. With countless manuscripts piled around the office, numerous phone calls with editors, quick lunches with entertainment lawyers, and complaining spouses who vent that they haven't seen one of their kid's soccer games, they don't have time for nonsense. As a result, you want to make sure you don't do anything that drives them nuts.

Avoid the following to ensure you don't get on their bad side:

- **Gimmicks:** Stay away from any gimmicks to get the agent's attention. For instance, one thriller writer wanted to give a prospective literary agent the same fear his super-spy agent felt when having to defuse a bomb in the climax of the novel, so the special delivery package the literary agent received (with no return address) was ticking. You can image how that literary agent felt about that writer after the office building had to be cleared out and the bomb squad called.

- **Packages that are impossible to open:** If you need a machete to hack through the packing tape and string, it's more than likely going in the trash instead of the "Read Now" stack.

- **Super small fonts:** Everyone in the book business has bad eyes. Don't make it worse. Use the standard size font of 11 to 12 points.

- **Funky fonts:** Make the story be your selling point, not the strange and possibly hard-to-read font. Use a standard font, such as Times New Roman, Georgia, or Arial.

- **Misspelling the agent's name:** If you misspell the agent's name, you may as well try another agent. The little details mean a lot. With a name like Van Cleave, I know this one personally. I am *not* Mr. Cleave nor am I Mr. Van. Call me either and I will ignore you. Literary agents can be equally petty.

- **Pitching more than one book at a time:** Unless it's a series, focus on one project, one book, and one thing at a time.

✔ **No return address:** Put your return address on the envelope and include your entire contact information — name, address, phone, e-mail, and website — on the cover letter or query. If you don't, you can expect your manuscript to go in the circular file (also known as the trash can, folks).

✔ **Lying:** It doesn't matter what you lie about — your background, your age, your writing credits, whatever. If you tweak the truth, or massage the facts, or engage in a little old-fashioned white lying, the agent can legitimately question whether your memoir is truthful. You're not ready to get published.

Trying some insider tactics

Although I don't have any surefire advice for landing a literary agent, I do know that most of the real movers and shakers in the writing world have done one or more of the following. Decide which tactic suits you and go for it. If anything here doesn't feel right, ignore it and try something else. There's no single blueprint for success.

✔ **Query more than one agent at a time.** Some writers hit up as many as a dozen at a time. You're not blanketing the earth because you should research every agent you query, but doing so does speed up the process of trying to find an agent.

✔ **Pitch an agent over the phone.** If you have the gift of gab and you can sell yourself and your book in less than three minutes, this option may work. Try calling at 8:45 a.m. Eastern Standard Time because most receptionists often show up at 9 a.m. You may get the agents answering without the gatekeepers running interference.

✔ **Tell agents that you'll be in town and would be happy to meet them at their convenience to discuss your manuscript.** Even if you haven't made a plan to visit the area where the agent works, if an agent agrees to meet with you for a short sit-down, you can quickly buy a plane ticket. If not, you haven't wasted any money.

✔ **Get a celebrity to write your Foreword.** Even if the odds are 1 in 100 that you can convince a celebrity to pen two or three pages for the front of your book, just think about how an agent will view it. Add Morgan Freeman or Grammy winner Mariah Carey to your book's pitch and people will notice. Don't lie about this, though. Only name someone who has actually agreed to write a Foreword or you have a reasonable expectation to get (and then name that relationship, such as Kim Kardashian is your cousin).

If an agency's guidelines specifically say *not* to do something, follow that advice. But if they don't mention it at all, you can consider that lack of direction as an invitation to try that tactic if you think it will help your cause.

Many literary agents are interested in signing writers for the long term. Sending a strong query letter is important (refer to Chapter 19 for what to include in a query letter). Adding a single sentence to your query that affirms you're working on a second project may suggest you're a career author (meaning someone who can make that agent money for decades) versus a one-and-done person. It won't be enough to seal the deal, but if you're on the bubble, it may help for the agent to know.

Feel free to invent other ways to get an agent's attention. Just be respectful of the agent's time and personal space. Consider these options: How about starting up your own writing contest and asking for the literary agent to judge it? How about sending some of your grandmother's secret mulberry muffins via special courier? How about writing an earnest thank you card for the agent's latest hit that you enjoyed reading without even mentioning your own book (yet)?

Being leery of a bad agent

Bad literary agents exist. Some are failed writers. Some are failed editors. Some are people who sincerely love books but don't have the right business IQ. Some see this as a get-rich-quick scheme ("If I can just sell one book like Stephen King's . . . "). Be extra careful as you research and vet agents to stay clear of bad agents.

Having a bad literary agent is worse than no literary agent because not only will your agent be unable to sell your book, your name will be sullied for being associated with her. And future agents won't want to try the same manuscript at a publisher who has already said no to it. If you decide to use an agent, do your research before signing up with any agent. And if the one you hired isn't the right fit, abandon ship!

Making Sense of an Agent Agreement

If an agent agrees to represent you, you'll need to sign an agency agreement. Basically an *agency agreement* spells out who is expected to do what as well as exactly how any proceeds are to be divvied up. A good agency agreement covers all contingencies, such that an author doesn't have to guess whether she's paying for photocopying or not — the agreement has it clearly in writing.

These sections explain in greater detail what information you can find in an agent agreement, provide questions you can ask before you sign, offer insight into what happens after you sign, and discuss when you may need to end an agreement.

Identifying what's in a standard agreement

An agency agreement comes in different shapes and sizes. It may be a one-page document that's easy enough for Homer Simpson to make sense of, or it may also be several pages long and awfully complicated where only a Stanford education and a legal scholar can decipher it. For example, one of my agency agreements fits on 1½ pages, and another ran 15 pages.

Agreements differ from agency to agency, but you want to be clear on these main points in the agreement:

- ✔ **What percentage of your book's income does your agent get?** Ten to 20 percent is typical.

- ✔ **What expenses are you responsible for regardless of whether the book is sold or not?** These expenses can include shipping, copying, using a messenger service, and so on.

- ✔ **What is the procedure for submission updates?** This point is important if you want to get regular updates on which publishers are currently looking at your work and which ones have passed on it. Some writers never want to know any of this unless it's an actual offer.

- ✔ **Is there a term limit to this agreement?** Having a year-to-year agreement isn't a bad idea so you can easily walk away if things don't work out.

  Even if you have a one-year contractual obligation with a specific agent, you may be working with the agency forever if your agent sells your memoir during that time. Even if you sign with a new agent to represent a second or third book (after your first agency agreement is up, of course), the first agent will remain the agent of record for your first memoir. This means that you have a business arrangement with that agency for the long term. Be sure you're happy with that first agent before you each make this type of commitment to each other.

All agencies have a boilerplate, or standard, contract, but that doesn't mean the agency agreement is a "take it or leave it" situation. If you have a request, ask. The smaller the agency, the more likely it is willing to adjust to your needs.

If your agent belongs to the Association of Authors' Representatives (AAR), it must follow a number of standards. Check out www.aaronline.org for details.

A legitimate agent that you've researched and feel good about isn't out to screw you. If you don't understand something you see in their agency agreement, ask for a clarification. And if you're especially paranoid, e-mail your question so you have written proof of their answer.

An author-agent relationship is a success-based endeavor. If the book doesn't sell, no one wins. You're in this together. The agency agreement should reflect that win-win relationship whether it's a one-person agency in Denver, a mom-and-pop shop in Scranton, or a fifty-person agency in Brooklyn.

Asking questions before you sign an agency agreement

Although having an agency say it loves your work is exciting, hold on. Before you sign any agreement, make sure you ask the following questions to gather more information so you can make the best decision:

- **What do you like most about my book?** Consider this question both a chance to feel good by having an industry expert offer some specific praise for your work, and also to serve as a quality control check. The agency should have clear ideas about what's good in your book. If not, why on earth are they offering to represent it?

- **What type of potential do you envision for my book?** Yes, you dream of hearing about the feature film potential and seven-figure advance that your story deserves, but is it realistic? Is the agency promising the moon? If your book has that kind of potential, other agencies should be fighting each other to represent you.

- **How do you plan to market my book?** Make sure the agency has a clear strategy. Will it be sent to one publisher at a time? Which publishers does the agent have in mind? Is there a Plan B if the first round of submissions is unsuccessful?

- **How often and by what method should we communicate with each other?** Some agents prefer to handle everything by e-mail. Some want to talk weekly. Some will send you a copy of every submission and every rejection. Find out what the agency typically does and see if that matches your expectations.

✔ **What commission rate do you charge, and are there any other fees?**
Ten percent used to be the going rate. Fifteen percent is becoming the
new standard, though 20 percent may be worth it for the right agency to
represent you. A good agent should make you more than enough extra
money to cover her fees. Make sure you know about other fees, such as
faxing, photocopying, shipping, and so on. Check to see if the agency
has a limit to these other fees. What happens if you accumulate a lot of
fees but the manuscript never sells?

Beware of an agent who insists on a *representation fee* (paying upfront
for the agent to represent you, which isn't the norm in the publishing
world), or will take your book on only if it's edited or developed by an
editing service they recommend. Think scam. In short, don't pay anything upfront for an agent unless you're 100 percent comfortable with
the situation and that you've done some research to ensure what you're
paying for isn't unnecessary. It's a sad truth, but plenty of people prey
on the hopes and dreams of aspiring authors for their own financial gain.

✔ **How many books in my genre have you sold?** It doesn't have to be a
ton, but the agency should have some kind of track record unless it's a
brand-new agency.

✔ **How many of your clients have you sold books for?** Like the previous question, make sure the agency has a track record. Some or a lot is
better than none. This number will give you a fair assessment of your
agent's sales ability.

✔ **What subsidiary rights sales have you made for your clients?**
Subsidiary rights — film rights, merchandising rights, audio rights, book
club rights, and so on — are big moneymakers. You want an agency
that knows which ones are worth holding onto versus signing over to a
publisher in the contract. Although many agencies don't have the staff
to cover all subsidiary rights sales in-house, they should have subcon-
tractor arrangements with agents who specialize in these areas who can
help sell them for a modest fee.

✔ **What happens if my book doesn't sell?** Is there a *sunset clause* in your
contract, meaning that if a sale doesn't happen by a given time, the relationship with the agency is over? Or will the agency continue to work with
you on the same project for longer if you both agree it's fruitful to do so?
Will the agent help you create other projects to pitch to publishers?

✔ **How do you pay out royalties and advances?** Anything that your publisher pays to you first goes to your agent, who takes her agreed-upon
cut before sending it on. Ethical agents should have a separate bank
account for these funds that is different from their personal accounts.
They should have a clear procedure and timeframe for paying out the
money that's owed to you. Two weeks or less is typical.

Looking beyond the dotted line

Think of the period right after you sign your agency contract as the early stages of dating. You're both excited. Possibilities abound. Be flexible to changing the way things work to better suit you. At first getting every rejection letter may have sounded great. However after you have enough of them to wallpaper the guest bedroom, you may think otherwise.

Your agent, too, may want to alter the agreement, which may necessitate an official amendment to the original contract. If you're game, sign it. If not, explain your hesitation and be willing to walk away.

This partnership is a lot like a marriage. If you're both less than fully committed, the odds of success are slim to none.

Know when your relationship is at the end (and what to do about it!)

As someone who has parted ways with four different literary agents during my twenty-year writing career, I promise you that a time may come where continuing to work with your current agent no longer makes sense. One time was my fault. One time was her fault. The other two? A combination of issues that are just the normal stuff of the world of writing.

What are the symptoms of an author-agent relationship that isn't working?

- ✔ Your agent can't sell your manuscript.
- ✔ Your agent doesn't respond promptly to your e-mails or calls.
- ✔ Your agent doesn't seem excited about your work anymore.
- ✔ Your agent tries to pass you off to a new, junior agent in the office.

Understand that sometimes a good manuscript being represented by an enthusiastic agent doesn't equal a book contract. That's not necessarily a sign that you need to dump your agent. But if you notice more than one of the preceding situations, then you may need to give this relationship some serious thought.

Before you officially end things, make sure that you have a clear, honest conversation over the phone with the agent. Yes, it will be uncomfortable, but an e-mail or snail mail letter can't properly deliver tone. Make sure you're polite and gentle. You may be surprised — the agent may agree that she has been less professional than expected and that she'll change. You may wish to stay on longer in that case and give her another chance. If not, properly end things.

Your agent contract will have a specific clause in it about how to terminate the relationship. Typically, it's just to officially notify your agent that you're moving on and at that point (or 30 days, 45 days, or whatever your contract specifies), you're now unattached. If for some reason your agency contract doesn't have a procedure for parting ways, then you need to send a clear note that says you're no longer happy with the relationship and choose to end things. This note doesn't have to be elaborate, and you don't even have to give reasons why unless you choose to do so.

Tapping into a literary agent's mind: Claire Gerus

Claire Gerus has been editor-in-chief of two publishing houses, worked for seven major publishers, written countless articles for US and Canadian magazines and newspapers, and taught corporate communications to such clients as IBM, Kellogg's, Mutual of Omaha, and Procter & Gamble. In 1996, she established the Claire Gerus Literary Agency, which represented such books as the *New York Times* best-selling memoir by Esther Williams and Laura Bush's first biography, *Laura.*

If you want to snare yourself a top agent like Claire, be sure to follow her advice. Claire says, "People write memoirs because they want to give readers insight into an experience they had that they want to share with others. Agents get many memoir submissions because more than ever, this category seems to be increasing in interest from both writers and readers.

As to what agents look for in memoirs? We look for experiences others can relate to that will result in strong book sales. Among today's successful topics are overcoming personal challenges, making fascinating new discoveries, and assisting others with a new approach to a problem or situation."

Agents tend to steer away from family-based stories, Claire warns. Beyond the immediate family, who wants to read *How Great Aunt Mary Immigrated from Australia to New York in the 1930s* or *My Life as a Potato Farmer in Boise,* *Idaho.* These will receive only limited attention from book buyers who don't identify with these topics.

Claire recommends that prospective memoir writers spend time researching what trends are happening now in the field. For instance, "Inspirational memoirs can attract large readerships, such as Laura Hillenbrand's *Unbroken: A World War II Story of Survival, Resilience and Redemption* and Anita Moorjani's *Dying to be Me: My Journey from Cancer to Near Death to Healing.* Both have sold thousands in a very short time. Adventure and survival are also appealing, such as Cheryl Strayed's *Wild: From Lost to Found on the Pacific Crest Trail.* Of course, celebrity memoirs continue to attract both fans and the curious."

After working for decades in the publishing business, Claire says, "The most important thing I've learned about publishing is to look for possibilities, even if an initial proposal doesn't work. Sometimes there's another more marketable book idea within the original submission that will work better. I tend to talk with the author to explore all possibilities if I sense there's another lurking there."

But Claire is a rare case. For most literary agents, it's a simple yes/no situation. Claire has a reputation for being a real champion for writers. It's easy to see why.

You want to be nice when you part ways. Don't burn bridges on your way out. Even if your agent was truly rotten to you, the publishing world is a small place. You don't need enemies. Exit gracefully and with the sincerest "thank you" that you can muster.

Another reason to be nice: If an agent has your work out at some publishing houses and it ends up generating a publishing contract, that agent represents you for that title *even after* you parted ways, so be nice on your way out the door, no matter what.

Chapter 19

Making Sense of Traditional Publishing and the Submission Process

In This Chapter

▶ Investigating traditional publishers

▶ Considering the advantages and disadvantages of traditional publishers

▶ Using effective query letters

▶ Discovering submission dos and don'ts

▶ Going with a subsidy/vanity publisher

*Y*our manuscript is complete and you're anxious to see it in print at last. You have a number of options on how to make that happen (refer to Chapter 20 for a couple of those options). Many writers choose to consider traditional publishers first because they pay for the privilege of publishing your manuscript. They also have editors, designers, PR people, warehouses, and distribution channels, which basically handles everything you need except for the actual writing of the book (that's still your job!).

Of course, because most writers want those benefits, the competition at publishing houses is understandably fierce. That's why a thorough understanding of the publishing world can help maximize your chances for success. This chapter delves deeper into how you can increase your chances for connecting with a traditional publisher.

Publishers are in the business of making money, not books. Keep that commercial bottom line in mind at all times, and you'll be better able to think like they do.

Researching Publishers

In the past, only a few significant publishers located in New York City published books. No longer! Now that technology has improved so that anyone anywhere can print and distribute a book, you can find quality publishers throughout the United States, in places such as Minneapolis, Minnesota (Graywolf Press), Ann Arbor, Michigan (Dzanc Books), and Chattanooga, Tennessee (C&R Press), as you can in the Big Apple.

These sections reveal the easiest ways to find the right publisher for your memoir. They also uncover everything else you need to know to move forward after you locate the right match.

Locating publishers

Publishers are surprisingly easy to find, or at least the bigger ones are. You can spot them by virtue of their books appearing on bestseller lists or the shelves at the front of the big chain bookstores.

Beyond checking bestseller lists or combing bookstore shelves, you have a lot of options available on finding publishers, both small and large:

- **Read helpful guides from**
    - The annual *Writer's Market* (edited by Robbie Lee Brewer)
    - Jeff Herman's annual *Guide to Book Publishers, Editors, and Literary Agents*
- **Go online**
    - Search for "book publishers" (or more specifically, "memoir publishers")
    - `Querytracker.net`
    - `Publishersmarketplace.com`
- **Ask for referrals from**
    - Your writer friends
    - Booksellers
    - Librarians

Not every book belongs at a big publishing house. Sometimes the best fit is a smaller press, a university press, or a foreign one. Be open to all options when you first start looking.

Checking out your prospective publishers

After you get a specific publisher in your crosshairs, see what kind of product the publisher puts out to the world. What it's publishing now is going to be similar to what it will do for you. You need to make sure it's a level of professionalism and quality that you're comfortable with.

In other words, if you can't find copies of the publisher's books in bookstores because the publisher has crappy distribution, think twice. And if the books regularly have typos or misprints, reconsider. If the publisher lets its books go out of print in a year, really rethink things.

If you go with this publisher, you're married for the life of this book. Don't assume that the publisher will get better, more prestigious, or nicer. Deal with the reality of what the publisher is and what it can offer you. To cover yourself, make sure you follow my advice in these sections.

Going for the real deal: The Internet isn't enough

When you're taking a closer look at the publisher or two that you're interested in, make sure you look at its website. Anyone can put up a slick website these days, so take the time to study the entire website and all its content. Don't get me wrong — it's great if the publisher has a slick website versus an obvious template website that seems pretty generic, but make sure you go deeper than just the home page.

Just because the publisher's website says something doesn't necessarily mean it's true. Do a little sleuthing and fact checking and carefully:

- ✔ **Read the "About the press" page.** Companies spend a lot of time and money on this part of the website to explain who they are and what they do. Don't neglect this important and readily available information.

- ✔ **Look at the list of current authors.** Are these authors writing books you'd be proud to have written? Would you be happy to have your name and book alongside theirs?

- ✔ **Check out the backlist.** The *backlist* includes the older titles still available from the publisher. Are these still selling long after the initial sales push that comes with a new book? Is the publisher letting older books just fall out of print?

- ✔ **Examine a few of the pages for individual titles.** Get a sense of how the publisher is promoting its own authors. Are they getting good reviews? Winning awards? Receiving media coverage? The individual book title pages on the website should tell you all that and more.

Although most people wouldn't dare lie in such an obvious manner, it's better to be safe than sorry.

A bigger deal now than ever before is web presence. See how hip the publisher is to social media and virtual PR. Is this publisher still in the digital stone age or is it on the cutting edge of e-publishing and social media campaigns?

Although most writers realize that badmouthing their publisher in public is self-defeating, you can still get a decent feel for things by checking out a writer's blog. Some will rave about their publisher. Others will be oddly quiet about it. Read into that what you will.

Doing a quality control check

In your sleuth work, head to your public library or nearby bookstore and find some of the publisher's titles. Hold a couple of the publisher's most recent books in your hands and ask some of these questions:

- How do the cover designs look? Are they attractive or amateurish? How would you feel if your memoir had a similar type of cover?

- How do the interior pages look? Are they thin or cheap? Do they look professionally produced?

- What do the interior images look like? Are they grainy or too light or dark? Do they bleed through to the next page, so when you hold the page up, you can see the image from the previous page?

- How does the text look? Is it sharp and in good contrast to the paper? Is the font and font size easy to read?

- How are the text margins? Are they consistent or does the text sort of slide when you flip through the pages?

- Does the book simply have the heft and feel of a quality product? Does it feel like it'll hold up well after years of heavy use in a public library?

If the answers suggest you go forward, submit your manuscript to this publisher by following its guidelines that you can find on its website (which are almost always more recent than anything in annual market books).

Working with a Publisher: The Pros

Traditional publishing is popular because it has a lot to offer for writers. Perhaps the most important thing, though, is prestige. An established company puts its own time, money, and effort into *your* book. It feels great when that happens. And it tells the world that your book is going to be worthwhile. In addition, here are some other upsides to working with a publisher.

Editors, well, edit

One of the clearest signs of a book done professionally is that it's well-edited, which means more than just dotting Is and crossing Ts. A well-edited manuscript features writing that is smooth, effortless, and a pleasure to read. For more information on how to do some of this work on your own, see Chapters 15 and 16.

Even though editors are often very good at editing, they're fallible. Don't rely exclusively on their edits. Re-read your manuscript as many times as you need to. Have some of your reader friends take a look too. You'll thank me when readers aren't sending you notes about the typos and geographical snafus in your published version.

Professional layout and design

Traditional publishers have pro layout and design people, which means that the books they produce look nice. Although your Cousin Herbert may be a wiz with InDesign at the local FedEx Office store, you're better off with a pro who creates dozens of book layouts and covers per year. Cousin Herbert can't avoid some of the problems that a well-seasoned book layout person knows.

See this for yourself. Compare a memoir by, say, HarperCollins with one that was self-published. The differences should be astounding.

PR plan and team

You can never have enough people in your corner when marketing your book. Traditional publishers have PR people (entire departments, in many cases), and their goal is to sell your book. The more copies they sell, the safer their job is.

You want people on your team whose job security is affected by how well your book does. They'll work hard. They'll also know what tends to work and what doesn't, so no one wastes time on PR goals that don't pay off in sales.

For ideas on how you can help your publisher with PR matters, visit Chapter 21. PR people at your publisher usually welcome your help, though you have to keep them in the loop. The last thing you want is for both you and them to put money, time, and energy into the exact same PR area, so communicate and then divide and conquer.

The bigger the publishing house, the shorter period it has to promote its current books. It's a simple numbers game; more new books are coming, and the publisher has to move on to them. Make sure you take advantage of those two or three months of PR support; they can be priceless!

Higher chance of reviews

Reviewers are deluged with books and no matter how much they may wish otherwise, they have to ignore 98 percent of the books that come across their desks. If you want the best shot of getting reviewed at major venues, having the backing of a traditional publisher will help immensely.

A traditional publisher has plenty of checks and balances that guarantee the majority of books they put out are worth putting out. That means reviewers are more likely to find books worth reviewing by sticking with books by traditional publishers.

Why be concerned with a review of your book? Reviews matter a ton. Garnering high-profile reviews is one of the best perks of working with a good traditional publisher.

Advances and royalties

Traditional publishers offer an *advance* to the authors of the books they sign, meaning these publishers pay money upfront against future expected royalty earnings. Pretend that a publisher offers you an advance of $10,000 for your completed memoir. Awesome! Take it and run, right?

At some point, though, you may start wondering why you don't get more money from the publisher because your book is selling. The reason you're not seeing more cash is because you have to pay back that $10,000 before you see another dime. If your royalty agreement comes out to you making $1 per book sale, then you need to sell 10,000 copies before you start earning money beyond the initial advance. In other words, you don't see more money until the sale of book 10,001.

An advance is a great thing because it's basically a no-interest loan that you never have to pay back, even if your book tanks. Though if your book doesn't *earn out,* meaning you don't sell enough to offset the initial advance, you're quickly labeled a sales risk and future book deals may become quite scarce. For this reason, you may want to go with a much more modest advance to assure that you're seen as a profitable author.

Instant books: Just add water

You may have heard about *instant books*, which are written and published within weeks of a major world event, such as Michael Jackson's death, the Black Hawk Down incident, or Occupy Wall Street. These books are created to quickly cash in on an extremely timely moment that has everyone talking. They tend to be a flash in the pan, though. The sales are terrific for a few months, and then the books fade away — often going out of print in a year or two.

Unless your memoir is about something amazingly timely, like you just escaped from an Al-Qaeda prison after being held for two years, and you got back to the United States by commandeering a pirate vessel single-handedly, expect to be on the same slow timeline as every other author.

Because the US economy has been less strong of late, the publishing industry has gotten thriftier. Although the number of $100,000 deals going on is the same at $5,000 advances, some publishers are offering publication with a *no-advance clause,* which means you don't get any upfront money. A no-advance clause isn't acceptable if you need rent money. But if you don't need money upfront, you can still make the same money down the road if you sell 15,000 copies versus having a modest advance to begin with.

Going with a Publisher: The Cons

Although getting a contract for your memoir from a publisher is exciting, you also have your share of concerns. Here are some of the main things to strongly consider before signing on the dotted line. Ultimately, you have to make a well-reasoned cost-benefit analysis that may come out different from what your significant other, your parents, or your dog would choose.

Acceptance to publication timeline

Your memoir took months if not years to write, so you want to see the book out as soon as possible, right? The truth is that even after you sign a contract with a traditional publisher, the book won't see the light of day for 12 to 18 months on average. Sometimes it can be a full two years.

Why does it take so darn long? The reasons include

- ✔ Publishers already have a season or two worth of other titles to publish first.
- ✔ Your manuscript requires multiple rounds of edits and revisions.
- ✔ The marketing people need time to create and prepare their materials.
- ✔ The major book review venues require six months of lead time before a book comes out.

In rare cases, you may be able to negotiate a faster publication timeline, though doing so is unlikely and usually not in your best interest. Although the publishers are slow, they have a process and it works. It just takes a *long* time.

Low royalties

The myth of the starving writer is still more reality than myth. *Royalties* are the monies paid to a writer after each sale of the book. With a return of your efforts of 10 percent *net* (the amount remaining after any discounts, which are traditionally offered to booksellers and distributors — for example, Amazon takes 55 percent off the top!) on average per sale, you're not going to get rich unless you start selling copies in the tens of thousands. And to be clear, with that being 10 percent net (versus off the actual cover price), the publisher can deduct discounts or expenses, such as advertising or printer's costs before shaving off your share of the ever-shrinking pie.

Publishers hold back a specific amount — often 15 percent — of any royalties owed to you as a reserve against potential returns. Books are always coming and going to the warehouse, and the publisher doesn't want to overpay you only to find out that the literature mega-class of 300 students at the University of Florida was cancelled so the bookstore sent back all 300 copies of your book. Just holding onto a bit of the money the publisher owes you is far easier than asking you to send it back. As a result, nearly all contracts now have this *reserve clause*.

Royalties can also be awfully confusing for a writer. Here I try to help explain these murky waters:

- ✔ **Many contracts have an escalator clause.** An *escalator clause* means that your royalty rate increases if sales hit certain benchmarks. For example, sales of 1 to 10,000 earn you 10 percent. Sales of 10,001 to 25,000 earn you 12.5 percent. Sales of more than 25,001 earn you 14 percent.
- ✔ **Different types of sales earn different rates.** Hard covers, trade paperbacks, and racksize paperbacks may all earn a different rate. The same is true of special sales (such as book clubs), mail orders, or electronic versions of your title.

- ✔ **A small reprinting — another printing of your book after the initial print run is sold off —may earn less.** Because it costs more per unit to do small printings, you may only get half your normal royalty rate if the print run is 1,000 copies or fewer.

- ✔ **Some sales have a zero royalty.** Books in Braille or used for promotional reasons typically earn you nothing. If either situation especially bothers you, you can negotiate after you've been offered a book contract.

- ✔ **Remaindered copies earn zero.** If the publisher gets tired of seeing boxes of your book cluttering up the warehouse, it may sell them off as remainders or overstock. Have you ever seen books for sale at dollar stores with a black mark on the spine or across the UPC? Those books are remainders and are sold in lots by the pound, as in "200 pounds of general cookbooks at 10¢/pound." You don't earn anything for those sales because they're being sold at far less than it cost to make them.

Your contract will spell out your royalty information in great detail, so look through it and make sure you understand exactly what you'll get for your book sales. If you're confused, make sure to ask questions. The last thing you want to have happen is to hear that Warren Buffett is going to buy 20,000 copies of your book to give away to his employees, only to find out that he's negotiated a 51 percent discount off the cover price and your contract specifies that you get nothing for sales discounted by half or more from the cover price. (You can bet that the publisher makes moolah on that deal, though, which is why it sold those copies to Mr. Buffett in the first place!)

As you can imagine, many authors have no idea what they're making. It's not inconceivable that the publisher's financial department may get a bit lost, too. Royalty statements typically come out once or twice a year, so make sure you scrutinize yours to make sure everything looks correct and that what's in your contract is what you're actually getting.

If you can afford it and your book is selling fairly well, you may choose to pay someone to audit your publisher once every three or five years. Publishers are notorious for keeping sloppy records, under-reporting sales, and being a bit light with the money all around. Not all are this way, certainly, but with so many of them being or becoming bottom-line driven, you may need to be extra wary.

One book/writer among many

Most writers get frustrated with this downside. Bigger publishing houses may have as many as a dozen books in the same genre as yours come out the same month. You can easily get lost in the crowd.

Beginning authors have more questions than experienced authors — they need more attention throughout the publishing process. At a big publishing house, beginning authors quite simply may not get as much attention as they would like. In a perfect world, beginning authors would get all that they need to succeed. The current publishing environment, though, is one in which many beginning authors have to fend for themselves.

Lack of control

In some cases, you don't have any input on book production issues, such as cover design, font style, and the incorporation of images/graphics. Sometimes you do, but they may ignore what you say.

On one hand, traditional publishers have been making books for awhile now and they do have a sense about what does or doesn't work. On the other hand, some books require a certain kind of attention to detail to make them stand out or highlight key elements of the story. A publisher may not be as sensitive to that level of detail when they have many other manuscripts to print that month. If you think that your cover designer actually read your book, well, I have some swampland just south of Miami that I'd be happy to sell you for a song.

Worse, your editor may agree with you about certain book elements, but the editor isn't the one doing layout or figuring out how to sell the title to book-stores and colleges and libraries. You may be at the mercy of the marketing people who believe they know how best to sell your title. Writers are under-standably upset when marketers shoot down a terrific manuscript or book idea for reasons that have little or nothing to do with story or writing quality.

Being the big kahuna in a big pond still isn't fun

A writer friend of mine who won the National Book Award once called up his big New York publishing house with a question. He could have been some random Joe Shmoe from Idaho calling, the way the receptionist didn't know him. The assistant to the editor also didn't know who he was and gave him the runaround. My friend got so irritated that he took his next book to a much smaller non-New York press who was ecstatic to land such a high-profile writer.

The National Book Award is one of the three top awards you can win as a writer — the other two are the Pulitzer Prize and the Nobel Prize for Literature. Winning any one of them

can make your career. In fact, being a finalist for any of them will get you on the high-paying lecture circuit for as long as you care to speak about yourself and your book.

If a publisher has someone like that in its stable, it should treat the person as publishing royalty and make sure that everyone knows who the person is. On the other hand, big publishing houses may have thousands of authors they've worked with in the past decade alone. It's understandable that they don't have much of a relationship with many of them, especially with the increasingly high rate of editor turnover.

Out of print

Having your book go out of print is the scariest part of writing with a traditional publisher. If your book doesn't meet the publisher's sales expectations, the publisher can let it go out of print, which means it yanks the copies off the warehouse shelf, remainders them, and sells them by the pound to dollar stores and book warehouses, just like I discuss in the "Low royalties" section earlier in this chapter.

If your book is out of print, used copies are what's available, which means no money for you no matter how many used copies sell. Sure you can take your manuscript and go self-publish it so new copies get out to the world, but if you wanted to self-publish, wouldn't you have gone that route in the first place? Worse, because all your friends and family already have copies, who is the ideal audience to buy your book? Your first publisher who decided to run when the going got slow took the easy pickings. Where are you going to sell copies now? And what traditional publisher is going to want your next book when your first one went out of print so fast?

Crafting a Winning Query Letter

When you're interested in working with a particular publisher, you have to write a query letter. A *query letter* is a short, professional business letter that pitches both you and your memoir to that publisher (you can also write a query letter to a literary agent; check out Chapter 18 for finding an agent). If your query letter kicks butt and the publisher responds with interest, the next step is the publisher asking to see a significant chunk of the book or perhaps the entire thing. If your query letter blows, everything stops here with this publisher, because it isn't interested in you or what you have to offer. Clearly you want a query letter that stands out from the crowd. Read these sections to see how to accomplish exactly that.

Querying more than one publisher (or agent) at a time isn't unethical or wrong unless the publisher has specific guidelines on its website saying it only considers exclusive queries. (Another way the publisher may convey this information is requesting that writers don't send *simultaneous submissions,* which is the term for sending out the same material to more than one place at the exact same time.) Don't blanket the earth with your queries, but do keep a few out at a time until you make a connection and sign a contract.

I recommend that you don't query both agents and publishers at the same time. If you're going after an agent, do that exclusively. If one signs you, the agent wants to be the first person to show your project to a publisher. If the agent finds out that you're already had it rejected from dozens of publishing houses, an agent may then decide to say no on a book that was otherwise a yes.

Naming the basic elements

You need to answer three main questions in a query letter for a memoir. Answer these efficiently in a well-written query, and you're on the road to publication. They are as follows:

- **What's the project?** Implicit in this question is "Why is it worth doing? What will a reader find useful, valuable, or interesting?"

- **Why am I the one to write it?** Here is where your biography comes into play. If you have writing credits or awards, name them. If you don't, don't mention that or lie about it. Do offer a few facts that suggest you're creative, easy to work with, and/or committed to doing what it takes to end up with a great memoir.

- **Why are you the one to take it?** This is your chance to show you've done your homework. If you're firing queries off blindly, it comes across like spam e-mail. Tell the publisher why you picked it. Some good reasons are that the agent has just sold a similar book to yours, the agent runs a great blog and you want to mention a particularly useful post, or the publishing house specifically likes books like yours (as you know from reading its website thoroughly).

A good rule of writing in general is "less is more." Utilize this idea in your query letter. Most good queries are no more than a page in length, so keep on track. Refer to www.ryanvancleave.com/queryletter.pdf for an example of a good query letter.

Do you need some additional help in creating a query letter? See if the following books give you the extra guidance that you want:

- Wendy Burt-Thomas's *The Writer's Digest Guide to Query Letters* (Writer's Digest Books)

- Lisa Collier Cool's *How to Write Irresistible Query Letters* (Writer's Digest Books)

- Literary agent Noah Lukeman's *How to Write a Great Query Letter* (Amazon Digital Services), which is free to read on Kindle

Recognizing what an editor (or literary agent) hopes for in your query

In order to get an editor's attention at a publisher, you want your letter to rise to the top of letters she receives. To do so, show your hopefully soon-to-be future editor some professionalism, good writing, evident research, considerateness, and reasonable confidence that doesn't slide into pushiness or braggadocio.

Editors want to know that working with you is going to be easy and fruitful (versus an ongoing battle with your neediness and handholding). Prove that you're a professional. Show that you understand how the publishing business works, or that you have a willingness to learn it.

Grasping the Power of a Proposal: Think like a Publisher

Although a book proposal is typically used for a nonfiction book, memoir writers can try this route as well. The reason novelists don't often sell a book via a proposal is that they don't really know how it ends. Not so with a memoir!

If you're a first-time author, submitting a proposal, which is a somewhat detailed description that tells the publishers what your book is about, probably isn't going to work for you. Too many writers have good ideas but have trouble reaching the finish line, so editors are reluctant to sign first-time authors this way.

Publishers are in the business of selling books. Convince them that your book has a sizable enough audience who will be motivated to buy your book, and you're home free. If you have written a book or two and can submit a proposal, then you're one step ahead of the competition. Having a record of published magazine articles or pieces in literary journals can help a good deal, too.

If you can create a couple of terrific sample chapters and a very clear, chapter-by-chapter outline, plus reasonably assess the competition and identify your own specific audience, you may be able to go this route. I sold my own memoir this way — two chapters and a 35-page proposal. It helped that I have been published in numerous periodicals and already had a number of books with my name on the spine, though. Still, I know of many authors — including this book's technical editor, Dinty Moore — who sold their first nonfiction book based off a good proposal alone. Moore and these other authors didn't have a big track record in book publishing and they made it happen, so don't be dissuaded at giving a proposal a try.

Even if you choose to never send out a book proposal, writing one can help you discover patterns, recurring themes, and organizational opportunities for your memoir. It forces you to put on your editor's hat and really examine your book, inside and out. Perhaps most importantly, it can help you see your book like the marketing people will.

After you start asking yourself "Just how is my memoir on teen drinking different from Koren Zailckas's *Smashed* or dozens of others on the same topic?" you realize that you need to put some effort into making your book distinctive and worth buying. Publishers don't invest in authors or manuscripts that are exactly like other books. A good book proposal proves to them that your book is enough like other good books to have a nice literary pedigree, but that it's different enough to stand out on cluttered bookstore shelves.

Quite a few books have been published on how to write a book proposal. If you want to go this route, check out the following to give yourself the best chance of success:

- W. Terry Whalen's *Book Proposals That Sell: 21 Secrets to Speed Your Success* (Write Now Publications)
- Michael Larsen's *How to Write a Book Proposal* (Writer's Digest Books)
- My own title, *The 48-Hour Book Proposal* (Writer's Digest Books)

Staying Away from Serious Submission Don'ts

Although numerous books on writing include chapters on how to properly submit materials to publishers, writers still get it wrong. Here are the most common reasons that a submission goes wrong and what you can do to avoid them. (This same information applies to sending submissions to literary agents; see Chapter 18 for more information.)

Generically referring to the editor

You don't like receiving junk mail and neither do editors. If you can't take the time to figure out the editor's name and then address her by that name in your submission, don't expect her to bother reading your submission. You're better off sending one properly addressed submission that is tailor-made for that recipient than ten that are generic and simply fired out to the world.

When you send the submission, make sure you take the time to correctly verify

- **The spelling of your intended recipient's name:** For instance, with a last name like "Van Cleave," I'm sensitive to misspellings, as are most people. It's a matter of respect. When I get a letter or e-mail addressed to "Mr. Cleave," I think of what would happen if someone spoke to Jean-Claude Van Damme by saying, "Hey, Mr. Damme!" *Pow!*

- **The gender of your intended recipient:** Sometimes "Terry Jones" or "Pat Richards" is *not* the gender you expected, so a "Dear Mr. Jones" or "Dear Ms. Richards" will earn you an instant rejection.

Shooting a shotgun

An old novelist friend of mine once explained that there are two ways to submit your work

✓ **The shotgun approach:** The *shotgun approach* is simply what it sounds like. Instead of using a single bullet, you fire off a ton of buckshot in any old direction in hopes of hitting the target. For writers, this means playing the numbers. You don't have to be a math wizard to realize that sending out 20 submissions offers twice as many chances for success as sending out only ten submissions.

The problem with this approach is that many book editors (and literary agents) request an exclusive submission. That means you shouldn't send the same materials to them and anyone else at the same time.

✓ **The heat-seeking, laser-guided missile:** These babies cost a fortune in time and energy, but they nearly always hit the target, which is a great outcome for a writer who is committed to getting his work published.

Instead of sending out 20, 50, or 100 submissions, try three. Research the target people and businesses to the point that you know more about what they like and don't like better than they do. Tailor-make your letter to showcase that knowledge.

Don't get me wrong — both approaches can work. I've done both, and I've succeeded with both. However for first-time authors who are trying to get a foot in the door or even for more experienced authors looking for something special to get an editor's attention, I suggest you go with the missile approach and stay away from the shotgun approach. The heat-seeking, laser-guided missile takes a good deal of time, effort, and patience, but your odds of success are significantly higher than the shotgun approach where you may end up hitting no target at all.

When you're putting together your information to send to the publisher, don't include more than you need to. You don't want to bludgeon them with data. And you most certainly don't want to look like a stalker, which is easier than ever to do thanks to blogs, social networking, and interviews.

Claiming that your book is the next best thing

Suggesting that your book shares a few qualities with an existing successful book isn't a bad idea. But making outrageous claims makes you look like an amateur, so don't do it.

For example, a few claims to avoid include the following. Go ahead and insert any author's name, book title, or hyperbolic statement:

- ✔ I'm the teenage David Sedaris.
- ✔ My memoir is the next *The Glass Castle*.
- ✔ I write as well as Stephen King.
- ✔ I'm going to make us both famous.
- ✔ This is the best book you're going to read this year.

If you're going to compare your memoir to another book, compare it to another memoir, not a space opera movie or a Michael Crichton thriller. And remember to point out how yours is going to be distinctive versus a second rate copy of the original.

Sending sloppy writing

Some writers have the idea stuck in their heads that editors will swoop in like some kind of beneficent literary genies and do the hard work of making your writing Shakespeare quality. Not so. Underdeveloped ideas, weak plotting, and cardboard-thin characters will do one thing — guarantee rejection.

On the most practical of levels, editors get swamped with submissions. Many of them are well-edited, well-developed, and competently written. They won't bother with a sloppy, undercooked one when other choices abound.

Submitting incomplete work

You may have finished 15 pages, and you start to send submissions to editors. Whoa. You're not even close to thinking about publication yet. Writers who haven't previously published a book need to finish most — if not all — of their manuscript before seeking publication.

Even if you're only including three chapters in a book proposal, you should keep writing the rest of the book. More than likely, a publisher (or literary agent) will ask to see more pages than what you initially submitted. Make sure you have a completed project to show them.

Using Subsidy/Vanity Publishers

If you like the idea of not having to submit your work for publication at a traditional press but dislike the idea of having to do all the legwork a self-published author has to (see Chapter 20 for more details), then subsidy or vanity presses may be the solution. If you give them your manuscript and pay them, they will accept it and print it. It's that simple.

Although the two are very similar, here is the main difference between them:

- ✔ A *subsidy press* foots some of the cost of publication, with half or more being the author's responsibility.

- ✔ A *vanity press* holds the author responsible for 100 percent of the cost. As the name suggests, these are books done out of vanity versus some other reason (like quality).

  Both types are essentially subsidy presses — one, though, is partially subsidized and the other, fully so.

Some traditional publishing houses are now creating separate *imprints* (a name that a publisher gives a group of books to help create clarity in their catalog) that operate like a subsidy press. Because subsidy presses have a healthy bottom line, you can see why traditional publishers are interested in them.

Who are these publishers? They come and go, and the names sometimes change, but here are a few of the more popular ones. You may hear otherwise, but the business model the following companies have set up make them a vanity press.

- ✔ AuthorHouse (www.authorhouse.com)
- ✔ iUniverse (www.iuniverse.com)
- ✔ Xlibris (www.xlibris.com)
- ✔ Vantage Press (vantagepress.com)

The pros with subsidy and vanity publishers

Subsidy and vanity presses have many of the same resources as a traditional publisher, which means they can make a handsome book. Some have connections to distributors. Some even provide no-cost or low-cost editing.

In addition, probably the biggest pro is that they do everything but the initial writing of the manuscript for you. You don't have to research printers, learn InDesign or Photoshop, or deal with any of the technical issues that always arise when assembling a book. Basically, they're convenient and easy.

The cons with subsidy and vanity publishers

With subsidy and vanity publishers, they often lack the quality control checks a traditional publisher has, such as where an editor and editorial acquisitions board all sign off before a contract is issued. (Often, marketing people are included in those meetings because if the sales team doesn't see how to sell a title, it's a no-go from the start, regardless of how much an editor wants the book.) Although traditional publishers are profit driven, they also want the reputation of being a proponent of quality books. Subsidy and vanity presses are far more concerned just with profit.

Book reviewers and people in the publishing world know which publishers are subsidy and vanity publishing houses, and those publishers aren't offered the same level of respect. Ever buy a carton of milk and some bread at a convenience store? A subsidy or vanity press is quite similar. You pay for the convenience factor of having your book all handled for you the same way you pay 30 to 60 percent markups at a convenience store for things you need *now*.

Furthermore, the contracts can be restrictive. You need to dissect the entire thing and make sure you know who's doing what (and for how much), as well as who *owns* what when it's all said and printed. Authors aren't offered much or any support in marketing so recouping the investment can be quite difficult unless you have a tailor-made audience available. A memoir on living well into your seventies may sell a lot of copies at regional senior centers and retirement homes, for instance, but one on your role in the invention of lip balm may sit in boxes in your basement, interesting though your story may be.

Chapter 20

Going It Alone: Self-Publishing and E-Publishing

*T*his chapter wouldn't have existed a decade ago because everyone already knew the two main options for publication. Back then, the only way to see your book in print was these two methods, which I discuss in Chapter 19:

✔ **Traditional publishing:** To be lucky enough to have a publishing company offer to publish a print copy

✔ **Subsidy or vanity publishing:** To pay a publishing company to publish it for you

No longer! The digital age has arrived, which means many grateful writers because it gives them a wider buffet of publishing options to use to present their memoir to the world.

In this chapter, I talk about the reasons you may want to take advantage of this digital publishing revolution. I also discuss why this option may actually not be the best for you. Ultimately, the choice is yours, though be warned — these nontraditional publishing options require a good deal of commitment and work on your part. The rewards may be worth it, however. Read through this chapter and make sure your decision is based on information and realities versus ignorance and myths.

The Lowdown on Self-Publishing and E-Publishing

Self-publishing and e-publishing (also known as *electronic publishing* or *digital publishing*) are attractive, affordable options to the old-school way of doing things.

Do you have time to figure out how to write query letters and proposals and potentially wait around for months to hear from a publisher when all you really wanted to do was get a darn book into print form? Do you want to let other people tell you if you can or can't publish your book or if it's worth publishing at all?

These sections answer these questions and provide a clearer definition of self-publishing and e-publishing and explain why some authors pursue these routes to get their book published over traditional publishing.

Defining self-publishing and e-publishing

Here I take a closer look at these two main options of getting around that traditional system:

- ✔ **Self-publishing:** With *self-publishing*, authors choose to bypass traditional publishers and take complete charge of the publication of their own work. In essence, the author creates his own one-person, one-product publishing house.

- ✔ **E-publishing:** With *e-publishing*, authors have their work published in a nonphysical manner, such as a format used for the various e-readers, a downloadable PDF file, or some other type of online venue. Authors can readily do this type of publishing, which means e-publishing is a type of self-publishing, though more and more traditional publishers create e-book versions of regular print books to maximize their own profits. (As a matter of fact, this book, *Memoir Writing For Dummies*, is available in several e-book formats.)

Self-publishing is fast becoming a popular option for writers. In 2009, nearly 70 percent of all books published were self-published. Some industry experts foresee drastic changes to the entire industry as self-publishing challenges the old paradigm of traditional publishing.

Seeing why some authors self-publish

Many authors self-publish because they want the control over the whole process — from layout to font style choice to the inclusion of color images to the trim size of the books. Others want their books done in a hurry (which isn't a very good reason to self-publish — getting your book published isn't a race). Still more can't face the idea of being rejected by traditional publishers so they don't even try.

Authors also self-publish if the audience for their book is too small to interest a regular publisher. And if your topic is extremely time-sensitive, you may self-publish to capitalize on the timeliness before the topic is yesterday's news. Topics that may merit this type of *instant book* are major world events (hurricanes), huge celebrity news (death of Michael Jackson or Lady Di), and significant societal/cultural upheaval (9/11).

Authors with an established platform of some type — a radio show, popular newspaper column, a highly trafficked blog, and such — may choose self-publishing to keep the lion's share of the profits versus letting some publishing house get it. Famous authors, too, already have a following, so some of them are going the self-publishing route to make more money. A few of the biggest names who have tried this route include J.K. Rowling, Tom Clancy, Deepak Chopra, Stephen King, and the estate of Ian Fleming.

Self-publishing has a long and storied tradition in the United States. Some of the most famous self-published books include the following (with the publisher who eventually bought the rights to the books listed in parentheses):

- *What Color Is Your Parachute?: A Practical Manual for Job-Hunters and Career-Changers* by Richard N. Bolles (Ten Speed Press)
- *Joy of Cooking* by Irma S. Rombauer, Marion Rombauer Becker, and Ethan Becker (Scribner)
- *Eragon* by Christopher Paolini (Knopf Books for Young Readers)
- *The Celestine Prophecy* by James Redfield (Warner Books, Inc.)
- *The Elements of Style* by William Strunk and E.B. White (Longman)
- *Dianetics: The Modern Science of Mental Health* by L. Ron Hubbard (Bridge Publications, Inc.)
- *Chicken Soup for the Soul* by Jack Canfield and Mark Victor Hansen (HCI)
- *The Adventures of Peter Rabbit* by Beatrix Potter (Puffin)

A real-life story: Reaching success with self-publishing

Kristen Brown decided to self-publish her first memoir after every literary agent she pitched (at least 40!) told her they liked her writing and platform but that she wasn't a celebrity so they wouldn't take her on. She explains, "I knew my story had a place in the market so I self-published *The Best Worst Thing* through Balboa Press (a division of Hay House) and the book hit the Amazon bestseller list the day it was released. I also hit No. 1 on Amazon's 'Movers & Shakers list.'"

Her book is about how she overcame major stress and change after her young, healthy husband died of a heart attack in his sleep at the age of 31 when their daughter was just a baby. Two weeks later she got a new, challenging boss at work and then the economy tanked. About that time in her life, she says, "I had major stress, but I started experimenting with stress management techniques and ended up starting a company called Happy Hour Effect helping others get through their own challenges in life. The book chronicles the journey I took and how I found the upside to a really lousy situation. And as a super-sweet bonus, after the book's success, I immediately landed a literary agent and got three offers from publishers for my next book."

But a success story like hers won't just happen to anyone. You have to write the book well and then be prepared to work equally hard on connecting with prospective book buyers. "I think so many writers think they can just write a book and the readers will line up to buy it," she says, "but the marketing of the book is 100 times harder than actually writing it. A good platform — way to reach people — is 1000 percent necessary to build an audience of buyers for the book." For more on book publicity and marketing, see Chapter 21.

- ✔ *Shadowmancer* by Graham P. Taylor (Putnam Juvenile)
- ✔ The Trylle Trilogy by Amanda Hocking (St. Martin's Griffin) (Search online for her name to discover one of the greatest e-publishing success stories!)

The following sections examine the pros and cons of self-publishing and e-publishing to help you figure out whether you want to pursue one of them.

Deciding Whether to Self-Publish: The Pros and Cons

You're considering to go the self-publishing route and join the ranks of Mark Twain, Edgar Allen Poe, Walt Whitman, Margaret Atwood, Rod McKuen, Louis L'Amour, Benjamin Franklin, and Anais Nin.

This section frankly reveals the pros and cons of the process. Even if you're already completely set on self-publishing, a review of these benefits and challenges can prepare you for what's ahead. So read on, take notes, and make the most of your self-publishing plan.

Dan Poynter's website, www.parapublishing.com, has a wealth of information on self-publishing. He even has tips on how to save on shipping by using a specific trucking service. He includes a contact name at the company and a phone number, suggesting that using them may save 50 percent or more on shipping. Cha-ching!

The advantages

The main reason most authors choose to self-publish is control. You control the look, you control the text, and you control the money. If you're going the route of self-publishing for any other reason than that, take a moment to rethink your decision. You have to want that control or you're missing out on a major reason to self-publish.

A few other good things about self-publishing include

- **Stronger sense of ownership and pride:** Because you handled all aspects of the writing, design, and publication, you'll feel more attached to the book. You'll also be prouder as the book succeeds with readers.

- **More money per sale:** You're not splitting the profits with anyone, so you make a lot more with each sale.

- **Updateability:** Because you're likely not filling a warehouse with copies, you can make changes and have those incorporated in the next reprinting you order from your printer.

- **Author-owned rights:** You keep all the rights to your work. Though you can always choose to sell them to a major publisher later, if your book sells enough copies to interest them. (A good number seems to be 10,000.)

- **Early release date:** You don't have to wait the two years it takes for a book to come out from a traditional publisher.

- **Author pricing:** With most traditional publishers, they choose the price which the book will sell at. Here, you set that number.

- **The number of copies:** You can have as many copies of your book as you want *at cost,* meaning you pay only the cost to produce it.

- **Always in print:** Your book never goes out of print (unless you want it to).

The disadvantages

On the flipside, self-publishing does have several downsides that you need to be aware of. Here I tackle each one:

- **Assumptions:** Readers, agents, editors, and reviewers will assume your manuscript was rejected so many times that you just gave up, which means they think it's likely defective in one or more ways (even if that's untrue). To be clear, the phrase "self-published memoir" for some readers equates to "poorly edited, poorly designed, overwritten, and self-indulgent." (Had those writers followed the instructions in this book, this wouldn't be the norm!)

- **Lousy track record for sales:** The average print-on-demand book sells fewer than 100 copies.

- **Lots of competition:** Memoirs are the most rejected type of book at publishing houses, so it's no surprise that many find their way into print via self-publishing. Convincing someone to pay money to give your story a chance is hard enough. When thousands of other self-published memoirs are clamoring for attention, yours can easily get lost even if your memoir is the best of the entire bunch.

- **Hardcovers are cost prohibitive:** To produce 1,000 hardcover copies of your memoir, it'll cost you around $7,500.

- **Libraries tend not to stock them:** Some do, but usually only if they have a very clear regional connection or include a super-timely topic.

- **Not easily stocked in bookstores:** You can get them stocked at independent bookstores, for sure, by showing up in person and pitching the manager. You may even be able to pitch bookstores via e-mail or snail mail letters. However getting self-published books of any type placed on big-box bookstores' shelves is getting harder and harder. If you're so lucky as to have that happen, don't expect the cover to be facing out on one of those racks or shelves at the front of the store. Publishers pay big money to rent those highly desirable spots. (An executive at Barnes & Noble once admitted to me that 80 percent of their sales are from titles in those front areas.)

- **You do the marketing and publicity:** Self-publishing without serious promotion is a lot like taking the only copy of the manuscript, putting it in a rocket, and blasting it off to Mars.

- **ISBNs, bar codes, and LCCNs are your responsibility:** These elements all belong on a book, and it's your responsibility to make that happen. I include a section specifically on ISBNs and bar codes later in this chapter. LCCN stands for Library of Congress Control Number. Without one, libraries can't order your book. It's not hard to get one (just visit http://pcn.loc.gov/pcn, make an account, and then request one for your book), but it's yet one more thing to do before your book comes out.

If you look at the laundry list of names of authors who have self-published, it can read like a Who's Who of the publishing world. Understand that their huge successes are unlikely to be repeated. They were the exception, and in more than a few cases, they were already famous prior to self-publishing. As they warn in commercials about investment firms, "Past performance does *not* guarantee future results." The chances of you having lottery-like success with your self-published memoir are remote. Your chances of that type of success with a traditional publisher? Much higher.

Facing the Reality of E-Publishers

A few decades ago, writers used manual typewriters and onion skin paper. Now they use desktop computers, laptops, and tablets. In fact, I've even seen one writer using a smartphone app to make manuscript corrections while waiting for a train!

With the increased reliance on the Internet, it only makes sense that paper books have been impacted. The e-publishing world is here and it's here to stay. So in these sections, I take a good look at e-publishing, including its different options and the pros and cons of going the e-book route.

Recognizing the three types of e-book publishing

Three types of e-books are available. They are

- ✔ **Fully self-published e-book:** This option is all about you. If you're even mildly tech-savvy, you can navigate the world of Kindle or Lulu easily enough. If running the whole show suits your personality, go for it. You can always upgrade to the next option later.

- ✔ **Self-published e-book with help:** This option is just like the previous option, except you're paying one of the e-companies (or a third-party company, such as BookBaby, Smashwords, or Publish Green) to help with the technical side of things. These companies are fairly new to the industry so do your research first. Ask questions like:

    - Do the royalties come directly to me or do they go through you?

    - Do you take a one-time fee only or a percentage?

    - How does the process work?

    - What if we decide to part ways after you help me put my e-book out?

✔ **E-book fully published by a publisher:** You obtain this option by sub-mitting your work to a publisher in the traditional sense. You create a query letter or proposal and go from there, just as you would if you were seeking regular print publication of your memoir. For more on this pro-cess, see Chapter 19.

With most publishers you'll want an e-book/print book combination, though some publishers are releasing only e-books of a title the same way that years ago some publishers skipped hardcover and did paperback-only printings.

If you need a little extra guidance to tackle the technical stuff on your own, check out YouTube. Tons of how-to videos that give you the edge you need to complete your project are available. Do check the amount of views and some of the comments first before viewing the video — more than a few of the videos are lousy and not worth watching. The comments about what other people are saying can alert you.

The 4-1-1 on the main e-book retailers

E-book publishing can get confusing because of two reasons:

✔ E-book distribution services, which for a fee, upload your book to major e-book sellers.

✔ E-book sellers simply sell e-books on their own website and in their own format.

To complicate matters further, some distributors (like Smashwords, for instance), have your book available on their own site as a retailer, but they'll also distribute your title to other e-book retailers.

Here's ultimately what you need to know. Readers looking for e-books can do so at the main e-book retailing sites, period. So that's where your book needs to end up. Whether you do it directly or pay a distributor to do it, that deci-sion is yours. Just make sure you get your e-book there however you can.

Here are a few of the most popular e-book retailers:

✔ Amazon Kindle/CreateSpace

✔ Apple iBooks

✔ Barnes & Noble e-books

✔ Books on Board

✔ Diesel

✔ Kobo

✔ Powell's Books e-books

✔ Sony

Before you commit to any e-book retailer, make sure you get these questions answered:

✔ **Is it an exclusive or nonexclusive service?** You can run into legal problems if you sign a contract that says one company is your exclusive e-book seller for a specific book, but then you make that book available through competitors.

✔ **Who controls the pricing?** Trust your e-book retailer's expertise but remember that price affects sales as much as it affects your profits. Make sure you have input on pricing.

✔ **Are there any upfront fees?** There usually are upfront fees. Make sure you know what you're getting for your money.

✔ **How are royalties calculated and paid?** This question is hugely important because you want to make money. You need to be certain about what percentage you get on each sale and how (and when!) you'll receive that money.

✔ **What file formats are acceptable?** Some writers have this issue. If you can't provide your manuscript in a specific file format, you'll be asked to pay for someone to make that conversion.

✔ **What if I want to make changes later?** With nearly every retailer, you do have the option to update the manuscript. It typically involves a new set-up fee and possible other costs. Avoid these costs by only publishing a truly well-edited and completely final copy of your manuscript.

Although you can sign up individually to all the major e-book retailers, be super savvy and combine services to maximize your coverage (and to save time). A common strategy is to use Amazon Kindle as well as the distributor Smashwords, which sends your title to all the major e-book sellers other than Kindle. Combined, you have great coverage over nearly every venue to purchase and read e-books.

Using DRM (or not)

DRM, which stands for *digital rights management,* protects your files to discourage or prevent pirating of digital texts. The fancier word for digital text theft is *data leakage.* If you've ever downloaded an image or text from the Internet and then e-mailed a copy to a dozen friends, then you know exactly how easy it might be to pirate an e-book.

Using DRM is something you need to consider. According to Google, there were between 1.5 million and 3 million searches *per day* for pirated books in 2010 alone, which shouldn't be a shock because the International Federation of the Phonographic Industry estimates that more than 90 percent of the music downloads done throughout the world are illegal.

Some e-retailers don't use DRMs. For instance, Smashwords' website claims "we think DRM is counterproductive because it treats lawful customers like criminals." The site also suggests that there's more evidence that publishers who forego DRMs completely end up with greater sales.

More and more authors are making their e-books available for free for a limited period. The reason is simple; getting a book out to readers can create buzz. That buzz can generate a lot of money-generating sales after the limited-time free e-book promotion is over, or it can lead to people buying a print copy of the book, too. A free e-book can also drum up reader interest in a forthcoming title by the same author. A final reason to give an e-book away for free is visibility. You may end up becoming an Amazon bestseller by having your memoir available for free. That's a distinction you can use to help promote your book from then on.

You need to decide how important it is for your books to have DRM or not. Your choice will limit some of the e-book retailer options, but it's your book. You need to decide the best way to offer it to readers.

Identifying self e-publishing pros

The real pro to going the self e-publishing route is cost. Unlike print self-publishing, which can run into the thousands of dollars, you can e-publish virtually for free. Even if you use one of the main distributors like Kindle, the setup fees are minimal and one-time only. If you go on to sell a million copies of a print book, you need to hit up your printer again and again, each time paying production costs, setup fees, and shipping. With an e-book, you don't do anything but watch the money roll in (digitally, of course).

Some of the other plusses for going the e-publishing route are as follows:

✔ **Your end product is portable.** If you've ever lifted a big box of books, you know the value of portability. On my Kindle, I have 600 books right now. How portable is it? It's about 5-x-8, and less than an inch thick. Even with a cover, it weighs 12.7 ounces. That's portable!

✔ **You can easily get paid.** No need to wait for royalty checks that generally come twice a year from traditional publishers. E-book proceeds get transmitted electronically to your bank account in a very timely fashion (often just a week or two from the sale).

✔ **You keep all the rights to your work.** Just as with self-publishing, you own all the rights. If you get a zillion-dollar movie deal, you keep that cash. If a German publisher wants to buy German rights to print your book, you keep that cash.

✔ **You control the price of your e-book.** As with print self-publishing, price matters. You set the price that makes you money but still is low enough to encourage casual readers to commit to your memoir. Remember that there are no printing costs, so your overhead is essentially nonexistent.

✔ **You can have as many free copies of your e-book as you want.** Need to show your grandma a copy of your book? You can send her a free digital copy. You don't need to mail her a print copy. Just press a button, and she has it in her e-mail inbox.

✔ **Your e-book never goes out of print (unless you want it to).** Having a book in print can be like an ongoing ATM machine that keeps delivering you money. An e-book is easier to keep in print because you don't have to order copies from a printer, pay for shipping to get them to you, store them in your garage, pack them when you have orders, and pay to ship them to the customer.

Considering self e-publishing cons

The biggest con with self e-publishing is that you won't have a physical book to put on your shelf, sign copies of, or show to pretty girls (or guys!) at parties. Part of the mystique and wonder of a writer, in my mind, is the actual artifact called a book that you can hold in your hand. I may be old-fashioned, but that matters to me.

A few of the other main cons of e-publishing include the following:

✔ **They're easily piratable.** DRM can combat this to a degree, but pirates know ways around any copyright protection for e-books.

✔ **They rarely get reviewed.** This will change at some point as e-books become more the norm, but right now, e-books simply don't get much coverage from the major book review outlets.

✔ **Libraries don't carry them.** This, too, is changing, but it's a very slow process for libraries to embrace digital copies of books. The libraries in my area only have a few options available at the moment. Librarians have logistical issues to solve about pirating, storage, distribution, and cost, that haven't been adequately handled yet throughout the country.

✔ **No one edits your work unless you pay for the service.** As I talk about in Chapter 16, sentence-level editing is crucial because readers avoid books with typos and formatting issues. It's so tempting to type "The End" and then instantly upload the file as an e-book. Resist that urge.

✔ **Many e-book formats are, quite simply, difficult to read.** With cheaper e-readers, the text is harder on the eyes to read. This will change as more companies work on this problem or as higher-end e-readers come down in price.

Researching Printers

If you have decided to go the self-publishing route and publish your book, I offer a congratulations for starting the final steps toward realizing your dream of being a published memoir writer. Part of this route is selecting a printer. Realize, though, that not all printers are created equal. Although you can hop over to your local copy shop, you're going to pay a premium for having them print your book (which they can't even do — they'll ship it out and pay someone else to do it).

TIP

If you want a book printed, go to someone who prints nothing but books. Of the 50,000 printers in the United States, fewer than 100 are primarily book printers. You want to consider them and only them. Skip the local joints; you can use those for promotional materials, including fliers, posters, and business cards.

These sections help you locate a printer, identify your options, and explain how you can get a great deal.

Finding the right printer

When looking for a printer, you need to understand that even though most book printers can handle any type of request, many specialize in one type. Before you select a printer, you need to know what type of book you want. The main three options include

✔ **Hardcover,** also called *casebound*

✔ **Softcover,** also called *perfect bound*

✔ **Saddle stitch,** where the book is stapled together

Look at the different types at your local library and see which you want for your memoir.

After you know the type of book you want and you have a sense of the quantity needed, start your online search. You'll find more printers than you can even imagine.

When you narrow the list down to a dozen or so that you think seem reputable and capable, send them a *request for quotation* (RFQ), which is a standard practice that has suppliers bid to obtain your business. The lowest quote isn't always the best option, though you'll want to start with that company first as you move forward and get ready to make your commitment.

Keep an eye open for unscrupulous printers who do shoddy work, have hidden fees, and are just less than ideal to work with. You can do an online search for "writer beware" to find the Science Fiction and Fantasy Writers of America list of shady publishers and printers; they keep it up to date. You can also do a little legwork of your own on any printer you're considering using even if it's not on that list. Are other writers happy with the work? Are any of the books they printed actually being sold? Do the books look good or do they have an appearance that screams "Amateur!"? Ask yourself these questions and really consider your honest answers.

Considering print-on-demand

In the past, self-publishing meant that you bought as many boxes of your books as you could (to lower the per-unit cost), and they filled up your garage or dining room for years. Print-on-demand (POD) printers eliminate that problem. With a POD printer, you don't print a book until someone orders one, so you don't have any boxes of stock taking up room.

Additionally, one of the biggest reasons to go with a POD printer is that you're not stuck with the current version of the book. You can send the printer a new electronic file, pay a small setup fee, and now every book the printer prints from here on out has those changes (refer to the nearby sidebar for an example).

Some of the most popular POD companies include

- www.lulu.com
- Amazon's CreateSpace
- www.bookmasters.com
- www.thebookpatch.com

The downside of a POD is that the per-unit cost and the postage required to ship the books is a little more because you're sending out books one, two, or three at a time versus shipping a box of 25 at once. A POD printer can do a big print run, which offers price breaks at certain increments (like other printers). If you're talking thousands of books, the per-book cost gets very affordable no matter what type of printer you're using.

POD allows cover updates in a snap

In 2012, I was at the governor's house in Tallahassee, Florida for a special banquet given for all the winners of Florida Book Awards. While there, I saw the cover for Caren Umbarger's bronze-winner *Coming To: A Midwestern Tale*, which she self-published via CreateSpace. On the front cover were the words "Winner of the 2011 Florida Book Awards Bronze Medal for General Fiction" along with a little image of a medal. Pretty cool! My book didn't have anything like that to show that it won a gold medal in young adult literature. Awards and honors like that do help sales, so I've been buying gold foil stickers to attach to the front, which is a huge pain. Any books that I don't directly sell don't have those stickers. Caren's choice of using a self-publisher really helped her out there. And if she gets a great review down the road, she can excerpt the best few lines and add them to the back cover in the next "reprinting."

A few POD firms can help you with the design work, but then they claim ownership of that design. Some even request a share of your profits. Make sure you know exactly what your agreement with the POD says and who owns what. In theory, everything your printer — POD or not — does for you should be *work-for-hire*, meaning you own everything after you pay for it. In other words, you hire them to do work for you, and after you pay them, they're out of the picture — you still own everything. The same arrangement should hold true of any deal with a freelance editor, too. (See Chapter 16 for more on freelance editors.)

Getting the best deal

Working with a printer isn't like buying a box of cereal at the grocery story. The price you're quoted is just the price you're quoted. The printer wants your business. Make sure you get the best deal. You can explain that you have a competitive offer elsewhere, and you're in a position to negotiate.

Realize, too, that printing prices vary depending on how busy that particular shop is. If the printer has a full docket, it has no motivation to give you a bargain basement deal. If the printer has a slow few weeks ahead, it badly needs the business and will really work with you. The printer's workers get paid hourly whether they're sitting around twiddling their thumbs or putting in a long day's work, so use that knowledge to your advantage.

Don't show your hand any more than you need to. In other words, you don't need to say what the exact estimate you received from a competitor is, nor do you need to say who that other company is. Sometimes doing so may make sense, but until that point, less is more. It's the same tactic for buying a car. Play it close to the vest.

Getting and using an ISBN and bar code

If you're using your own printer to self-publish, you need to supply the printer with a bar code and an ISBN (International Standard Book Number), a 13-digit number that uniquely identifies your title. The bar code, when scanned, pulls up the ISBN, the title of your book, and the price. That's why books without bar codes often don't get stocked at book retailers; retailers like to scan items versus type things in manually.

You need an ISBN if you intend to have any sales at big-box bookstores and even most independent bookstores. Libraries also won't stock a book without an ISBN. If you intend to only sell copies by hand, then you don't need an ISBN or bar code. If you want to sell at Barnes & Noble, Amazon, or your local bookstore? You do need one.

Contrary to what you may read on the Internet, the *only* place to buy an ISBN in the United States is through Bowker. You can't buy or borrow one from someone else; it has to be specifically generated for your book. Check out Bowker's website (www.isbn.org) for more information about obtaining and transferring ISBNs.

If you go the POD printer route, POD printers have their own blocks of unused ISBNs (and bar codes) to sell you, which is fine. Whoever is fulfilling the orders counts as the publisher, and the publisher puts the ISBN on the book. An added plus is that purchasing a single ISBN on your own costs $125. A thousand of them only costs $1,000. Odds are that your POD bought the 1,000 pack so they can mark it up 10, 20, or even 50 percent, and you're still saving a ton.

Pricing Your Book: Two Philosophies

Although you're near the finish line, you still have an important decision in terms of pricing the e-book. Charge too much and you scare off thrifty readers. Charge too little and you have to sell oodles to make anything substantial.

To help you figure out where to find that middle ground, consider these two main philosophies of book pricing:

- ✔ **Market penetration:** You want to maximize sales and create a loyal reader base. If you have more than one book to sell, this method works better so you can make the most of all those new customers you've created. Some authors sell books at a loss to generate the most readers. The downside of doing so is a low financial return.

✔ **Premium pricing:** This model seeks to grab a much smaller market share, but because your prices are high, the profit margins are proportionally high, too. This model only works if your book is truly new, exciting, revolutionary, revealing, or otherwise unique. And even then, you can't keep gouging readers forever or your sales will plummet to zero.

For an unknown — which is what any first-time-at-book-length author is — you need to tempt prospective readers with a low-risk price. I think anything under $5 is reasonable. Ninety-nine cents is a popular how-can-you-go-wrong? price. Although you may be tempted to go with $9.99, getting any sales for a first-time author at that price is difficult unless you have a very strong publicity and marketing strategy in place already. See Chapter 21 for options on how to do this.

In addition, you need to do the following when pricing your book:

✔ **Consider the psychological factor.** Sales people have been doing market research and speaking with psychologists for decades to figure all this out. Consider the actual numbers in the price. For instance, $14.99 sounds better than $15, and 99¢ feels a lot cheaper than $1. End your price with whatever number you want, except a 1 or a 0.

✔ **Offer a free bonus.** Doing so makes whatever price you have more attractive because you're offering something for nothing. You can offer an exclusive downloadable audio interview of the author, for instance, a bonus chapter, or free bookmarks that you sign and mail to the purchaser.

You can promote the special free bonus offer on your own website or in the description of the product at e-book retailers. Some readers will ignore it, but some will find the something-for-nothing idea too enticing to pass.

If you try the something-for-nothing idea, try rotating the free bonuses to keep things fresh. Work up at least three different options. Maybe you can have special periods where buyers get multiple bonuses.

The price — no matter what it is — is always a turn-off. Pro designers know to bury it at the bottom of the back cover so potential buyers don't see it until after they've read all the sales material.

Letting Amazon Distribute Your Book: You Need to Do More

Amazon is the biggest book seller in the world, whether it's print copies or digital copies. Having your book available on Amazon makes sense. Whether you use Amazon's Kindle service or want to sell print copies that you made via CreateSpace or through another printer, you can get your books listed for sale on the site. Selling on Amazon is important and easy to do, but just having it there isn't enough. You need to do more.

Here's why: In 2010, the total North American sales numbers for bookstores were $14.3 billion. How much of that was from Amazon? Just under $8 billion. That means that 43 percent of sales occur elsewhere, which is a lot of book orders (and mugs of coffee, too!). As a result, for the best results, you want to make sure you get your book available in multiple retailers, both online and offline.

Even in terms of Amazon's site alone, you can do more. You can maximize the selling power of your own Amazon book page in the following ways:

- **Ensure that your page has quality book images.** Include a clear photo scan of the front cover and the back cover. Readers like to be able to see what they're buying. Covers also communicate a sense of the book's overall quality.

- **Update the book description with quality sales copy.** Unless you've invested heavily in marketing and publicity, most of the readers coming to your Amazon page don't know you or your book. This book description has to sound exciting or they'll find another option. Read a lot of them from other memoirs to see how they should look and read.

- **Participate in the "Look Inside!" program.** Doing so requires a bit more work than some of the other things listed here, but it's a valuable resource. Readers like to test-drive a book. Giving them the option of actually seeing inside your memoir provides exactly that.

- **Encourage reviews of your title.** Encourage people who've bought your book to write a review. Don't tell them what to say, but rather just say you welcome their thoughts via a review. Maybe offer a giveaway via your social networking site or Goodreads.com for the 10th or 20th review?

- **Regularly update your Amazon Connect author profile.** Amazon is like a free website where readers can get to know you better. You can embed video, link up a blog, add hyperlinks to other pages, and include lots of information about you and your book. Keep it current.

- **Add keyword tags to your book page.** If you've ever done much with website building, you know that *optimization* is a word that means *more easily findable by a search engine*. A search engine looks for keywords. If your book doesn't have any (or too few, or inaccurate ones), how will it know when to include yours as a result?

- **Review related books.** Because you're researching and reading other memoirs in order to do market research in the genre, you should post a few reviews. At the same time, you're supporting other writers. You can possibly strike up friendships with people who read and respond to your reviews. Authors need as many book-reading friends as possible.

✔ **Create Listmania lists.** These lists get pulled up often via search engines. Not only is it good literary karma to recommend readers try out books you didn't write, but anyone visiting your Listmania lists has your name and book right there too.

Noting Common Self-Publishing Issues

I review books for a number of different venues, so I have stacks and stacks of print books, advance reading copies, and digital copies throughout my office. I can always tell which ones are self-published at a glance. Why? They typically have one or more of the following common self-publishing issues that you want to make sure you avoid:

✔ **Poor cover design:** A clip-art style or poorly laid-out image says, "I spent ten months on the manuscript and ten minutes on the cover."

✔ **MIA info:** Make sure your cover has an ISBN, bar code, and the book's price on the back. Ensure you also have a copyright page in the front of the text that has the same type of information that the most recent book published by a famous author has. Make sure you also have an LCCN.

✔ **Cheesy author photo:** Unless your memoir is as funny as the writing of David Sedaris, a silly or cheesy author photo announces that it's amateur hour. Don't skimp on something like this when you've invested so much time in the writing itself.

✔ **Production issues:** You want to make sure the book fans out when standing and that the pages are properly cut and glued. Make sure the margins are consistent and correct throughout. (Old printing machines can get a little sloppy from time to time.)

✔ **Typographical issues:** The little things stand out. Make sure you use curly quotes rather than straight quotes in dialogue.

✔ **Formatting issues:** You should have one space after punctuation and not two. Make sure other conventions of the book are formatted consistently.

Take the time to ensure that your memoir isn't being sold or sent off to reviewers with any of these errors. You and most other writers are overworked and you're looking for excuses to say no to something — even if you spent three years of your life working on it. That's just the reality of the book business.

Chapter 21

Promoting Your Finished Product (and Yourself)

. . . .

. . . .

*A*fter you finish your manuscript, the hard part begins. How do you convince people to pay actual money to buy it? It doesn't matter whether a big name publisher published your book or you had it self-published. Short of a big five-figure publicity budget (which is rare even in the biggest commercial publishing houses these days), the problem remains: Your book can easily get lost in the noise of hundreds of other books coming out the same week as yours.

Technology, though, saves the day. Twenty years ago, the idea of promoting your own book was a fool's errand. Unless you had your own radio show or television show, you didn't have a chance. With social networking, digital cameras, faxes, e-mail, and the Internet, you have many tools to publicize your book so people want to read it. Even a novice can now make a good showing. This chapter explains what to do, when to do it, and how to make the most of your marketing efforts.

Grasping the Difference between Marketing and Publicity

In order to promote your hard work, you want to market your book . . . or wait, you want to publicize it. Okay, which is it? Although many people use these terms interchangeably, there's a crucial difference. *Marketing* is when you create impressions with an audience. It's about directly contacting target markets with an eye toward creating sales. It's where the hard sell takes place. Publicity, on the other hand, is about interacting with the author. It's the soft sell. It's all about creating buzz, exposure, awareness.

Allow me to clarify this distinction even further. Marketing generally costs money. Publicity generally doesn't.

Make sure you understand the value of publicity. It's the best option for memoir writers to try first because it's budget-friendly and it's something you can be proactive with. You can feel publicity happening because you're directly involved with it and you can often see the results immediately. Publicity is less obvious to see than marketing, but it's not less important. Resist the temptation to just spend money on advertising. Getting your name out to the world (publicity) is more lasting, less pushy, and might create other opportunities beyond selling a single copy of your book.

Some examples of marketing include

- ✔ Ads in newspapers
- ✔ In-store displays
- ✔ Billboards
- ✔ TV commercials

Some examples of publicity include

- ✔ A guest spot on a morning TV show
- ✔ A radio interview
- ✔ A book signing
- ✔ Social networking

Writers and publishers have a prickly relationship when it comes to promoting a book. Unless the publisher specifically mentions money or efforts in the contract, the marketing and publicity usually fall in the writer's lap to handle. Although you may think it's short-sighted and unfair, publishers don't tend to offer much marketing or publicity support and expect you, the author, to generate your own buzz. That means that promoting your memoir is up to you. That's just the way things tend to work in the publishing world. The next section focuses on some ways you can publicize and promote your book without much (or any) help from your publisher.

Recognizing Free Ways that You Can Promote Your Book

You clearly want your book to be successful. After all, you spent hundreds of hours, perfecting it. Now the book is published, and its promotion rests on your shoulders. If people are going to buy and read it, you have to make sure they know about it.

The bad news: Publicizing anything (by spending nothing or very little) isn't easy. The good news: I've successfully promoted several of my own books that I've written, and you can too. The following suggestions are surefire ways to help you cheaply get out the word about your memoir so it starts flying off the bookstore shelf or virtual bookshelf.

On the wall across from my desk is a sign that reads: "Do something every single day to promote yourself and your books." You can easily get wrapped up in the writing and the editing. But unless you're making sales — thereby generating an audience — there's not much point. So do one publicity thing every day. It may be merely speaking to someone new about your book. It may be sending out a press release. It may be pitching the local media.

If you're shy, you have to get over it. Publicity is a must. As the Nike ad says, "Just do it."

Getting local author appearances

Setting up local author appearances works well at independent bookstores where you can call up the manager and explain your situation. Doing so at a big chain bookstore is less likely to happen, although not impossible.

Don't limit author appearances just at bookstores though. You can arrange author appearances where you sign copies for readers (who buy your book on the spot). Consider these less conventional options that may connect your book with eager readers:

- ✔ Churches
- ✔ Coffee shops
- ✔ Hospitals

- Prisons
- Senior centers
- Women's shelters

More and more books are being sold in unconventional venues, so make sure you take advantage. Get creative and stand out. Look at what niche your memoir may stand out in. The question isn't what have you got to lose by trying these alternative venues, but more about what have you to gain.

Inviting friends to buy the book

When you're promoting your book, you don't want to be shy. You've put a ton of time and effort into the writing of your book, so take pride in it and ask friends, family, coworkers, and so on to purchase a copy. You may be surprised at how many people you know actually want to get a copy of your memoir — *your story* — after it's available. They know you, so selling it should be fairly easy.

Just know that asking them to buy once is never enough. I suggest you pitch all your friends by following these five steps.

1. **About two months before the book comes out, send notice to everyone in your e-mail contact list, offering a discounted preorder opportunity.**

   A *preorder opportunity* can come directly from you or worked in conjunction with a publisher. Basically, you offer a discount to get readers to commit now to buying the book. These are guaranteed sales.

2. **The day the book comes out, hit up the e-mail list one final time, announcing the publication and offering ordering information.**

   This ordering information may be a link to your own website where you can take orders via a Paypal link, or it may be a link to Barnes & Noble, Amazon, or to your publisher's sales page. On a business side, all you need to do is have a way to take orders and collect money. After that, you need copies to ship and nice slim boxes or padded envelopes to ship the books safely in.

   Check out my own sales page at http://www.ryangvancleave.com/nonfiction.html for a sample where I have brief descriptions and sales links for my nonfiction books. I can easily send this same information (with or without graphics) in an e-mail or via social media. If this seems too tricky for you, offer a tech-savvy friend a free lunch if he'll help you create and send your own sales information.

3. **That same day, create a Facebook post about the book's availability that includes ordering information.**

   Post on your own Facebook page, but you can also easily create a separate fan page just for the memoir. Check out *Facebook For Dummies* by Carolyn Abram (John Wiley & Sons, Inc.) for more information.

4. **That same day, tweet about the book, including a shortened link to an ordering page.**

   If you don't have a Twitter account, go ahead and make one — it'll take you no more than ten minutes to do so. Check out *Twitter For Dummies* by Laura Fitton, Michael Gruen, and Leslie Poston (John Wiley & Sons, Inc.) for more information on how to turn a Twitter account into a marketing machine.

5. **Put up a permanent link to a sales page on your own website.**

   Refer to the later section, "Developing a website for your book" for creating a website and what to include on it. Want to see how Felicia Ricci did it for her theater memoir, though? Visit `http://www.unnaturally green.com` to see how Felicia Ricci did it for her theater memoir, *Unnaturally Green.*

When I've done all of these options, I average a 20 percent conversion rate. (A *conversion rate* is the percentage of people who see your deal who take advantage of it.) Just to give you some perspective, some of the biggest internet ad-click conversion company's rates hover around 5 percent.

Getting copies to word-spreaders

While the media is indeed a vehicle to spread the word about your book, so too are influential people. As a result, do what you can to get your book in the hands of people who have influence and can promote your book.

For instance, if your memoir is about your against-the-odds success in the business world, consider sending a copy with a handwritten note to Warren Buffett, Bill Gates, Mark Zuckerberg, and Tony Hsieh. For a book that details your life of rescuing dogs throughout America, send a signed copy to Luke Gamble, Cesar Millan (the Dog Whisperer), or the president of PETA. Maybe even fire one off to Dog the Bounty Hunter!

People selling non-book products pay huge money for companies with access to A-list celebrities to deliver samples of their goods. Why? A single paparazzi photo that runs with one of those products clearly displayed in the celeb's hands is worth millions. The same is true for a book. Imagine how many people would run out and buy a copy of your memoir if Facebook maven

Mark Zuckerberg sent a Facebook post: "Hey, just read 'Insert your memoir title here.' It's the best book I've read in a long time! Check it out!" Your book would skyrocket on Amazon faster than it takes you to read this sentence.

Famous people get inundated with requests, gifts, and product samples. To give yourself the best chance, include a very brief, handwritten personal note. And if you know a way to bypass the traditional front door way to reach these folks, try that. Celebs have *gatekeepers* (assistants, receptionists, agents, and managers) who filter 99 percent of what tries to get through. Anything (short of illegal acts) that you can do to increase your odds of the celeb at least seeing your memoir may be worth considering.

Suggesting people give your book as a gift for the holidays

Whether you hit up your friends or not when your book initially came out, the holidays (Christmas, Hanukkah, and Kwanzaa) are a great time to (re)mention your book as a potential gift-giving item. And if your book lends itself well to other holidays (Father's Day, Mother's Day, Easter, and so on) and even special occasions (graduation or birthdays), you can suggest it then as well.

A writer friend of mine did a bonus Christmas e-mail blast to his entire list. Ten percent took him up on his offer, even after passing on various offers and announcements he made before. Ho ho ho indeed!

Don't be pushy with your pitch. You want to make sure your friends and family know they have the opportunity to buy the book for themselves or others. Don't try to guilt them into spending the $14.95. If they do fork it over under duress, they may be ticked about it.

Offering a free reading or discussion to local book clubs

When you suggest your memoir to a local book club and offer to lead some discussion sessions, you can increase your book sales. By working with a book club, every member who reads the book has to buy a copy, so a single sale actually becomes however many people are in the club.

Book clubs are some of the most loyal readers out there. If you can get enough members to know about you and love you and your book, you may start to see the sales numbers improve dramatically as people talk more about your book. Better yet, they'll buy your next book, and your next one. And they'll tell all their reader friends about you.

You may wonder why a book club would be interested in you or your book. Most clubs never get the chance to interact with any author, so one coming to them is unexpected and appreciated. The truth is that the words "free discussion with published author" are also quite compelling. Insist on working around the club's schedule. If the club cancels at the last second and asks you to come back another time, do it, and smile the entire time. Be the easiest author they've ever worked with.

Making a book PR signature line for your e-mail

Creating your own book signature line for your e-mail is an absolute must and it's super easy. No matter what e-mail service you use, you can set up a signature line that promotes your book. Your signature will then automatically appear at the bottom of each e-mail, every time you hit "Compose."

When you figure out how many e-mails you send in a day or a week (I send at least 100 e-mails a day, and only half of those are to people I already know), you can end up informing a boatload of new folks about your memoir who see the information on your memoir. That's what people call free PR, my friend.

For example, the e-mail signature that I have right now is

Ryan G. Van Cleave

www.ryangvancleave.com

Check out Ryan's latest Young Adult book, *Unlocked*,
a Gold Medal winner in the Florida Book Awards
and a Gold Medal winner in the Florida Publishers' Awards!
www.unlockedthebook.com

The best part is when my next book came out, I easily switched that second part to

Check out Ryan's latest illustrated humor book,
You Know You're a Video Game Addict If . . .
www.videogameaddictbook.com

You may also want to embed an image of your book's cover in your e-mail signature too. That way, every e-mail recipient sees your book's title, the URL to your book's website and perhaps an online link to purchase it, and your cover image. However, I do urge some caution if you do consider placing a book cover image. I used to use a book cover image in my signature line, but I stopped doing so when some spam e-mail filters started blocking my e-mails more often. I'm not sure why it happened, though it likely was because the image was hosted on another website. If you consider adding your book cover's image, just be aware that this may occasionally happen.

Writing a newspaper op-ed tied to your story

No matter your memoir's topic, you can easily translate it into a newspaper op-ed. An *op-ed,* which is usually about 600 to 800 words long, is rooted in your opinion, which in turn is rooted in your experiences.

If you're interested in writing one, research your local newspaper's website to see what its requirements for an op-ed are. Living in a smaller town or market may make it easier to get an op-ed published, especially if you're a published author. Just know that the op-ed market can be fairly competitive. To stand out, be both controversial and timely. (Pass on being outrageous for the sake of being outrageous.)

When writing one, remember that they're short. You don't have time for some throat-clearing or warming up. Start with your conclusion. After you make your strongest point, move to your next strongest point, and so on. Make sure your op-ed is persuasive. Don't leave your best evidence and argument until the end, where you re-state the conclusion. Good op-eds often have a call to action (or a call for change), like "So call your congressmen and insist they support Proposition 35."

You can also consider writing a letter to the editor. A good letter to the editor can help get your name in the news, and you may get people talking about issues that your book brings up.

Making yourself available to the media

Another way to publicize your new memoir is to tap into the media. Unfortunately the media won't come looking for you. As a result, you need to look for them. The media can help get you face time with the public.

The two easiest sources for connecting with reporters who are actively writing stories are www.helpareporterout.com and www.reporterconnection.com. But if you need more ways to hook up with journalists, more than 90 percent of them have a LinkedIn account. And if you can chase people down via Twitter or Facebook, then you have all you need to keep tabs on most of the media figures you'd ever need to speak with.

If the media comes looking for you, respond immediately. Deadlines make most opportunities a now-or-never situation. A friend of mine learned the now-or-never lesson. She received a call around lunchtime one Tuesday from Oprah's producers to see if she wanted to promote her home relocation how-to book on the show. She didn't return the call until after dinner. She was too late in responding. The producer went with a different show idea that was easier to contact. She missed her one shot because she wasn't available when the media needed her.

Writing your next book

A great way to get publicity for one book is to write another. Even if your next book isn't a sequel or obviously connected to your first memoir, you'll still be mentioned as the "Author of [your other book]." That's more free publicity.

Don't feel that you have to write another book today. Just be open to the possibility to one day writing another one, even if you don't consider yourself a writer and never intended to write a single book in the first place. Some of the most successful authors I know don't really consider themselves to be writers even after two, three, or five published books.

Marketing Your Memoir: A Little Monetary Investment Can Pay Off

Sometimes in order to get people's attention, you need to spend a little money. To market your book and get people to become aware of it and inevitably buy it, you probably have to invest some cash. These sections offer you some ideas that I've used. I invested a little cash in the marketing of my book, and many times I earned big returns with more books being sold.

Developing a website for your book

Creating a website that touts your memoir is essential, even if you don't have a tech-savvy bone in your body. Having a website for your book does require some monetary and time investment, but it will be the best investment you can make. These sections discuss what the benefits are to having a book website, how you can go about creating one and what to include on the website.

If you already have a personal website, I recommend you getting a website just for your book. Although you may be able to use your personal website, if it has tons of family photos, video game high scores, and political rants on it, then you shouldn't use it. I like to keep my websites focused versus trying to serve a lot of functions at once. Running multiple websites is easy and fairly cheap. The last thing you want to do is have a messy, busy, confusing website that makes it hard to find out more about — or order — your book.

Eyeing the benefits of a book website

A website gives potential readers a place to get good, authoritative information about your book. It's a place to compile all of your reviews. You can also offer a teaser sample of the text, a book trailer, a blog, and other materials that readers want, such as reading group guides, an author bio, and a book synopsis. Having a website also make you look like a pro. An additional bonus is that if the media wants to find you, that contact may well be through your website.

Figuring out how to create your website

Today developing a website has never been easier. You don't need to be an IT master to create an interesting and interactive site that can promote your memoir. All you need to get things rolling is to follow these three steps:

1. **Find a company to do your web hosting.**

   A web host stores the data on your site. You can't have a website without having a web host. You can find one by searching online in your favorite search engine with "web hosting," though check for customer reviews before committing to one. Some of the more popular ones include GoDaddy, www.1and1.com, www.fatcow.com, and www.bluehost.com.

2. **Locate a program that allows you to build and update your website.**

   A wide variety is available, and many are easy to use. You can buy one and load it on your computer, although some are entirely web-based. Companies like GoDaddy and Wix.com have free or inexpensive subscription-based online programs, plus you have good software options like WebEasy, Web Studio, and WebPlus.

3. **Select a domain name.**

   A *domain name* is a unique address that you type into your Internet browser. For me, the domain name I bought was www.unlockedthe book.com. Even if www.unlocked.com was available (it wasn't), I see some advantage to having some clarity in a slightly longer domain name and specifying that my site is about a book versus locksmith services.

To get your website up and running, skim through the manual and/or complete the tutorial. Find out all that your software is capable of. Then start by making the index page, also called the *home page* or *landing page* — this is the front door to your website, the first page visitors will see. Figure how your specific software allows you to manipulate elements on the page before trying to make other pages to website.

Knowing what to include on your website

When putting together the subject matter for your book's website, make sure you include these following elements:

✔ Your name

✔ Your book's full title and ISBN

✔ At least one ordering link (at your own e-commerce site or through a site like www.bn.com or www.amazon.com, though many people like to support independent bookstores, so do include a link to one of those that carries your book, if possible)

✔ Your speaking and reading schedule

✔ A clear way to navigate your site

Other useful information you may want to consider adding to your site includes the following:

✔ **Testimonials:** If someone (anyone) says something nice about your book, prominently include it as a customer testimonial. After you have a couple of them, start to be selective — go for other authors, celebrities, and high-profile reviewers first. Relegate the lower-tier testimonials to a less prominent place in your website. Keep the high-profile ones front and center to lend their credibility to you and your memoir.

✔ **Book news:** Have a prominent place on the home page to announce updates, awards, reviews, and other book-related news.

✔ **Good, professional PR photographs in a variety of styles, formats, and sizes:** I'm not talking snapshots your spouse took, but very nice, professional-looking photos like you'd see on a dust jacket of a bestselling hardcover. Make these available in various sizes and file formats.

✔ **Social media integration:** If you're using social media of any type to promote your book, find a way to connect it to your book's webpage. Think one-stop shopping — have it all handy in this one place.

One mistake I see more than any other is having a cluttered website. Too many widgets, too graphics heavy, too much stuff. When in doubt, keep it simple. To help keep it focused, develop a firm mission for the website that addresses exactly what you want to accomplish by having the site. Some reasons may be to connect with readers, build your brand, or sell books. Decide what your top priority is and shape the entire website around that goal.

If you can find a way to offer some value (preferably free) to your viewers, they'll keep coming back. What are a few options? A short, free, downloadable "how to" article a month, free original music, fun quizzes, and a place for visitors to post information, thoughts, or images and have a two-way conversation.

Throwing a publication party

You finished your book, so celebrate. What better way to celebrate than throw a party to commemorate the publishing of your book. Have an ice cream cake, buy a big box of party hats, and invite every family member in driving distance and your friends and coworkers. And if you're in a writing group, absolutely have them attend and share in your success. Be aware though that everyone who shows up will likely want a copy, so have them available for sale or for free.

You can also offer to your guests some tchotchkes, such as bookmarks, key chains, bumper stickers, or even USB drives with an excerpt of the book (doing so is cheaper than ever to add a book cover or even the first chapter on a USB drive).

Sending out book cover postcards

To market your book, you can also mail postcards, depicting your book's front cover with important information, such as your website and a few other details on the back to garner more interest in your memoir.

For instance, to promote my memoir *Unplugged* (HCI), I had 5,000 postcards printed up for $119. At 28 cents to send via first class postcard rate, sending postcards was a ton cheaper than sending bulk mail. One side featured a full-color picture of my book's cover. The other side had some sales information, a nice endorsement from a US Senator, and a space to write in the recipient's contact information.

A perk with sending out postcards is that you get address updates because undeliverable ones come back to you for free. The yellow sticker they put on it often has the updated address, which isn't a bad way to keep your mailing list current.

Making and distributing business cards

Having business cards are an absolute must for any aspiring author. When you're out and about, whether attending a writers' conference or meeting with a prospective agent, you'll surely meet a few people who want your card, and anyone you ask for theirs will expect one in return. You can utilize business cards in two ways:

- ✔ **You can market yourself as an author with it.** This type of business card looks a lot like the business cards your working father or mother likely used. You want to include the basic information: Name, address, phone, e-mail, and website. You can even put "author" under your name. If you don't plan on writing another book for awhile, you can even add "author of [your title]."

- ✔ **You can specifically market your book.** On one side, include a big, clear image of your book cover. On the flip side, have sales information about the book including a working e-mail and a good book URL for your book's website. You don't need much more than that.

Although you can buy a DIY business card kit that works with your home printer, spending the $20 to have a printing department make professional-looking ones on sturdy card stock is worth the investment. If you plan things early enough, you can get twice as many for half the cost from an Internet printing company like www.vistaprint.com. (Be sure to plan for a two-week shipping period unless you pay a ton.)

Using Others to Market Your Book: Hiring a Freelance Publicist

Sometimes you may need to bring in the big guns to help market your book. In other cases you may be busy (writing your next book or living your life) and marketing your book seems too much to handle, so you prefer to let a pro handle things from the start. Either option is fine. A freelance publicist's job is to take whatever you've done already and go a lot further. These sections explain how a publicist can help you, how to find a publicist, and how to hire one.

Knowing what a freelance publicist can do for you

Every author wants to be on CNN and the early morning talk shows. No publicist can or should promise such a thing. Here's the honest truth — the media doesn't care about you or your book. They have too many deadlines and too many other obligations. That's where the publicist comes in. A publicist pitches you and your book to the media and makes them care, or at least tries to make the media care. In other words, the most important task a publicist does is to make your book relevant to the media's needs, whether it's CNN, a morning drive radio show, or any other venue that's appropriate for your memoir and your topic.

A good book publicist can do the following for you, all of which create publicity about you and your memoir (which can lead to sales):

✔ **Write media releases.** Formerly called *press releases*, these are written communications sent to members of the media to alert them to newsworthy information.

✔ **Create more detailed pitch letters and press kits.** *Pitch letters* are short, pithy letters a publicist can use to tempt the media on its own or accompany with a media release. A full *press kit* has a pitch letter, a media release, and promotional materials such as a professional headshot photo, a list of past press coverage, a brief biography of the subject, a business card, or a marketing postcard.

✔ **Send out galleys to the media.** *Galleys* — also called *proofs* or *ARC/ advanced reading copies* — are an early printed version of a book used to generate publicity, endorsements, or pre-publication reviews. The media wants to see books before they agree to talk about them.

✔ **Set up events and interviews.** Not only do publicists know how to speak to event schedulers, but they know which events are likely to feature you. They also have access to event schedulers. Let a pro put you and the media in the same room.

✔ **Develop talking points/interview scripts.** *Talking points* or an *interview script* tells you exactly what to say when you're there in front of a microphone, a camera, or a reporter taking notes. Long, rambling answers from authors won't work.

✔ **Obtain and archive your media clippings.** Having *media clippings*, which are copies of every time you've been mentioned or featured in the media is helpful. A good publicist will keep these together and use them to generate new publicity opportunities.

✔ **Help you create an elevator pitch.** An *elevator pitch* is usually a 30-second spiel that you tell people when the opportunity arises. Media folks are busy, so if you can't sell them in 30 seconds (the typical amount of time in an elevator ride), then you can't sell them period.

Because publicists have established relationships with members of the media, the odds of success are greatly increased. They also can find unexpected, unconventional ways to get you, your book, and your message out to the world. That's what you're paying them for.

Finding a freelance publicist

You want a publicist, but you're not sure where to find one. To locate one, consider these options:

- **Ask for referrals:** If you know other writers, ask them if they use a publicist or if they have any suggestions for qualified individuals.

- **Network at a writers' conference:** You can meet all sorts of individuals, including literary agents, publishers, other writers, and even publicists, at a writers' conference.

- **Do an online search:** Go online, search, and pick out a few. The next section can help you narrow down your list.

The way the industry relies on phoning and e-mail and video conferencing now, you don't even have to insist that your prospective publicist live in New York or Los Angeles.

Hiring a freelance publicist

Like hiring most professionals, you have to go beyond the surface. Many look alike at first glance. After you narrow your list of prospective publicists to a few, ask them questions such as these to find out if you have a match:

- Are your fees on a monthly basis, or do I pay for each confirmed booking?

- Do you require an upfront retainer?

- What type of publicity (TV, radio, and so forth) is your specialty?

- What percentage of your work is for books versus other things?

- What type of involvement do you expect from me?

- What potential angles/hooks do you see in my book?

- Can you show me some of the results you've gotten for clients with a book similar to mine?

Don't make a decision on which publicist to go with until you've spoken to at least three and you've had every question answered. Then take a few days to really mull it over. Your best chance to get publicity for your book is the three months before and the three months after it comes out. You have one chance to utilize that time. Make sure you have a partner you can work with and whom you can trust.

Getting advice, directly from a professional book publicist's mouth

Maryglenn McCombs (www.maryglenn.com) has worked in the book industry for more than 20 years, and one thing she's learned about memoirs is that celebrity memoirs tend to get lots of ink, meaning coverage in the media. "Usually, the bigger the name or celebrity, the more ink," she says. "With that in mind, non-celebrity memoirs have to be extra compelling and timely."

One way to make that happen, she says, is to have a good hook, a unique component, or an unusual subject. "There has to be something about the memoir that draws people in — both the media and actual readers — and makes them want to know more."

In her years as a freelance book publicist, she's seen a lot of writers who've made mistakes, with the two biggest mistakes being the following:

✔ Writers try to promote a book that's poorly designed and/or inadequately edited.

✔ Writers try to get reviews of a book before the entire memoir manuscript is available. Trade review journals, such as *Publishers Weekly* and *Kirkus Reviews* do provide advance reviews or *forecasts* of upcoming books, but in general, consumer media reviews (basically all other book review outlets) shouldn't run before consumers can buy your book. Proper timing is everything.

Maryglenn recommends that any writer — especially memoirists — get good, solid, honest feedback from unbiased sources. She emphatically recommends joining a writers' group and/or critique group. "Too many writers rely solely on the input of friends and family. Not to say that input from your friends or family *isn't* important, but all writers need to make sure they're receiving honest feedback on their writing."

Finally, she admits that self-publishing does *not* have to be the kiss of death, so long as the book is created in such a way that it'll be taken seriously. She explains that "any author thinking of self-publishing needs to make sure that their book has every chance of success — and that means hiring a top-notch editor, cover artist, interior designer — and making sure that the end product is absolutely stellar." With that, a PR pro like her can drum up a lot of interest and attention, indeed.

Whether you hire a freelance book PR person or not, you may still want more information on how it's all done. Give Carolyn Howard-Johnson's *The Frugal Book Promoter* (CreateSpace) a try. It has more grassroots ideas than you'll know what to do with. John Kremer's *1001 Ways to Market Your Books* (Open Horizons) is so chockfull of ideas that you'll almost certainly find a dozen PR tactics you've never imagined before. Try either, or both!

Part V
The Part of Tens

The 5th Wave   By Rich Tennant

"Oh, Will — such passion, such pathos, such despair and redemption. I've never read a more moving grocery list."

In this part . . .

Here are a few quick reference chapters that work well on their own or as a way to reinforce some of the best ideas from previous chapters on planning, writing, revising, publishing, and promoting your own memoir. Sure, these are short-and-sweet little chapters that are great last-minute checklists, but they're also fun to read through. From myths about memoirs to reasons memoirs are rejected for publication to tips for writing your first book, this part is jam-packed with good stuff!

Chapter 22

Ten Myths about Memoirs

*T*hanks to folks like Sigmund Freud — who famously said that a five thousand dollar advance offered to him was 1⁄100 of what was needed to tempt him to foolhardily share his own story — the memoir has a reputation that makes it seem more like one of those cousins you shudder to think you have to invite to your wedding.

To readers and nonreaders alike, some consider a memoir to be full of horrors, betrayals, vices, and embarrassing self-exposures. These naysayers claim that memoirs are simply the work of people trying to grab their 15 minutes of fame. They suggest that the vast majority of memoirs are bland, boring, and better off having not been written.

They couldn't be more wrong.

This chapter debunks the most prevalent myths about the memoir, starting with the myth that it's not a commercially viable genre and ending with the idea that the time to write one is now.

No One Reads Memoirs

Nothing could be farther from the truth. People do read memoirs. Consider the sales figures for the following memoirs, which all found a readership that even top novelists may envy:

> ✔ Mitch Albom's *Tuesdays with Morrie: An Old Man, a Young Man, and Life's Greatest Lesson* (Broadway) — more than 14 million copies sold

✔ Tony Blair's *A Journey: My Political Life* (Knopf-Doubleday) — 92,000 copies on the first four days of its release

✔ Jaycee Dugard's *A Stolen Life: A Memoir* (Simon & Schuster) — 175,000 copies sold on the first day of its release

A well-written memoir — like a good film, a great painting, or a first-rate restaurant — can find its audience after it's been made available to the world (in this case, by being published). Any book that's poorly written inevitably will find a home on the remainder shelf soon enough. Or more realistically, a publisher will never publish it in the first place.

To be a great memoir writer, you should be reading great memoirs because they can inspire you. They can show you how to handle challenges specific to memoir. They can reinforce the idea that anyone's story told interestingly and with passion is worth hearing. After you start looking for memoirs at your public libraries and local bookstores, you can see that the form is alive and thriving, too.

You Have to Be a Celebrity to Write One

Writing a memoir was once reserved for the most noteworthy people — actors, athletes, musicians, industry tycoons, government figures, and similarly beloved (or reviled) figures — that society had to offer. Today that is simply no longer the case. More than ever before, readers are open to reading ordinary people's compelling stories. You don't have to be a celebrity first to succeed with a memoir. You just need to write well and be creative in finding what elements of your story will be of interest to readers.

"Big issue" memoirs are always a hit with publishers because they have ready-made markets. What are some of these memoir hot topics? Divorce. Loss of a child. Mental illness. Sexual abuse. Addiction. War experiences. If you have one or more of these stories to tell, just remember to make sure your story is different from others on that same topic. Do your research to see what's out there and then figure out what can make yours different in an interesting, useful way.

Here are three memoirs from non-celebrities whose lives aren't the stuff of myth and legends, yet each is a terrific read:

✔ **Jeanne Marie Laskas's *Fifty Acres and a Poodle: A Story of Love, Livestock, and Finding Myself on a Farm* (Bantam):** This fun tale covers her first year of transitioning from city life to country life. It also follows how she moves from being a single person to living with someone to being married. Along the way are sheep farmers who shoot dogs, tractor attachments, and satellite dishes.

✔ **Abigail Thomas's *A Three Dog Life: A Memoir* (Harcourt):** This poignant story details how a wife's life changes when her husband's car accident leaves him brain damaged and needing to be institutionalized. Through it all, love stands strong.

✔ **Julie Klam's *You Had Me at Woof: How Dogs Taught Me the Secrets of Happiness* (Riverhead Trade):** Klam's memoir reveals the life lessons she learned from adopting and fostering Boston Terriers. Through those experiences, she muses on how our lives are defined by the animals that people love.

My Family and Friends Remember Things Differently

Whether you're writing a tell-all memoir or not, worrying that your memory doesn't jive with what your friends and family members recall is common. Life is subjective and so are your memories. That's not to say you have carte blanche to make things up, however!

If you're concerned that family members will remember things differently, have some conversations with them (see Chapter 17 for ideas on how to go about having these conversations). Ask them what they recall. They may be right. Of course, you may be right instead. Jot down notes on what they say and spend some time thinking about it. Are the differences minor or major? Which version feels the truest? Trust your gut.

A memoir is a promise to readers that says, "This is what happened, and it's exactly how I remember it." As long as you truthfully write and revise your memoir, you don't have to worry too much about the memory of others.

People Will Hate Me If I Include Them

If you portray people in a less-than-glamorous manner versus just including them as a background to your life, you may be afraid that they'll hate you. The best thing you can do is to remember that the truth matters. You also need a sense of respect and empathy for the people in your book. If you can manage all that while presenting the faults of others, it's unlikely that they'll think you're out to make them look bad.

If they're ticked off because you wrote a memoir that brought you a bit of notoriety or a little money, that's their problem. Anyone who dislikes you for a sliver of success probably also dislikes you for a dozen other reasons. Just remember: Ignore the haters. Those people thrive on ill will and complaining.

I Can't Write an Entire Book

As Confucius said, "The journey of a thousand miles begins with a single step." This quote also applies to writing your memoir — one word, then one page, then one chapter, one draft of your memoir — and so on.

If writing your memoir takes you as long as it did Mary Karr to write *The Liars' Club: A Memoir* (Penguin) (2½ years), that's okay. If you bang the thing out in a couple of weeks like Jack Kerouac did with his autobiographical novel *On the Road: The Original Scroll* (Penguin Classics Deluxe), then terrific. Writing isn't a race, and no speed is right. All that matters is that you finish it.

I wrote *Memoir Writing For Dummies* with the goal of two pages a day, which was 14 pages a week. If I missed a day like I did when my daughter cracked a tooth on a popcorn kernel, which required an unexpected visit to the dentist, no big deal. I worked a little more over the next weekend to get back on pace. And when I was invited to deliver a writing workshop in Vermont, I brought my laptop and wrote in the hotel room and on the plane.

Many memoir writers discover that they have so much material and ideas that it all fits in more than one book, which is a great situation to have. For inspiration, look at the work of Nick Flynn, who has written a couple of terrific memoirs on different aspects of his life.

I'm Going to Be Rich and Famous

Writing a memoir won't make you famous. Although your memoir possibly can make you scads of money and get you a seat on a TV talk show, the odds are roughly a gazillion to one or maybe worse. The main reason to write a memoir is for self-discovery. Money isn't the reason to write a memoir. And, quite frankly, money shouldn't be the reason to write a memoir. Everything else is merely a bonus.

Keep your expectations under control. Limit them to things you can control, such as discovering more about yourself, creating a family legacy by writing your memoir (whether you publish it or not), and telling a story with truthfulness, empathy, and wonder. If something else happens, be grateful.

My Life Is So (Insert Adjective Here) that It Will Be a Bestseller

Just because your life has had enough drama to give you the drama queen or king title or it has been serene and not exciting doesn't mean your memoir will be a bestseller. What makes a difference is how you focus on those experiences in your writing.

Having had an interesting experience or two in your past is enough to write a memoir. Everyone has all had experiences that, when properly revealed to tease out meaning and emotional power and irony, prove interesting. In fact, if you've gone through childhood, high school, a relationship, or a job, you have more than enough source material for a memoir. The key to your success is in how you handle that material.

I have students tell me all the time that "My life is so *crazy* that it's certain to be a bestseller." Having had truly unique and amazing experiences that others will want to know about may help. The caveat: Make sure you properly tell your story. Writing something people will want to read is a lot more like eating a peanut butter and jelly sandwich versus a gourmet meal. Both will feed you, sure, but one will keep you talking about it for the next few weeks. That's what a bestselling memoir is like.

I Don't Have Any Writing Credentials

You don't need a license, degree, or permission from a famous author or teacher to write your memoir. All you need is your past, a computer with a word processing program (or even just some paper and a pencil), and a little gumption. Everything else is just gravy.

I tell my writing students all the time: "There is no writer's jail." Basically you won't be punished for choosing to be a writer (at least not in the United States). What you choose to write, how you choose to write, and where (or if) you choose to publish is all up to *you* and only *you*.

Even if you do have some credentials doesn't guarantee that your memoir will be successful. For instance, having a PhD in American literature, being married to a New York literary agent, or winning a creative writing award in college mean nothing. Having written successful books prior to attempting your memoir may have taught you a thing or two about effectively creating scenes on the page. All that truly matters is that you live your life well, write about it well, and are willing to generously share it with others. Those credentials are enough for a successful memoir. Don't let anyone else tell you differently.

I've Been Journaling for Years So Writing My Memoir Will Be a Breeze

Keeping a journal is a great way to record your experiences and save them from the dark whorl of forgetfulness that so much of history can easily become. But taking material as is from your journal and sticking it in your memoir doesn't work. People don't write journals with a clear audience in mind beyond themselves — journals simply don't work the way a memoir needs to.

A journal can get you started, but a memoir needs focus and fully-developed scenes that are powerful enough for strangers who read it to feel like they know you and your life. A journal offers a lot of mundane stuff that's on a variety of topics. A memoir is centered on a specific theme. Check out Chapter 5 for how you can use a journal to write your memoir.

I'll Get to It . . . Later . . .

Planning to write your memoir later isn't a sound plan because later never really arrives. If you're really interested in writing your memoir, then figure out what is holding you back from fully committing.

People hold off on writing a memoir for two main reasons:

- ✔ **They want to live more, so they have more (or better) stories to recount.** You already have enough life experiences to fill the pages of a 400-page memoir. Trust me.

- ✔ **The idea of writing intimidates them.** The writing part is a lot more bark than bite. By that, I mean that as soon as you get started, you discover that it's nowhere near as bad as you thought.

I write to find out what I think and believe. Writing your own memoir can help you do the same. And the results may be profoundly enlightening.

Today is a great day to write page 1. Or page 399. Or anything you want. Just take a deep breath, pick up a pen (or a keyboard), and put down those stories that have remained shelved in your head for too long. People look forward to reading them.

Chapter 23

Ten Reasons Memoirs Are Rejected

More than 98 percent of all books submitted for publication are rejected. This statistic includes memoirs, novels, poetry, textbooks, and even books on how to repair airplane engines or make a zillion dollars in the stock market by using the wisdom of Sun Tzu — all of them. But the reasons for this intimidating rejection rate vary from the editor had a bad hair day to the publisher just bought a similarly-themed book to your submission having one of a variety of common manuscript problems.

Understanding what the common manuscript problems are is important so you ensure that your book doesn't have any of these pitfalls. Knowing them can dramatically increase your chances of publication success. Think of this chapter as your final troubleshooting template that's perfect to use right before sending your work out or if you've already sent out your work but keep meeting the "Thanks, but no . . ." response, you can use it to revise it to get an acceptance letter.

Insufficient Editing

I can't emphasize enough the importance of thoroughly editing your manuscript before sending it to agents or editors. Unfortunately more than a few authors choose to submit sloppy work instead of polished, professional-looking manuscripts. Chapter 16 discusses the importance of editing your work and how to edit with the help of writing classes, editors, and writing conference discussion panels.

Sending sloppy work gives the impression that you don't care. A sloppy manuscript, with careless use of language, lazy writing, haphazard development, grammatical errors, and so on, also creates a lot of extra work for a publisher. Furthermore, a sloppy manuscript likely means you're sloppy. And a sloppy author misses deadlines, forgets to do what the marketing department asks, and shows up late to book signings. In short, publishers prefer not to work with sloppy authors.

Would you rather work with a sloppy person or one who has everything in order? Editors at a publishing house who are considering making a huge investment in a new memoir certainly prefer the latter.

Data Dumping versus Storytelling

Writing a memoir means you craft the most interesting and revealing moments of your life into a powerful and coherent story. You aren't dumping everything that has happened to you. A memoir is more like a connect-the-dots version of your life rather than a complete birth-to-death report of one. (Chapters 1 and 2 discuss in more depth the particular characteristics of a memoir.)

As a memoir writer, you have to take the material of your life and manipulate it to a desired effect. To do so, you use the tools of novelists, who are very skilled at turning events into powerful stories and moments into stunning, memorable scenes.

These tools can help you decipher which type of information about characters is relevant to the story and makes for good reading. A barrage of facts, dates, and numbers doesn't make a compelling story. For example, the following shows a poor example of a data dump that includes way too much irrelevant information:

> And then Jim solemnly approached the dilapidated porch of the boarding house at 185 West Ridge Road, Chicago, IL 60067, where he lived from September 12, 1983 to January 3, 1994, when he moved to Menomonee Falls, WI to be the general manager at Beckman's Drug Emporium on Jacobson Drive.

Lack of Focus

Your memoir is your story, so you can decide what the focus is. *Focus* is the richly-developed, thematically-interesting main story element that's going to be the backbone of your memoir. Ever lost someone to another man? Or to cancer? Or to a love for hiking up distant mountains? You can write a story about loss. Ever succeed against all odds? Tossed the winning touchdown at a division I college playoff? You can write a story with a *Rocky*-like triumphant moment. Ever fought in a war? Been in a violent bank robbery? Got kidnapped and managed to escape? You can tell a survival story. Ever discover that you have a great, important relationship with God? You can tell a story about spirituality and religion.

Just make sure you don't write all those stories at the same time. Each of those preceding areas of focus may make a fine story, but you need to be choosy. Select one focus and stick with it.

If you're not sure what the focus of your book is, enlist a reader or two to give your their impressions. Ask them questions like the following:

- ✔ What do you see is the most important message of the book?
- ✔ If you had to describe my book in a single word, what would that be?
- ✔ What is the mood of the book?
- ✔ If part of this book were excerpted to run in a magazine, what specific magazine would you expect it to appear in? Why?

Whatever information your readers offer, take a good, long look at it. Odds are they probably have zeroed in on the focus your book has (or should have). Keep working until your book's focus is its clear selling point. Refer to Chapter 3 for how you can focus your focus.

Improper/Incomplete Submission Procedure

When you submit your manuscript to publishers, make sure you follow the publisher's submission guidelines. Every publisher on the planet has taken the time to state its complete submission guidelines on its website. You can also find those same guidelines in the yearly marketbooks (like F&W's annual *Writer's Marketplace*) and in blogs and websites for writers about the process of submitting work. Check out Chapter 19 for more information about how to find information for submitting your manuscript.

Sending work outside the open submission period or in the wrong format isn't the only way writers can go wrong. If publishers ask for an initial 10-page sample, don't send 25 pages because "page 21 is where it gets really good." If you can't follow directions, don't expect anything more than an automatic rejection for breaking their rules. Think about how welcome your mother-in-law is when she doesn't bother to call and just shows up on the doorstep, suitcase in hand, as you sit down to dinner. Don't let your own work arrive with the same sense of irritation and dread.

Skips/Avoids the Juiciest, Most Interesting Parts

A part of human instinct is to protect yourself. So make sure you don't underplay your mistakes, ignore your faults, and hurry over the most difficult and painful times in your life, which are all the juicy parts. These parts make your story worth reading.

Readers don't know you. Unlike your friends and family, they haven't heard your stories a hundred times. They simply don't know your world beyond the words you put on the page. Sure, *you* know exactly what happened and every time you think about that fraternity house hazing incident that went horribly wrong, your brain summons up every memory, fear, emotion that plagued you for years. But unless you put the details of that event in your book, the reader misses out. So make sure you give them the goods, even if doing so is a difficult thing to write about.

If an event is difficult to write about, then it's probably the right thing to write. The day-to-day events are easy to handle. The truly trying times? Those are a challenge to live through, and even more so to reflect back upon and then capture in words. But if you do it, readers will thank you with book sales, with good word-of-mouth reviews, and with respect to you as an author.

Incredibly . . . Slooooow . . . Pace

If your memoir's manuscript creeps along at the speed of a snail, then more than likely your readers won't stick with you until the end. Some writers consider *pace* — which is what I'm talking about here — to be like the story's heartbeat. Quite often, that heartbeat is calm and steady. At times, though, it's banging away like a machinegun. If you don't know how to manage the variations of pacing in your story, you're going to lose readers. The most common issue with pace is slowness, or not knowing when to rev things up.

Although readers want a full, rich experience that creates a movie in their mind, they're happy to do some of the work of creating that movie for themselves. Good writers know that pace matters. Try doing 30 mph on the highway — or 120 mph for that matter — and you can see that there are consequences to working against the norm.

Lack of a True Emotional Experience

Because you're likely not famous, a reader will expect the emotional payoff — the true emotional experience — from your story. If your memoir thrills and chills them, or makes them wish they were in love like you were, that's success no matter who you are.

The poet Robert Frost said that if the writer isn't crying when he writes it, the reader won't be crying when he reads it. Dive deep into the emotional world of your story. You'll know it when you get there — you can feel it in your gut.

Theme Bludgeons the Readers

Having a great theme is important in a memoir. (*Theme* is really about a story's meaning, which is typically shaped by a writer's vision of life; check out Chapter 14 for more on this.) Readers, though, don't want you to come out and smack them again and again with the theme. Trust the reader to know that the human spirit is amazingly resilient by reading your story about a three-time cancer survivor who runs marathons and feeds inner city orphans through your own nonprofit food program. That theme of that story or anecdote is already embedded deeply in the narrative.

If you give readers 1 + 2, they'll say, "Aha! That's 3!" Even better, they'll feel a little bit smarter for having figured it out. They can locate the theme just fine.

Although having a theme is a must for memoir, you can have too many themes. So make sure you limit your memoir to one or two main themes, and perhaps a couple key sub-themes. Readers want to care. But insisting on having them care about a whole host of things equally isn't a good strategy.

The Story Is Overly (and Unnecessarily) Complicated

You're in charge of writing your memoir, so make sure you keep things simple. You don't need to turn your life into a soap opera (at least on the written page), so you don't need to make it confusing or difficult for readers to follow along or understand what's going on. Readers shouldn't have to figure out whether Joe is Maria's true love or not while struggling to know if the hidden secret is about lost treasure in the Atlantic or just a joke Uncle Mikey is playing on Sam in return for the affair that happened nine years ago, but no one wants to openly admit, while the family company's impending buyout is being thwarted by a tycoon who . . .

You get the picture. This story is a mess and feels like a mess. You want to keep the story easy to follow. Making someone feel lost or stupid is *not* a recipe for success with any book. Keep it simple. Keep it clear.

The Writing Is Merely Competent versus Exciting

Exciting writing makes agents and editors leap out of their ergonomic office chairs in Manhattan. They're in this business to bring great new books to the world.

On the other hand, a competent manuscript is like having lunch at a fancy restaurant and afterwards announcing, "That was an extremely acceptable meal." Not exactly a 5-star endorsement, is it?

Which would you rather read? Of course, you want to read an exciting manuscript, so make sure your manuscript is exhilarating and stirring.

I save this pitfall for last in this chapter because the difference between a good book and a great book is a series of small things that you did well. Perhaps you took the time to find the best verb, the best structure, the best title. Perhaps you put the book away and came back six months later with fresh eyes only to notice issues with atmosphere, pacing, and dialogue. Perhaps you brought in an old schoolteacher, a bookish friend, or a professional editor for advice. And then you took the advice to heart and the book improved as a result.

At some point the book is simply the best you can make it at this point in your life. You can hold off and hurry through an undergraduate or graduate degree in creative writing, in which case you could probably find more things to improve on. But that's pretty unrealistic.

If you're done with the book, you're done. Just make sure that if you dropped dead tomorrow, that you're proud of the manuscript and it's exciting. If you can honestly say, "Yes!" to that question then you're ready.

Chapter 24

Ten Tips to Writing Your First Book

In This Chapter

▶ Believing that you're a writer

▶ Planning and planning some more

▶ Staying off the Internet

A surprisingly large percentage of memoirs are written by people who've never written a book before. I didn't realize that until my own literary press started taking on memoirs. The first two we did were by first-time authors. As a result, I started talking about this phenomenon with other writers, publishers, writing teachers, and students. Sure enough, nearly half of people writing memoirs have no real writing background. The memoir they want to write is their first leap into the ocean of book writing.

You may be in the same shoes at some stage of writing your first memoir and your first published work. And you're probably reading this book because you want more guidance with the writing process. This chapter details ways to navigate the general challenges of writing a memoir (or any book for that matter).

Whether you're an old pro at writing or new to it altogether, the following tips can help you deal with all the things that writing a book entails.

Thinking of Yourself as a Writer

Want to know the big difference between you and Charles Dickens? He has written a few more books than you. Big deal. Being a writer starts with committing to the process of writing. That's all. If you're reading this book, you're a writer. Just like Charles Dickens. Or Elizabeth Gilbert. Or your favorite author. Maybe they're a little better at writing than you . . . at the moment. That'll change though with a bit of practice on your end.

For example, while I was waiting on a bench for my wife and daughters, I started talking with an elderly woman who joined me to "catch her breath." After a few minutes of small talk, she revealed how she went to France to help with the Allied war effort during WWII, was captured by Nazis and fought her way free, and then she lived for two weeks in a tunnel before an English tank patrol rescued her. Some of the other life events she shared were even more movie-worthy. "Why don't you write these down?" I asked. She laughed then said, "I wouldn't consider myself a writer."

With that attitude, those amazing real-life stories will be lost to the world in just a matter of years because she's in her late 80s and her health's a real concern (she admitted as much). And to not record those kinds of experiences is a true loss for everyone else. Change your mindset and give yourself permission to share your story. It's really that easy. Flip the mental switch from "regular person" to "writer." You'll be glad that you did, even if you never quite catch up to Dickens's tally (he racked up 34½ books during his lifetime).

Getting Some Writing Momentum

Ask any pro writer what her writing process is like. No matter what idiosyncrasies she has, she writes on a schedule. It's the same reason that taking a formal writing class requires you to write daily. You get better at it, and you figure things out as you go. Best of all, the more writing you do, the easier it becomes. So get writing on a regular schedule, even if it's ten minutes a day. That's momentum.

Failing to Plan Is Planning to Fail

Working with a plan in mind can help make the entire process of writing a book go much smoother. The plan doesn't have to be insanely detailed. Just make sure you have a plan. (Chapter 5 discusses how you can put together your own writing plan.)

Your writing plan may be as simple as the following:

- Write three pages of my memoir each week.
- Read one new memoir every month.
- Attend one writers' conference in the next year.
- Take one class in literary editing from the local community college during the next year.

If you work with a plan similar to this one, your chances of succeeding are ten times greater than someone who writes when he feels like it and just "goes with the flow." Certainly some people have made it with the latter strategy. Most, though, are best served by adhering to a specific plan. Your life is busy, and writing can somehow get de-prioritized. However, with a clear, actionable plan, you're on your way.

No single plan will work for everyone. Make your own plan that suits your life, your personality, and your goals. Push hard and get things done or go at a more leisurely pace. Just have a plan and follow it.

Stopping in the Middle of . . .

You can incorporate this trick that many pro writers use. When you're writing, just as you reach those last few sentences before finishing for the day, you make an unexpected choice. Instead of pushing through to the end of the paragraph, typing that period, and saving the file with a full sense of closure, you stop right in the middle of typing that last sentence. Why? So the writing session the next day starts without taking much brainpower. For instance, how hard would finishing the following paragraph be versus writing something completely new from scratch?

> The more I listened to her explain why she failed every test on purpose, the more I began to realize that I didn't know my child at all. Here she was, sixteen going on thirty, and she was okay with tanking her high school career just to tick me off. Worse, I'd been bragging just the week before to a coworker about how

When I finish, I choose the mid-sentence stop every time. Doing so is a great way to get into the flow of writing without insisting your brain is firing instantly on all cylinders.

Having the Courage to Write Badly

If you're worried about being embarrassed that your first draft is unprofessional, sloppy, or a hot steamy mess, don't be. If your first draft is bad, you don't need to fret. You can just tweak, revise, and edit to your heart's content (refer to Chapter 16 for help with editing). What's more important is that you finish your first draft, no matter how good or bad it is. After you finish the first draft, you can feel free to keep it to yourself or show people your first draft. If they say, "Wow, this is *really* some rough stuff," you can just laugh and say, "Yeah, you should've seen the previous draft."

If you shoot for perfection, you'll never get there. And because you can't achieve perfection, you'll get frustrated and maybe even quit writing altogether. All you can do is do the best that you can with your writing. Do that, and then revise to make it better. You can also get some outside input for areas that you can improve.

Even the classics have hiccups. Many classic memoirs are great, but each came about from muddled early drafts and pretty strong middle drafts that ultimately transitioned into terrific final drafts that left each of them with the well-earned reputation of being a classic.

Knowing That Plenty of Good Blueprints for Writing a Memoir Exist

Every writer has her own style. You need to make sure you find yours. For instance, your next door neighbor paid a lot of money to go to a writer's retreat and live with other creative types for two months to write his memoir. And your office coworker wrote a single page at a time, longhand, on a big yellow pad while riding the train to work every single day. And someone else in your health club went to college to get an undergraduate or even a graduate degree in creative writing.

Some memoir writers will have lottery-like success, no matter how they started. Others will struggle for years (or even decades) in ways that make you want to weep. So what's right for you? All that matters is that you finish the writing, in your way. Be your own person and your own writer. Be the success that you want to become and do it in the way that makes sense for you. If something isn't working for you, change it. Take charge of your writing life and make it efficient and inspirational.

Celebrating Small Victories

When you're writing, you need to take a moment and rejoice in your successes, no matter how small they are. You just finished a chapter? Enjoy a red velvet mini-cupcake with cream cheese frosting and some rainbow-colored sprinkles. Maybe toss it down with an icy glass of milk. Then immediately get back to work.

Feel proud and satisfied for a quick moment with your own efforts about what might seem to others to be rather small accomplishments. You may have finished writing your first chapter or sent your first query to a literary agent.

No matter what the accomplishment, reward yourself in a small way for these small victories that, taken together, mark your progress toward the success of your memoir. Find a way to make the process pleasurable and you'll have an easier time with it.

Keep the celebrations in proportion to the completed task. Did you finish a chapter? Stick with a single mini-cupcake. Did you finish the entire manuscript? Splurge with surf and turf at your nearest steakhouse. There's nothing wrong with acknowledging your own hard work. As long you don't go overboard and celebrate more than you write, you're fine.

Stealing Writing Time

Your day is full of wasted time, so make sure you wisely use your time. Make writing a priority, which means finding ways to put enough time in it to finish the work.

For me, I typically grab about an hour a day in this manner, getting writing done while waiting in the car line to pick the kids up from elementary school, sitting in stand-still traffic, or putting in my mandatory office hours each week. I could daydream or send funny text messages to my friend, but those are luxuries. For me, writing is a priority, and with my life being busier than I want it to be, I need to get this extra time in or there'd be some days that nothing gets done on my current book project.

Killing Your Internet

The Internet is a wonderful and amazing thing. At times, it can be a godsend in helping you research or write parts of your book. But the rest of the time? You may be better off without it. If you want to be a successful writer, you need to remember that the Internet is *not* your friend. In fact, the following aren't helpful for writers who want to actually write:

- Checking your e-mail
- Playing one more video game
- Surfing sports websites
- Watching YouTube videos
- Tweeting
- Writing snarky comments on your friend's Facebook posts
- Checking your e-mail again

If you have to, yank the ethernet cable from the modem, or turn off the wireless card. Get back to the digital stone age if that's what it takes to eliminate the siren call of your Internet temptations. Check Chapter 5 for more help.

Reading and Reading Some More

Because I write for a lot of magazines and also go to lots of writers' conferences, I get to interact with a lot of professional writers. I always make sure to ask them what's the best thing a young writer should do? Perhaps half of the time, I get some variation on "Read everything you can get your hands on." I believe in that, too. Chapter 2 discusses some advantages to reading.

If you're going to write a book, read books. You can read within your target genre, but I suggest that you read beyond that too. Read what other writers are reading. Read what catches your eye. Make reading your hobby, your passion, your job.

Index